Bringing Aztlán to Mexican Chicago

José Gamaliel González

Bringing Aztlán to Mexican Chicago

My Life, My Work, My Art

Edited and with an Introduction by
Marc Zimmerman

UNIVERSITY OF ILLINOIS PRESS
Urbana, Chicago, and Springfield

Manufactured in the United States of America
1 2 3 4 5 C P 5 4 3 2 1
♾ This book is printed on acid-free paper.

Unless otherwise noted, rights to all visual materials are
held by the González Collection, Alicia González, director.

A Project of the Latin American and Latino/a Activities
and Studies Arena Series (LACASA) of the Department of
Modern and Classical Languages (MCL) of the University
of Houston. Director, Marc Zimmerman.

The editor wishes to thank the Office of Small Grants of
the University of Houston for providing funds for photo,
interview-transcription, and indexing costs.

Library of Congress Cataloging-in-Publication Data
González, José Gamaliel, 1933–
Bringing Aztlán to Chicago : my life, my work, my art /
José Gamaliel González ; edited and with an introduction
by Marc Zimmerman.
p.   cm. — (Latinos in Chicago and the Midwest)
Includes bibliographical references and index.
ISBN 978-0-252-03538-8 (cloth : alk. paper) —
ISBN 978-0-252-07735-7 (pbk. : alk. paper)
1. González, José Gamaliel, 1933–
2. Mexican American artists—Biography.
3. González, José Gamaliel, 1933– —Themes, motives.
I. Zimmerman, Marc. II. Title.
N6537.G626Z2   2010
709.2—dc22   2009039067
[B]

Contents

Preface

Marc Zimmerman

In the fall of 2002, during my first month of living in Houston after some twenty-two years in Chicago, I attended a Museum of Fine Arts postconference party at which Tomás Ybarra-Frausto, Gilbert Cárdenas, and Nicolás Kanellos, major players in U.S. Chicano and Latino cultural studies, ganged up on me, drinks in hand, to tell me that they understood that I was a friend of José González and that it was my duty as a writer to put together a book on his life and work.

José had not been well for some time; it was not clear how many more years of health and life he had to go. I'd been his friend for years, and I had developed book after book in that time. I'd seen him get ill, and I'd seen many friends drop off along the way. I'd also seen him lose the preeminent position he'd had in the Chicago Mexican arts community and above all seen his dream of establishing a gallery/museum space give way to the plans and successes of a more mainstream Chicago Mexican group that had the know-how, connections, and commitments to plot out and get funding for an ambitious museum project that would virtually transform Chicago's Mexican cultural ambience. Why in all this time had I never thought to tell his story—the story of his struggle, his great efforts, his tragedy?

Surely one answer lay in the nature of my own career and ambitions—the fact that I'd devoted myself to participating in national and international discussions of Latin American themes and problematics. I also did some work on U.S. Latino themes and even Chicago Latino ones. But I was not focused enough on this dimension of my interests to produce any major work on local themes. In addition, José was a friend who had seen his world torn apart as he got ill and others went on to do the things he'd dreamed of doing. I empathized with him in his frustration and pain; but I never sought to objectify or "exploit" his story or our friendship to the point of actually making it the basis for one of my books.

And yet when I explained all this to my three famous interlocutors, they were not sympathetic, telling me that I was selfish—and that, given my history of taking on and carrying out book projects, I should do this one, and do it as soon as possible before José or I got too ill or old to finish the work. I didn't fail to notice that those urging me seemed more concerned about José's health than my own. But I have to admit that I was both embarrassed and flattered by their urgings. And I agreed to take on the project.

So began a series of interviews that came to occupy my every trip to Chicago between 2002 and 2008, as José went in and out of hospitals, suffered failing health, and finally had to give up his home in Chicago's Mexican Pilsen neighborhood to live among Puerto Ricans and Cubans in the Casa Central Retirement Home in Chicago's Humboldt Park, and even as an illness in 2008 sent him on to still another site where he now resides.

Each year, as I managed a complex academic department with multiple problems, and as I received a grant that enabled me to complete a large series of other book projects, I never stopped visiting José, interviewing him and gathering materials for this volume. Even as he had his illnesses and severe ups and downs with his health, to the point of his institutionalization, José kept me on my toes, insisting that I complete the interviews and do the final edit of my interview and related materials. The result includes an edition of those interviews and a series of photos and scanned images selected by both of us as examples of his work as an artist, graphic designer, and cultural promoter. Indeed, the documentary material began to overwhelm the flow of the narrative, and therefore much of it had to be consigned to appendices that ended up being longer than the narrative proper and will have to appear in another publication[1]—which will supplement, round out, and in many ways go beyond what we have been able to include in this volume.

Some comments about my editing of the interviews would seem in order. For years I have been party to theoretical discussions about *testimonio* and the role of the interlocutor-interviewer-editor. Now in this volume I found myself faced with all the practical considerations involved in editing an extended interview with many testimonial elements and with many problems stemming from the different experiences and issues that developed over the years. In this role, I, like others before me, had to make choices large and small.

My first goal was to help José tell his story in detail but with clarity as well. It was sometimes hard because of José's bouts of illness, his periods of depression, and my own state of energy.

In the editing process, I wanted to eliminate my questions and comments so that the story would indeed be his. There is no doubt that my prejudices, preconceptions, and ideological orientations influence every page. However, it must be said also that José read the first, crude version that included every intelligible sound that our transcribers could capture; that, as noted, he participated in the initial and final corrections; and that he also intervened in all the key decisions that have resulted in this book. There is not a picture or image he didn't choose; there is not a word that didn't have his final approval. And indeed, in his next-to-last reading, he decided to develop his own extended commentaries on certain themes that he felt were underplayed in our interview sessions, writing them out in a longhand that seemed to get more determined, firmer, and clearer with each page. As much as possible, then, this book is his. And as such, this collaborative effort is finally a work of Latino and Chicano autobiography[2] with virtually all the characteristics ascribed to that genre.

It is true that José was and perhaps still is somewhat frustrated with the result, first because each day he recalls more details, and I told him that we had to finish—that we could add no more and that to do so might overcome a narrative line that was already in jeopardy from the weight of added detail. But perhaps a greater source of frustration is his sense that we have overemphasized his charcoal and line drawings, perhaps driven by my sense of the expense involved in producing a volume of color, and maybe too by my personal prejudice that his work in black and white represents his best. There has been a temptation to look for more of his works in color (his pastels, watercolors, and oils) and perhaps some more work of his youth; but all these materials are now buried in piles of artwork, posters, and archival materials that were placed in a small storage space when José entered the Casa Central Retirement Home. Many valuable works are now difficult to retrieve. They may or may not come to light by the time we bring out the supplementary collection of documents, thereby perhaps modifying the way he will be seen in the future.

I wish also to note that, as the readers for the University of Illinois Press pointed out, this is one of the few existing life histories or "autobiographies" of a Latino arts organizer and is a contribution to the study of Latino arts movements and the overall connection between art and community, art and politics, and so on. It is a rather special example of "Chicano autobiography" and only one of three examples of the genre that I know of from Chicago;[3] it is also only the third about a Chicago-based Latino visual artist.[4] These qualities alone, I believe, give the book some importance, as does its elusive but also present consideration of the relation between the arts and mental health.

However, our readers requested certain changes and additions that we could not fully realize, and I should comment upon these here. First, one of the readers wanted more clarity on how José earned his money as he developed community projects. Suffice it to say that José sometimes had regular jobs as an arts coordinator and teacher, but his main source of income over the years was freelancing. He was often without work and indeed very poor. In the past several years, he has been on disability and social security and living in subsidized homes for the elderly.

The same reader also noted that while "the narrative is striking . . . in recounting his marriage and divorce, it frequently calls out for more personal detail which would enhance the story [by providing] a greater sense of his family, friends, and relationships." Here, however, I have been able to go no further than I have gone. The narrative is as intimate as José wished it to be, since he saw and continues to see it as centered on his role as an artist/activist. Indeed, the fact that this activist dimension comes to be more central to his text than his own art and personal life is the essence of the story José is trying to tell. As he narrates it at the end of chapter 2, he left his own art projects and also his potential future as a more mainstream arts organizer to one side as he became swept away by his activist role. José didn't wish to go into any significant fleshing out of the personal in the narrative for fear that it would undermine or dilute the central story and get into areas he preferred to keep private. As his interviewer, I frequently probed the personal and found him unwilling to go into the deepest detail; it was difficult, for example, for him to bring a close woman friend into the narrative, partially because he didn't want to do it, and also because he respected her wish not to be included in detail.

This same problem comes up when a second reader expresses the wish that we develop a more detailed narrative and analysis with respect to José's illness and its effect on his daily functioning as well as his goals and achievements. There is no question that José's illness hurt him as an artist and affected his activism and every aspect of his life, but the full fleshing out of this matter will remain beyond the range of this book. José only wanted to go so far in this direction. I address this issue as best I can in the introduction. But even there, I have chosen to respect his limits.

The second reader also asked for more information or perspective about politics, artists, artist groups, and movements in Chicago's Latino communities. The reader wished for "a greater sense of Chicago politics, which would be most helpful to those not familiar with [these matters]," and more discussion of the "perspectives, goals, and limitations of varied groups or individuals . . . and of the political contexts involved in each major phase of José's career" as well as "some overall sense of where Latino/a arts were in 1970 in Chicago versus today."

Surely the central theme of José's story is how a group of cultural producers attempted to bring a uniquely Chicano/a perspective to the attention of a larger population that is largely of Mexican origin and orientation. At least certain sectors of this Mexican population took on Chicano and pan-Latino positions as they sought to transcend the divide-and-conquer patronage tactics typical of Chicago ethnic politics and to develop a more militant agenda, inspired by the Chicano movement of the 1960s and tied locally to the efforts to forge a militant independent Mexican and Latino politics in relation to the emergent movement that would bring Harold Washington to power. Local Chicano and Latino arts groups and the artists themselves were very much part of all that—connected to *mexicano* leaders like Rudy Lozano, Juan Solíz, Juan Velásquez, and Chuy García and also to Puerto Ricans like Luis Gutiérrez, Miguel Del Valle, and others as well. In one sense, the story of José's MIRA years is tied to the partial collapse of that convergence— to the deaths of Lozano and Washington and the failed efforts of Solíz and Velázquez. Above all, the story is tied to the articulation of Richard Daley's politics in the 1990s and beyond. My comments here and in the introduction aim to make all this quite clear.

While we seek to bring in a "more political perspective" on disagreements and conflicts, my initial effort to provide considerable material on these matters (including documents and images related to other artists and art groups) took us too far afield and would have made for a cumbersome book that might have been richer but would have suffered from a lack of focus. The development of a documents-archive supplement as a separate text ran the risk of leaving us with inadequate context here. And this risk points to the fact that there has been no overall volume on the development of Mexican or Latino Arts in Chicago or the Midwest—and this has been so perhaps because the people best qualified to write such a work (and edit this one, for that matter) have chosen different career paths. This book cannot compensate for another book that does not exist; all it can do is tell one of the key stories that a more general book would have to take into account.

It is also true, however, that as I finish this revised preface, I can now note that a book has finally appeared and another is on the horizon that indeed place José's story within this broader context. First, the Institute for Latino Studies of the University of Notre Dame published Olga Herrera's book, *Toward the Preservation of a Heritage: Latin American and Latino Art in the Midwestern States* (2008), which includes sections on MARCH, the National Task Force on Hispanic American Arts, and MIRA, with at least some measure of credit to José. Second, in the same year, Francisco Piña began a follow-up to his book on Marcos Raya, centered on Chicago Mexican artists, including José. In light of these developments, I seek only to provide enough general context for Chicago Latinos and their politics and art to make this narrative understandable to most readers by bringing into the introduction certain themes I have developed in other publications.[5]

Questions of politics and of feminist views, to be discussed in the introduction, lead to some final comments about the perspective presented in this book, especially with regard to the start and breakup of MARCH, as well as the rise and decline of MIRA, in relation to the development of the Mexican Fine Arts Center Museum (MFACM), now named the National Mexican Museum. Herrera's narrative underplays José's role as cofounder and leader of MARCH in the 1970s and provides the most neutral description of the MIRA/MFACM struggle. José's own story places him center stage during MARCH's formative years; it clearly provides his version of the MIRA/MFACM story. I believe that José's versions are closer to the truth than Herrera's. However, it would be fascinating to read other versions of the developments and struggles in question by other participants and observers. One such narrative we do have is my interview with Carlos Cortez, which will be included in the documents archive (Zimmerman forthcoming).

The views expressed in the narrative are José's, and there are many other ways to see what took place. But this is José's story as he wished to tell it. Here we may return to one of the great questions in José's life: the role of his illness. Did his disappointments push his illness? Did his illness lead to the problems he had as artist and artist organizer? With reference to a hidden gender narrative detailed in the introduction, I have sometimes felt that José suffered from depressions resulting from the breakup of his marriage; but his mood shifts and growing mental problems also led to the breakup. So, too, his other problems, including those with Juana Guzmán and Helen Valdez, were most probably a matter of interacting causes and effects.

These are difficult questions to ponder in each case, especially for a reader who may wish objectivity in relation to the story told and the organizations and people discussed. Although a fuller account of all of these gender concerns might go a way toward explaining José's achievements and failures, their full elaboration would require an expertise in psychodynamics far beyond this writer's capacities and far beyond José's wishes for what is, after all, his story more or less as he wishes it to be.

However judgment may rest with regard to these matters (and I shall take some of them up again in the introduction), it gives me great pleasure to present José's life and art to his readers. May it give José a sense of joy and accomplishment to imagine you reading his words and seeing his images, thinking about your own lives in relation to his story.

Acknowledgments

Marc Zimmerman

I wish to acknowledge the help of Nicolás Kanellos and his staff at Arte Público Press for finding key materials and scanning many photos from José's private collection. Thanks to Mario Castillo, Jeff Huebner, Lennie Domínguez, and Gilberto Cárdenas, as well as José's former wife (and my former colleague), Mary Kay Vaughan, and members of his immediate family—above all, his daughter, Alicia, and his brother-in-law, Cayetano García—for providing and preparing key materials. Also I wish to thank Paul Lister for transcribing most of the tapes; thanks to Elizabeth Cummins for her transcription of the first González tape; and to my granddaughter, Jacqueline Javior, for transcribing a final tape on MARCH.

I also want to thank the Chicago photographer Jim Prinz for his digital photographs of José's artwork and related materials. Thanks to the Small Grants Program of the University of Houston for providing funds for the photos, transcription, indexes, and other costs. Thanks to my staff in the Department of Modern and Classical Languages—to Maricela Villanueva and, above all, to Flor Velásquez, who deserves credit for her help in inserting José's original corrections of the interviews, for working on José's many handwritten additions to the interview transcriptions, and for many other key tasks she carried out. Thanks to Tiffany Javior and Marquesa Macadar for their "volunteer" photographing help. Thanks also to Joan Catapano, Rebecca McNulty, Tad Ringo, and other staff members at the University of Illinois Press for their work in seeing this volume through to the end.

Thanks to the readers of this text for the University of Illinois Press; their encouraging words and insights helped shape the final version of the book. Thanks also to Frances Aparicio, the director of the Latinos in Chicago and the Midwest Series, for her encouragement and for enabling me to see that cutting materials made this book more focused. I am responsible for the final editing and form that the interviews took as I shaped them into a volume that I believe tells José's story as well as I could tell it.

Introduction

Marc Zimmerman

MARCH, MIRA, THE CHICAGO MEXICAN ART WORLD, AND THE MEXICAN FINE ARTS CENTER

I first met José Gamaliel González when I began working as coordinator of the Rafael Cintrón Ortiz Latino Student Cultural Center at the University of Illinois at Chicago. Part of my job was to meet and work with people in the community, and one of my new colleagues, Mary Kay Vaughan, told me I had to meet her ex-husband and father of her child Alicia, José González, an artist and the cofounder of the Movimiento Artístico Chicano (MARCH), the major Latino arts organization in Chicago and the one who seemed most likely to establish a Mexican gallery or museum in the city.

Very soon I realized that José had left MARCH. The graphic artist and poet Carlos Cortez told me that José had broken with the organization in a split based on personalities and policies. Then the young Chicano poet Carlos Cumpián, who had worked for MARCH as a Comprehensive Employment and Training Act (CETA) employee and was now beginning to assume a leadership role in the group, described José's last MARCH days as marked by his fears that MARCH was seen as a communist or left-wing front and that the FBI was out to get the group. Cumpián felt that José was watching his every move. There seemed also to have been a struggle over the place of literature in an organization that José primarily saw as a visual-arts group.

Though never a large group, MARCH had indeed been the prime organization of Chicago Mexican and Latino artists from the early 1970s. It was involved in many community struggles, developing mural projects, exhibits, and presentations throughout Chicago's Latino world. José was one of the better-known artists of the group, even though inside and outside of MARCH there were already several established and emerging artists like Ray Patlán, Mario Castillo, Alejandro Romero, Aurelio Díaz, Salvador Vega, and Marcos Raya, some of whom were technically more complex and far more prolific painters than José. Carlos Cortez stood somewhat apart because of all the artists, he was the one who did political woodcuts and drawings in the tradition of José Guadalupe Posada. González's talent was more focused on his gift for line-drawing portraiture in ink as well as charcoal, with few finished oils or watercolors and a small body of important mural works that seem on the road to extinction. As the pictures reproduced in this collection show, his was an art of intense simplicity with touches of Vincent van Gogh (his favorite painter), German expressionism, and, among the Mexican painters he so loved, Diego Rivera and José Clemente Orozco.

José was born in 1933 in Iturbide, Nuevo León, Mexico, a small town some miles from Monterrey. Soon after his birth, his mother, separated from his father, brought her children to the Mexican enclave of the steel-mill town of East Chicago, Indiana, where she and her husband had gone some years before, and found permanent employment with the Inland Steel Company. After high school and some rudimentary art training, José, like many steel-mill children, served time in the military. He was sent to Germany and had the chance to travel in Europe and to visit some of the major museums. When he came back to the United States, he sought to pick up on his early interest in art and break with his Mexican working-class background by developing his artistic abilities though a stint at Chicago's American Academy of Art, a six-month art program in San Miguel de Allende, and a scholarship-funded degree program at the School of the Art Institute. In all these situations, José produced impressive drawings, paintings, and sculptures; and at the Art Institute School, he came to know the artist/activist students John Weber and Mark Rogovin, as well as the artist Mario Castillo. Then came José's time as a graduate student in the Master of Fine Arts program at the University of Notre Dame. A devout Catholic, José loved being at this center of Catholic learning, but his growing identification with the national Chicano movement and the Notre Dame student branch of MECHA (El Movimiento Estudiantil Chicano de Aztlán), which he founded with Gil Cárdenas, a graduate student from the West Coast, resulted in a new militancy that was unprecedented in his prior trajectory.

It is difficult to grasp José's transformation at Notre Dame from someone only gradually identifying as a Mexican artist to an impassioned Chicano-arts activist willing to risk all for the empowerment of his marginalized and oppressed community. José himself does not fully explain the transformation in his narrative. It is clear that "the answer was blowing in the wind," as national and primarily southwestern currents, personified by Cárdenas, stirred smoldering resentments into a blazing fire. But there may also have been in all this mixture some early presence of the chemical imbalances that would take center stage and perhaps indeed propel José, as he became a sometimes volatile activist leader throughout the 1970s and into the 1980s.

In what must have been a great life defeat, José was forced to leave Notre Dame. Returning to northwestern Indiana and then Chicago, he began finding his way first as a community activist influenced by César Chávez and the national Farm Workers movement and then as a Chicano-arts activist influenced by Saul Alinsky–style organization tactics, seeking to transform the situation of fellow artists and his community.[1] José lived on freelance work in the 1970s and early 1980s, but he increasingly devoted more time to political activity and arts promotion than to his own work and indeed his personal life, as he emerged as the organizational leader of Chicago Latino and Mexican artists—the one who wrote the proposals, organized the events, and represented Latino Chicago on the Hispanic national boards for the National Endowment for the Arts and other arts funders. He worked as the cover-art designer and overall arts editor for the emerging *Revista Chicano-Riqueña,* which, from its home in the northwestern Indiana Chicagoland area, represented Latino artists throughout the country. However, on a more local level, González's achievement lay with his cofounding and development of MARCH, making it one of the more significant local artists' groups in the country, ever with the goal to enrich Latino and above all Mexican poverty communities through bringing and promoting the production of great art. It was through MARCH that José established an impressive record of arts activity, recruiting key artists and arts advocates and coming to national recognition as the midwestern repre-

sentative in the forging of the National Hispanic Task Force on the Arts in the late 1970s. But partially because of his work on the Task Force, he ran into conflicts of agendas and personalities to the point that he felt compelled to leave the organization he had cofounded and with which he was so identified and embark on a new path.

José exiled himself from MARCH. By the time I arrived in Chicago, he was serving as the Latino representative on the Chicago Council of Fine Arts, encouraging and developing Latino city arts projects. As I got to know him, he ran into a conflict on this job and was fired. As the newly appointed coordinator of a campus Latino cultural center seeking to work with José, I called his now ex-boss, Mary Cunningham, and protested this move, but was quickly rebuffed: José was difficult, José was impossible, he might even be crazy—he was certainly manic or schizophrenic, she told me. My protest was useless; José had already picked up his belongings, and Juana Guzmán, a close friend of the writer Ana Castillo and an artist in her own right, had already taken on a post she was to hold for the next several years, playing her part in the formation of a museum that would be both a tribute to José's efforts and the site of what he felt to be his undoing.

In the early 1980s, before the museum project came to the fore, José launched Mi Raza Arts Consortium (MIRA), which, in spite of its Chicano-sounding name, attempted to represent Latino as opposed to specifically Mexican artists in the city and the Midwest. José published several issues of a carefully laid-out newsletter that verged on being a journal, as it not only gave information about upcoming events, projects, and grant possibilities but featured articles on local artists and programs. José tried to build his arts organization with the aim of establishing a cultural center, museum, or gallery in Chicago's Pilsen neighborhood. He and his organization were instrumental in bringing in the artist-promoter Felipe Ehrenberg from Mexico and establishing the Day of the Dead as a major citywide event extending from Mexican households to public spaces in the Anglo-American art world. Other major events helped place MIRA on the map. But as ethnic politics heated up in the city, and as Latinos sought their own agenda in relation to the emergence of a groundswell in the African American community for the mayoral candidacy of Harold Washington, José became identified with the pro-Washington Mexican progressives, fund-raising for Washington and Washington-linked Latino candidates like Rudy Lozano, Juan Solíz, Juan Velásquez, and Luis Gutiérrez. As the Washington campaign continued, José was instrumental in leading a virtual constellation of artists and arts supporters in a series of fund-raising and solidarity-building events in support of the Washington campaign.

José González's efforts to support Mexican, Chicano, Latin American, and Latino arts in the city and to link these concerns to overall community development would be crowned with success in the coming years. However, that success would not be his, and he would for several years be obscured and almost forgotten in the process. He and those supporting him would not benefit from his work in the Mexican community because, at least as José sees it and so argues in chapter 4, Harold Washington reached out to extend his political base, and those interested in promoting the arts for a growing Mexican population in the city sought to direct their support to other arts promoters in the Mexican community.

In the midst of all the fervor attendant to these developments, I became aware that a man who was more and more my friend was indeed getting sick, and that sickness in the early years involved constant bouts of agitation and depression with visions of persecution. In the mid-1980s, José had one of his fiercest attacks, which left him hospitalized and debilitated at the University of Illinois Hospital and other Chicago health facilities. Meanwhile, as he sought to adjust to what turned out to be a deepening mental health problem, the Mexican Fine Arts Center (MFAC) began to develop under the leadership of the public school teachers Helen Valdez and Carlos Tortolero. With the support of the Illinois Arts and Humanities Councils; the Chicago Council of Fine Arts, represented by Juana Guzmán; and the Mexican consulate's cultural attaché, represented by Argentina Terán de Erdman, it won increasing recognition as the city's center for those wishing to be identified with Chicago cultural developments bearing a Mexican name.

From the mid-1980s, as his health declined and the MFAC began institutionalizing its program, José González began to fall by the wayside. His illness came to dominate all that happened to him. His last concerted effort to remain a key person in the Chicago Mexican arts scene was his campaign, taken on with his friend, the art historian Victor Sorell, to bring an ambitious, nationwide Chicano art exhibit, the CARA (Chicano Art Resistance and Affirmation) show, to Chicago's Field Museum. However, even though they had long championed a more conservative Mexican as opposed to a Chicano model (indeed, that was their supposed allure in relation to González's efforts), Tortolero and the Mexican Fine Arts group put the brakes on a major Chicano-centered art event that seemed to marginalize or minimize the growing importance of their organization. The CARA show never came to Chicago, and the MFAC, now entrenched as the representative of things Mexican, could begin to develop a more populist Chicano dimension, honed to their own vision of *mexicanidad*. So began their work on the national Chicano scene and in the local community. But, as José was always quick to point out, they never used the word "Chicano" in their exhibits.[2]

As the new organization rose, José was written out of the prehistory of Chicago Mexican art. Until the mid-1990s, no exhibit of community art at the Mexican Fine Arts Center Museum (MFACM) reflected his role. Only a bit of his record of achievement slipped into the museum surreptitiously as part of a large-scale show dedicated to the life and work of José's friend Carlos Cortez in 1996, in which José's early role as founder and head of MARCH could not be completely ignored. Then a positive reference appeared in the MFACM's book on Mexican Chicago; and finally the MFACM sponsored a student-centered publication including a highly positive interview with José.[3]

As the museum grew and José's health problems deepened, he continued to struggle to win support for a new Mexican cultural center at the Smyrna Temple and then Thalia Hall in the Pilsen neighborhood. He struggled to change the name of Harrison Park, the site of the MFACM, to Zapata Park, and he struggled against gentrification in Pilsen. José supported Bill Luna's effort to establish a modest Mexican history museum; he struggled to mount occasional shows and planned comebacks that never went too far due not only to his illness but the drugs he took to combat it. For a time, Louise Año Nuevo Kerr, a key historian of Mexicans in Chicago and an administrator at the University of Illinois at Chicago, was able to land him employment in my old position as coordinator of the Rafael Cintrón Ortiz Latino Cultural Student Center, but the effort failed as his mental health had its ups and downs. Increasingly on medication for his illness, he could no longer

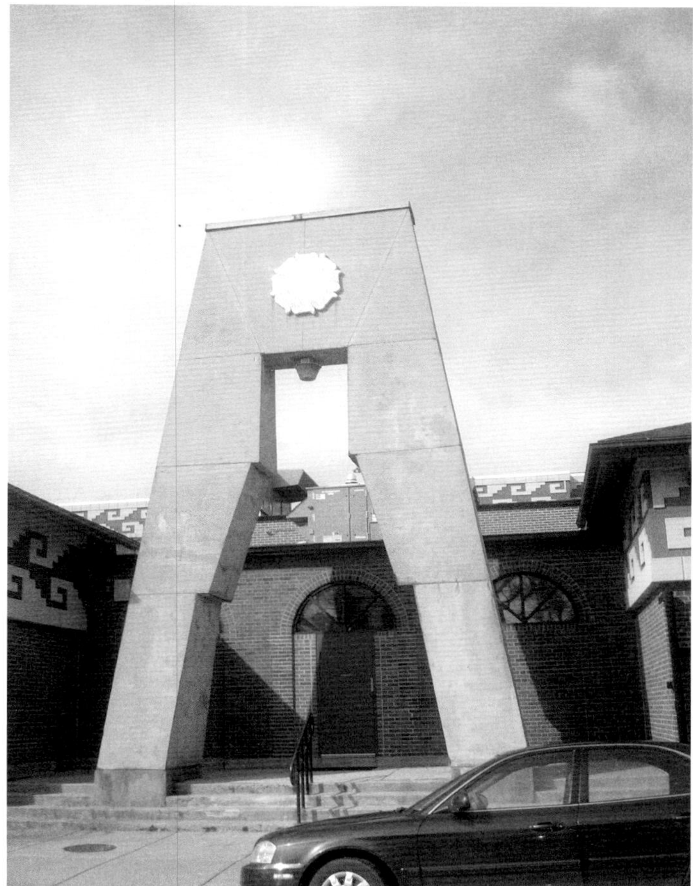

complete a major project, hold a job, or even complete a painting or drawing. His personal production, on the decline since his MARCH days, with one small burst inspired by the Van Gogh centennial, now became reduced to a woodcut of Siqueiros he carried out with the help of Carlos Cortez and some sketches he managed to produce in one of his stays at Chicago's Northwestern Hospital.

In all of these developments over the years, I remember happy and joyful days in José's life. But above all I remember the days of illness—days of hallucinations, the cold days of winter when he would disappear only to be found wandering the streets without adequate clothing, days when he thought the FBI planted microphones in his sneakers or that he was being watched for the crimes he'd committed, days on dialysis, days of loneliness. During those years

Fig. 1. Mexican Fine Arts Center Museum, on Nineteenth Street, east of Damen Avenue, in Chicago's Pilsen neighborhood. Originally the Harrison Park Boat Craft shop, it was converted in 1986 to house the new museum, which was later expanded and renamed the National Mexican Museum in 2006. Photo: Marc Zimmerman, March 2007.

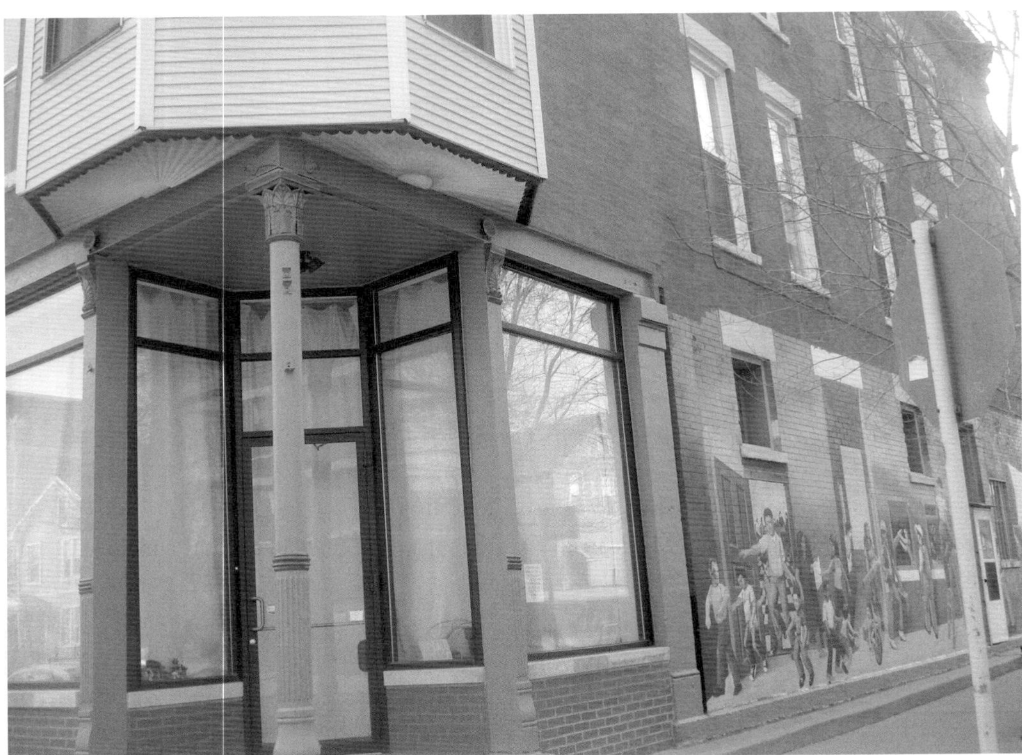

Fig. 2. José's street-level apartment at 1901 South Carpenter Street in Chicago's Pilsen neighborhood. The mural was designed and painted by Guillermo Campillo when the apartment was used as the gallery Calles y Sueños in the early 1990s. Photo: Marc Zimmerman, March 2007.

from the mid-1980s on, some of the veteran Pilsen artists like Ray Patlán and Aurelio Díaz left Chicago, and others, like Mario Castillo, Alejandro Romero, Marcos Raya, and Carlos Cortez, achieved considerable local and international recognition. Meanwhile, new arrivals like Héctor Duarte and women artists like Diana Solís and Esperanza Gama came to the fore. Even as the Mexican Fine Arts Center became the Mexican Fine Arts Center Museum and then the National Museum of Mexican Art, so grew smaller, counterorganizations, like the Taller del Grabado,[4] the Prospectus gallery on Eighteenth Street, and the Calles y Sueños gallery operating out of an apartment where José had once lived.

A new generation of Latinos launched one publishing project after another. A group of younger artists emerged to form Polvo, and a few artistic coffee shops emerged in the Pilsen area even as gentrification continued. All of these were guerrilla-like actions on the mar-

gins of the MFACM project—movements the larger organization sought to bring under its wing, even as they tried to resist and keep their distance and autonomy.

One of the saddest recollections I have of José is when Victor Sorell and I, along with several other friends, helped move him out of his house on Carpenter Street to a smaller apartment a few doors away. But it was even sadder for me when, only months later, I attended the first of several Calles y Sueños gallery shows that took place in what had been his apartment: a modest version of the great museum/gallery space José had sought for years had been right under his nose, in the space where he piled up the disordered archives of MARCH, MIRA, and his own personal projects. But with big dreams and illnesses only heavy sedation could cope with, he had not even seen the possibilities that had lain under his feet (see fig. 2).

In one sense, the story of José is one of his generation replicated throughout the United

States—a grassroots Latino visionary with more dreams than know-how, perhaps, whose great efforts get trampled on, coopted, and negated as a new generation of college-educated Chicano professionals comes to maturity. More so than Chicago, Indiana was typical of other midwestern spaces in that the Chicano dimensions were at least as important as the *mexicano*.[5]

Even though José was Mexican-born and increasingly oriented to Mexican art, his story represents how those most influenced by the Chicano movement clashed with Mexican and Mexican American sectors in their communities—as they brought in more rebellious currents having weight in other regions, but not in their own; as they struggled, sometimes successfully, to bring new vision and commitment to their people. The story here is also one of artists who are economically, socially, culturally, ideologically, and artistically marginal but who seek to be seen and heard, to make and maintain a difference, even in the face of changing times and changing sensibilities in their own immediate communities. The story told in this book is significant in its own right, but also in the larger network of stories that make up the history of grassroots, minority, Latino and Mexican American or Chicano arts in Chicago and the United States.

MEXICANS IN MIDWESTERN AND CHICAGO LATINO CONTEXTS: A BRIEF OVERVIEW

The Midwest has long been a destination for migrant farm workers to rural areas and settler Latinos in urban settings. While the largest ethnic group involved in midwestern Latino migration has long been Mexican and Chicano, Chicago migration has been more specifically from Mexico, something that is now becoming true throughout other midwestern urban centers as well.

The Chicago area's Mexican population grew in relation to labor demand in the steel mills, railroad lines, and packing houses. First, Mexican immigrants served as a buffer against strikers and African American encroachment. Many with or without papers were deported during the Depression, and many returned, but we have no clear sense of continuity in this evolving process. The Puerto Rican migration was primarily in the 1940s and 1950s in response to a program called Operation Bootstrap. By the 1970s, the city had become a major U.S. Latino center, with the core Mexican and Puerto Rican immigration waves constituting the majority in the overall national Latino aggregate, and increasing numbers of Central and South Americans, as well as Cubans and Dominicans. Chicago had become a locale in which cross-acculturation patterns were leading to the kinds of transformations in gender, class, and national identifications that enabled new pan–Latin American and explicitly Latino identifications to emerge and become rooted. Indeed, the city became one of the U.S. vanguard centers of post-national Latino identification.

By the 1980s, Central American wars and, above all, Mexican economic crises led to a virtual explosion in Latin American immigration at a time when Chicago was entering a postindustrial phase. The Mexican immigrant wave was by far the greatest, involving a larger middle-class dimension in an immigration not directly tied to labor demand. The effect of the new immigrants was an upsurge in Latino creativity and entrepreneurship as well as an intensification of Latino relations and identifications, even as group enmities emerged and as tensions with other minority communities intensified. As the population grew and became involved in local concerns, Chicago experienced a burgeoning Latino cultural infrastructure of restaurants, organizations, newspapers, radio stations, and music and film festivals—all of which signaled the full emergence of Latin American identity in the city, even as Mexican immigrants experienced transnational processes, and the overall configuration of Midwest Latino life changed radically. Also in the 1980s, Chicago underwent an intense political struggle leading to the election of the city's first African American mayor and the forging of an independent Latino group intent on breaking with the patronage system that had prevailed for years. But this movement became modified and weakened in the wake of Harold Washington's death and the rise of Richard Daley. Many of the political, economic, and cultural advances were thrown into crisis by a national backlash that intensified after September 11, 2001. Intergroup struggles over economic restructuring, gentrification, and affirmative action have shaped Chicago's emergence as a global city.[6]

The new politics and culture building of the 1970s cultivated a core of young artists, writers, and cultural workers who responded to movements from their own locations of family or personal origin, national Latino and Chicano trends, and their local circumstances to forge a new set of aesthetic responses marked by a drive toward the creation of patterns of resistance and change.[7]

CHICAGO LATINO ARTS AND THE STRUGGLE FOR SPACE

An understanding of the history of Chicago Latinos, including Latino artists like José, has to portray interactions throughout the larger Chicago region, including acculturation and transculturation processes, leading to lateral interchanges with other Latino and non-Latino groups. These processes involve racialization and stigmatization, accommodation and resistance, Latinization and reflexive nationalism, as well as gender relations and identities related to spatial struggle, displacement, and cultural and political empowerment. Such studies have to emphasize the relation between expression and experience, artistic representation, and social context.

Chicago Latino and specifically Mexican arts development can be related to efforts of group affirmation and empowerment. On the most general level, this book portrays struggles over conflictive efforts to win turf or space in a world in which large-scale forces are leading societies from industrial to postindustrial, post-Fordist globalization. For Chicanos nationally, this concern became centered on efforts to recuperate a presumably lost relation to sacred space known as Aztlán and involving spiritual and spatial values, as opposed to the money- and time-centered values imputed to dominant material culture. José's obsession with establishing a gallery or museum is mediated by the Chicano movement's emphasis on Aztlán, as he grew to understand that poetic trope in the late 1960s and tried to bring it to Mexican Chicago in the 1970s.

The literature on Aztlán is immense; however, its articulation as an indigenous *axis mundi* or sacred space is perhaps best set forth by Juan Bruce-Novoa, first in *Chicano Poetry* (1982) and then in *RetroSpace* (1990). Over the years, the Aztlán myth was severely criticized as part of a critique of identity politics and nativism, as well as a growing conviction that the construct concealed a patriarchal, male-centered orientation. The counter to this construct was Gloria Anzaldúa's *Borderlands/La frontera* (1999), which tended to "feminize" or reappropriate every dimension of the Aztlán trope in function of the "new Mestiza." However, in one form or another, the theme persists as a central one of the Chicano experience. Over the years, it has been coupled with the question of resistance, as in Ramón Saldívar's *Chicano Narrative* (1990) and in Raúl Homero Villa's *Barrio Logos* (2000), where the struggle for space takes place in relation to industrial restructuring, gentrification, and other urban processes finds its expression in literature and the arts. A Chicago version of spatial concerns (in relation to Latin American as well as national and local considerations) is best conceptualized in Nicholas de Genova's *Working the Boundaries* (2005); however, the Chicago story has been most richly portrayed in feminist and artistic terms in Sandra Cisneros's celebrated *House on Mango Street* (1991).[8]

In Chicago, the Mexicans' drive was to own property, to leave factories and sweatshops and establish restaurants and other businesses bearing the name of their hometowns or regions, affirming identities supposedly lost through immigration and the configuring of Mexican immigrants as members of a racial minority. Only a few "vanguard" intellectuals and artists could take on the Chicano construction of Aztlán as a kind of ultimate metaversion of the spatial trope. But the spatial obsession has had a point of convergence between Mexicans and those Mexican Americans who came to call themselves Chicanos. That point of convergence has also been one of conflict, as various sectors struggled for the small spaces allotted by an economy that provided minimal opportunities for longtime resident and recently arrived Chicago Mexicans.

Nowhere are the struggles for space more intense than in the arts, especially painting. For Cisneros, narrative time could be "spatialized"; she could seek her house, or "space of her own," on the written page. However, for visual artists, the question is much less metaphorical, much more direct. In José González's case, the struggle extends from his own space in the sketch book or the mural to that of a space for all the artists in the barrio world of Pilsen, which had become

his home, his *axis mundi,* in Chicago. His defeat was an inability to stave off the competition for the space of art and culture in his world.

On this local level, José's story is enmeshed with the failure of the Harold Washington movement and the mayor's Chicago Mexican allies to end Daley family hegemony over ward and ethnic politics in the city. This failure is in turn tied to the growth of neoliberalism internationally, the emergence of Reagonomics nationally, and, in the midst of it all, the inability of the Mexican community and its grassroots organic intellectuals and artists to fend against the pressures brought to bear by John Pomadjersky, the University of Illinois at Chicago, and other gentrifiers, to counter the force of the MFACM in its drive for Mexican cultural hegemony and, finally, to win out against the Daley-allied United Neighborhood Organization (UNO), led by Danny Solís, whose own vision of community "betterment," involving a revisionist take on Alinsky-style community organizing, frequently meant forming alliances with the non-Latino gentrifiers and the cultural "hegemons." Such forces were beyond the artists and intellectuals caught up in them; they would have probably been too much for José González even if his health had held out.

The stories of how MARCH rises in the 1970s and how MIRA develops in the 1980s, only to lose out to a new organization, the Mexican Fine Arts Center Museum, now renamed the National Mexican Museum, are central to this volume. Here I wish to note only that these stories took place in the midst of others—for example, developments in the Puerto Rican community and the emergence of other arts groups, galleries, and publications in the 1980s. The early developments occurred when the arts infrastructure in place today did not exist; they took place in a hostile political atmosphere and developed initially as a new wave of politicization swept through the Latino communities, leading to struggles over the arts and creating pressures that led to the development of that minimal infrastructure that has made recent developments possible, even as city politics changed and as new leaders struggled against growing forces of disempowerment and gentrification that affected the core communities where Chicago Latino and Mexican arts developed.

In relation to the political matters invoked here, a question arises with respect to the sexual politics of the groups involved—most specifically about the presence and activity of women in what seems to have been mainly male arts movements in the 1970s and 1980s. José does mention a few female artists in and around MARCH, MIRA, and other projects; his narrative includes such women as María Almontes and María Enríquez de Allen, the mother of the artist Mario Castillo but also, as José indicates, an artist in her own right. Marguerite Ortega and Susan Stejni are mentioned (though not much discussed) as early MARCH members. Marta Ayala, a Chicago Mexican actress, and the Chicago Rican poet Salima Rivera worked with MARCH, while another poet, Beatriz Badikian, of Argentine-Greek descent, worked with MIRA. The Chicana poet Sandra Cisneros, the photographer/artist Diana Solís, the school principal Angela Miller, the community mover Amy Horton, and the activist-professor Teresa Córdova were among several women who had some positive involvement with José's antigentrification projects. It is also true that there were far fewer women artists publicly showing their work in the 1970s and 1980s than in more recent years. José's role in encouraging women artists and promoting overall feminist consciousness cannot be dismissed. Shows by MARCH and MIRA focused on Mujeres, on Frida Kahlo, and on Sor Juana Inés de la Cruz are probably his best defense in this matter.

However, women's presence is probably not as strong in his life narrative as it should be, while the true heroic figures are Emiliano Zapata, Pancho Villa, Vincent van Gogh, Diego Rivera, José Clemente Orozco, and César Chávez. José may well have had a male-centered perspective, and it is interesting to note how this Chicano artist likens MARCH recruitment methods to those of Robin Hood with his merry men—with Carlos Cortez as Long John and Mary Kay Vaughan as Maid Marion.[9] Indeed, the struggle between "professionals" and "activists" so central to José's narrative may have "sometimes masked gender conflicts."[10] Some of Ana Castillo's early poems (1995) mock the male-centeredness of early Chicago Chicano cultural workers, although the butt of her sarcasm is clearly not José but other, younger Latino males of her own generation. Nevertheless, a crucial point in José's narrative is when Castillo's close friend Juana Guzmán replaces him on the Chicago City Arts Council and when Guzmán, along with the Mexican cultural attaché Argentina Terán de Erdman, helped the budding MFAC in its developing efforts. Another moment of tension, now forgotten by most, was when a recently arrived arts entrepreneur, Diana Berticini, with the support of Margaritte Morton and José's friend Marta Ayala, began to mount shows and eventually open a space in Chicago's gallery district, promoting Latino arts and, to Jose's discomfort, inadvertently establishing distinctions between the important artists like Marco Raya and lesser ones in the community. Berticini's efforts eventually failed, giving way to the more successful enterprise of the Nicaraguan artist/promoter Aldo Castillo to mount and sustain a distinguished mainstream Latino gallery in the 1990s. However, the tension with Juana Guzmán seemed to persist over the years in the midst of moments of cooperation, and José's difficult relationship with Helen Valdez, one of the two key figures in the development of the MFACM, is probably underplayed in José's narrative, as it centers on the Mexican figure who also became a key player to both women, Carlos Tortolero. It may well be that the gendered dimension of José's struggle and narrative is underplayed in his own account and in the questions I asked that had their role in shaping the narrative. But a full exploration of this theme would require a closer look not only at his wife and women artists as organizers and cultural workers, but also at his mother and his daughter—and, to name a last, crucial figure, the Virgen de Guadalupe.

The failed efforts of community artists, Chicano artists among them, make for the sad narrative on the pages that follow. There is, however, another way to see José's story: as one of triumph in spite of every defeat, as one of fidelity to one's deepest impulse. So all his frustrations and failures have another side, and there are also the small victories along the way. As a father, perhaps his greatest day was when his daughter Alicia graduated from Brown University. As an incapacitated artist, perhaps his greatest recent triumphs were when the Pilsen art group Mestizarte arranged an homage to him at their Eighteenth Street gallery space in 1998; or when one of his sculptures became the virtual centerpiece of one of the more important Day of the Dead exhibits at the Collage Gallery run by this writer's wife, Esther Soler; or when Arturo Avedaño arranged a Carlos Cortez/José González retrospective at Avedaño's La Llorona Gallery on Chicago's North Side; or when Gil Cárdenas purchased one of his best charcoals and then contributed it to the MFACM's permanent collection and their 2006 Day of the Dead show; or, most recently, in 2008, when José's daughter won recognition as a Chicago Latina marathon runner and announced her plans to develop a program centered on Latino fitness.

It is my hope that this book, which those more knowledgeable than myself convinced me had to be done, now joins and confirms José's previous victories, as readers come to know and hopefully understand one of the most significant figures in the making of Mexican Chicago and its relation to the U.S. Chicano art world, but also one of those key U.S. Mexican artists whose work seeks to express the richest aspirations of his community. This book may well be the key space achieved by José's struggles.

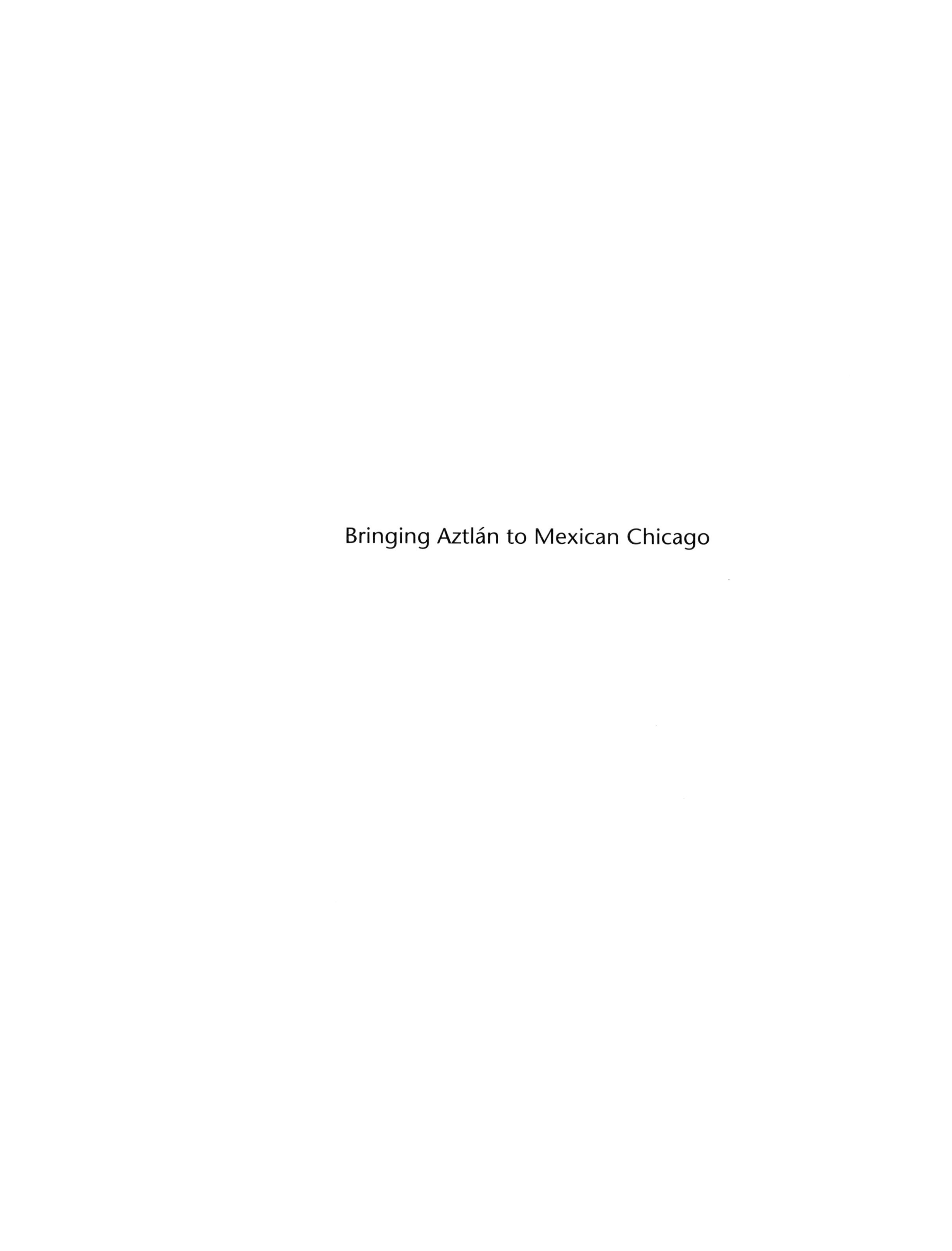

Bringing Aztlán to Mexican Chicago

Invocation

Some Framing Thoughts

This will be the story of my life—my work as a Mexican artist and arts promoter in Chicago's Mexican community. There's so much to tell, and I'm not sure I can tell it all. Sometimes I think I'm losing memory. I remember the order and dates of things and the things more or less, but I seem to leave out the details. Then I remember the smallest things, but the details are confused or kind of hazy—I can't quite get it, or I guess I don't get at the importance some of these things might've had for me or others. I would never have told this story, but Marc Zimmerman told me how three Latino leaders ganged up on him, saying it was important to have my story, and that he should do this book, and Marc said he'd try. I'm proud of what they said, because they're important and knowledgeable Latinos, and I guess they made me feel that Marc should try too, so I decided not to let illness or any problems stop me from doing my best to tell my story. I guess I'll leave for others to say if I got it right or not.

Some will argue that this is a happy story of a man who did some important things in the face of difficulties. Some will say it's the sad story of a man who failed—a failure who didn't achieve what he wanted to and could have or couldn't have succeeded. Others will say it's the story of a community pioneer—but someone who didn't do as much as he wanted and wants to cry about things that stopped him from doing the great things he would never have been able to do anyway. I know I've always been a dreamer—a Catholic dreamer and artist, I guess, trying to do what God made it maybe possible for me to do as best I could. And, of course, I've always been a Mexican trying to do my art for my people as much as for myself. But this is my story as my friend Marc got me to tell it. You and I will have to judge what to make of it.

1
The Early Years (1933–55)

FAMILY ORIGINS

My family is from two places. My mother is from Texas—a *texana*—and my father is from Iturbide, Nuevo León, Mexico, a small village about thirty miles from Monterrey. He was born there, and then I was, on April 20, 1933.

My mother's father was from Durango, Mexico, I think, but he'd gone to the Midwest when she was pretty young. My father came up to East Chicago, Indiana, as a migrant worker. They met in the early thirties, during the Depression, at a time when a lot of Mexicans were being sent back from Chicago to Mexico. That's exactly what happened to them. My father went to work in the steel mills as a strikebreaker. Soon he met my mother, who was only seventeen. He courted her for about two years. Then he went to my grandfather and asked for her hand, and they finally got married. The day after, he said, "We're going to Mexico, because we've got a free trip." That's how quickly she left. And she didn't have time to settle down. I

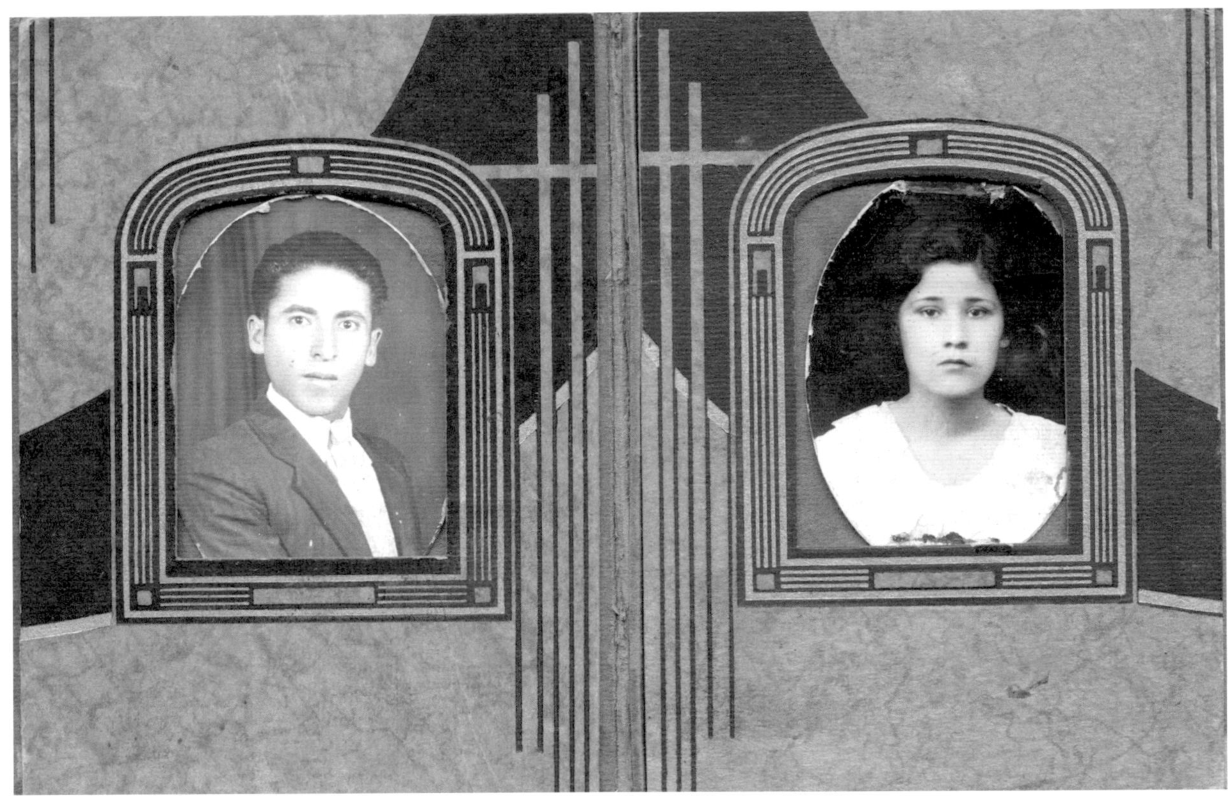

think they left by cattle car, which is how a lot of them left. That was the Repatriation. And they were part of it.[1]

My ex-wife, Mary Kay Vaughan, a historian of Mexico, once told me how colleagues of hers had done some studies of the Repatriation in the Chicago area, including East Chicago and Gary, Indiana. And it's always been a big question: "What relationship is there between the early people who came to Chicago from Mexico and those who eventually were there in the forties and fifties?" One theory being that a lot of people were sent out and never came back. That was my father, but not my mother. Sometimes the historians can't get it right because life's too complicated. In my case, my family was broken up by the patterns of immigration and separation. My father let himself be repatriated back to Mexico, and he took her with him. She was a U.S. citizen, but the *migra* didn't care. She was Mexican and was married to him, so they went together to Mexico. And he went to live in Iturbide and then Monterrey, while my mother moved back and forth to Indiana until she finally decided to stay in the United States.

ORIGINS, BIRTH, AND BAPTISM

My father's parents were born in Iturbide, and his grandparents too—so there are several generations back, probably. I don't know where his family may have initially come from. Some of them may have come from Spain. He was named Gamaliel, and it was a strange story. When he was born, someone said he should be called Gamaliel, who was a Jewish rabbi and St. Paul's teacher. St. Paul is the one who decided to take the teachings of Jesus to the Gentiles, to the non-Jewish people. He said the Jews aren't all accepting Christ. We've already got as many as we can get from them. There's not really anyone else to convert—we'd better go and seek some converts elsewhere. So he revolutionized Christianity from the day he went from being Saul and became Paul, spreading the gospel as he traveled the world. And his rabbi Gamaliel had a kind of spiritual influence on him. Gamaliel was the one who was famous for saying not to do anything to Jesus, because he said, "If he's a fake, he'll be discovered, but if he's not a fake, then we're fighting against God himself." So Saul took it upon himself to fight against the Jewish religion—or for Christianity. This maybe became part of me, fighting through art for my faith. My father wanted me named Gamaliel too. But my mother wanted José. She wanted a simple Christian name and chose the name of a man of faith, a carpenter who could believe it was God who got his wife pregnant. And yes, I believe in the Immaculate Conception and the Virgen de Guadalupe.

Anyway, my parents compromised, and I was baptized José Gamaliel González in December 1933 when I was six months old. My mother was Flores, but she left that off my name in the American and not the Mexican way. So no one knows me as González-Flores. And I wasn't baptized in Iturbide, but in Mexico City. There was still persecution of the church during the years when Calles was in power. I think my parents took me off to Mexico City so no one would know about the baptism.

ITURBIDE MEMORIES

Iturbide was and is a small town. And at that time, the town had no light, no running water.

We had a well from which you could draw up a bucket of water, and we had corn, oranges, apples—different things. My mother said my paternal grandfather was a saint, and he was very good to me. He planted an orange tree and said, "This tree is just for you." But it wasn't for my father. You couldn't even get to the town unless you had a jeep, or at least a horse or mule. So first, after my baptism, he looked for work in Mexico City. And when he failed, he took us back to Iturbide and headed for Monterrey. There he started a scrap-metal business with his three brothers, Arturo, Gustavo, and Octavio.

My uncle Arturo was the oldest of my father's brothers. He had married and gone up to Indiana, where he had a rooming-house business, with a lot of *mexicanos* living there—and him giving them room and board. Maybe "gave" isn't the right word. I've heard a lot about people who had those boarding houses. Some of them weren't so nice. Maybe my uncle wasn't so nice either. He got a dollar a day from these poor people, and they were stacked up like pancakes in a small room while they were trying to send the *remesas* back to Mexico, and they were saving on their rooms there because they didn't have much anyway, and they were hired mainly as scabs. But my uncle Arturo didn't work in the mills. He had the rooming house. That was enough.

Now together in Monterrey, he and his brothers went into scrap metal during the late 1930s and early '40s, as the Depression winded down and World War II began. They did very well during the war because the U.S. needed the iron. So they were going all around the Monterrey area gathering up bits and pieces and getting them to the border. I guess they did well enough so my father never felt the need to go back to the United States or to Iturbide, so we hardly ever saw each other till I got out of the army in the 1950s.

ITURBIDE STORIES

I'm not sure I remember much about my years in Mexico, but I remember the stories that my mother told me about those Mexico times when I was about eight and we were living in Indiana. So I'm not sure I remember Mexico or if I remember my mother telling me stories about Mexico. If I close my eyes for a minute, I can see myself as a little kid in Iturbide, but maybe that's because I have pictures of me there. In one photo you can really see my face—it's the picture of a baby boy, but he looks like me even though he's only around three and dressed in a baby boy sailor suit, the way they always dressed up kids in those days. And yes, my baby brother is there with me too. We never learned to be great sailors, but maybe we learned to keep afloat. I guess I don't remember all that—I remember my mother telling me about things, and showing me photos of things. But that's not the same as remembering the things themselves.

Maybe the first thing I do remember in Iturbide is when a group of Mexican soldiers came by on horseback. My brother Arturo and I were swimming naked, and we got scared and ran to the house when we saw the men and horses, because in 1937 and '38, there were still divisions in Mexico, and we were told the federal soldiers were dangerous people. It wasn't the Mexican Revolution, of course, but the Cárdenas period had its problems too.

I guess the stories I remember most are the ones my mother told me. She suffered a lot from raising us, especially me—because I was a pain in the neck to start with. She told me a story about when she was pregnant with me, and she went with my father on horseback in Iturbide, and she fell off the horse. But she survived, and so did I, she told me—and I guess I've no reason to doubt her because here I am, whatever and whoever I am.

Another story of hers was when my father was driving an old station-wagon jeep in Iturbide, and there was a hill, and he couldn't put the brakes on. I was sitting in the front seat as the truck kept moving and moving, and my mother was praying. She was really scared. And she prayed for me, and the jeep hit against some rocks. But we didn't get hurt at all, because the jeep just bounced off the rocks, and I was okay. I guess what the stories are about is how we all survived and bounced back in spite of it all in that little town.

But my mother kept going back to her family in East Chicago, Indiana, and my father kept on living and working in Monterrey. And my mother finally decided to stay in Indiana and took us for good when I was almost six years old, with my father staying in Mexico for good—or ill.

RETURN TO INDIANA

My mother traveled back and forth all the time, so my brother Arturo was born in East Chicago, Indiana. My sister Helen was born in Mexico, and my sister Mary was born in Indiana. The last time my mother was pregnant was when she was carrying Mary, who's about eight years younger than me.

My mother worked cleaning house and cooking and sewing for the Garzas, a rich Mexican family that opened a factory making cheese and other things in East Chicago. And then Mr. Garza started selling sewing machines, and my grandfather, her father, bought her one. So she began to sew for these people, but then she finally got a job at the Inland Steel Company, where she worked for over thirty years—from the start of World War II to the day she retired. She left the sewing behind her.

Arturo Rosales wrote some things about Mexican Chicago and especially East Chicago,

Indiana—what they call Indiana Harbor, near Lake Michigan. He also did a long interview of my mother, but only a little note about her appeared in his book, *Chicano!* [2] My former wife, Mary Kay, and our daughter, Alicia, interviewed her too, but the interview was never published, even though it probably still exists in tape form. They asked her about coming back to Chicago after being repatriated—about all of that, including how she raised us alone, because my father and my mother got separated. She didn't divorce him, because she was a Catholic, except that many, many years later she divorced him, because her lawyer said, "If he wants to take the kids, he can take them from you, and so you have to divorce him, so he can't do anything to you." But he wouldn't have done anything like that anyway, because he wasn't that kind of a person.

Meanwhile, in East Chicago, we lived with my grandfather on my mother's side, and I got to know other family members. There was my Aunt Helen. She was older; she joined a religious order, and they sent her to Colombia for a year or two to work with the sisters. Then there was my Uncle Pete, who went off to Europe.

My Aunt Candy—Candelaria Flores, my mother's sister—was a singer and sang well enough to perform opera in Grant Park. She won a competition—there were three people that competed, and all three were offered scholarships to the Metropolitan in the 1930s. But I guess something got in the way for Aunt Candy.

My grandfather was an orphan. He was raised by monks. He wasn't mean, but he was very strict and had to have his way. I was born left-handed, but when I got to Indiana, he changed me to be right-handed, because he said, "The left hand is the hand of the devil." I know that's supposed to have a very special effect, because your body's nervous system is geared to whichever hand is dominant. And if you're left-handed, the creative part of your brain is what's supposed to be on the right side, which coordinates with the left hand. I don't know all the details. I just know that my grandfather taught us that the left hand was evil, that the monks raised him and told him that that's the hand of the devil. So he forced me to change, and now maybe I'm a right-handed painter who should be a lefty. Maybe I might have been a better or at least a different painter if I'd painted with my left hand. I didn't know the story until later. But sometimes I feel that when I'm painting somehow part of me wants to be painting with the other hand. It was a long time ago that I was changed. It was when I was very young, when I was six, soon after I came back to Indiana. And I think that change was also the cause of my starting to stutter. I stuttered as a kid for many years, and as a young high school student I still stuttered. I still stutter to this day, and with medications today it's sometimes worse.

But I think I'm almost naturally a stutterer. I think there've always been moments where I pause or stutter, when there's some kind of break in my thought or speaking. Maybe it's because of stuttering that I need to draw and paint. Maybe that's part of my art, too, some gap or break I try to fill by working my images and details.

One thing I should emphasize, though, is that my grandfather was a musician. He started the first orchestra in East Chicago, Indiana, and he taught his brothers and sisters and their kids to play musical instruments. My grandfather not only taught my mother to sew but also to play the violin. She really didn't want to play, and he forced her. She said she wanted to play the piano, and she couldn't afford a piano anyways, but he said that her hands weren't wide enough to reach all the keys. So she had to learn to play

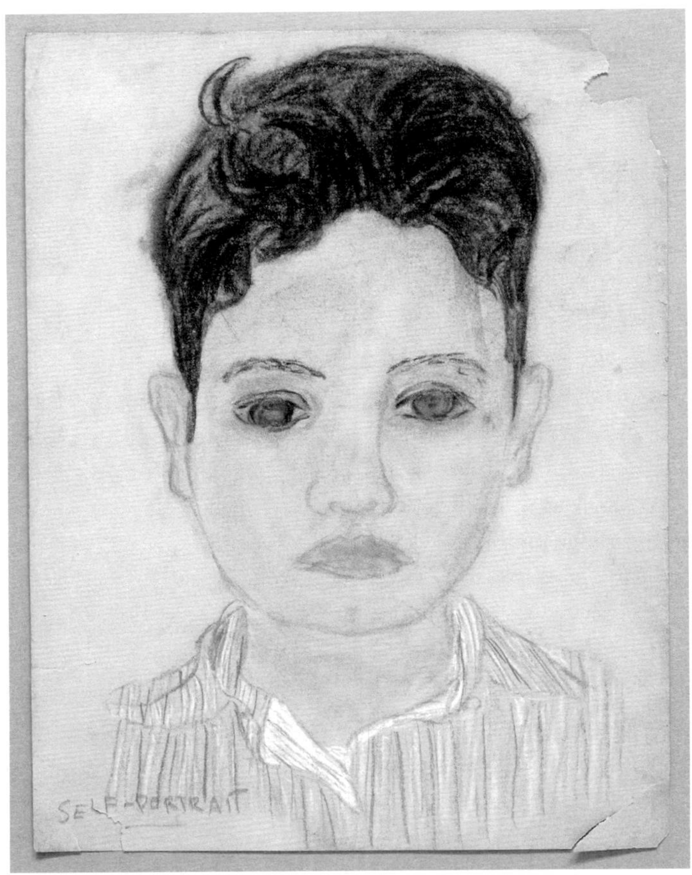

Fig. 4. José Gamaliel González, self-portrait, early 1940s. 8"×11". Color. Pastel.

the violin. My Uncle Joe played the trumpet. My Uncle Peter also played, though I don't remember what. And my aunt was the opera singer. She and my mother used to go to the opera in Chicago when they were young, at the old opera house at the Auditorium before the Lyric Theater took over. In *Citizen Kane,* Orson Welles's wife screeches at the huge Auditorium theater, and her terrible voice rises up into the balcony, but that's not the way my aunt sang at the opera.

So my family is really not an artistic but a musical family. And maybe it was all that music that went into my art. That was the main thing—that every kid had to play an instrument, like Selena's family, where every brother and sister played something, and they ended up backing her up in her songs. Really, we all played instruments. As for me, my grandfather taught me to play saxophone. But I also played

clarinet in the marching band of Washington High School. I was in the band, but I don't play anymore. I was kind of proud about playing. I liked the teacher we had. He was Hungarian and had a very difficult name—he had to sign a declaration that he was going to change it to "Young." We're talking about the forties in East Chicago, Indiana, where I graduated in 1952. I was always the Indiana kid from the time I was six to my graduation date. Some of my better courses were math and U.S history. My grandfather taught me algebra when I was twelve. But English was very frightening to me.

When I got to kindergarten, I was a year older than the other kids, because I was six already, and I was going on seven when I began. I got scared. School frightened me, because I didn't understand a word people spoke to me. My family spoke Spanish in the home—even though my mother taught me English, because she spoke English. And no one taught me Spanish; we just spoke it. To this day I feel that my understanding of Spanish is pretty good, even better than when I was a kid, because I can read now more than I could before. Then, I couldn't read. But English is still my first language, then Spanish. In fact, I think I write pretty well in English—even with style, some people have said so. Some of the things I've written on gentrification, some of the proposals I wrote for MIRA, have won me some praise. So I guess there's a strong English emphasis in what I learned. I didn't learn the history of Mexico; I learned U.S. history. I learned the history of Mexico on my own. But that came later.

From my early childhood, I had a sense of being Mexican, of being in a Mexican family and also being in a Mexican community that was very Catholic. My general sense was of feeling Mexican in the Indiana part of the Chicago area. I felt like a minority because there was a lot of prejudice where we were living, and we were in the so-called ghetto. There was a part that was literally across the tracks, where you had blacks and Mexicans living. There was a time before I was born, in my mother's time, when you couldn't walk on the same side of the street, down the main part of Main Street, without some problems happening. Mexicans weren't supposed to walk there in East Chicago. And there was prejudice against us, too, even in grade school. About 20 percent of the students were Mexican, black about maybe 25 percent. And I guess we all felt sort of inferior—that we weren't on the same level as the white kids, try as we might.

Us Mexican kids used to play games against the Anglos—soccer or other games. But we always won, and the *güeros* used to say, "You cheated. You counted in Spanish. Besides, you're playing soccer, not U.S. football. So that's cheating in itself." It was very Mexican of me to play soccer. But even when I played U.S.–style football, I felt *mexicano* because of my grand-parents and my mother. She and I identified as *mexicanos*. I knew that the *mexicanos* were a minority. I knew they were not treated the same way in the steel mills. I knew they didn't have the same job opportunities. And this was part of my sense of who I was. I was going be one of these guys who would be caught in that trap, or I was going be somebody who was go-ing to fight against that trap. I saw they were prejudiced against us, and of course we were prejudiced against them. I guess it's not the first time where the Mexicans win something, and the whites say that it's because you do some-thing Mexican-style so even when you win you lose, somehow.

MY BROTHER ART

I felt very good about being the oldest of my brothers and sisters. I was the one who had to take care of them—especially my younger sis-ters. But with Art, my relationship was kind of funny. Art never learned to play an instrument. Even though his name was Art, he never was artistic. I found a drawing he did of a dragon, and it's a really good ink drawing. I told him so, and he was surprised. He didn't remember it at all. I didn't remember either until I found it. It's like he blocked out his artistic side, or maybe gave it over to me.

Arturo was only a year and seven months younger than me, but we were going in two dif-ferent directions. He was into the male thing and the peer group thing. And without knowing it then, I was going toward the arts. Of course, we were kids in the Depression. Being the oldest, I went to work as soon as I could—dishwashing, working in a boarding house, and doing milk and paper delivery. My brother had some of the same jobs, but he didn't work every place I did. I bought a couple of little things, but I really brought most of my money home to my mom and my sisters. I was the older brother working for the family, but Arturo was a spender. He didn't bring much money home. All he made he spent.

I went to public school, and Arturo went to Catholic school—in the first graduating high school class of Our Lady of Guadalupe church. But he was never very religious, and he was the one who got involved in gangs—not me, though I sometimes went along for the ride. He was always in trouble or looking for it; he took to the streets and joined a gang pretty early. It was hard to get him to see reason; he was a little bit of a problem. He was very popular with his friends because he was a good fighter. A lot of the guys he went around with admired him and considered him a hero. Gary Mexicans didn't want to deal with East Chicago Mexicans—and least of all, Indiana Harbor Mexicans like us. We were always conniving to see which one of us could get the better of the other. One thing we knew: you didn't go to Gary and go dancing in dance halls—you showed up there, and you might not get out alive. But one night in our late teens, we just couldn't resist—and off we went to a dance in Gary anyway. Some Gary Mexicans pulled up next to our car and gave Arturo a bad time. He got out and jumped on their car, banging on it for them to get out. I asked my brother, "What are you doing? You're looking for a fight with these guys?" And he said, "If you don't like it, then you can fight with me." So we went at it—the only time I fought with my brother. His buddies started swinging, but they weren't able to beat me up—I really kept them at an even draw. And that surprised them, because I wasn't supposed to be the fighter. And then they stopped fighting, and they separated me from Arturo, maybe because I would have gotten beat up sooner or later.

There's the thing about my brother: he was very prone to problems and accidents. When he was about seven or eight years old, he was running across the street, and a Cadillac hit him and ran over his knees. I saw it all myself, and I remember it very clearly. The tires stayed on top of him, but they couldn't completely roll over them. Two big guys picked the car up, and they pulled him out. His legs were bruised and battered, but they weren't completely broken— even with a Cadillac on top of them. That was on Block Avenue near the Indiana Harbor Guadalupe church. And it was a miracle. But not even that could keep Arturo serious about religion, let alone art. But we weren't Cain and Abel. We've always been different, but brothers.[3]

RELIGIOUS QUESTIONS

It's also true that though I never went to a Catholic school, I studied catechism after school and on weekends. I was really close to the church. I was an altar boy, and so was my brother. But he didn't go very much. It was a Mexican church with a Mexican priest for a while. But he died, and after that all the other priests were Irish or English or German or whatever. I always felt very religious. And that was normal for altar boys—you were vehicles of the church. I used to serve mass at different churches, including a morning mass at an orphanage. I was very close to the church. I wanted to be a priest at one time. I went to the seminary for a weekend to see if I liked it or not. And I said no—but only after a while.

A lot of my religious education was in English with the liturgical materials in Latin, but there were also services in Spanish. The three priests took part in the mass, with the priest in the center leading the ceremony. Once when I participated in the mass, the tassels on my cassock caught fire. At first I felt warm and sweaty, and then I got very hot. The head priest caught on, and he got the Bible and hit me to put the fire out. I didn't fall down. I never fainted. But it was like I caught on fire with my religious faith, and he put it out by hitting me with a Bible. Of course, I had feelings of reverence and religiosity, and I went to the seminary when I was about sixteen or seventeen, after six or seven years as an altar boy. It was important for all of us young boys to aspire to be priests.

I didn't feel like, "Oh, Mexicans can't do that," or, "Only Irish kids can do that." I never felt neglected or put down by the church. I know the historians emphasize how a lot of Mexicans in the Chicago area left the church and joined Protestant sects because they felt they were not treated right by the Catholic hierarchy. But we were treated very well, first by two young priests—one from Poland, and another who'd come from another part of the United States— and then by an Irish priest, Father Kennelly from New York. He was a great guy. He had a

Brooklyn accent, and he was short. I was very close to him. We used to go picket the movies that had too much sex or violence. I never thought it was wrong to be on those picket lines, and it turned out to be good training for my Chicano activism later.

By the time I graduated high school, though, my religious fervor was gone, and being a man in the world had taken over. Being Catholic was not the main thing; being a playboy was. I did not come out of high school feeling I had a religious mission or feeling that my future was tied up with religion in any way, but I had a religious background. I did not feel discriminated against in the church. In fact, I felt encouraged to be a good Catholic, and even if I decided not to become a priest, I had a very strong and positive experience in the church as a young boy.

I was very close to the church, as was my mother. We were all religious, except for my brother. He was kind of distant—he was so busy with his gang and cars. I lost some of my religious spirit when I went to art school at the Academy of Fine Arts in Chicago, even though I sometimes would go to the Holy Name Cathedral, which was very close to the academy.

BEGINNING INTERESTS IN VISUAL ARTS

I do remember being interested in the visual arts almost from the start. As a very young kid, I used to draw a lot, and my teacher, Helen Carter, kept me after school when I was about eight or nine and gave me supplies to draw and paint. And I have drawings that I did when I was a kid. I had some, and I lost some. I don't know what happened to them. But in northwestern Indiana, I lived right near a city called Chicago, and I knew early on that being from northwestern Indiana was being part of the Chicago world. I first went to the Art Institute as a young kid, about ten or eleven years old. My mother brought me to Chicago, and I went to the institute on Saturdays. And then I learned how to go by myself, and I got interested in going to the openings and special shows there.

I discovered Mexican art later on. At the beginning, my favorite artists were Michelangelo, Da Vinci, Rafael—the Renaissance period. Those were my first interests, and I wanted to learn how to draw the way they drew; and when I look at my notebooks, I see efforts to draw in a certain kind of style—neoclassical or something like that. Even as a boy and then a young man, I often thought, "I'm going to be an artist."

I kept on drawing always, all the time, through eighth grade in 1948 and then through high school, where I won many awards for drawing and painting. My teacher used to pick an artist a month, and I was one that was always picked a lot. When I was just entering my freshman year of high school, a teacher saw my work and said, "This is pretty good. You might make it as an artist." And that stayed with me. I thought about it all the time. And I thought, "That sounds really good." So I came to know I wanted to be an artist from the time I was about sixteen.

There was probably something else that made me think about being an artist from 1948 on. That was the year when the Art Institute brought a huge one-man Van Gogh show to Chicago, and it just floored me. It didn't bother me that he was Dutch and not related to my world very much at all. As a matter of fact, it was the opposite, so that he became the artist who most affected me. I even went to the big show in Amsterdam in 1990, and I did a Vincent and I exhibit at four galleries when I came back. I felt that I knew the man, that I suffered like him, when I saw his paintings.

Of course, I didn't see myself as suffering in high school. On the surface I was just having a good time like other kids seemed to have—in

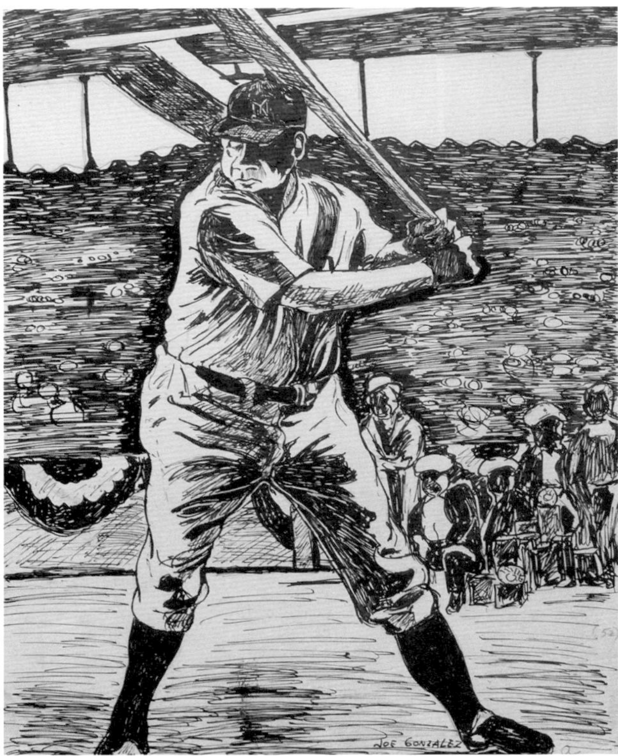

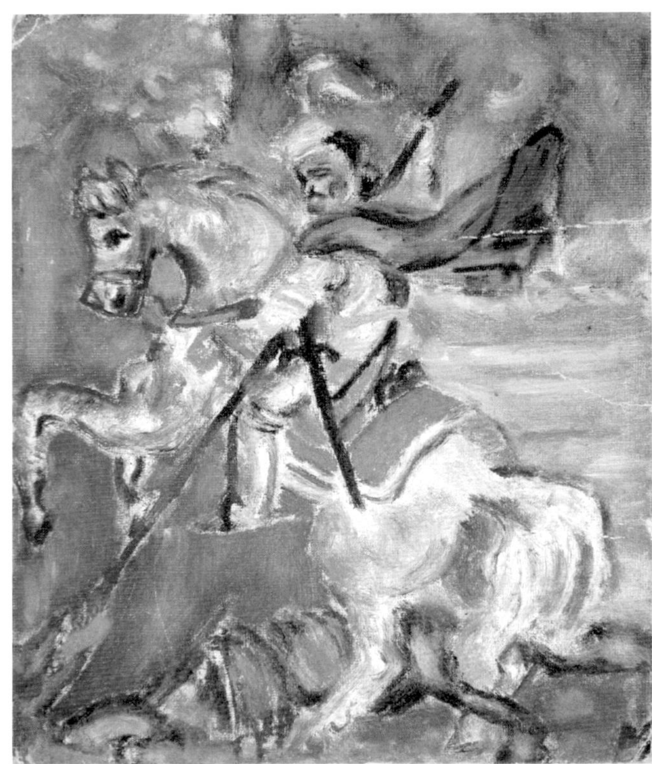

fact, I was really a trouble-maker. I had a history teacher who was kind of comical, and we made fun of him. Really, we were the ones that were comical or absurd. And one time when the teacher was in his room on the second floor, I went up to the window and threatened to jump, and he got scared. So I was a kind of a trouble-maker, but I never got the whip—though maybe I should've.

But I also took up oil painting in high school, or even before. My teachers gave me oil colors and brushes, and I did a portrait of Heddy Lamar playing Delilah. I got into oil painting and sketching, too. Drawing, sketching—I did a lot of portraits of students and of my sister, Mary. I've lost most of the pictures I had from grammar school. My mother saw that I had artistic abilities, and she got a correspondence course for me. She paid for it out of the money she kept aside, and I took correspondence courses for about three or four months. I got tired of it, though—I didn't like it that much. It

was good, though. Today I see the confidence they gave me. I had to do horses and animals and people, and then they made corrections of them, and they almost always demanded corrections. Sometimes I got an "okay," and I had no corrections at all. Sometimes I had corrections of the horses' hooves, for example (fig. 6).

I also went to work. I went to work in the mills in the summertime. And I worked two summers in a labor gang, but they were very easy with me. I had times when they'd tell me to go, just go hide by the rocks and by the lake—"Don't kill the job, kid, just take a nap."

When I was finishing up high school in 1951 and '52, a lot of kids were starting to think about going to college. Other kids were thinking about getting jobs; others were thinking of joining the military. I won a math scholarship to Purdue University, and I didn't take it, because I wanted to be an artist. There were counselors that were prejudiced against Mexicans, and they advised us to go work in the mills. They said that I could

Fig. 5. José Gamaliel González, Babe Ruth, 1952 (high school). 8"×11". Pen and ink.

Fig. 6. José Gamaliel González, Saint George, 1952. 8"×11". Oil on canvas, color.

earn good money—better than I could make by going to college. And I knew nothing about Purdue. I didn't know they had a good art department and that I could take classes even if my scholarship was for math. I figured, "I don't want to be an engineer, so why should I go?" One of my best friends, Louis Sander, went to Purdue and became an engineer. Purdue had scholarships for *mexicanos*. There was even an organization, a "Sociedad mutualista mexicana," that was something like LULAC (the League of United Latin American Citizens) and that gave scholarships to a few Mexican students. But I didn't get one because I wanted to go to art school, and so they gave the award to someone else. I won a scholarship from the teachers who knew me—Helen Carter, my grammar-school teacher, and Frances Boomer, a high-school teacher of mine. They raised some money for me. But I was very proud. I thought it was a handout, and I said, "Give it to someone else."

I didn't take either scholarship that I'd earned. It was a big opportunity, and I'd turned it all down—lost forever. I should have taken one of the scholarships, I know. But maybe I wouldn't have become an artist if I'd taken it. Or maybe I'd have become a better-trained artist. Who knows? I didn't go to college, and then I had to decide what to do.

As soon as I got out of high school, I thought maybe that the painting would fade as something I wanted to do—I doubted my calling, dismissed it as something that I'd wanted to do, without realizing that I was only cut out for that. I tried to leave art behind me, but I couldn't help it. I started drawing and painting again.

THINKING BACK: LOVE, ART SCHOOL, AND MILITARY SERVICE

Thus far, I've talked about my early days in Mexico and Indiana—how I became a high-

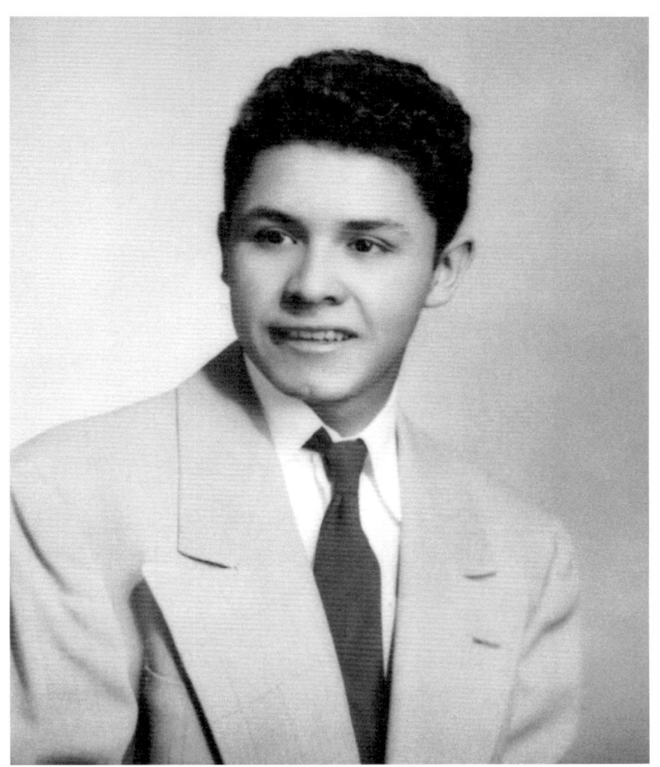

Fig. 7. José's high school graduation photo, 1952.

school kid, probably a bit of a troublemaker; how I became interested in Renaissance art and Van Gogh; how I did some artwork; how I had an opportunity to get a scholarship that I didn't take, which, thinking back on it, might have been an important moment in my life. In all of this, what I did know, what I was constantly reminded about was that I was Mexican—our society doesn't let you forget that. But I have to say that I never thought I was "a minority." I didn't think about minority/majority then. I didn't know about that idea. But somewhere inside me I somehow did feel, "Us *mexicanos*, we have it rough." I knew that I was part of a group that was put upon, victimized, and exploited. I saw what was happening to people in the steel mills. My mother was working all those years for Inland Steel. She probably even had a good job there, in a way. She was a clerk, and she worked in the stock room. The company went under just a few years ago. Until then, I could still drive by there and see the mills and the smoke pouring out of the stacks—the whole thing. Of course, I'm the son of a woman worker in the steel mills. Even though the Mexicans in the group suffered a lot, my mother had a good situation within the Mexican working-class world. And that privileged situation gave me the chance to take an interest in art, to develop that interest into the passion I felt by the time I graduated from high school.

But no, I never thought of myself as a Mexican artist. Not then at all. I had no idea of what that could mean. I didn't know anything about any famous Mexican artists—I knew nothing. I knew Van Gogh was a great artist. I wanted to be like Van Gogh. I know Van Gogh is a very unusual model for an artist. He's a brilliant painter, but he's also kind of like a disturbed painter, a painter whose visions come from maybe a little bit of emotional imbalance, some passion—that's what makes him stand out. Maybe I sensed I was going to have problems like him. I can still remember the impact on me when I saw the one-man Van Gogh show. I felt I knew the man. I stood there frozen when I saw the works. It was just incredible, the impact he would have on my art and life.

I remember too when I saw *Lust for Life,* it was interesting because Anthony Quinn, the *mexicano,* plays Gauguin, not Van Gogh. And so that's a very funny twist for me. Kirk Douglas, the actor with the cleft chin, is the one who plays Van Gogh. Yes, I have a cleft in my chin, too. But I think there's something else—maybe the intensity of his vision and also his religious or spiritual passion. His work has an almost mystical power that goes beyond "good" or "bad" technique. The bad thing about him, though, is what happened in his life: how he was going to be a preacher at one time—he was an evangelist like Paul—and then he turned all his passion to art, and he was alone inside and cut off his ear and later shot himself. He didn't die right away. He died about

three days later, and he never had Last Rites. That has stayed with me in my own dark nights—that I couldn't let that happen to me and my family because of our religion. I mean, his friends had a big funeral for him. They hung up his paintings on the wall of his yellow house, and they were just stunned at what he had done, at all the wonderful paintings that he had left.

But let me just repeat that I knew nothing about Diego Rivera. I knew nothing about Orozco. I didn't know who Siqueiros was—he could've been the plumber down the street, as far as I knew. And I'd never heard of Frida Kahlo. Over the years, I learned about Mexican art on my own, way before art school. I'm trying to remember when I learned of the Mexican artists, when my passion for painting deepened, when I considered them really great artists. Oh yes, I know when it was—when I was at the School of the Art Institute. I'm surprised myself by the late date, but maybe I shouldn't be. The Americans and Chicago artists couldn't care less about Mexican art. They were into Jackson Pollack and all that came after him. In 1952 I knew nothing about that.

Finally, I guess I should say something about my early loves and my relations with women, because I know it's important in the lives of most men and artists, and I'm no exception. Of course, there was my puppy love for a girl named Carol when I was a little boy. My young uncle Joe told me she had a thing for me. And I was very shy, but I got up the courage to approach her. I don't know what happened, but I seem to remember holding hands with her and maybe even kissing her. Then there was my first Mexican flame—a girl from East Chicago who was named Rose Mary. I really had a crush on her, and I took her to my senior prom (fig. 8). After the dance we drove to Chicago with my friend Tony Peña and his date to the Chez Paris, where we saw Frank Sinatra and had a great time. I remember that Tony's girl even caught the eye of a B-movie Romeo, Zachary Scott, who was at the Sinatra show. But nothing came of it, I think, and nothing happened between me and Rose Mary either, though I hear she's alive and would like to write to her if I can find her address.

In fact, I lost my virginity later than most men of my time. And though I was always crazy about women, I just didn't get carried away by them very often. I guess the pull of art was too strong. There was one girl—I can't remember her name, but she was from South Texas and had come to stay with her Indiana relatives in the house next-door to mine. I could tell she liked me, but nothing happened, and then she moved back to the borderlands. But she stayed on my mind. Once, during the year after high school, I took a trip to see her. I remember trying to find her house, and I figured I wasn't far from it. But it was raining hard. I was wading through mud in a storm. I kept wading and wading, trying to find her. But it was too much. I fell asleep by the train tracks, and when I got up it was still raining. And I just gave up. I went back to the Chicago area. She never even knew I looked for her, and I never saw her again. I really don't know why I did all that—I liked her a lot, and maybe I knew if I'd found her I'd have

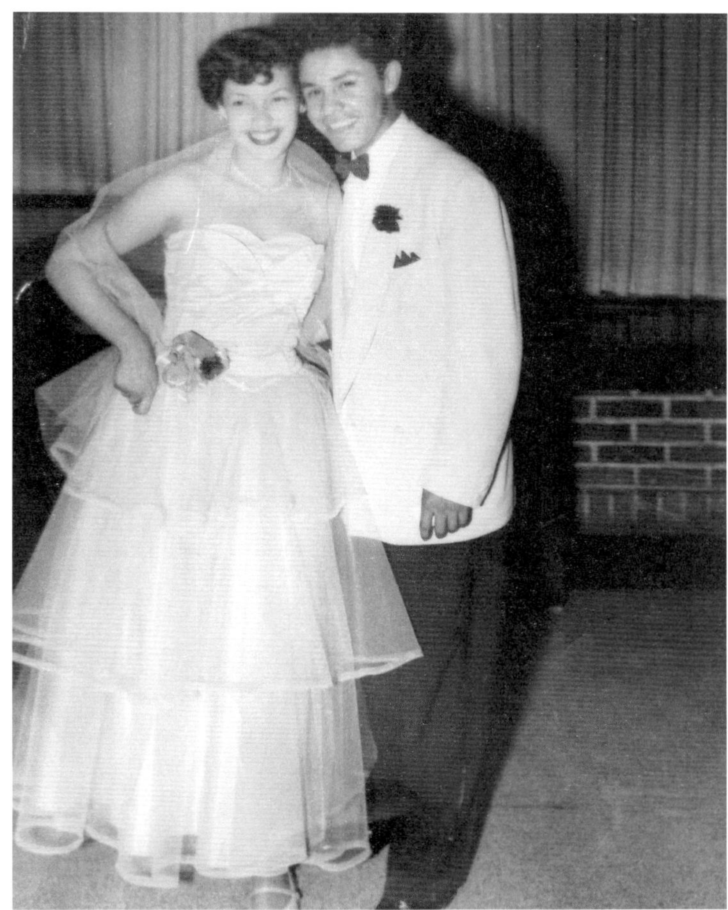

to marry her and maybe even live on the border or in Mexico, and that might not be good for my life or my becoming an artist. Or maybe it would have been good, maybe too good—who knows? But I guess not finding her maybe set up my life to go where it went.

Fig. 8. José with Rosemary Oría, prom picture, 1952.

2

From High School to Notre Dame (1955–71)

I graduated high school, but I didn't go to work. Instead I went to study art at the Chicago Academy of Fine Arts for a year. The school no longer exists, but it was near the corner of Rush Street and Chicago Avenue in the heart of the Gold Coast, the city's key nightlife area for tourists. It was there that I learned to draw and paint watercolors (fig. 10). We did some oils, but we didn't do many because of the expense.

Most of my experiences were commercial in the early years. I didn't think of art school the way the bohemian students did, then or today. I thought, it's not going to be that good—I can only go so far. I don't think I consciously thought that these were all just a bunch of white kids gone crazy over there—middle-class kids who are free to be crazy, where I had to be more practical.

I was always more practical—that was one thing, I couldn't relate to the students at the School of the Art Institute. Later on, I finally went there, when I was much older and probably more bohemian too. But I wasn't the typical student because I had been working for ten years in the advertising field.

Back in the early fifties, we were at war. My brother had gone off to fight in Korea, and I felt ashamed that I was the older brother, and I was not in the service. So I volunteered for two years, and I was a little scared because it was a rough war. But I was a fast typist in high school, so when they sent me to Missouri for basic training, they had already earmarked me for office work in Virginia, and then they shipped me over to Germany instead of Korea. And I was a little apprehensive about the German people at first. I thought, "They're going to dislike us because of the war. And they might hate Mexicans the way they hated the Jews." We were supposed to set up a new supply office for Europe. But when I got to Germany, they sent me to the post in Kaiserslautern, in the Rhine River wine region. They made a mistake and put me on an assembly line, where I worked with Germans and got to be very good friends with them. And I learned some German—I practiced on the radio. And all this meant that I never got reassigned properly because I became too valuable in establishing good relations with the German workers. I went all over the country. But I wasn't like most Americans. All they did was go to the bars—the Chicago bar, the Cowboy bar, the New York bar. And, of course, there were prostitutes galore at those places, but I never became a *pecador,* or sinner, in those days. Instead, other things happened.

First of all, an Italian friend, Fazzio, started what was like an orphanage for some German kids we kind of adopted. On Sunday afternoons, we used to take the kids to see the sights. And on Christmas day, we played Santa Claus, took them out, bought gifts for them. I was almost twenty years old, and there I was having it pretty good in Europe, while lots of guys and lots of Latinos

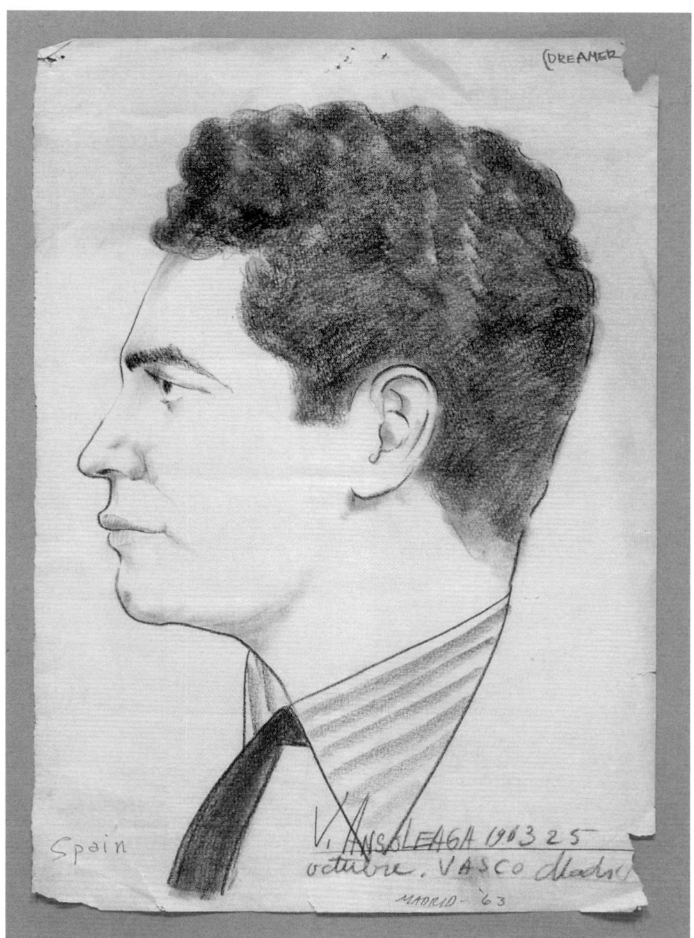

Fig. 9. V. Ansoleaga, Dreamer (Sketch of José). Madrid, October 25, 1963.

were in Korea. And meanwhile I was hanging out with different soldiers, including some Mexicans, Puerto Ricans, and other Latinos, doing cold war duty in a pretty safe place (fig. 11).

During my military service, I did have a few female friendships that almost led toward sex or love, though nothing really happened. Once, I went to a town along the Rhine at wine-harvest time, when visitors come by the droves to join in the fun. I remember I went to the village by bus, and I ended up staying very late because I was enjoying the white wine. A girl I met said, "Don't drink too much—it's real strong." And I said, "No, it's weak." I just didn't know it was stronger than the wine that's been already fermented, and I just drank too much after all. I drank and drank till I got sick, and she made

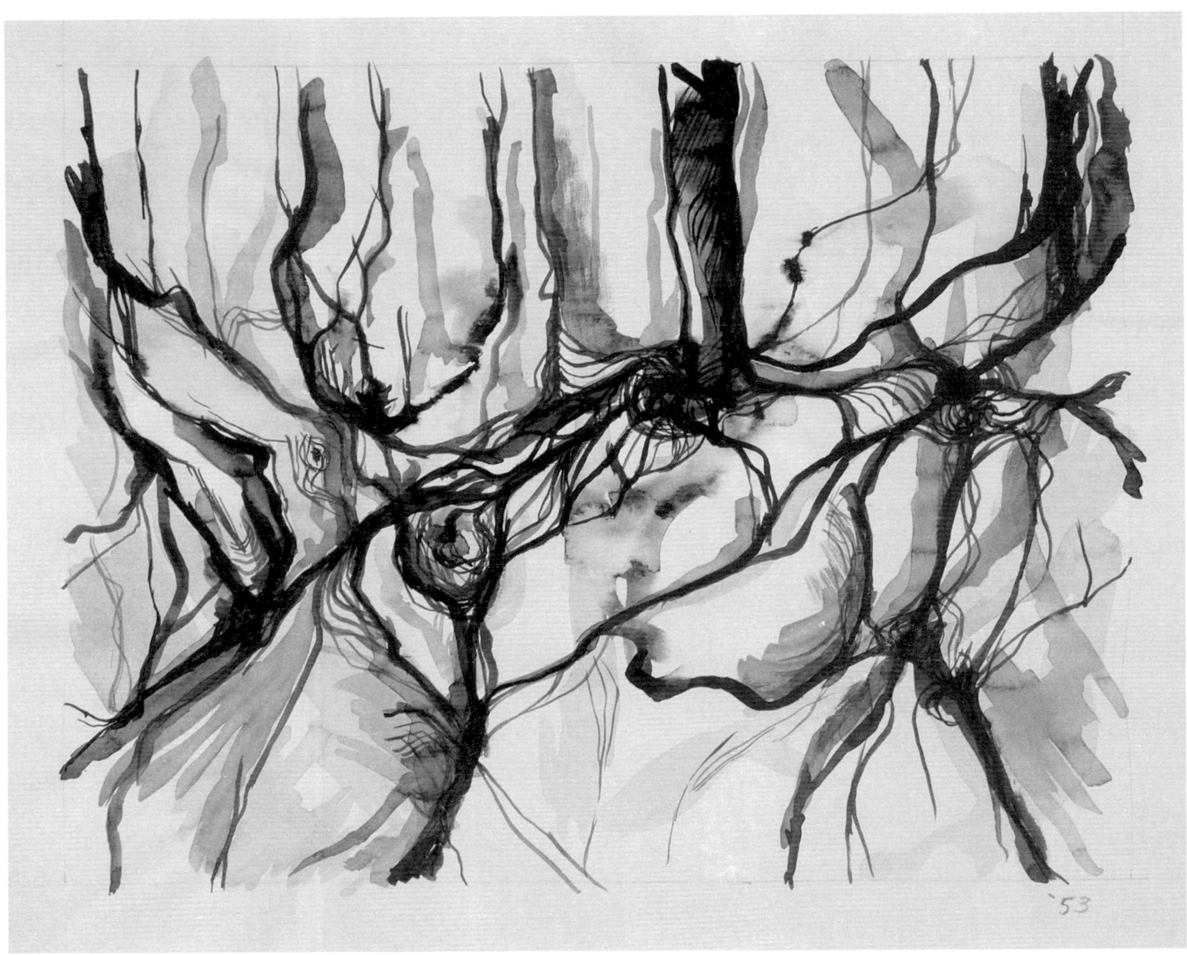

Fig. 10. José Gamaliel González, abstract landscape. 18"×24". Water color. Black and white. Chicago Fine Arts Academy, 1953. Owned and provided by Mario Castillo. From the collection of Mario Castillo.

me throw up to help me get well. It was pouring, and I don't know what happened to her, but all the buses had gone, and the hotels were full, so I stayed overnight under a bridge. I couldn't really sleep with the rain and chill air and my head still ringing from the wine. Finally, in the morning I found a bench and fell asleep. I was lucky, or God was with me, because I got up in time to take the bus back to camp, even if nothing happened with the girl who helped me.

Then, on a trip to Barcelona, I met a young woman from Madrid, but not much came of it because she was going with someone else. I did meet up with her again in Madrid, but she was still involved with the same guy or someone else. I spent more time at the Prado than I did with her.

In fact, those trips out were the most important part of my service time. I traveled all over Germany and then all over Europe, too. A few of us went AWOL, traveling without passes to Luxemburg. But for me, the best trips I took were to Italy and Spain. I remember being affected so much by the Renaissance art in Rome and Florence. I saw the Moses, the Pietá in Rome. Seeing the Sistine Chapel was overwhelming to me—the power and vision of Michelangelo were just remarkable. To see all the works by Rafael, Fra Angelico, DaVinci, and all the other masters—and maybe above all the David—was something I've treasured ever since. My trips to Barcelona and Madrid were also key events—seeing the paintings of El Greco, as intense maybe as the Van Goghs. Then seeing Velásquez, Goya, and other artists whom I felt seemed to have something more in common with me than with the Italian masters.

But one of the things I most remember was seeing all the young artists copying images from the Vatican and the Prado museum. Seeing all those students trying to learn from the works of the masters humbled me. How could I compare myself with these young artists, let alone the masters they copied? Even if I had some talent, how would I develop it? How would I find the time to grow as a disciplined artist? And did I have anything special to say? And if I had something to express, what would it be? And how would I learn how to say it? I left my military years with a sense of expectation and anxiety about my future in art and life.

WORKING IN THE COMMERCIAL WORLD AND LIVING THE URBAN LIFE

I got out of the army in 1955, after just a year and ten months of military service. Pretty soon after, I took a month to travel to Iturbide and Monterrey to visit family and get to know my father, who turned out to be a pretty good person after all. He offered to set me up in his scrap-metal business, get me a house, a girl to marry, and I would live a northern Mexico life. But as much as I was tempted, I told him I had to get back and help my mother in Indiana. I guess I also knew that my dream of painting would end right there. But I did visit him several times over the next few years, including once just weeks before he died.

Back in Indiana from that first trip to Mexico in June 1955 (fig. 12), I had to make my decision, and I enrolled for a year at Chicago's American Academy of Art. I got the G.I. Bill and could've gone to the School of the Art Institute, but I felt that it was too "beat"—too many kids with long beards, long clothes, long hair. So I didn't go over there.

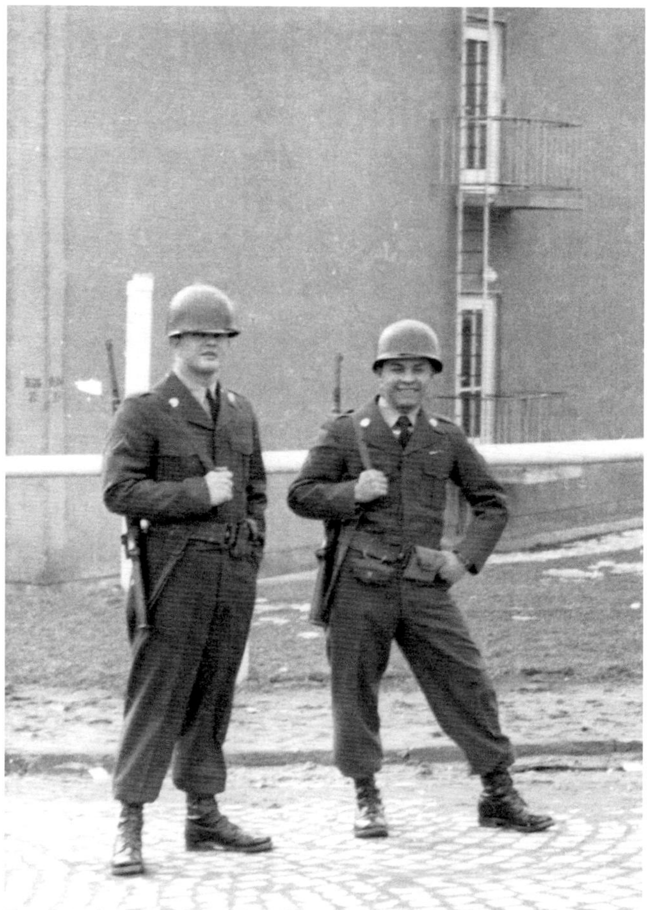

Fig. 11. José (right) as a soldier, with a friend. Kaisserslauten, Germany, 1954.

The Academy is where I learned to paint with oils. I did some work in oil years before; but in the Academy, I had a very good art teacher who taught me a lot. We did color schemes with all the colors using oil paints and making little squares, and I gradually worked up visual images from the dark tones to the light ones (see figs. 13 and 14). Then I took commercial art and drawing. I finished there, and I finally got the diploma in commercial art I'd started working on after I got out of the military.

Then, as the year came to an end, I thought it was time to go to work, because I asked myself, "What am I going to do? Keep on going to art school?" But I didn't have enough money to go on. So I went looking for a job and took one in the Handelan and Pederson Studio on Michigan Avenue's Magnificent Mile, where I worked for

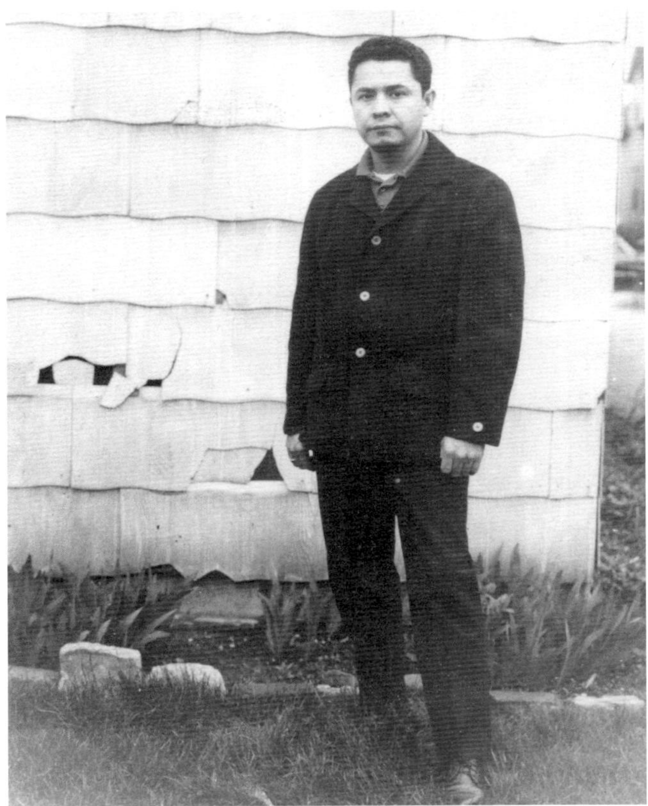

the next two years. It didn't pay much. In fact, I was lucky to get paid at all, because my work was considered as learning experience for an apprentice who was trying to become an artist. I felt lucky that I got thirty-five dollars a week for a job that usually paid twenty or twenty-five. So began many years of work—two years on the first job, doing all the errands and helping clean up the artists' materials and spaces, then another and another, getting better and better pay and work assignments. Meanwhile, I did my own drawing and painting in my spare time, keeping it all a little on the back burner.

In that first stint, my employers didn't look at my artwork that much. Finally, Wally Presprin, one of the heads of the key-lining department, wanted to put me to work on layouts, so I was ready to leave my apprentice work. But a friend told me, "Don't go with Wally. He'll work you to death when you come on board." So I stayed with Handelan and Pederson. It was very good—it was really terrific. The salesmen treated the apprentices really well and always said, "Thank you, sir." One day I asked, "Why are you so polite to us?" And he said, "Well, the thing is that in time you may be my boss."

After two years, I got a job for another studio run by a man named Sorenson in the key-lining department. Sorenson was the owner, coordinating staff work in ad books printed for different companies on contract. We did a lot of hardware products—I did the key-lining and all the publicity work.

All of this was going to help me later when I went on to do artwork with MARCH, *Revista Chicano Riqueña,* and then later with *Mirarte.* But I hadn't a clue about that at the time. I just kept on working and pushing ahead, taking a job next with the Boris Hamilton art studio. We had three people in the key-lining department and about twelve people in the layout department. We were faster than anyone in turning out the finished product. In fact, one thing that the owner did which was kind of difficult was that we met the deadlines. We had three clients—Admiral, Zenith, and Motorola—and it was no easy job. We worked a lot of overtime, and I made good money there. But it was hard work and didn't leave me much time for my own artwork.

LIFE DURING THOSE ADVERTISING YEARS (1955–66)

When I went to the Academy, I got an apartment with some other art students on the near North Side of Chicago—where it was very cheap to live, though now there are big condos there. But then, when I got into advertising, my mother left East Chicago, Indiana, and went in with me fifty-fifty on a house in Gary. I guess I was still set on being an Indiana boy rather than a Chicago kid. I worked in the city and commuted, buying a new car each year as my salary went up.

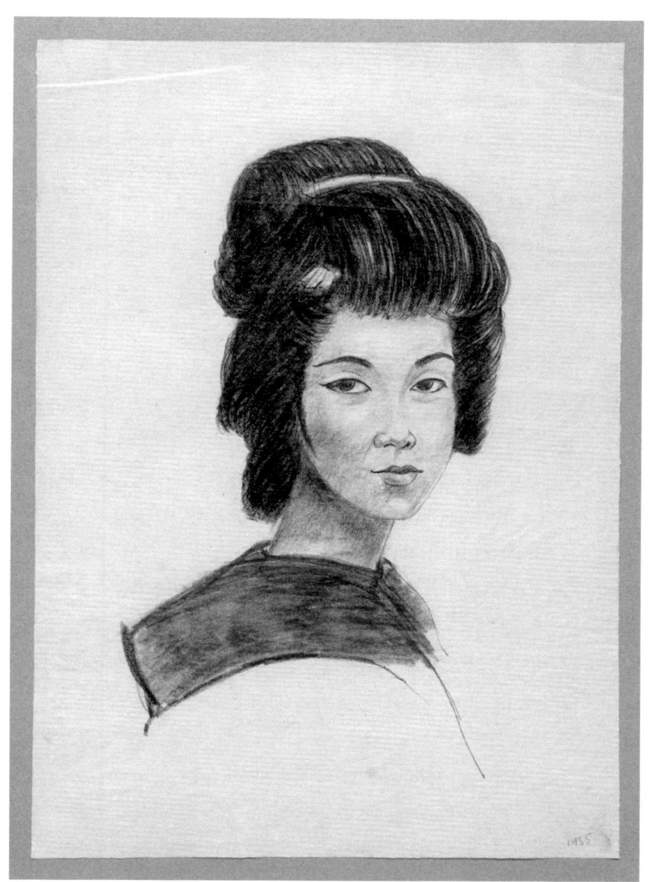

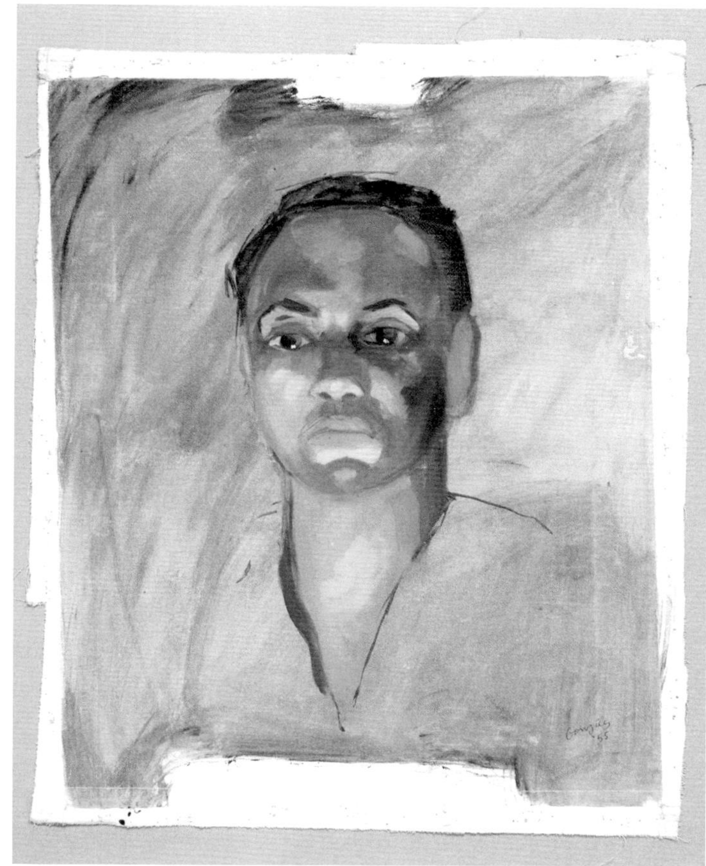

I saved money driving some women to work for much less than it would cost them to take the train. I would pick them up and drop them off by work, and I picked them up and dropped them off at their homes. So it was very beneficial to all of us because I could pay off my car and get repairs, and I got help with my parking costs. I was also dating some of these women. And I wasn't worried much about anything because I'd grown up poor, I guess, and now I had a job which gave me a good basic wage plus a lot of overtime. I was working up to ninety hours a week and making around twenty thousand dollars per year, which wasn't bad for someone in his twenties in the late 1950s. In fact, my mom and I bought another house together in Hammond—a large brick building with a bungalow and two-car garage that we could rent out. So on top of my salary I was making some money in real estate, too.

I had one nice car after another, including a convertible Mustang and a Pontiac Firebird. I had nice clothes, and I was a dancer. I started going out to some of the clubs around Chicago. One of my favorites was a Latino club, Mambo City, where a friend of mine, Victor Parra, used to perform.[1] Some of my Indiana friends and I used to come in to Chicago to dance the latest dances in the Anglo world and the latest dances in the Latino world. We used to win twist contests. They used to give a bottle of champagne to the winners, and I drank a lot. We went to Calumet City to dance rock and roll, the mambo, and cha-cha-cha. One of the musicians was a brother of my friend Geno Muñoz.

This was the most Latino or Mexican part of my life in those days. There were not many Latino magazines or radio stations; there just weren't many Latino outlets that I knew of at that time. There was no way to have what we can have today—an actual feel of *la raza*. I didn't feel I was part of a Latino world somehow, except sometimes, like when we went to dance. We made a point to go to the best dancing places, and there was a big dance ballroom on Rush Street where one band played rock and roll and another played Latin music to a crowd that was more Anglo than Latino. There was a mixture of people, with a lot of very good dancers. Mostly the women who went to the places in Chicago were not Latinas, but I used to date more *mexicanas* than *güeras*. I even began to make money organizing dances, hiring *mexicanas* and *güeras* to dance. So during those years, I led my single life as a young urban Latino with a good income and a normal enough social life. Of course, when I started going to the dances and coming back at four o'clock in the morning, I wasn't getting up for church; and my mother was very depressed about that. But I was young and did what I did. And now that I think about it, those dances we organized and the posters and costumes we designed (fig. 15) may have given me some experience for the art and cultural events we'd develop through MARCH in the 1970s.

It's true, though, that something was going wrong for me. I worked for Boris Hamilton for more than three years. I used to work overtime for him, and even when the department lost clients and he let workers go, he kept me on, working what we called a Photostat machine—one of those pre-Xerox systems that made stacks of photos fast. But there was less and less joy in the job. It became so mechanical, and I had to work long hours, even delivering the copies to clients all over the Chicago suburbs. I was dating a *mexicana* named Mela at the time, getting kind of serious; and two times in a row, Boris called in and said I had to stay late. The third time he didn't call in from the suburbs but arrived just before I was leaving. I told him I had a date, and he was really upset; but I just picked up my materials and my supplies, and I left. I quit without having any other job offer in sight, but I had a lot of money in the bank, so I was okay. What happened was that I needed to look at myself from another perspective because I saw myself being in commercial art, and I had grown more and more sure that I didn't want to be a commercial artist after all.

I had kept my hand in and did some things (figs. 16–18) that told me I still wanted to be a true artist—it was something I had felt from the time when I got interested in Van Gogh. Coming from a poor family, I thought I couldn't take the chance. I was trying to help my family, and the commercial jobs gave me the chance to do it. But as I got older, I regretted it all and felt a loss of focus on my work as a genuine artist. I was at a crossing point. I felt I had lost my way and had to find a new start.

And it's true, something new had been stirring in me. I had become aware of Mexican artists. I used to go to book sales and began to buy books on Mexican art. I felt myself more and more drawn to the artists—I felt there was something of myself in them, the way I felt when I saw the Van Gogh show when I was twelve or when I was working in oils at the Academy of Art, or when I read and then saw *Lust for Life*.

I recognized something of myself in the Mexican artists. At the Academy of Art, reading of Van Gogh's life made me become very despondent. The book was so well written that the author really captured Van Gogh's feelings and his disappointments. Another art student read the book because it was very popular. But he couldn't finish the book; he was so depressed, he put it down. I finished the book, and Van Gogh again asserted his great influence for

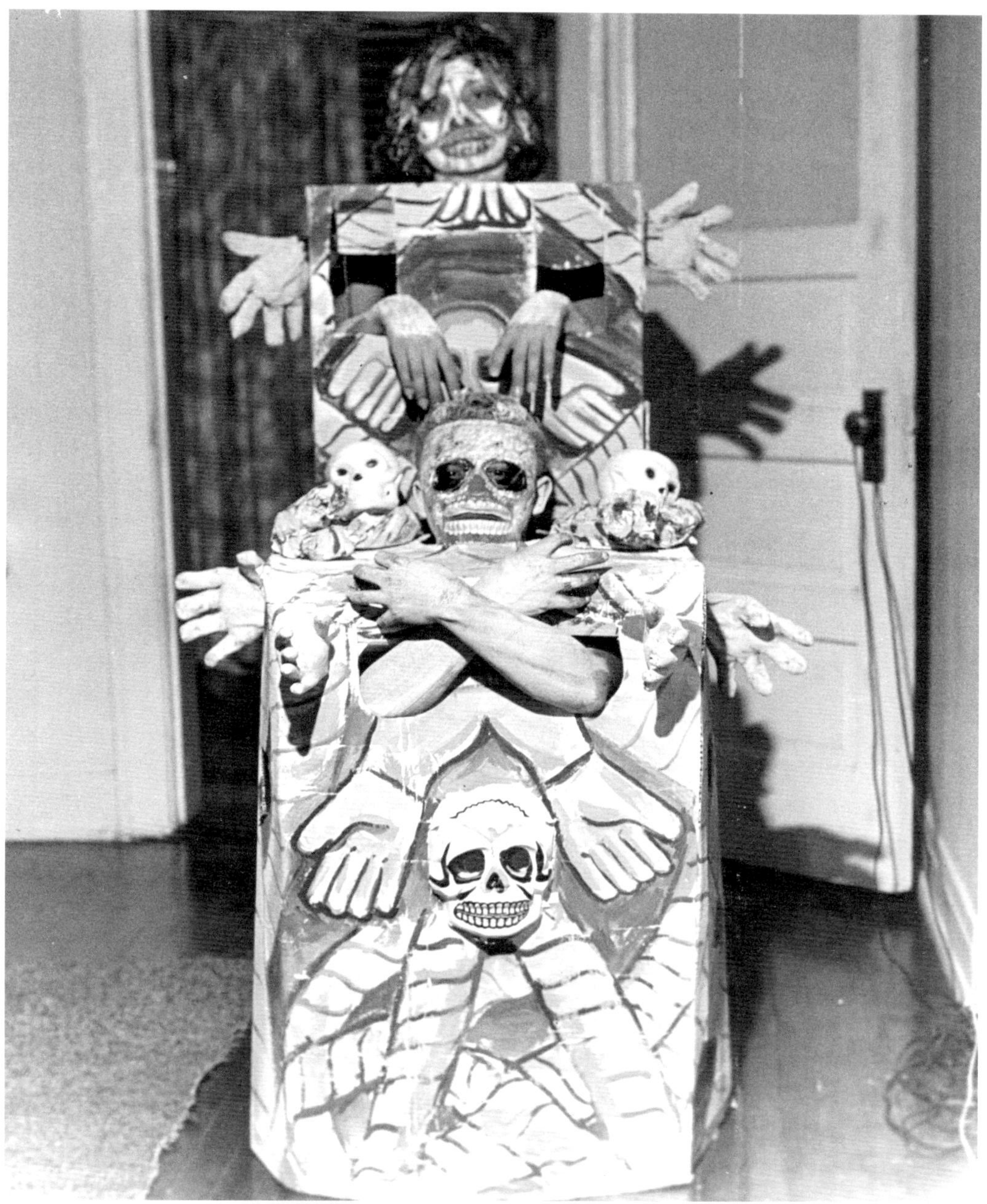

me. I felt that reading his life, I really could feel all the pain of becoming a serious professional painter. And the urge just grew and grew even more intense as I read of the Mexican artists. I decided that if other Mexicans could become serious artists, I wanted my chance, too. So I took all the money I'd saved, said goodbye to Mela, and off I went to Mexico.[2]

SAN MIGUEL DE ALLENDE

I knew about San Miguel de Allende as a place for artists to develop. An artist friend of mine knew about San Miguel too and got there a year before I even thought of going. I wrote him to say that I'd decided I had to go too. I also told him that I wanted to be around him and the

Fig. 15. José Gamaliel González, costume featuring José and woman in mask and costume. Designed for Halloween dance in East Chicago, Indiana, early 1960s.

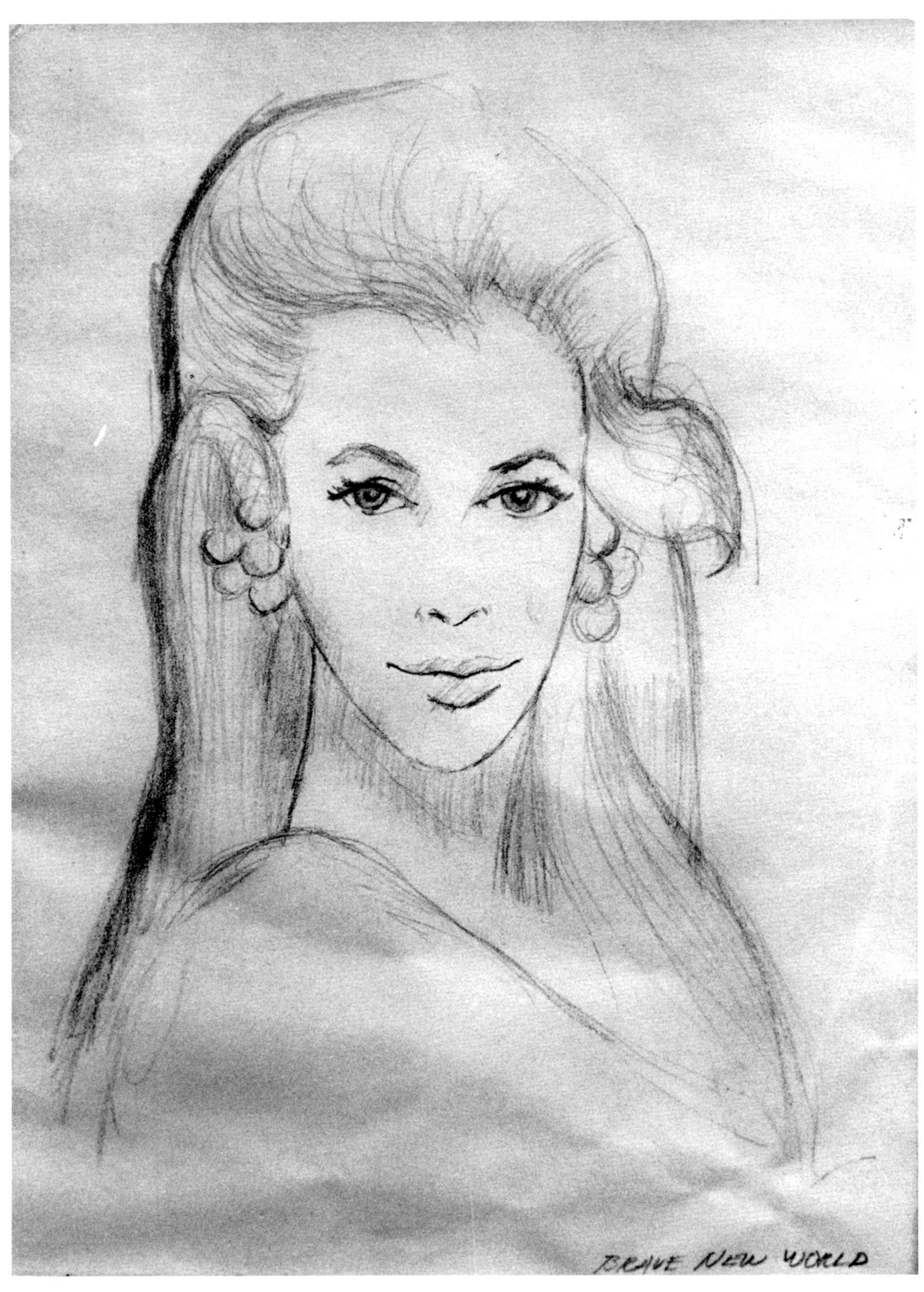

Fig.16. José Gamaliel González, Miranda (from Aldous Huxley's *Brave New World), 1965*. Pen and ink.

24

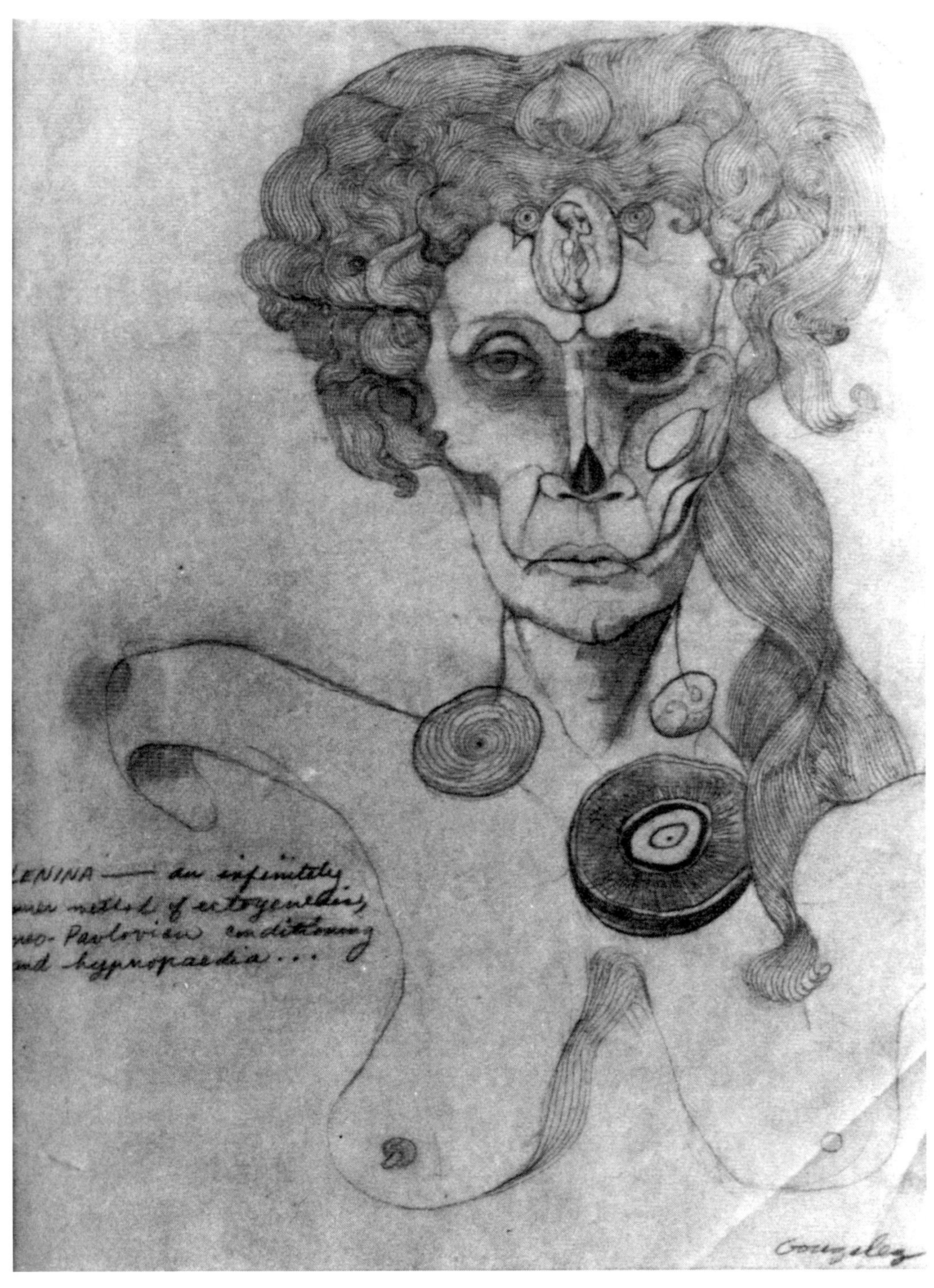

Fig. 17. José Gamaliel González, Lenina, 1965. Pen and line drawing with writing on the side (a quotation from Aldous Huxley's *Brave New World*). Lost drawing; saved as a photograph by González and published in *Revista Chicano-Riqueña* 1.2 (1972).

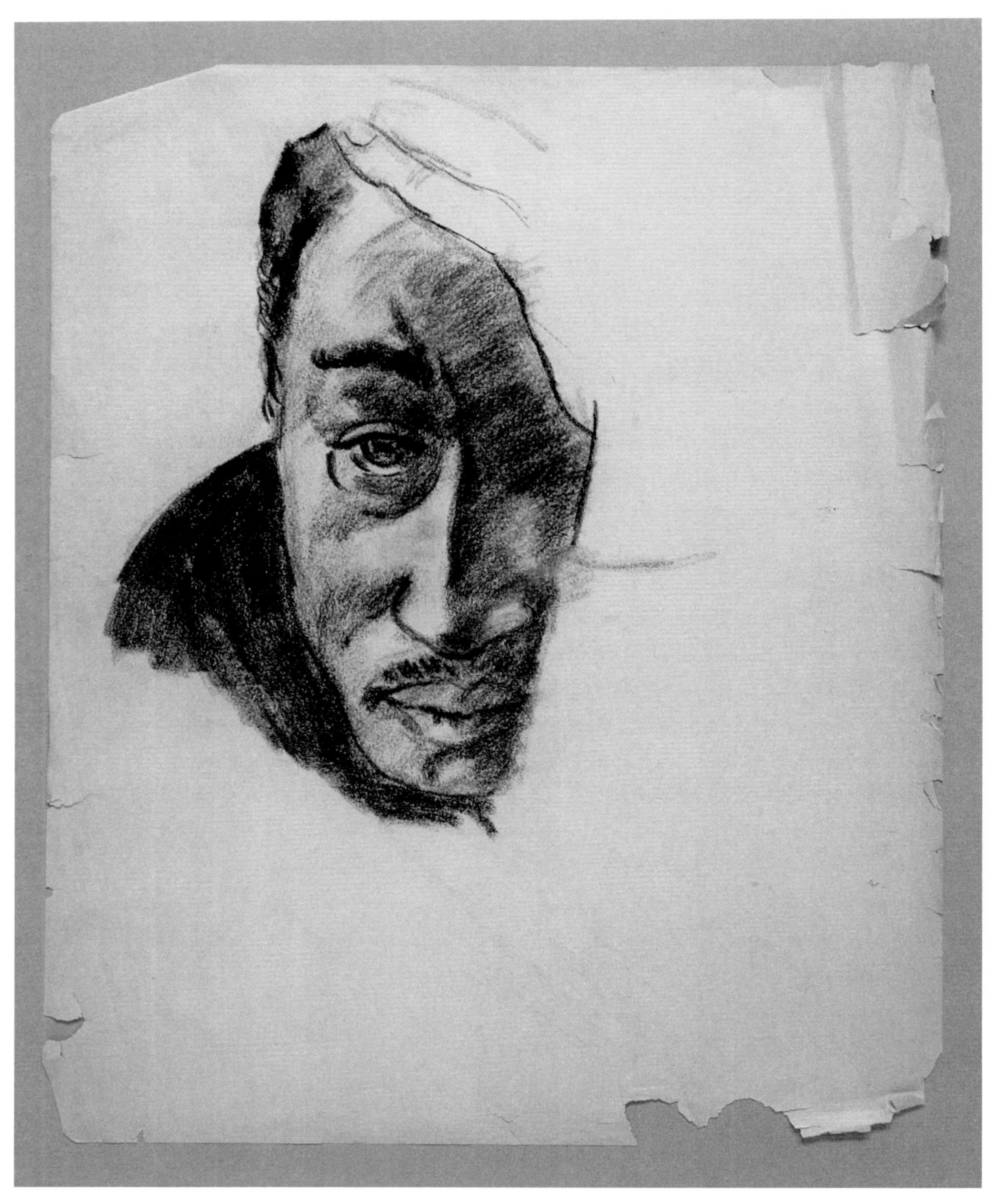

Fig. 18. José Gamaliel
González, Duke Ellington,
1965. 10"×10". Charcoal.

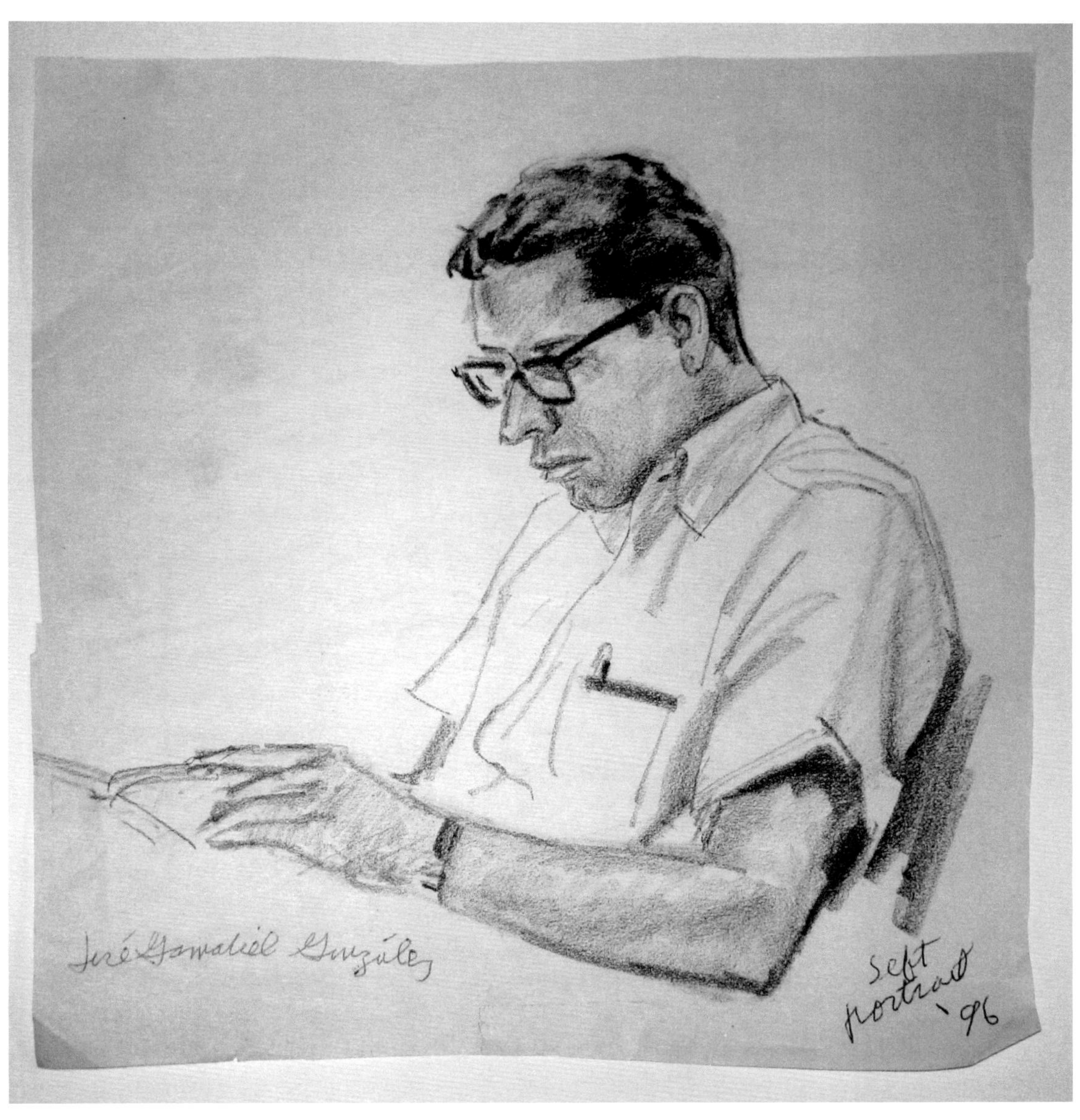

Fig. 19. Portrait of a Young Artist at the Crossroads. According to José, this drawing, while bearing his signature, labeled "seft [*sic*] portrait" and dated 1996, actually is a 1965 effort by John Price, a layout artist for Boris Hamilton, drawn just prior to José's quitting the firm. 10"×12.5". Pencil.

other young artists who could show me the ropes, but I didn't want to room with him or anyone else—I'd get my own place. Maybe I was thinking of Gauguin and Van Gogh in Arles. But anyway, he invited me to stay with him till I could find my own place, and in fact I gave my mother his address so she could get in touch with me if anything important happened.

So it was off to Mexico. But I didn't go alone, and I didn't go to San Miguel right away. Instead, I went with two friends of mine, driving all over Mexico in my good old gas-burning Oldsmobile station wagon—down to Monterrey and then to Guadalajara and Acapulco, then back to Mexico City, and back and forth from D.F. to Acapulco once again. It was like my last spree, but at least I saw my father, who seemed much older and sick. When I came back to the city, I told my friends that it was time for me to go to San Miguel. I knew I couldn't stay with them and the wild life we led if I was going to get anything done. So I took them to the airport, and they flew back. Now I was on my own in Mexico, and that's when I drove on to San Miguel, where I'd applied to enter the best art school there.

I went right to my friend's apartment. And sure enough, he gave me an already dated telegram from my mother saying that my father and my grandfather on my mother's side had died, one right after another—just one day apart. I called up my brother Arturo and asked him if I should come back, and he said, What good would that do? They were both buried now, and I might as well stay and do what I'd set out to do.

I felt a little guilty that I hadn't made it to the funerals of people so important to me, but staying turned out to be a big turning point in my life. I went and found an apartment to rent way far out from the main part of town. It had a kitchen, a shower, and a large living room with a fireplace. Outside there was a brook and also a well and clothesline to wash and dry my clothes. It was probably the biggest and best place I'd ever lived in. And, of course, it didn't cost much, so that I could last maybe six months on the money I'd saved from my jobs. So I took all the money I had in my Chicago North Side bank, deposited it all in a Mexican bank, and drew on the money to pay my registration fees and living costs for a half a year—enough time to get to know most of the local artists, to know what was going on and maybe learn what I needed to learn.

I ended up studying those six months mainly with Jaime Pinto, a *mexicano* veteran from the States who had studied with Siqueiros. In fact, a lot of veterans were showing up in San Miguel to go to art school. Pinto had gone down there and had decided to stay for a while. He's probably dead now, but he was maybe my key teacher in San Miguel, along with a very good *mexicano* painter from Los Angeles whose name I can't remember, but who did a magnificent one-man show there for his M.A. featuring all kinds of work in a variety of styles, with only some of it very much in the Mexican tradition.

Almost right off, I got very sick in San Miguel. It was late February, and it was very cold. I showered and washed my head, and it was still wet when I went out in a dress shirt, without a sweater or anything, to an open-air dance at nighttime. And I caught something that made me very sick, and there was no one to attend to me, so I used to buy penicillin and pay for a nurse to give me a shot. But I took my medication four hours apart to keep myself awake so I could continue with my studies. I remember I lay by the fireplace, and I didn't sleep—I lay awake all day and night. I was sick, but I was still studying—just getting started with my school work. Little by little I recovered, and only when I was almost well again did I find out I could've died from what I'd had and the way I treated it. I never found out what I had for certain, though it was strep throat compounded by something else. Maybe the illnesses that I was to have later on, and that have affected so much of my life and work, began there.

But nothing would stop me from learning what I had to learn—above all, the greatness of the Mexican painters and artists. We had a number of *mexicanos* from the States, but most of the students were *güeros*. There were two academies there—one in English and the other in Spanish. I made friends with most of the few Mexicans there, and we made trips on occasion, taking my Olds to Colima and other places, seeing the murals of Orozco in a small village there.

In my courses I discovered for myself that I wanted to be doing work in the line of the great Mexican masters. My sense of Mexican-ness was coming out, and I wanted to be an artist in the Mexican tradition. Of course, that was already behind my decision to go to Mexico anyway—a kind of growing affirmation of Mexican culture. In one of my first classes, we studied fresco and mural techniques, and my teacher liked my work. The murals we did were always painted over to make way for new efforts. But he said to me, "Your mural is really good, and if you stay another half a year, we can give you a wall for a permanent work." Of course, I was very flattered. But by this time I had run out of much of my money, and I knew that I could only stay the half year. The law was that with my visa, I had to go back and cross the border again anyway if I wanted to stay another six months. But I knew that was the time when I'd have to go.

This was my major stay as an artist in Mexico, and the key moment in my life when I turned to Mexico to grow as an artist. Of course, I knew I wasn't exactly *mexicano,* because I was very American too. One *mexicano* called me a *pocho,* making fun of my accent. But it was my first and only extended time in Mexico, and here I was

learning mural and fresco painting. I also did some drawing in watercolors. I did a few oils on that trip, but oil paints were really expensive to buy. Still, I got enough experience to understand that my Mexican background was helping me decide what kind of artwork I should be doing. I decided I wanted to project Mexico and Mexican visions in my artwork. I really absorbed so much from this time in Mexico. Above all, I saw that I was making progress—that my drawing was getting better and better. There was a certain style of painting peasant women which I guess was from the tradition of Diego Rivera, and I did a lot of sketches in that tradition that many people said were very good. So I began to draw more and more. I drew a lot of pictures, many of which have survived, including some drawings of indigenous women and other Mexican themes. Mary Kay Vaughan has three of them; Gilberto Cárdenas has some; Nicolás Kanellos has one; and I still have some. I know some people think of them as among my best work (see figs. 20–28).

It's funny that my San Miguel work looks like it's in the Diego tradition, when it was Orozco who impacted me more when I saw his work in Guadalajara, in Mexico City, and other places, too, though I didn't know his work in the United States at that time. And I guess I felt some kind of connection between Van Gogh's work and Orozco's. Van Gogh was expressionistic, and so was Orozco. Orozco had that fiery intensity we associate with Van Gogh, while Diego had the influence of cubism, which gave a certain cool formalism to his work on folkloric and indigenous themes and even his most political paintings. Orozco had a freer, more explosive style—it was sometimes pretty grim, but there was also a fair amount of caricature and humor because he was drawing on José Guadalupe Posada's work, too. I knew Posada from books and classes, but he wasn't that important to me

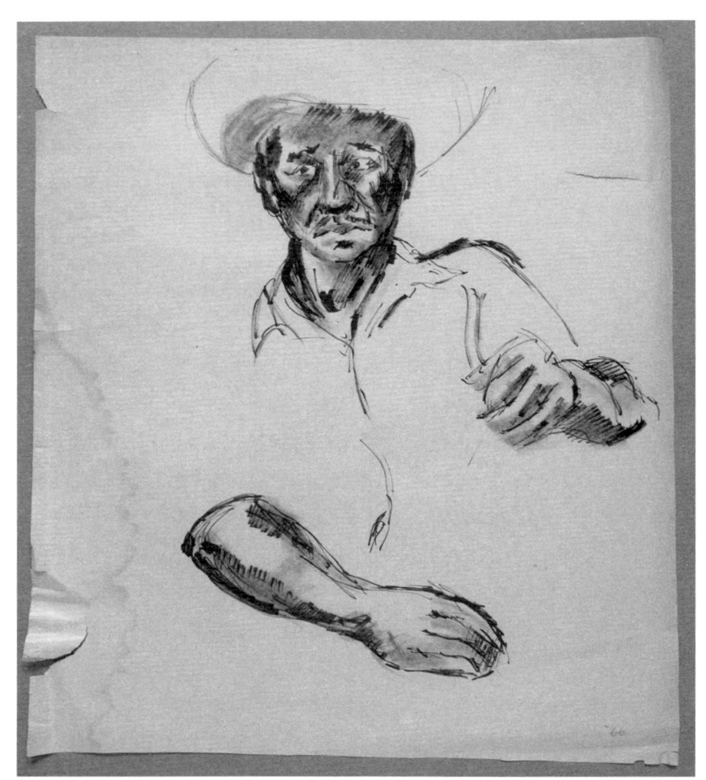

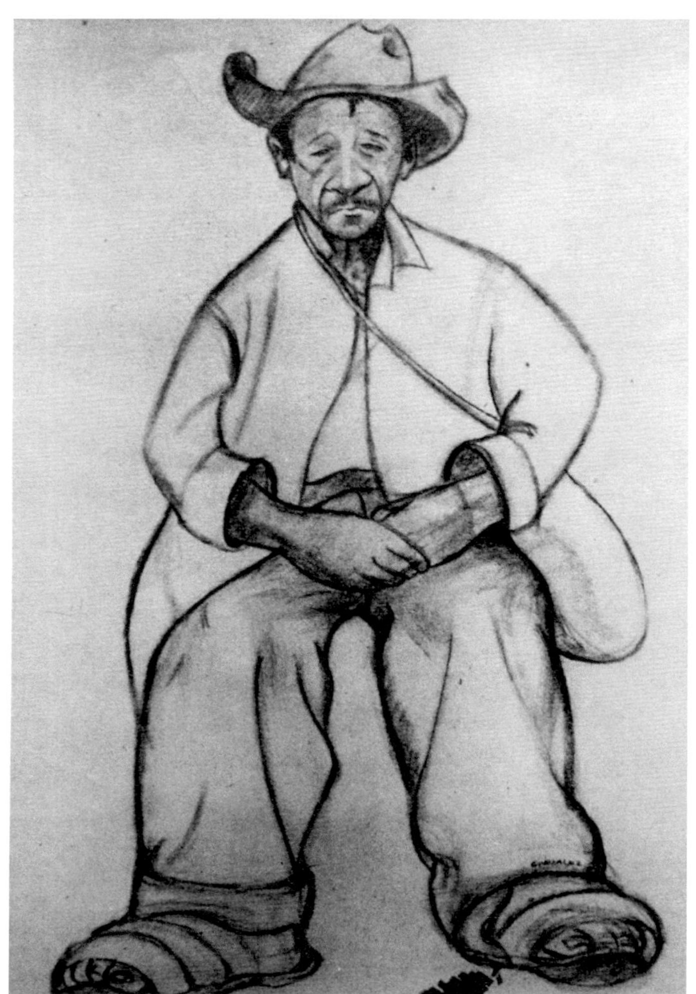

Fig. 20. José Gamaliel González, Campesino. San Miguel, 1966. 18"×24". Charcoal.

Fig. 21. José Gamaliel González, El Viaje Fue Pesado (The trip was heavy-duty), San Miguel, 1966. 18"×24". Charcoal.

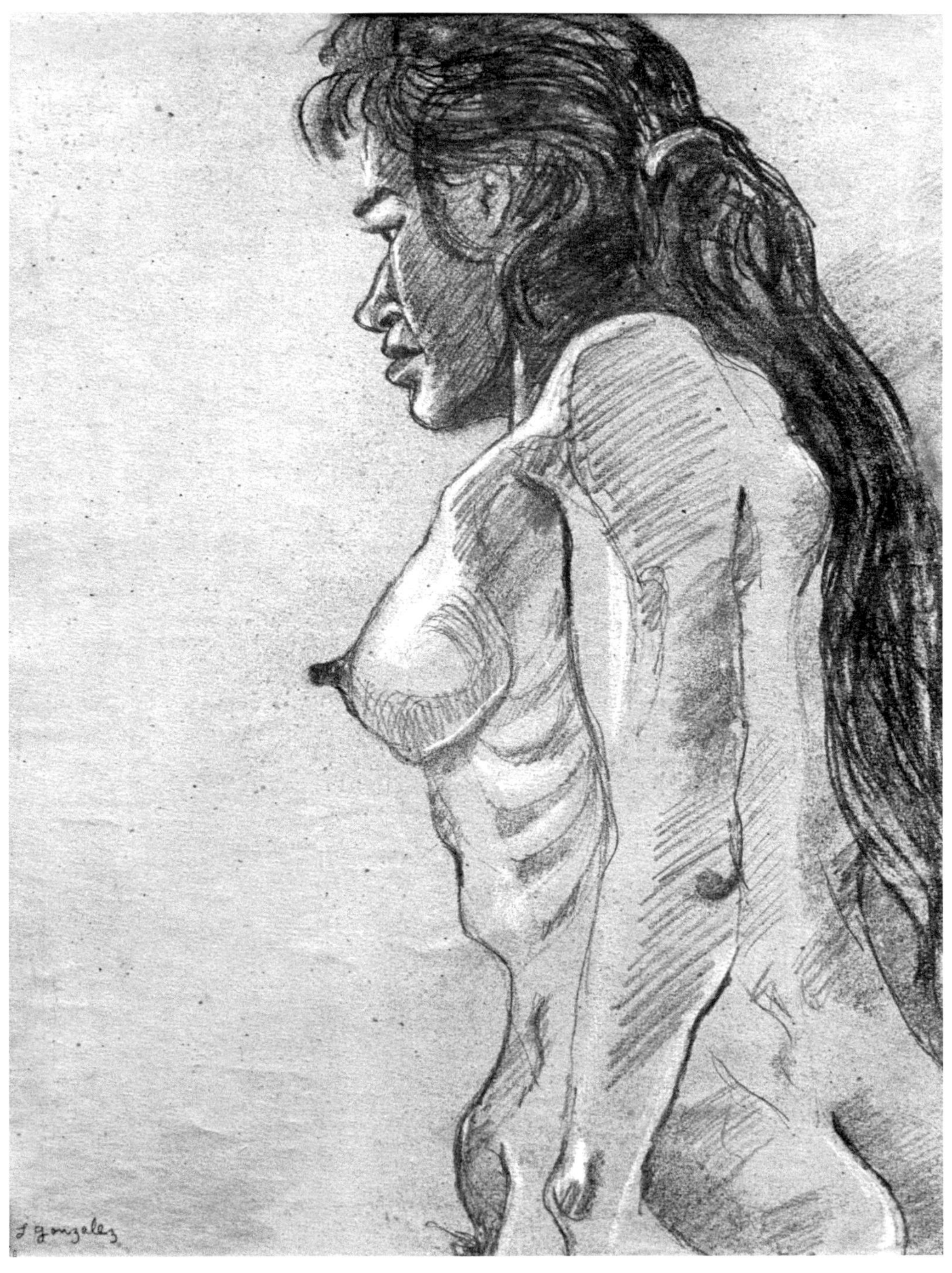

Fig. 22. José Gamaliel González, Nude Woman, side view. San Miguel de Allende, 1966. 18"×24". Charcoal.

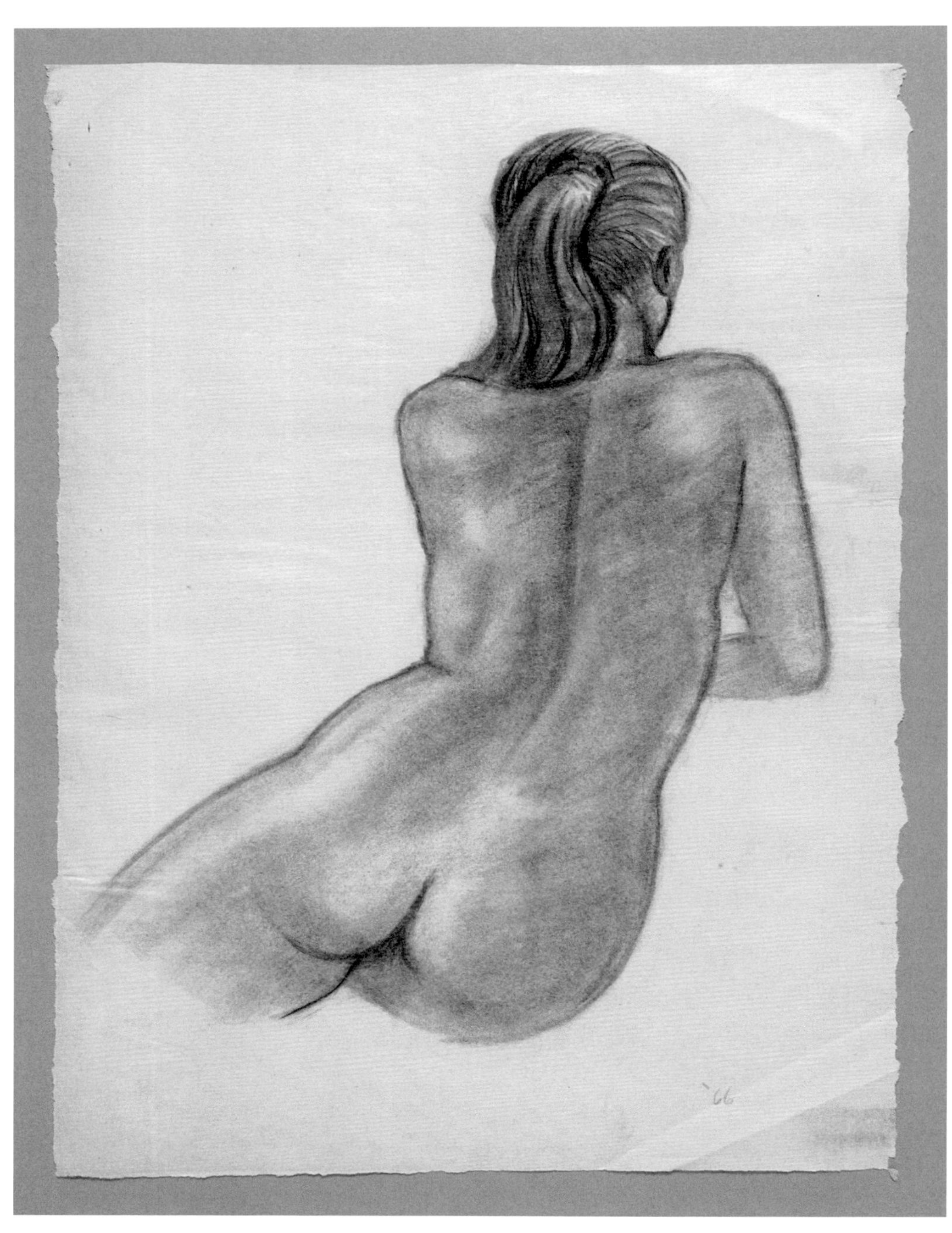

Fig. 23. José Gamaliel
González, Nude Woman,
back view. San Miguel de
Allende, 1966. 18"×24".
Charcoal.

32

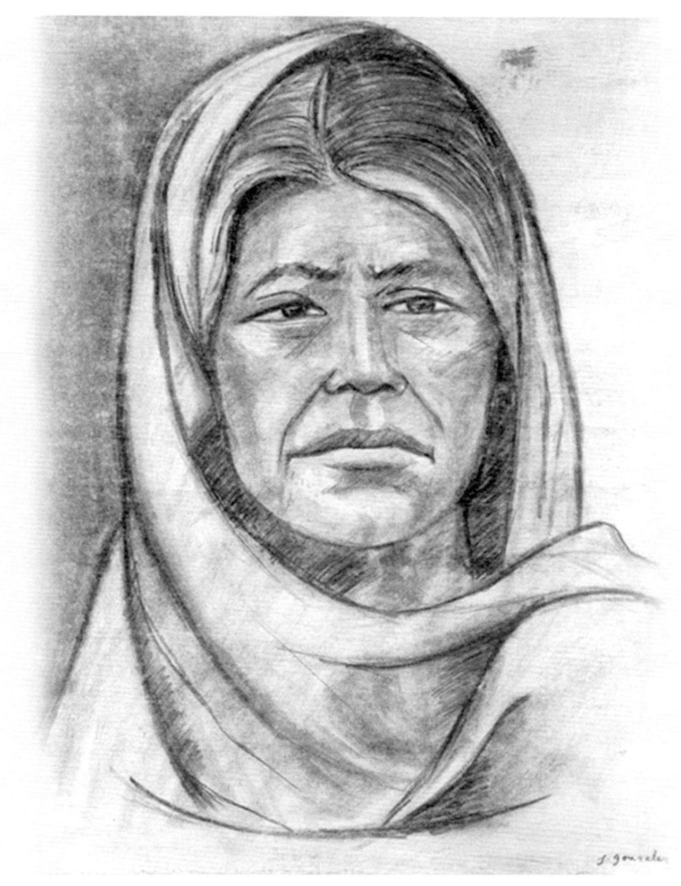

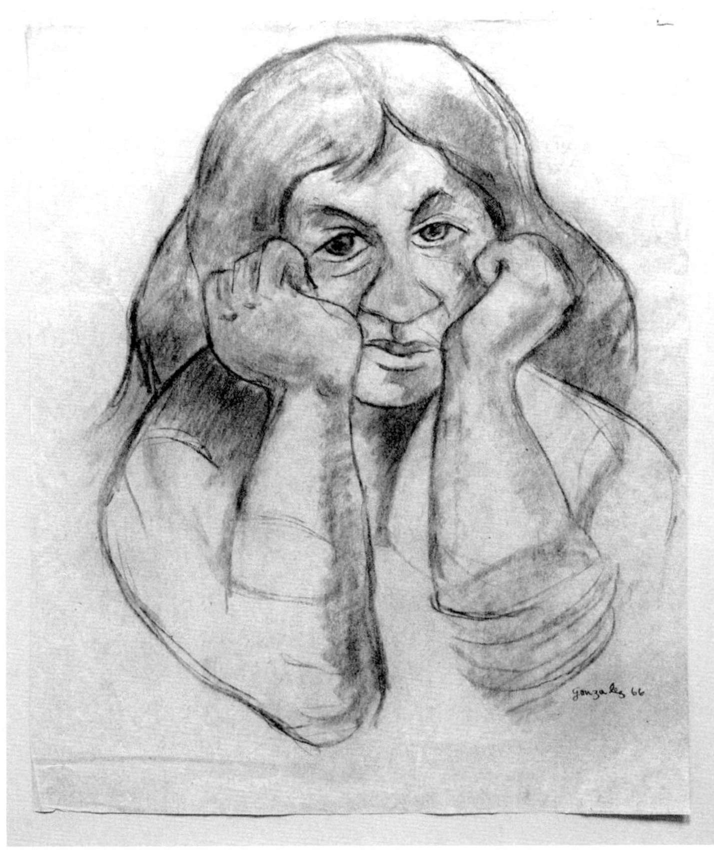

Fig. 24. José Gamaliel González, La Llorona. San Miguel de Allende, 1966. 18"×24". Charcoal.

Fig. 25. José Gamaliel González, Campesina Woman I, head resting on hands. San Miguel de Allende, 1966. 18"×24". Charcoal.

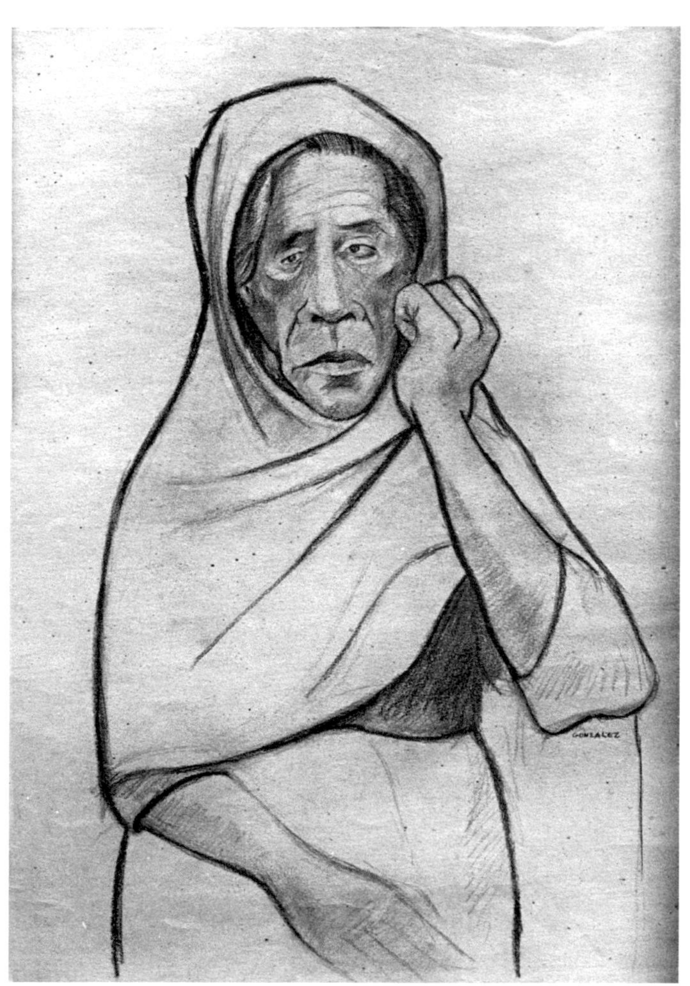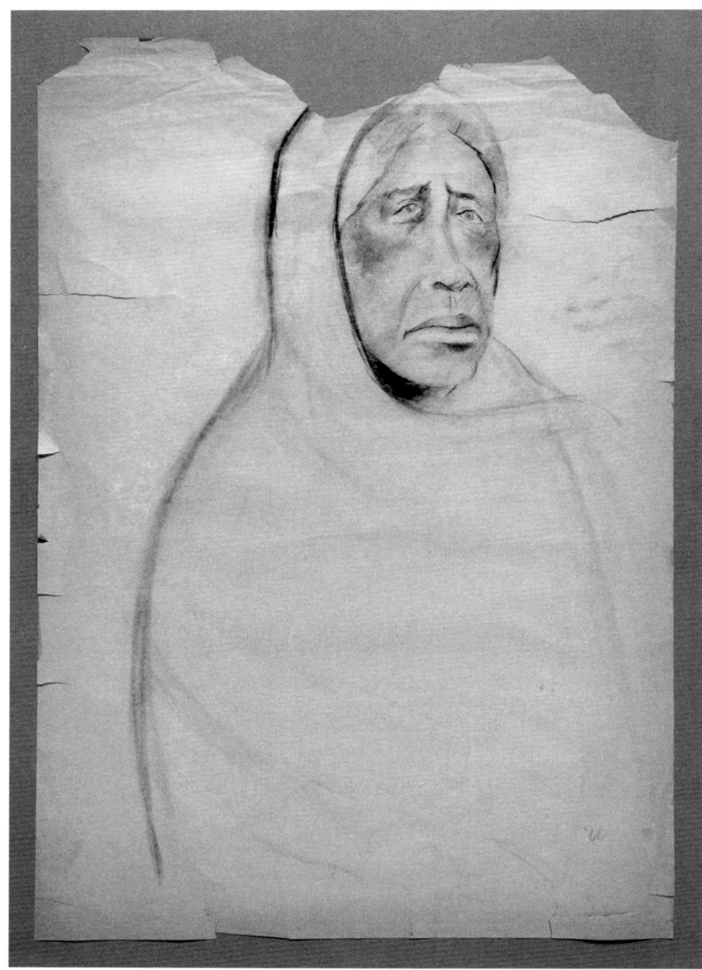

Fig. 26. José Gamaliel González, Campesina, head on hand. San Miguel de Allende, 1966. 18"×24". Charcoal.

Fig. 27. José Gamaliel González, Campesina. San Miguel de Allende, 1966. 18"×24". Charcoal.

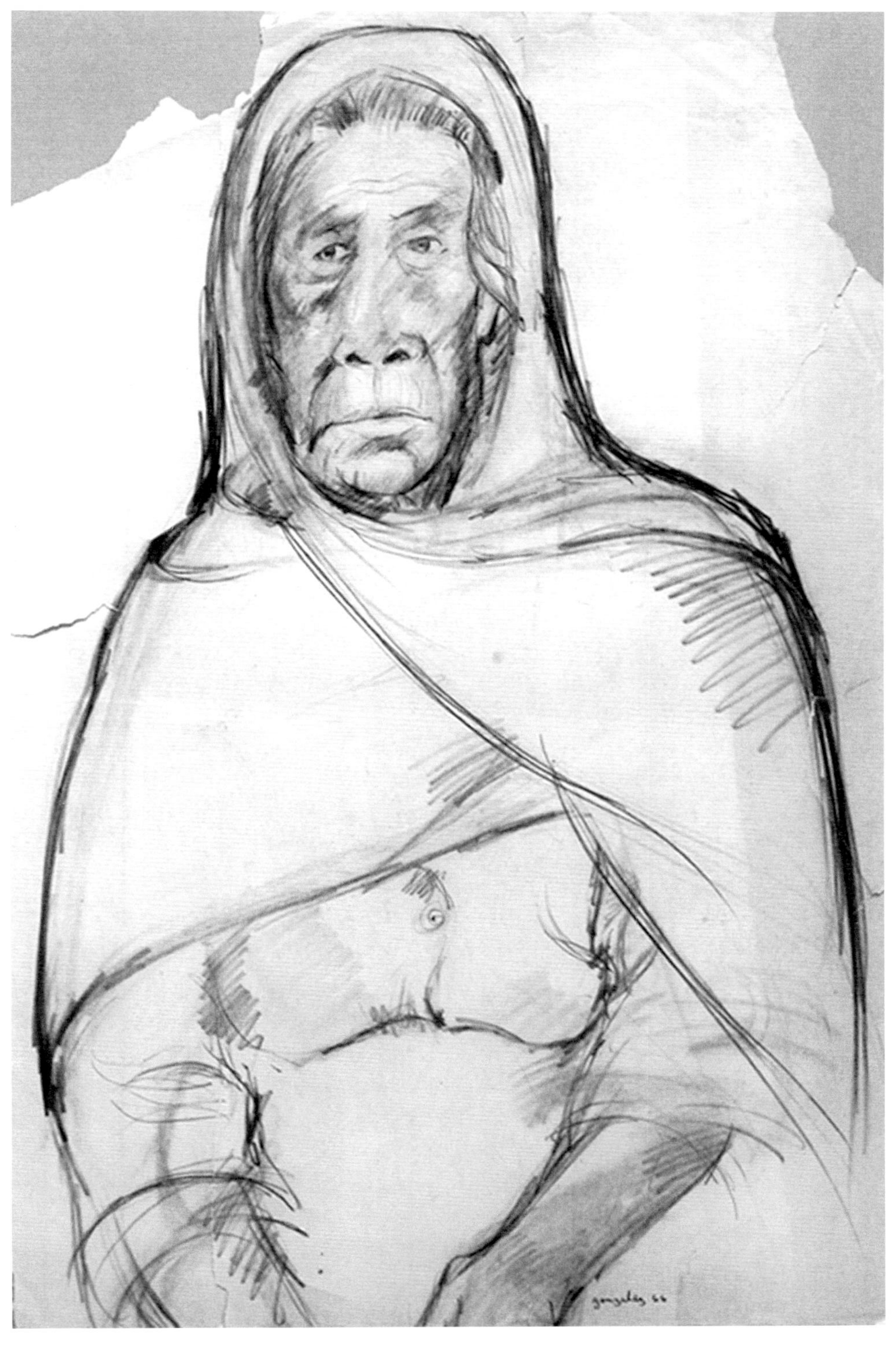

Fig. 28. José Gamaliel González, Campesina Woman VI (torn image). San Miguel de Allende, 1966. 18"×24". Charcoal.

at the time, even though I knew he'd influenced most of the Mexican painters, including Diego, too. He became more important to me when I founded MARCH because I recognized that he was political, as I hoped to be.

One of the things I learned from that time is something people don't talk about too much. You have the white academically trained artists, many of whom work as teachers and professors and whose income and life situation may not be so great, but it enables them to spend months in Mexico, sopping up Mexican culture, the *paisajes* (landscapes), the churches, the people on the streets—they can even pay people to be models for their classes, and so on. They have a lot of time to develop their artwork because of their economic and social situation within U.S. society. The U.S. Mexican artists were usually pretty poor without much formal training and having to work for a living, with much less time to be in Mexico and absorb Mexican culture. Thinking about all this was what helped me make up my mind to go to the School of the Art Institute. I wanted to be more of a fine artist. That inspired me because I figured I could make a living after all. I could be a teacher. I figured that if I went back to art school, I could get a degree and then go into teaching on a full-time basis and get the time off in the summer.

My notion was suddenly to become an artist, or I should say a Mexican artist in the United States. A Mexican artist—that was it. But the thing that I also recognized when I got back from school was the reality. The reality was that I couldn't pursue that dream purely—that I had to make a living.

WORK AND STUDY AT THE SCHOOL OF THE ART INSTITUTE

When I came back from San Miguel de Allende in July 1966, they gave me the money I still had left in dollars, and I realized it wasn't as much as I thought I'd have. I wanted to leave the world of commercial art behind me, but I was going to have to work in commercial art to support my education.

I shopped around and finally landed a job in one of the most ritzy art venues in Chicago. The Albert J. Rosenthal agency was very plush, with thick, red carpet and antique furniture to impress the clients who came by. Right off, one of my bosses, a Jewish guy named Phil, saw how good I was, and I told him my schooling plans, and he said, "Great, we'll hire you an assistant so you can get on with your education." This is 1967. There is already an antiwar movement going on. There is a Chicano movement beginning, but I wasn't focused on any of that. Politics were still not in my head.

So I went to the School of the Art Institute and filled out an application and got together my portfolio of drawings, photographs of paintings, and pastels. And boom! I was accepted—and with a scholarship, which didn't cover my living expenses but covered all of my school tuition. I went from being from Indiana City to being a Chicago North Sider when I went to school again for my degree. I had a North Side apartment a friend helped me get where I paid $150 a month for a small living area and a large studio. I remember doing a huge charcoal drawing at the beginning of the school year. It was ten feet high and four feet wide—a drawing of Plato's Cave of Shadows that covered up nearly a whole wall of that apartment. It was my "logo" for my Art School studies. I was to lose it, though my photograph of it has survived, even if it's a bit fuzzy (see central image in fig. 29).

I went to the school day and night, so I earned my four-year degree in three years. The program was connected with the University of Chicago extension. We took all our basic non-art courses—in psychiatry, English, French,

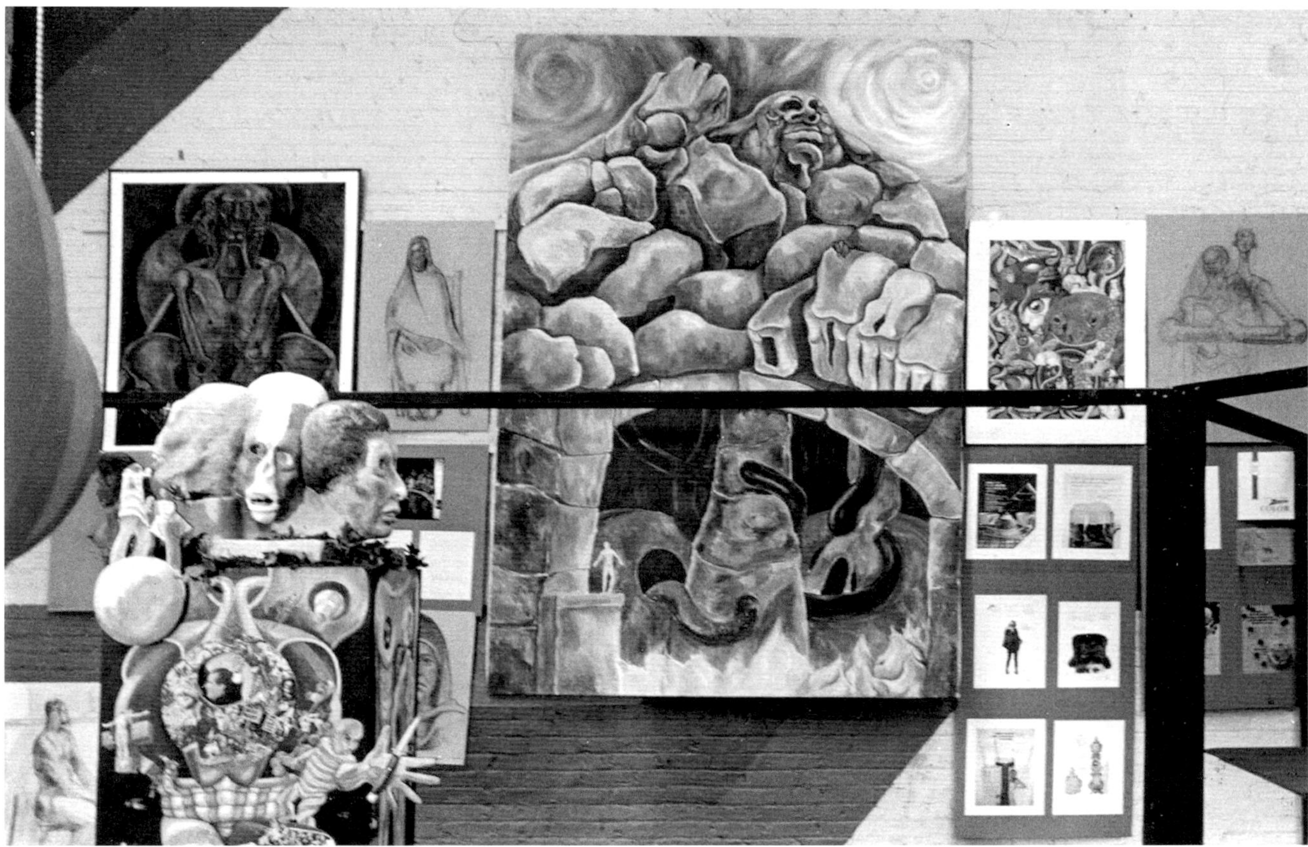

whatever—through extension. But all our art and art history classes were taken at the School of the Art Institute itself. There were several great teachers in the program, and Bob Loescher was one of the best. He influenced me in many ways, and so did many of the other teachers and fellow students.

When I got to the school in 1967, I was not part of the Mexican art world in Chicago. I was not connected with other Mexican artists. I didn't know anybody in the Mexican community doing artwork, and I thought I was the lone Mexican in most of the events that I went to. Then I met Mario Castillo, who was younger than me but was already an advanced student artist at the time that I started school. Mario graduated a year before I did, in '69, and I didn't

get to know him until his last days at the school. He was probably the first of all the ones we know today—the first Chicago *mexicano* to begin on the path of becoming an artist. I really got to know him much better after we attended school, and I've always felt connected with his work. But Mario wasn't showing much Mexican influence in his student days—the influences were basically U.S. art. And to this day, there are many influences in his art, although many of his paintings show what many would consider a Mexican sense of primary colors and overall design.

I actually got to know Mario by way of another artist, Ray Patlán, a friend of his who also went to the school, whom I'd first gotten to know in San Miguel, and who was to become one of the pioneer muralists of Chicago. Ray was from

Fig. 29. Display of José's artwork at graduating student show, Chicago School of the Art Institute, 1970. Left: Charcoal study of African American male; lower left: Cycle of Man charcoal and sculpture (heads plus body extension); center: Plato's Cave of the Shadows (acrylic on canvas, 10'×6' [lost]); right: multiple fantasy painting—Elizabeth Taylor and other images; lower right: commercial art images. Photo: José Gamaliel González.

Pilsen, the key Mexican neighborhood in Chicago, on Eighteenth Street. But when he came back to Chicago from San Miguel and was about to start at the Art Institute, he got drafted and was sent to serve in Vietnam. In fact, he did an early mural on Vietnam very much under the influence of the visual artist Robert Anderson. Later, when he came back from the army, he went back to the School of the Art Institute. And I was to get to know him again as we got involved in public art projects. But in those years I also met some non-Latinos whose work and projects were to profoundly affect mine.

By the summer of 1969, the Vietnam War was still going on; the uprisings of 1968 had taken place in Chicago, Mexico City, and other places. Over the months that followed, Cambodia, Kent State, and Jackson State would come to the fore. There was a lot of controversy and activism at the School of the Art Institute, and that's when I met Mark Rogovin and John Weber, two fine public artists with political visions. Mark later became the founder of Chicago's Peace Museum, and John was cofounder of the Chicago Mural Group. Later on, I was going to feel very connected to both artists, but when we were in art school, I just wasn't focused on politics. Weber was very active in school, and his artwork dealt head-on with social issues and antiwar themes. He was going for his master's now; he was way ahead of me. I got my BFA and he got his MFA in the same year. Another old friend of mine who got his master's was Paul La Mantia, an Italian American who became well known later on and whose work was influenced by the Chicago Image Group. I first met Paul when I worked at the Handelen Pederson art studio. He was a very good friend of mine; in fact, my North Side apartment was one he set me up with.

The artists I've mentioned were very affected by the times. The political atmosphere had a big impact on their artwork, but I wasn't active at all

yet, I guess. I was still deep into Michelangelo and Van Gogh, and then Orozco and Rivera, but not so much Siqueiros until later on, because he was too directly political and a Stalinist at that—his painting is very powerful and structured, but it's also kind of rigid, like his politics. I know that several students turned political because of the war and began to stress the social dimensions of art. There was lots of talk about the artist's social commitments and the needs to overcome abstract expressionism. That began to affect me and would become important as the years went by, but it wasn't so important to me at the time. I didn't even know much about César Chávez and the early years of the Chicano movement, though I was aware of Casa Aztlán's opening in Chicago's Pilsen neighborhood, and I guess my first modest political act was to pressure School of the Art Institute faculty to give some time in their courses to Mexican artists— and some of them did it. They even thanked me for my art activism.

I got a broad education at the School of the Art Institute. I had a great education in art and art history—very good teachers, bright students. My work in that period was getting stronger and stronger. Each study I did seemed to have something—each one seemed to be a gem. I think I produced some of my best work (see figs. 30–37). I got scholarships every year, and I won a good one my junior year. I even won a summer scholarship to Yale University, but then I reviewed the rules and saw that you had to be twenty-five or under, and I was in my thirties. I told the dean that I'd made the dean's list and qualified in every way, but that I was over age, and he said, "You'll be disqualified, and we'll be discredited if I process your papers." So I had to miss that boat. I think today I could sue for "ageism."

I was more and more interested in pursuing my art education beyond the BFA. But as

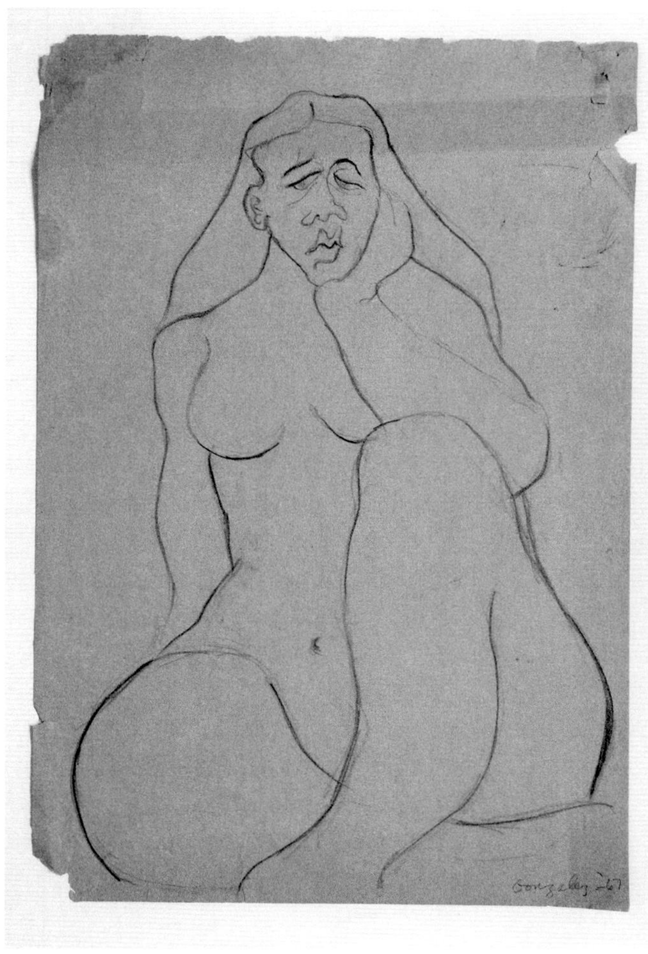

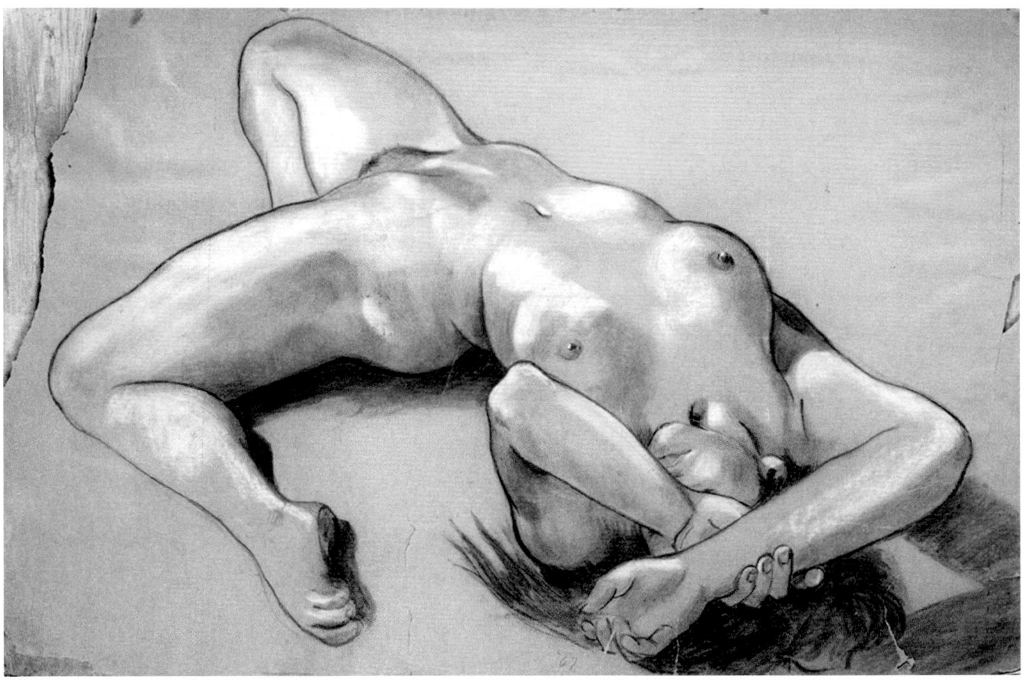

Fig. 30. José Gamaliel González, Nude Woman, after Picasso, 1967. School of the Art Institute of Chicago. 24"×36".

Fig. 31. José Gamaliel González, Nude Woman, arms over face, 1968. School of the Art Institute of Chicago. Charcoal.

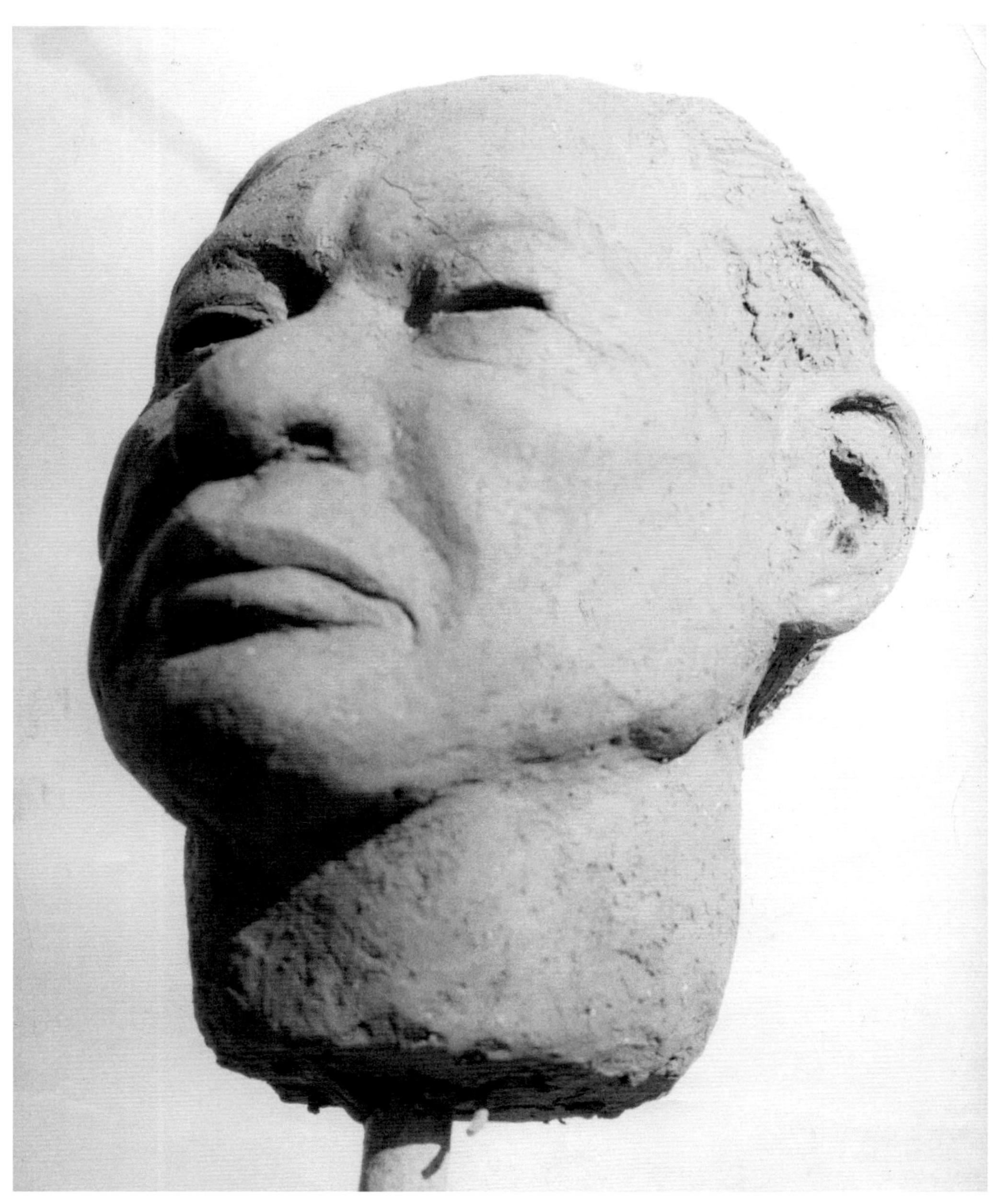

Fig. 32. José Gamaliel
González, Head of African
American, 1969. School
of the Art Institute of
Chicago. Clay sculpture.

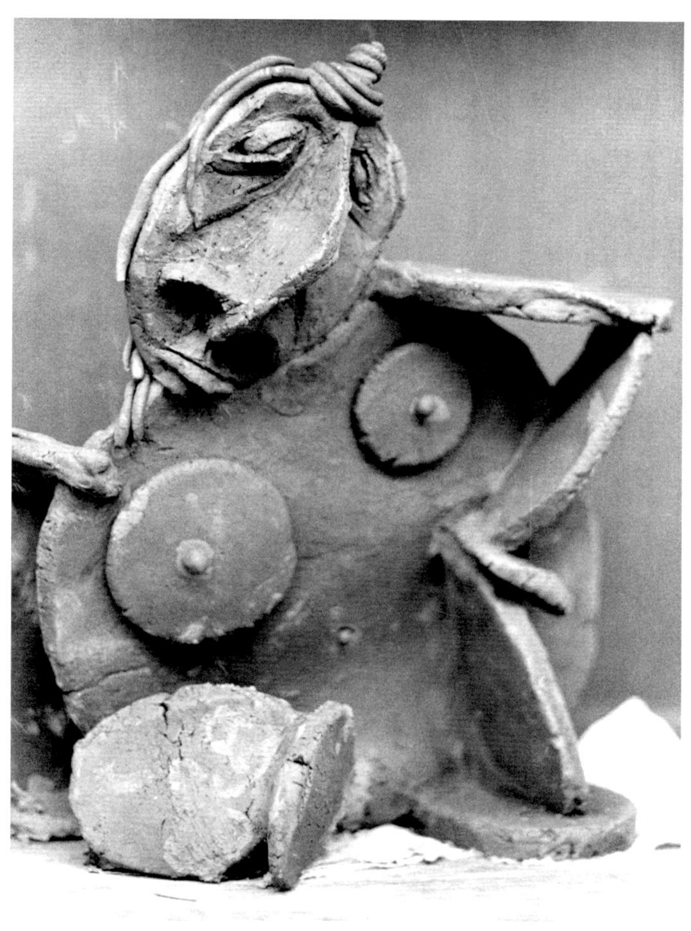

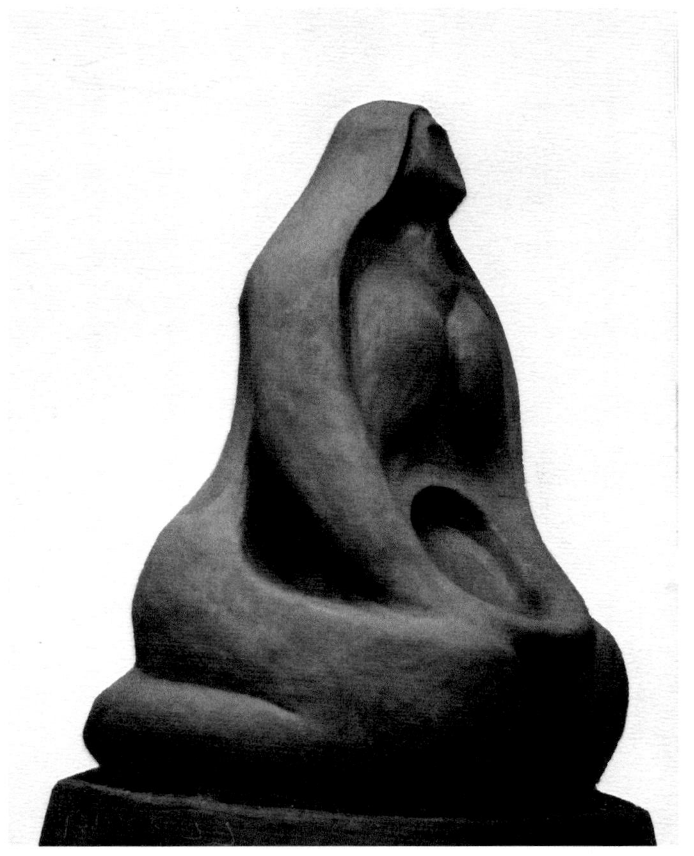

Fig. 33. José Gamaliel González, Nude, 1969. School of the Art Institute of Chicago. Ceramic sculpture.

Fig. 34. José Gamaliel González, Mother, 1969. School of the Art Institute of Chicago, 1969. Ceramic sculpture.

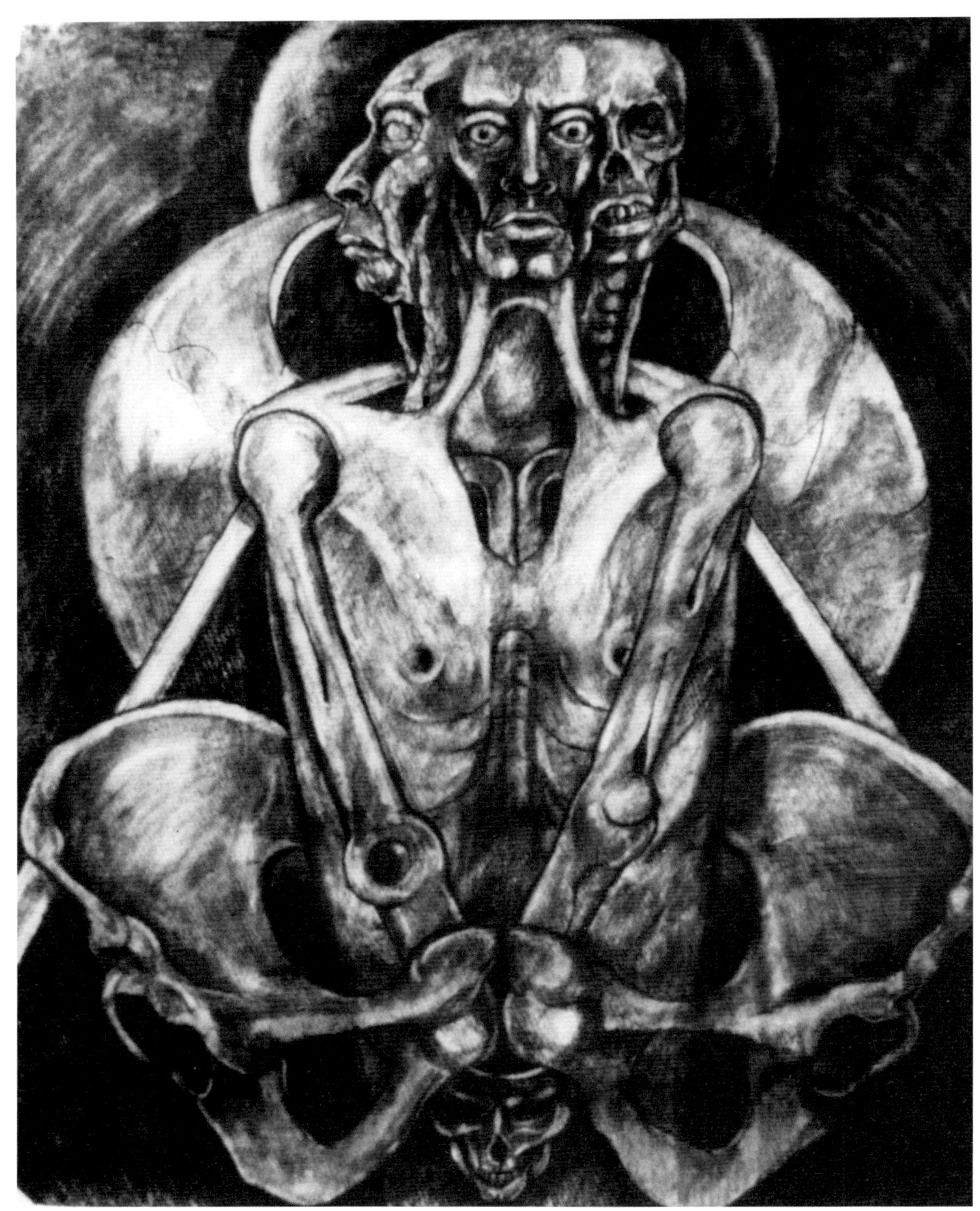

Fig. 35. José Gamaliel
González, The Cycle of
Man: Birth, Death, and
Regeneration, 1970.
School of the Art Institute
of Chicago. Donated by
Gilbert Cárdenas to the
collection of the Mexican
Fine Arts Center Museum
(now the National
Museum of Mexican Art).
Charcoal.

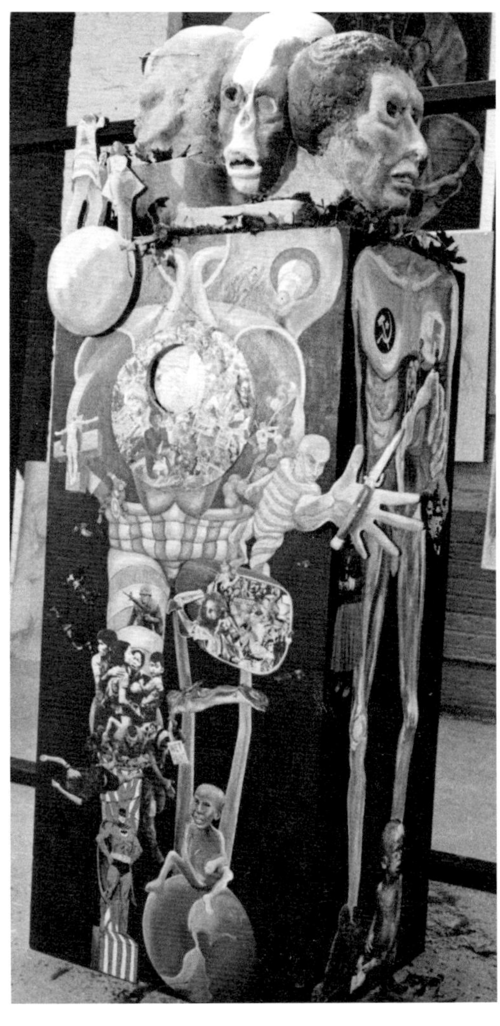

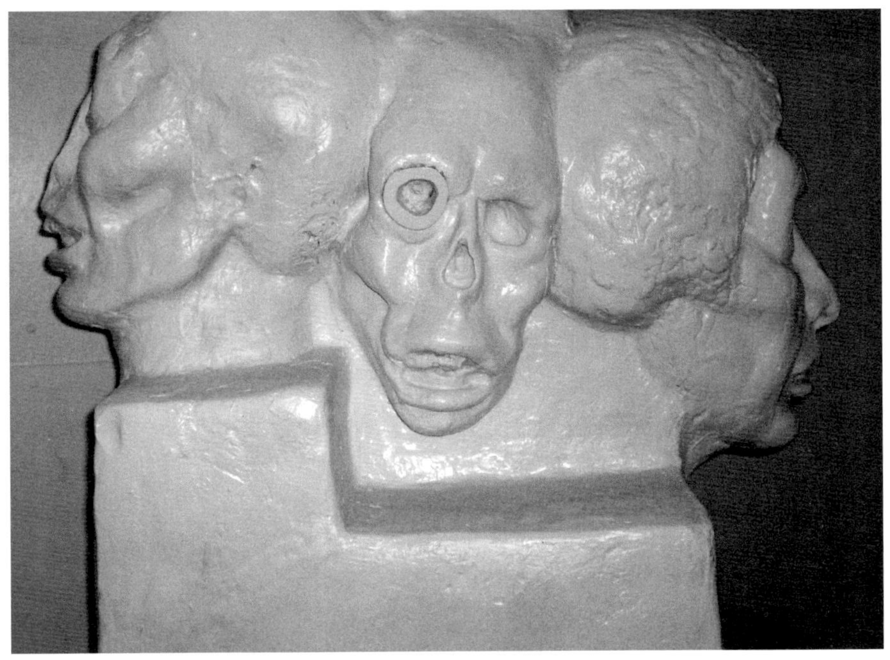

Fig. 36. José Gamaliel González, The Cycle of Man. School of the Art Institute of Chicago. 5'×3' with extended base. Sculpture in polyester. Photo: José Gamaliel González.

Fig. 37. José Gamaliel González, The Cycle of Man, 1970. (restored by Rey Vásquez, 2004). Photo: Cayetano García, 2008.

43

I got ready to graduate from the School of the Art Institute, I only applied for one place for graduate school, and that was Notre Dame. I always thought of Notre Dame as the best place for me—my ideal place because of its emphasis on Catholicism and its growing interest in the education of Latinos as their biggest new Catholic population.

I worked that final summer on call, freelancing for studios and agencies. I was getting twenty dollars an hour, which was good money at that time. And then came the fall, and it was time for me to go to Notre Dame. But it had nothing to do with football.

NOTRE DAME

It was September 1970 when I started. Notre Dame was one of the few universities that didn't have uprisings in the late sixties—the center of Irish Catholic education in the United States, now with its eyes on recruiting key Latin Americans and Latinos. I was there to get their education and pursue my work in art. But before you know it, I met Gil Cárdenas, a young California *mexicano* student activist who went recruiting other *mexicanos,* found me, and got me involved in helping him found and develop the Notre Dame branch of the national Chicano student organization, MECHA (El Movimiento Estudiantil Chicano de Aztlán).

Really, by 1970, the Farm Workers movement was in full swing, and then there was the Chicano Moratorium in Los Angeles. The reporter Rubén Salazar was shot in a bar, and MECHA was the spearhead of a Chicano consciousness that was spreading from campus to campus. Julián Samora had already set up his Chicano research at Notre Dame, and Gilberto brought all the excitement of California in the middle of all this, looking around for other potential al-

lies and finding *mexicano* students like me who now began thinking of ourselves as Chicanos.

Jorge Bustamante, who had come up from Mexico and later became famous as an immigration expert, was also a good friend of Gil and me, though he never joined MECHA. In fact, I did a very good charcoal drawing of Orozco, and he asked me for it, and I gave it to him—I wonder if he still has it, but I never saw it again. Of course, Gil was to later become a famous academic and a big collector of Chicano art, but in those days he did a lot of photography, and he photographed lots of MECHA activities, including the art projects I began to develop for our organization (see Zimmerman forthcoming).

The Latino students at Notre Dame used to hang out together. And we weren't just Chicanos, because there were Mexicans from Mexico and lots of other students from Central and South America. A lot of them came from good families, and some of them stuck their nose up at us. There were more of them than there were of us anyway, and that was our argument, of course—that Notre Dame didn't admit many Chicanos or Latinos. They wanted Mexicans like Bustamante but not Chicanos like Gil or me. So sooner or later Gil told us about MECHA, and we right away said yes—we would be a wing or chapter or branch of MECHA. The California MECHA wanted Chicanos to found a chapter on every college campus with the goal being to have more Chicanos admitted to the university, to fight for their rights for educational opportunity and cultural affirmation, for their right to a budget for programs and events that fostered the identity and advancement of Chicanos and other Latinos.

So we joined with Gil in forming the Notre Dame MECHA. And I guess for the first time I found myself identifying as a Chicano. Soon after, Olga Villa joined up, and we used to joke with her and call her Pancho Villa's wife because she was such a firebrand. Olga was very good with farm workers and with the Mexican communities in South Bend or neighboring towns that had lots of *mexicanos.* Another woman got involved very early—Dalia was her name, and she was going for her doctorate with Samora. I remember wanting to date her, but we were too wrapped up in politics to follow through on personal things. She and Olga held a conference in Michigan, and that's when I became more Chicano because I met David Torres from Saginaw. Right away we became very close, because we were both Chicanos and artists. David was a pioneer in Chicano-movement art. So we embraced each other like brothers. He was much younger than I. But David is dead now; he had just died when I began telling my story for this book, in 2002.

From the sixties, you hear of Rupert García as maybe the first major Chicano artist. Rupert was very good, but David was from the Midwest, and so he just wasn't as much in the limelight as the East L.A. artists. And sure enough, he was painting Chicano themes much influenced by the California style. He did murals of *mexicanos* and César Chavez, and he had an exhibit on Chicano history that took months to put together.

He did this in Michigan, and he somehow got me thinking that I could do things like this too. He influenced me a lot because he was doing the work I came to want to do. I remember an exhibit he entitled *Mexo-América* and another one on Chicano history. He and another artist he got to know in Saginaw decided to do a series of portraits of Lee Treviño, Jim Plunket, José Angel Gutiérrez, and other Chicano athletes and activists—they called the series "The Chicano Hall of Fame." But I wasn't doing anything like that—I was doing Orozco and Rivera. For a

long time, my focus had been on Mexico. Only gradually did I pick up on Chicano art, influenced artistically by David Torres and ideologically by my work in MECHA with Gil Cárdenas. Julián Samora was the MECHA faculty advisor and patron, and he probably influenced me with his ideas and attitudes. But I never studied with him as Gil did, because I was too much into my art. And that's what I was dedicated to: my work on Latino, Mexican, and Latin American art events—but above all Chicano work with the Three M's: MECHA, MARCH, and MIRA.

First I designed a small brochure for MECHA with a black and red cover and probably my first picture of Zapata (see fig. 39, lower center), a pencil drawing for the cover of the brochure that also had a little logo that I designed for the Notre Dame group. Then I started pushing the MECHA board for a big MECHA-sponsored exhibit at Notre Dame on Chicano art and artists. I said it would be a surprise for us to able to mount a big exhibit, but we could do it. I don't remember all the people—there were nine board members, and I just can't remember everything, but there was Gil, Olga, Dalia, and others—they all went for it, thought it was good too.

There was a hallway in the art department that was just for exhibits. The university had a show going on in the hallway, so I approached the art faculty dean, Thomas Fern, and told him about our MECHA group and what we did and stood for. And I told him that we wanted to bring in Chicano artists to do a show in the same locale. He told me that he was in charge of the space, but I had to talk to the man who was in charge of booking it—Mr. Beckman. So I did that, but Beckman said, "You've got to talk to the dean," and I said, "I talked to him, and he told me to talk to you." But I went back to Fern anyway. I asked him about it, and he said, "Well, tell him that he is in charge."

They were bouncing me back and forth, and I figured they were just playing games with me. So I went to a MECHA meeting and told them that they had to come with me so the administration would see we were serious and committed. "They're just denying me as an individual, but if you come with an organization they are denying the organization, and we may get permission to do it." So that's what we did. This time I went with three MECHA members—all three of them really young, going for their bachelor's at an early age. I mean, I was much older than they were—I was in my thirties. We went back to Beckman, and they just couldn't keep saying no. We finally got permission, but they made us agree to do all kinds of work that was going to benefit them and the hallway long after any show of ours. We agreed we'd have three MECHA members painting the showcases and the hallways, to make everything look like new. So I got two more M.A. students to help paint everything, and I went with them to paint on certain days and hours. But then the two students said that they were tied up with their master's work, so I painted up the showcases by myself. I finally went to Beckman to tell him the showcases were done. "That's fine," he said. "But now that the showcases look so good, you can't just put anything there, and I don't want you to mess them up with your artwork." I guess Chicano art made him think of a mess. As usual, we were good for the gutwork, but for nothing of any artistic or cultural value.

Well, I decided to do us proud. So I went out of my way to bring together pieces I'd gotten from Chicago and Indiana artists—some I'd known at the School of the Art Institute and other places. I wrote David Torres—he was my big contact—and asked him if he could send me something for the exhibit. He offered a piece he'd done on *Miss America,* but I didn't want that. I wanted something related to Chicano art history. So he sent me his whole portrait group of important Chicanos. And I put them in the showcase along with some pre-Conquest handicraft pieces from Colima and other parts of Mexico.

I also wrote to Mark Rogovin and John Weber, and I asked Mark to come and give a lecture and slide show on Siqueiros. I organized a dance, and I got a lot of people from Indiana. A guy I knew, Angelo Muñoz, played Latino piano for us—cha-cha-cha, mambo, and the rest. It was a huge success, and in fact it was so popular—I put Torres's Jim Plunkett image there when he and Joe Theisman were going head to head for the Heisman trophy, and Plunkett beat him out.

I did advertising for the show, designing flyers, passing them out all over the school. My best slogan was "The Chicanos Are Coming," and the show was called The Chicanos Have Arrived. I did a silk-screen poster and put that in the exhibit along with the artifacts, the portraits by David Torres, and works by another artist whose name I can't remember.

I didn't really do any painting of my own for the show, but I did an Aztec calendar (fig. 38) as part of the poster for the show, and I mounted a big collage as a contribution to our effort. We divided up the show in two places. We used our renovated showcases, as well as the art department and club-sites located in old campus buildings, where each of us student artists had a place for our work. There were maybe thirty to thirty-five pieces in the show beyond the group of some twenty portraits David provided. And I mounted it all and did all the advertising, and then the arrangements for the dance that was a key part of our plan.

All of it turned out to be a big success and a smash hit with the student body, which was all male in those days. But it was also popular with the women at St. Mary's College—a place we thought of as kind of a Notre Dame women's annex. And maybe the dance was the most popular event, but people were impressed by the artwork too. And my collage was one of the biggest hits. It was a pretty big three-dimensional construction with lots of old objects in the design: a wooden horse harness, an ice pick, and a wooden frame with a short-handled hoe hanging down—all this collaged with nailed-up photo images of farm workers and César Chávez pasted on in one corner, along with my Zapata drawing. I nailed and pasted everything together and then tied them up and hung them all with rope. It was a very impressive piece, I think, and I called it "Frustration" (fig. 39), a name that just about summarizes all that happened to me at Notre Dame. Eventually it was stolen after I exhibited it in several Indiana locales, but a few photos have survived. I have one, and Gil Cárdenas may have photos, because he was all over the place during the exhibit, photographing everything there. He had boxes of those photos, and my guess is he still has them now.[3]

I just couldn't seem to stay out of trouble at Notre Dame, much as I loved being there. It's just that I was becoming militant about things Chicano and my art. There was an art teacher from a visiting university who was going to come to campus to show his artwork and talk to the M.A. students as an adviser. So I was told that we had to get our exhibit work down because the art teacher was coming on Sunday. Our show was set for the whole weekend, and here we had to rush around dismounting the whole thing. The great artist showed up on Sunday night, but he didn't come with his work framed. His work was not very impressive to me—it was very simple, minimal. Some teachers said it was trendy, but it was nothing to me. He came at the last minute, after we were pushed to take down our exhibit; he came with unframed

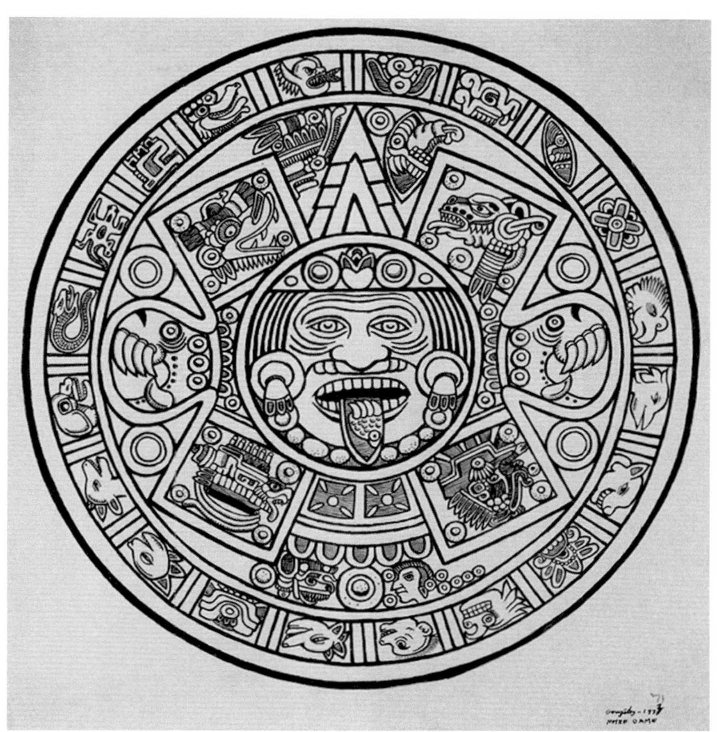

work, and we had to stop taking down our show to frame his pieces on Monday so they could go on display sometime on Tuesday. Meantime, Beckman came and took down the entire Chicano exhibit on Sunday afternoon. But he had no place to put them down, so I complained that they tried to take down our work earlier than they needed to without any plan or sense of order—and all this to put up some trendy junk. And I said I'd sue if anything was stolen or broken. I went to the student newspaper and told them what was happening, and they said they were going to interview the art department that day and then me the next day. So I came back the next day, and they had a sign on their door: "Closed for the rest of the year."

That was the way they did things at Notre Dame and its art department. And that led to my second big awakening. My first awakening was at San Miguel de Allende, where I discovered my roots. My second one was at Notre Dame— my call to become a real Chicano and to join in *la lucha* of the Chicano movement, of MECHA,

Fig. 38. José Gamaliel González, Toltec calendar for MECHA poster. Notre Dame, 1971. 16"×16". Pen and ink.

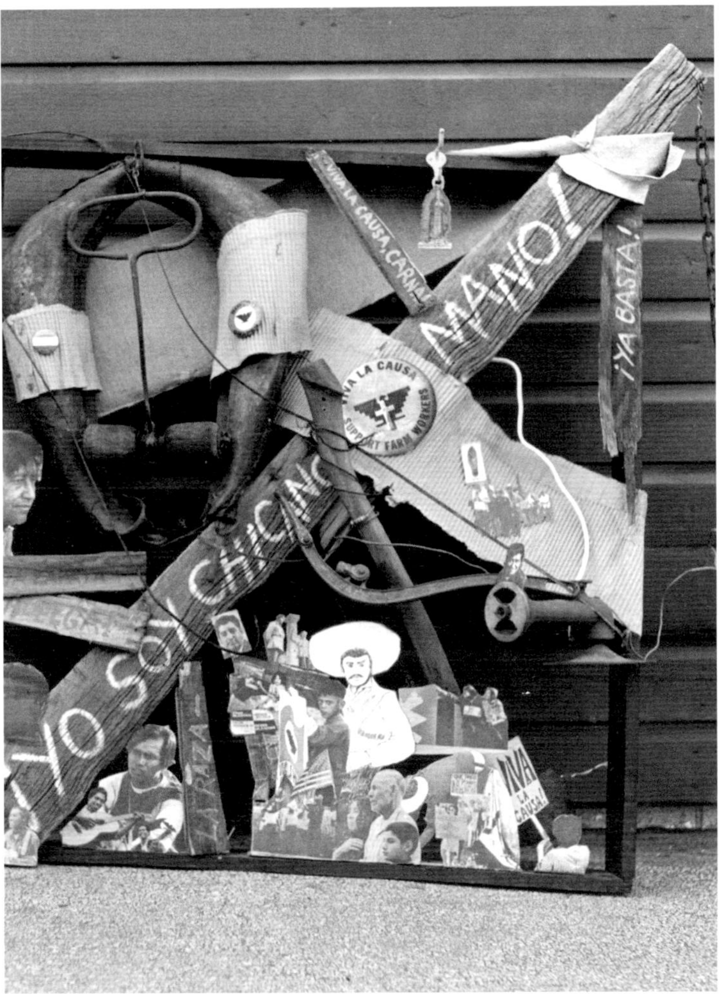

Fig. 39. José Gamaliel González, Frustration. Notre Dame, 1970–71. Collage, mounted (nailed and pasted together—including José's first drawing of Emiliano Zapata). Photo: José Gamaliel González, which appeared in the MARCH Calendar of 1977. (A photo of the collage by Andy Carrillo appeared in *Latin Times,* August 20, 1971.)

and the farm workers. Now it became fully a part of me. And it was almost like a religious conversion. I'd never gotten involved in politics, even in the late sixties, and now suddenly it was like Saul on the road to Damascus. I'd become a Chicano activist, and my great love of art would be central to that, but even my art and maybe my living, my love, and my very life would be sacrificed to the activist fire I felt within me.

Of course, it didn't happen that fast. The first step for me was to start a boycott. So I went with Dalia to the small campus art gallery, where they were showing a one-man MFA art student's exhibit on Sunday. She brought a tape recorder, and I got on top of a chair so the people could see me. "I'm boycotting the university," I said. "I'm not going to go to my classes because of the discrimination against us leading to the premature ending of our show." The students heard me, but they didn't say anything. They were stunned; no one said a word.

It probably wasn't a good thing to do, but I was in a state of anxiety. Up to this point in my life, till this very moment, I had not really been a rebel. But MECHA politicized me and led me to my awakening; and my awakening cost me my MFA and my one chance for a normal arts career. I wasn't expelled from Notre Dame, but I was going to have to leave. I had been getting straight A's in all of my classes, and I was a student teacher in ceramics. Everything was going great. But I said to myself, if I don't boycott my painting class I'll be a hypocrite, because if I'm not boycotting all of my classes, then what am I really doing? So I boycotted all of them, and I took my chances with what I would get. And I still ended up with A's and B's, except for the painting classes, where I got an F for not doing enough work. They didn't say that what I gave them wasn't good work, but it was based on my failure to produce. But it wasn't really that I hadn't produced. As I said, one of my key works was stolen, and a lot of my drawings had disappeared too.

I remember that our group somehow got the honor of being interviewed by NBC's channel 5 for an hour-long TV show called "First Tuesday." NBC came because they were interviewing the only large university in the country that wasn't having revolts, supposedly because, as Notre Dame officials claimed, there were no disenchanted students on campus. But when NBC got there, MECHA art students made sure we were interviewed, and we made a point of saying that there were a small number of Chicano and *mexicano* students there, and that

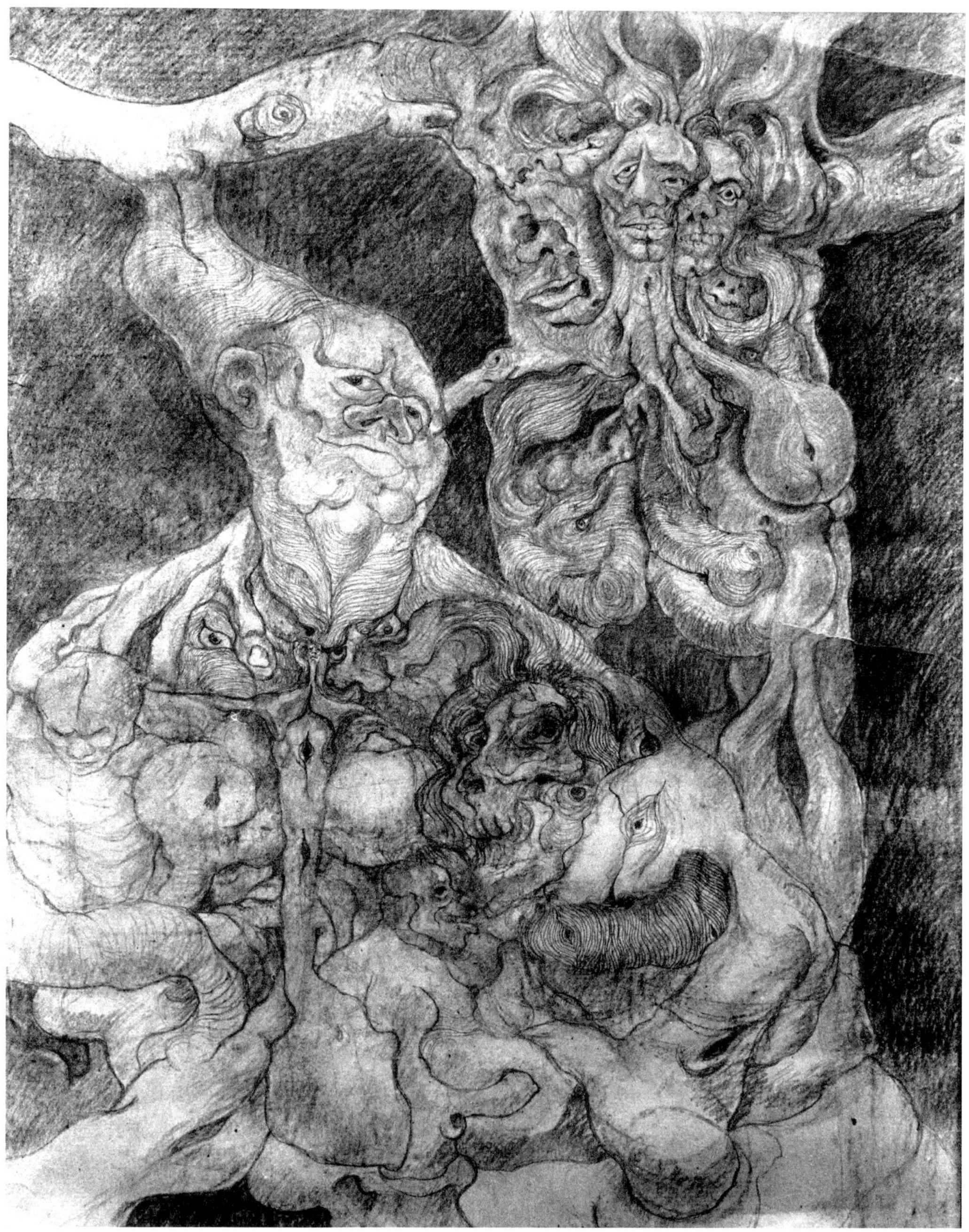

almost all of us were unhappy with the ways things were going. They took a photograph of my drawing that is on the cover of one of the old issues of *Revista Chicano-Riqueña*. I don't have the drawing anymore, but it was a picture of my struggle with the devil (fig. 40). I guess it felt like that kind of life-and-death struggle—a fight for body and soul. I wasn't going to church much at that time, and I was struggling with a lot of different problems. I was struggling with

Fig. 40. José Gamaliel González, Struggle with the Devil. Notre Dame. Charcoal. (Used for *Revista Chicana-Riqueña* 1.2 [1972]), cover.

my Catholicism, my work for the Chicano movement—everything.

I'm at a major Catholic university that is supposedly not politicized. I'm a part of a small group of Chicanos becoming aware and connected with the national Chicano movement and becoming very politicized and militant. So, sure enough, another thing I became militant about was that they didn't have anything Mexican in the church at Notre Dame. Our Lady of Guadalupe is recognized as the patroness of the Americas, she's our lady of the Americas, but Notre Dame had no representation of her. So for me the struggle over art images was also a struggle over recognition and inclusion in the heart or center of American Catholicism. But in all this, I didn't want to make my concerns into something that would create problems for the Mexican or Chicano students. I told them I didn't want them to support me because I figured that I could mess up their scholarships. So when I told them about the boycott, I told them that I was doing this alone and I didn't want anyone to support me because it could be detrimental to their careers. So I did it on my own and took my chances.

My boycott was the one that made a change at Notre Dame. It did some good because it got more scholarship money for Chicanos, and it looked at the problems of the campus. But it was going to have an adverse effect on me in lots of ways, because it was very hard for me to oppose the university which represented my church and my god. And I knew that my boycott meant that I could not stay at Notre Dame, and that almost broke my heart. I suffered deeply and mainly alone because of my refusal to involve others.

It was very painful for me, but it was also very important. I left the university but didn't want to leave a bitterness in my heart for a place I loved so deeply, so I went on a pilgrimage to the campus church asking for forgiveness, not from the university, but from "Our Lady." I practiced running long distance, walking, fasting—and then I did it on a Sunday. I went with my brother and mother. We drove all the way to the university. Then, as we got close to the church, we saw that we were showing up just in time for the noon mass. So I knelt on my knees; and I went forward on them with my mother and brother to the Grotto and lit a candle. We went to the front with my mother and Ricardo Alonzo, another Mexican artist who'd gone to the School of the Art Institute. We went to the altar and then the podium, and I said, "We are here in peace, and we ask for forgiveness for things that occurred in the past, and we ask *Nuestra Señora de Guadalupe,* Our Lady of Guadalupe, to forgive us for our past sins." No one moved; everyone was frozen, and the priest came out ready to do the mass, but he stood in the back till we were almost out of the church. And only then did he come in and start the service.

A few days later, Gil Cárdenas called me and told me he'd heard about what had happened in the church—that there'd been a big demonstration with a lot of people. And I said yes, but they weren't our people, they were their people. It was packed full of *güeros,* I told him, because the Mexicans didn't feel at home in that Irish church. But I told him that I had already quit Notre Dame because, the way it was, I couldn't have a Chicano agenda there. I felt that the only way we could express ourselves as Chicanos was to do it ourselves. And that's how it was going to be for me. In fact, when I decided to leave Notre Dame, I was, without knowing it, also deciding on my next project—which was to do some things for ourselves.

3

The MARCH Years
(1971–79)

NORTHWEST INDIANA ACTIVITY AND THE FOUNDING OF MARCH (1971–72)

I left Notre Dame in 1971, and in 1972 I gave birth to the Movimient Artístico Chicano (MARCH). I'd like to tell the story of what happened as I went quickly along a path that led to MARCH.

First, I went back to Hammond because that's where I lived with my mother, and it was in Hammond that I began to get involved with some local Latino organizations. There's no question that leaving Notre Dame meant a long period of confusion and disorientation for me. I supported myself by taking on part-time freelance work in Chicago. I was literally bouncing between Indiana and Chicago. I had a car in those days, whipping around back and forth. But I was very depressed, and I felt that if I kept on being depressed, I was going be unproductive. So that's when I became the opposite—I became super-involved in Hammond and East Chicago, Indiana, working in different organizations try-

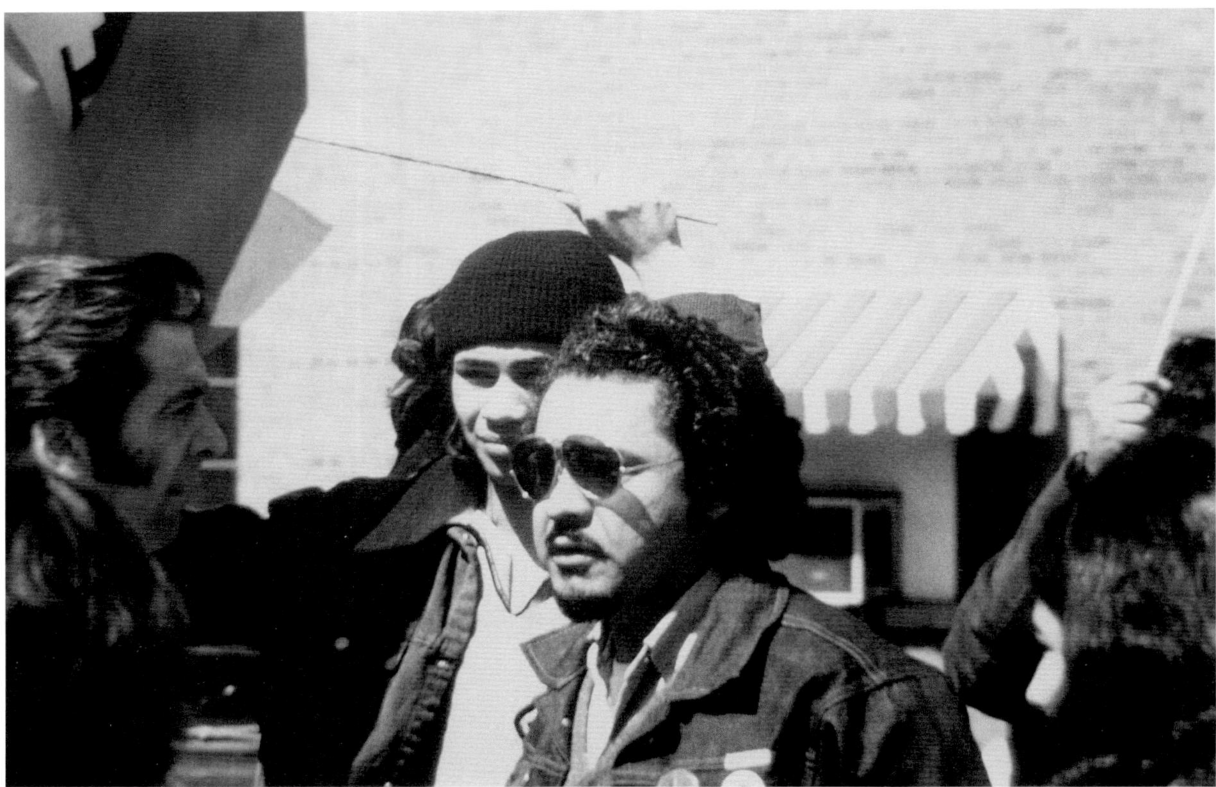

ing to find myself and get over the pain of Notre Dame. First, I became very active in Northwest Indiana Chicano politics—with anything Latino that seemed to be worth fighting for.

I don't remember exactly how I got involved in so many Indiana organizations. Almost as soon as I moved to Hammond, I joined the United Farm Workers (UFW) and became the Northwest Indiana coordinator for three years, working as a volunteer. The UFW had started forming picket lines, and I joined some of them and stayed involved with them even as I participated in other organizations and developed MARCH in the years to come. I helped form the Calumet Boycott Committee as the local UFW support group involved in grape and lettuce boycotts (fig. 42). I later cofounded the Concerned Latins of Lake Country (CLLC); later I broke away from that group to form the United Neighborhood Organization (UNO); and still later I got involved with the local Brown Berets,

who liked a few of the murals I was doing in the early 1970s.

I was inspired by César Chávez and the Farm Workers movement, but there was another person who came to have a direct influence on me, a community organizer named Ernie Cortez. Ernie was from San Antonio, where he went to college and then worked for the Mexican American Unity Council. In 1972, he went to the Industrial Areas Foundation training center in Chicago, where he learned community-development techniques worked out by Saul Alinsky, a famous professional organizer whose methods influenced Chávez and the UFW. Graduating in June 1972, Ernie started organizing Mexicans in Wisconsin and then moved on to Northwest Indiana, where the Bishop's Commission gave him his startup monies to organize full-time among Chicago-area Indiana Latinos.

The first time I met Ernie, I sensed right off that he was very astute (he later won a Mc-

Arthur Genius Award, so I guess I know how to pick them). He pretended to let it slip that he didn't meet me by accident, but he was a real recruiter. When he came to the Harbor area, he went to the local library and spent hours there looking at a lot of articles from the East Chicago newspaper, the *Latin Times,* to see who had appeared in the past few issues and who could be potential members and leaders. I was in the *Latin Times* a lot because of my boycott work. And that's how he found me and some of the others he convinced to join him—at local meetings, at dances, and of course in the steel-mill neighborhoods. And that's how he went about founding the CLLC as an Alinsky-style organization, and he convinced me and others to be cofounders and members. The CLLC was involved in attacking the administrations in three cities, Gary, Hammond, and East Chicago, for different things related to jobs, housing, safety, schooling—you name it. We would go to city hall meetings in East Chicago, and we would sit down in protest. For some reason, we never got arrested. But we did get a fair amount of news coverage in the local newspaper.

In all my Indiana political work, and even in my work as an arts activist in Chicago, Ernie was a great inspiration to me. He was a gifted organizer and an excellent mentor. He not only taught me how to spot talented coworkers but how to work with the community, Alinsky-style, by relating to their core values in religion, community, and art. He helped me to learn how to organize to do what we had to do. He taught me to think strategically and relate strategy to tactics—to understand where people were and convince them to reach for more. But in spite of all I learned, I also learned that Ernie and Alinsky methods could sometimes go too far.

All my artwork was now at the service of my political involvements. But even as I was involved in it all, I was thinking, How can I

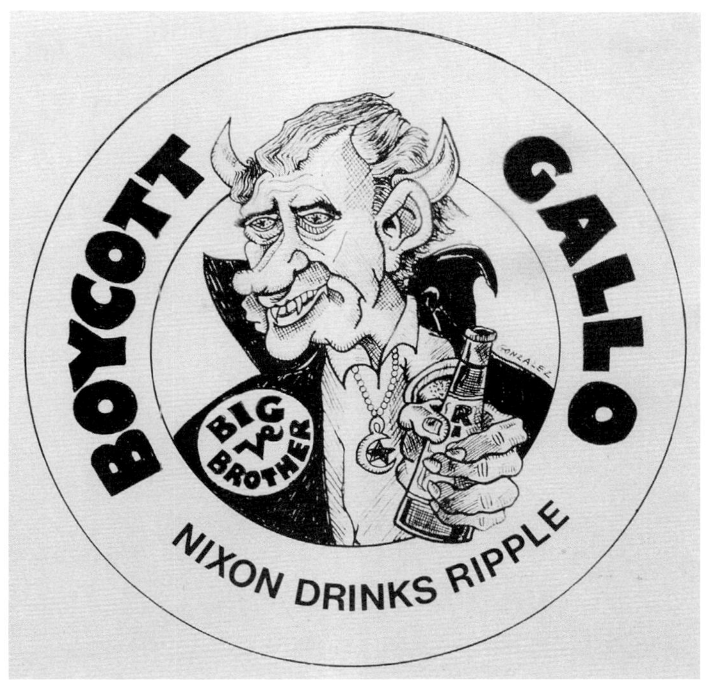

Fig. 42. José Gamaliel González, UFW Gallo Boycott, 1972 (design for Nixon button). Pen and ink.

bring together this political work with the artistic work that I wanted to do? It was a very political time, but I was also an artist, and somehow some of this activity for the UFW, for CLLC, and still other groups crystallized my new orientation toward my artwork as I developed during this period. I did the logo and posters for the CLLC (figs. 43, 44, and 49); I was designing and passing out flyers for the UFW boycott (figs. 45 and 46). I did artwork in relation to other Latino groups and causes. But somehow that wasn't enough. I needed to develop the organization I had been thinking about the most—an organization that linked artistic and political work. And I sensed that Northwest Indiana could not be the base for the new arts project I was thinking about.

I was talking a lot about my ideas on the phone with David Torres in Saginaw, Michigan. And one day he called me up and said, "There's a guy named Gilberto Martínez who's very interested in talking to you, so I told him we should come and see you." Gilberto and David drove all the way down to Hammond, and when they got there it was already night. But we

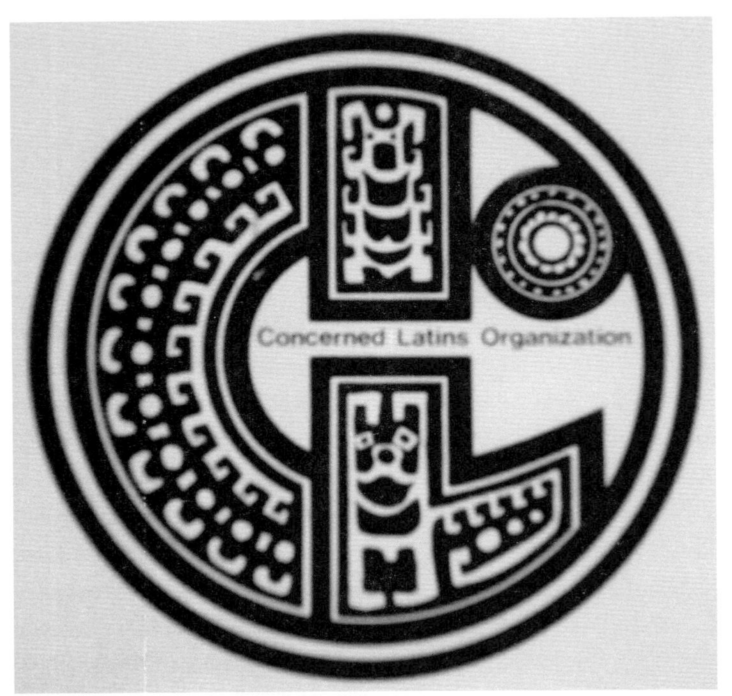

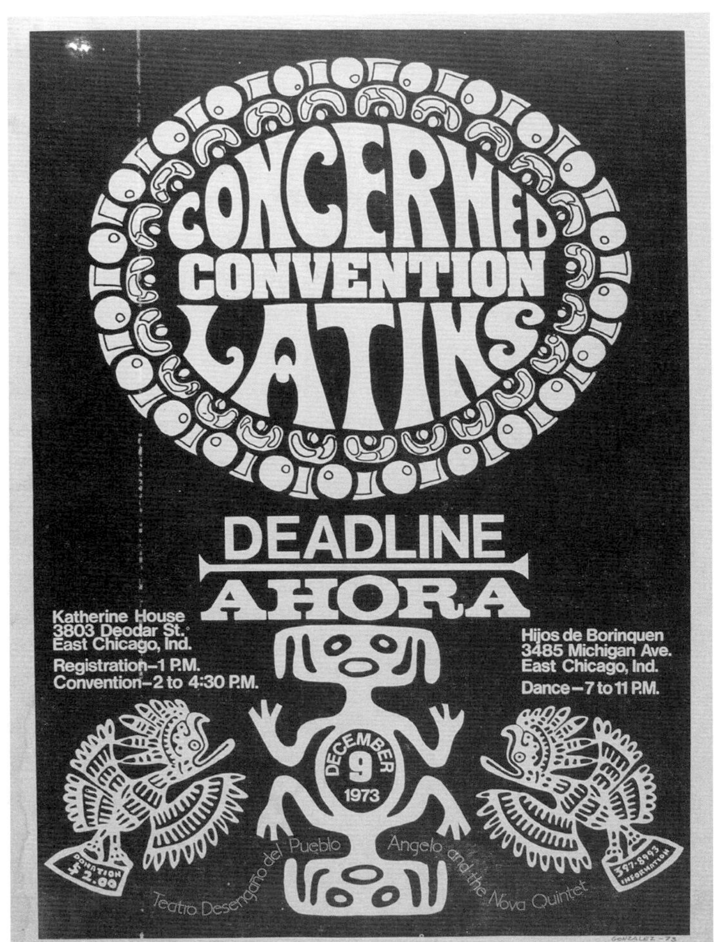

Fig. 43. José Gamaliel González, Logo design for Concerned Latins of Indiana, 1972. Pen and ink.

Fig. 44. José Gamaliel González, Poster, Concerned Latins Convention, December 1972. Pen and ink.

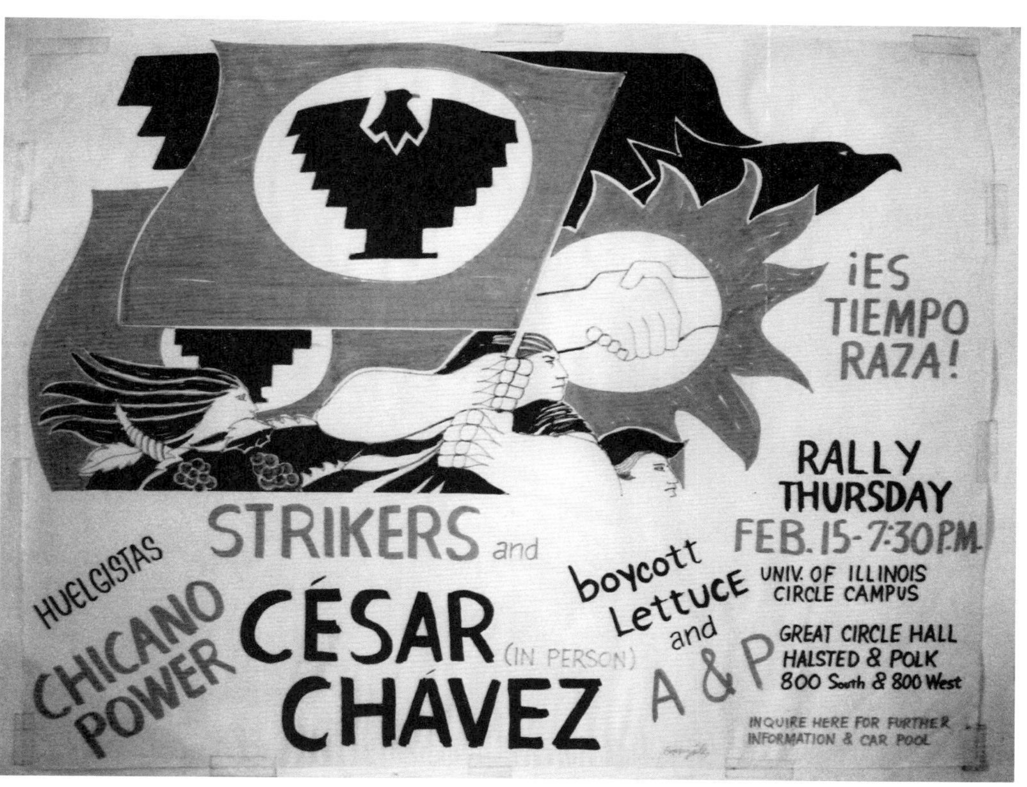

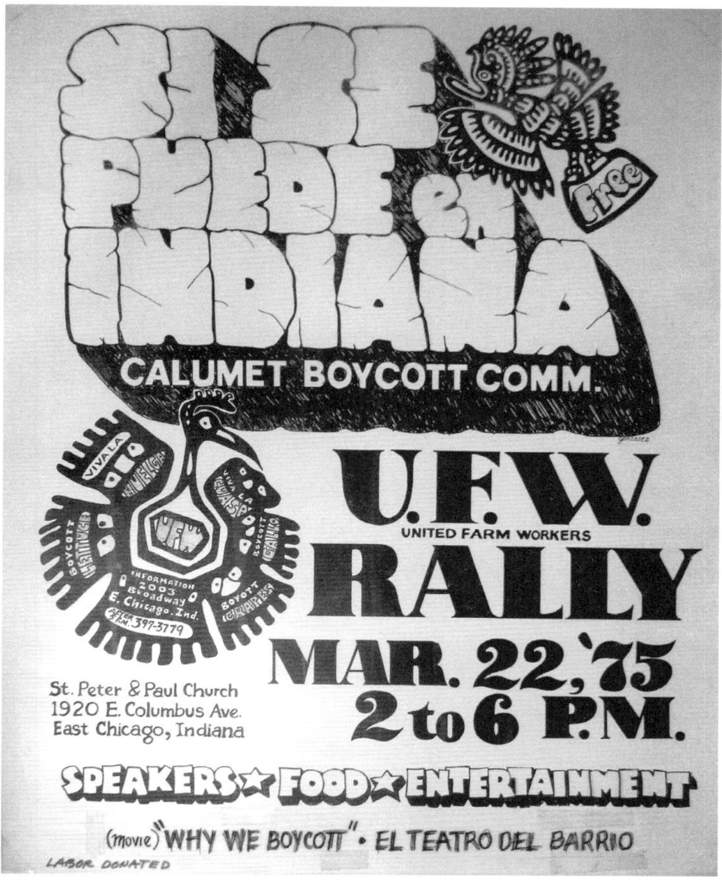

Fig. 45. José Gamaliel González, Poster/flyer design, modeled on UFW California poster for Calumet Boycott Committee, for an event at the University of Illinois at Chicago Circle campus on February 15, 1973. In black and red.

Fig. 46. José Gamaliel González, UFW poster, March 1975. An indication of José's continued UFW work in Indiana even after he had launched MARCH in Chicago.

stayed up and talked for hours. And that's when we decided that no matter how midwestern the arts organization we dreamed up might be, we would eventually have to center that organization in Chicago—preferably in the emerging center of Mexican cultural life, the Pilsen barrio in and around Eighteenth Street.

MARCH came about because at Notre Dame and then in my community work in the early 1970s, I recognized that we had to start to do our own thing to promote Chicano art. Even though I lived in Hammond and would do lots of things in Northwest Indiana even after MARCH was formed, I was constantly going to Chicago to pick up freelance artwork. That's when I began to think about art shows and art exhibits, and I also began to produce some art. And then I thought of the name MARCH because it was springtime after my long winter without Notre Dame and MECHA; and I thought of a militant kind of spirit for the group I could develop—something like, well, "soldiery"—kind of MARCH, with MARCHing feet. I thought of MARCH that way, and I thought of *Movimiento*. So that is one of the things I could imply by the MARCH anagram. Jessie Jackson had formed Operation PUSH, and so I thought of Operation MARCH. To cap it off, I designed a button with a logo that was red with a man's black hand and yellow lettering. The image maybe had too much red, and I was involved with many picket lines, so maybe that's why I was called a red by a lot of people who thought I was a Communist. But I never was, even though some Communist party members might have tried to join or "infiltrate" all the organizations I was involved in, including MARCH. So that was why I decided that MARCH needed a special logo—in black and white and without the red (fig. 47).

Even then people asked what community I was signaling by our anagram and logo—always

suggesting that the red was still really there. At first, I'd have to admit, I wasn't really sure who or what my real base would be—Indiana and Chicago Mexicanos/Chicanos/Latinos and then anyone who supported them, I guess. It's true, some of the initial members were political friends from Gary, East Chicago, and the Harbor, who became a part of the cabinet committee I had founded to help out-of-funds workers. But none of them were artists, and none of them lasted with us for long. Even Torres and Martínez were never going to be that much involved—though Martínez would play a role in three of our major projects. There were also some people from the Calumet Boycott Committee and also, later, some Northwest Indiana Brown Berets who became very excited about our project. The fact is, I still lived in Hammond and only moved MARCH to Chicago in 1974, even as I began to expand MARCH's agenda.

By the early 1970s, there was a cultural renaissance under way in the Mexican and Latino communities of Northwest Indiana and Chicago. Maybe not everybody was fully aware of it, and MARCH would become one of the biggest indicators. But there were other things happening in Chicano arts. In 1968, Carlos Cortez had made it to Chicago and was producing artwork, but not as a Chicano till he hooked up with MARCH. Other Mexican-style and Chicano artists began to emerge in the early seventies—some people I'd known earlier, like Ray Patlán, Mario Castillo, Ricardo Alonso, and other Mexican artists like Alejandro Romero, Aurelio Díaz, Marcos Raya, and Salvador Vega. Then there were Chicano poets like Carlos Morton and Ana Castillo. There were also Puerto Rican poets like David Hernández and Salima Rivera and artists like Gamaliel Ramírez, who developed in the same period and formed the group El Taller and later another group called ALBA (Association of Latino Brotherhood of

Artists). At that time, also, two young professors, Luis Dávila and Nicolás Kanellos, a Nuyorican graduate from the University of Texas now teaching at Indiana University Northwest, founded a nationally recognized literary journal, *Revista Chicano-Riqueña.* Then too there was the theater group, *Teatro del desengaño del pueblo,* which Nick founded and acted in along with his first wife.

I only became fully involved with this Latino arts renaissance when I moved MARCH to Chicago in 1974. However, the involvement began in Northwest Indiana earlier in the seventies through the work I took on for Nick and his fledgling *Revista.* I first met him in 1971, when the first two or three issues of *Revista* came out, and some of my work appears in an early issue. But Nick knew those first issues were not designed very well, and he asked me to help out by redesigning the logo for the next issues and by staying on as his art editor. This was more of an individual thing. I did it not as a member of MARCH, but Nick did ask me sometimes to find artwork for given issues, and so I began doing something MARCH would be known for: finding Latino artists and artwork for given projects. I should say that Nick was never a regular member of MARCH, even though he joined us in spirit and was our translator for MARCH's *Abrazo* publications in 1976 and 1979.

As far as MARCH itself is concerned, I kind of launched the organization by doing a mural with some kids at Washington Park in Indiana Harbor in 1972. The city didn't pay me, but I told a Mexican guy at the Park Commission that I'd volunteer my labor if they provided the paint. I figured that the commission might help me get this project going, and it did. I started the mural with my nephews and nieces, all smart kids between eight and twelve years old. The mural itself wasn't very big—it was about seven or eight feet high, I think. I don't remember all

of it, but it dealt with the four elements—fire, water, air, and earth—and there were animals and fish. That's why the kids could paint it, because it was very simple. The forms were easy to fill in. The colors that I had chosen for them to paint were all primaries—except for the Aztec sun, which I painted myself and made much brighter than the rest, so that it just shined out beyond everything else in the mural.

In those days, maybe it was common to paint an Aztec sun in a Chicano mural in Los Angeles, but not in Northwest Indiana. There was a Brown Beret group starting up in the area, and when two of the members, Gary and Roberto, saw the MARCH button and our mural project, they got excited about joining MARCH and bringing some Berets with them. I supported the Berets, but I never joined them. The Berets said they wanted to add an artistic and cultural dimension to their work through collaboration with MARCH, so some ten Berets joined. None

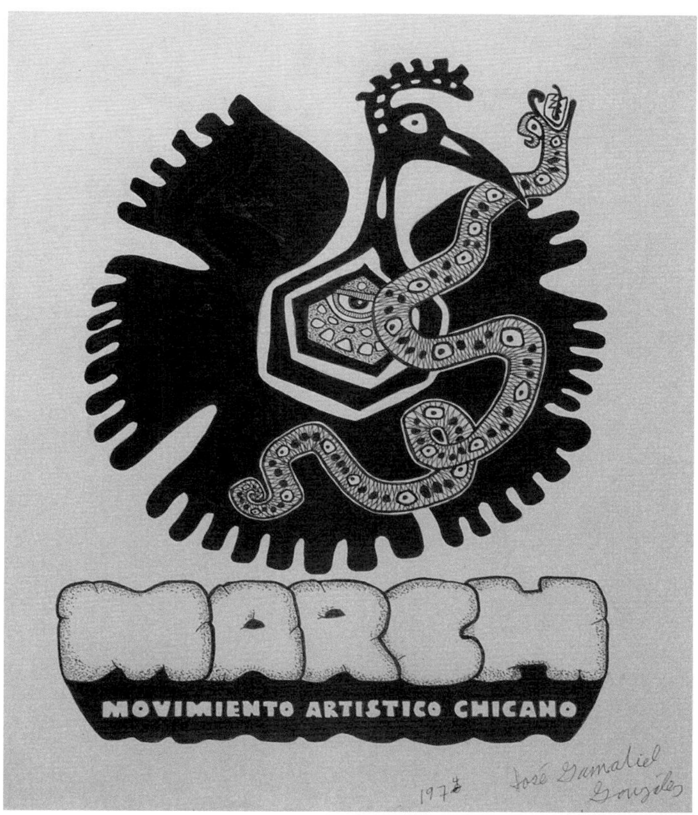

Fig. 47. José Gamaliel González, MARCH logo, hand dated 1972, but probably a work of 1973. Pen and ink.

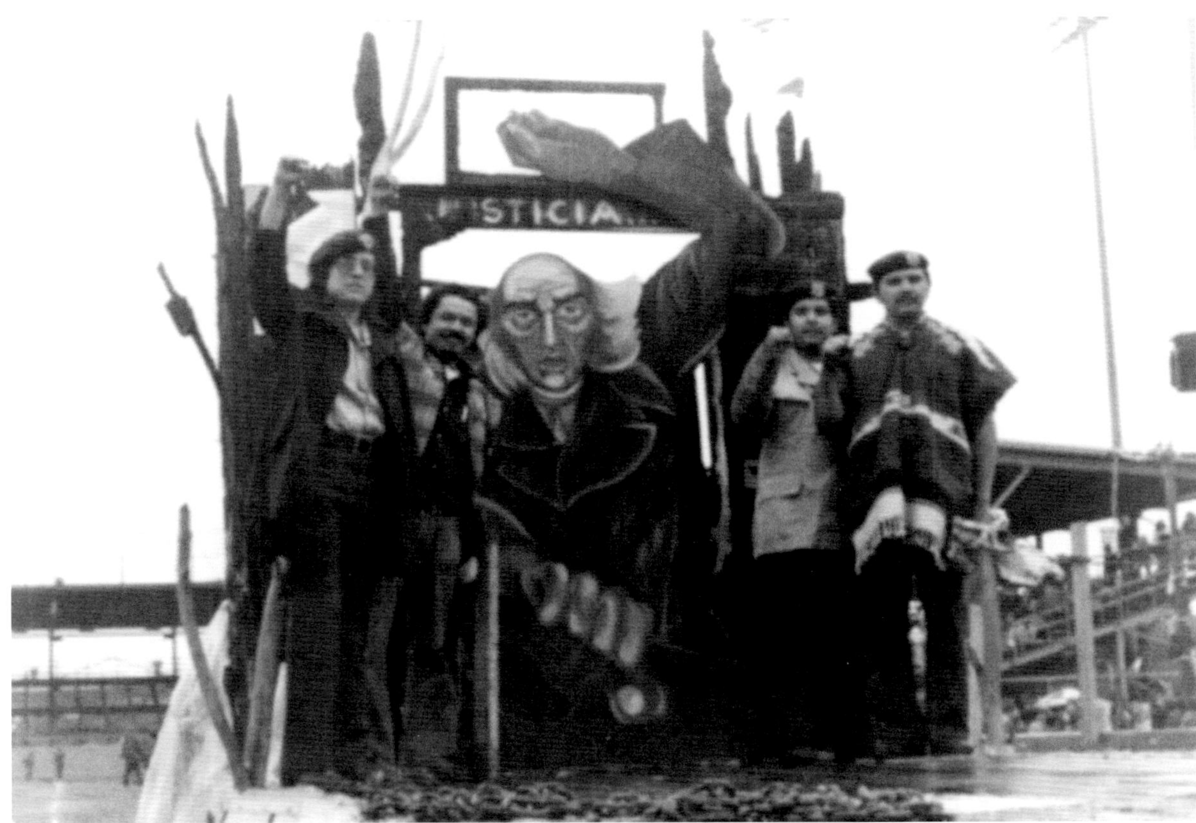

Fig. 48. Float with image of Hidalgo, with Brown Berets, designed by José Gamaliel González. Photo: unknown, printed in *Hammond Times,* 1973; reproduced in 1977 MARCH calendar. Courtesy of José Gamaliel González collection.

of them were artists, but they just enjoyed helping out on some of MARCH's first art and culture projects. I guess that made MARCH look like a militant organization.

In 1973, MARCH did an Independence Day float with a big image of el Padre Hidalgo (fig. 48), based on Orozco's famous image of him that you can see at the Guadalajara government palace. Pictures of the float still survive in some archives; one made the front page of the *Hammond Times.* In 1984, the *Northwest Extra,* a Chicago newspaper published on North Avenue between Pulaski and Cicero, reproduced the float image as the cover for a special Mexican Independence Day edition. But the best picture is reproduced in the MARCH calendar of 1977.

In 1974, the Brown Berets participated in another MARCH float that I designed for September 15—this one centering on the UFW, with images of César Chávez and Dolores Huerta. But a lot of the Berets were frightened because they were being hounded, and some of them were getting killed off by the FBI. After that they broke away from MARCH. But our militant image stuck, so MARCH and I personally would always be harassed by the police and the FBI. People were saying that I was a Communist because of my involvements; people were saying MARCH was Communist. It wasn't true, but the rumors followed us, and so did the harassment.

By the early 1970s, Concerned Latins began making strides when it grew to about fifty active members representing our three core cities. We would meet in East Chicago, mostly in Indiana Harbor. We picketed the police stations, the civic centers. We got lots of Mexicans and other Latinos involved in our organization. We joined farm- and steel-worker boycotts and picket lines; we spread leaflets and allied with different groups in making waves in all we undertook, attempting to build a popular base that could fight against the established politics in the region. But somehow I became unhappy with certain things Ernie and the CLLC did. They seemed to be all for boycotting everything without considering who might get hurt. Once they picketed the house of East Chicago Mayor Robert Pastrick at a time when he wasn't even home, and the only ones to get intimidated were his kids. When I complained about this, I was told that the publicity was too important to miss. I guess they were saying, "You can't make an omelet without breaking some eggs." But I and some others came to feel the need to leave the organization. We came to feel that in the name of community, Concerned Latinos sometimes imposed its will on the people. On the other hand, we still believed in the struggle for Latino rights. So I led them in forming a new organization, the United Neighborhood Organization.

As part of my work with UNO, I produced a huge mural projecting the role and vision of UNO in relation to the history of East Chicago, and I did it with the help of only one other artist, Frank Alfaro, an East Chicago Mexican who'd served some time for smoking marijuana.

The mural has disappeared, but I still have my color sketches for each panel. Overall, it represented many aspects of the local history: the plight and struggles of railroad, steel-mill, and farm workers; breadlines in the Depression; airborne paratroopers fighting in World War II. Featured to the far left of the mural was the figure of Cuauhtémoc, leader of the Aztec resistance against the Spanish. Almost right next to him, but in the distance, is an image of Pancho Villa riding on horseback, followed by an image of Mexican farm workers picking lettuce with the symbol of Mexican eagle on a banner. Later comes the image of a big fat butcher straight out of Carl Sandburg. Then there was a tribute to the East Chicago Wash-

ington Senators basketball team (working-class heroes, all of them). Then the last part of the mural in sequence was an image of two boys and two girls huddled hugging and praying, all four wearing t-shirts bearing the name of Jesus. But what I remember maybe the most was my portrait of two local Mexican Vietnam War heroes on tombstones (fig. 50). José Núñez, driving a cab while on furlough from the army, saved a boy by jumping from his car and pushing the boy away, only to be hit himself by a train and dying in his heroic effort. Emilio de la Garza, a Marine in Vietnam, received the Medal of Honor for falling on a hand grenade

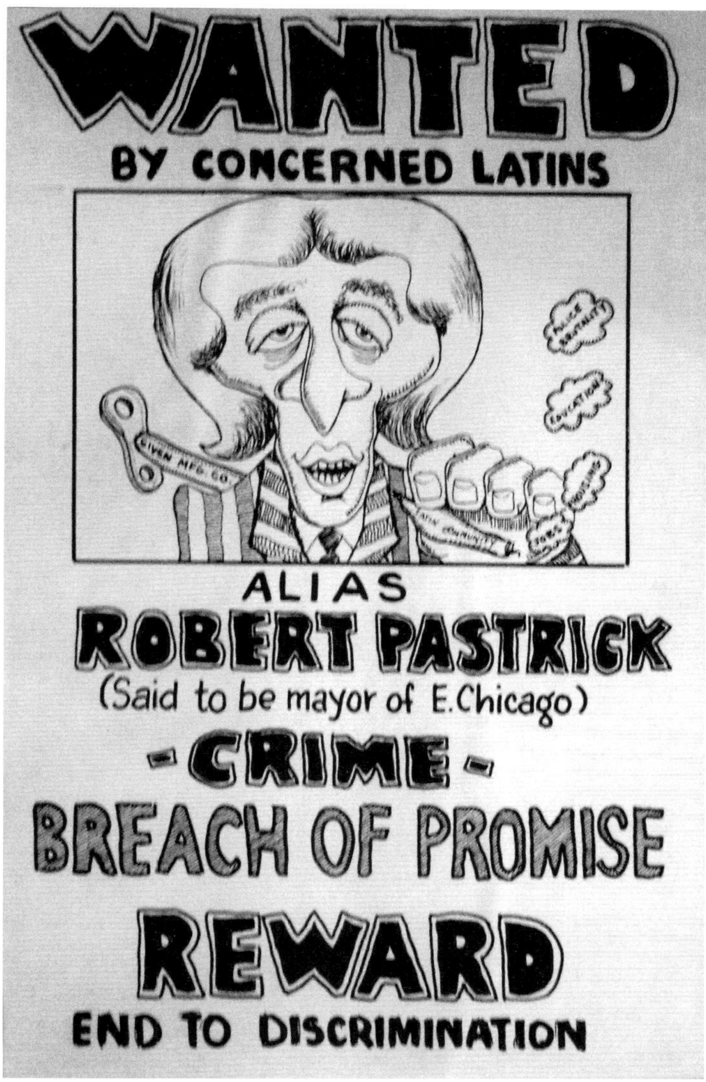

Fig. 49. José Gamaliel González, Poster for Concerned Latins of Indiana, 1973.

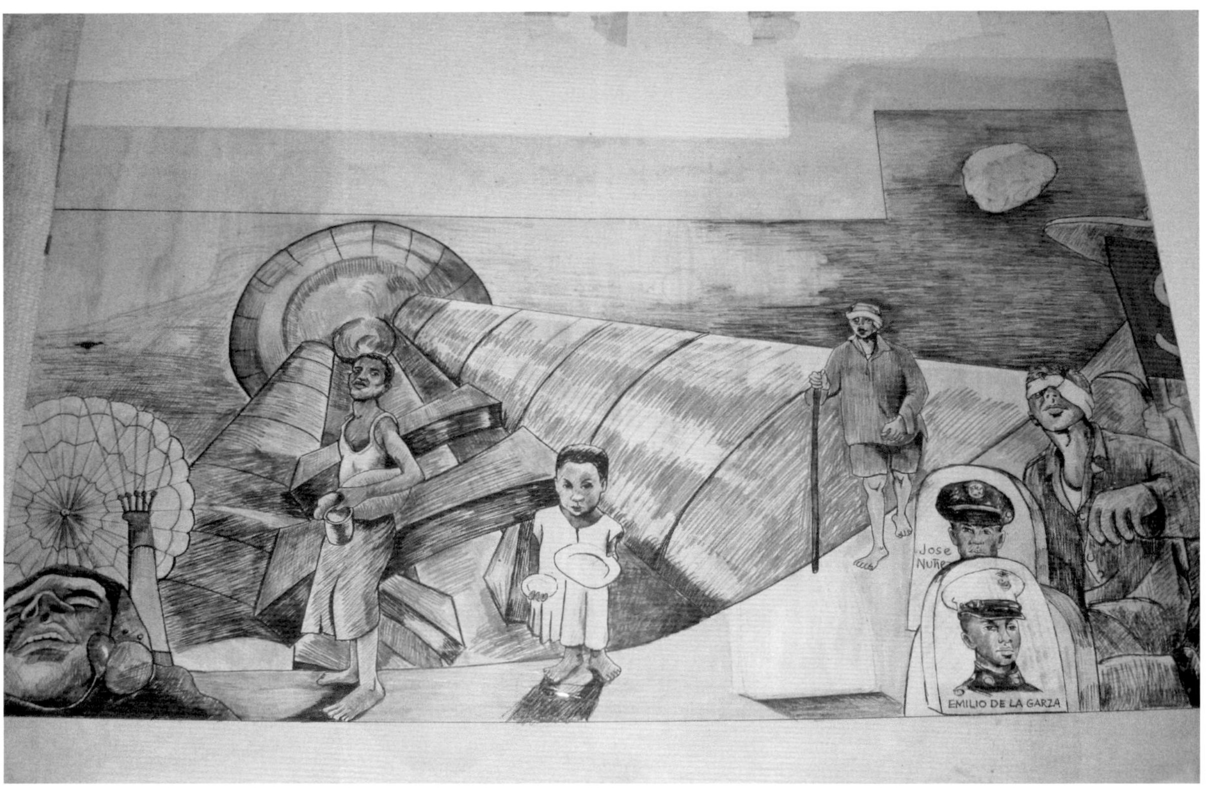

to save the lives of three soldiers as he gave his own. Finally, at the far right of the mural is a large image of the sponsoring organization's name and its anagram, UNO.

But that was my last major activity with UNO and in Indiana, an activity that showed me once again that my future was combining arts and community—but that future I would now pursue with MARCH and in Chicago.

MARCH IN CHICAGO (1974–79)

It was only in the late fall of '74 that I finally moved MARCH to Chicago and began to recruit Chicago MARCH members. Really building MARCH was all like Robin Hood gathering up his merry men—and merry women, too, I should add. I got to know Carlos Heredia in those first days. He was a young community organizer with some interest in the arts, and he found us a meeting space in Centro de la Causa on Seventeenth Street in Pilsen. Here-

dia went to some of the meetings, but he never joined MARCH, though he remained a friend and tried his hand at a Latino literary/cultural journal called *Imágenes,* in 1976, I think. Gilberto Martínez never really joined, but he always worked with us and brought in his brother, Efraín, who worked in the Justice Department and had lots of contacts in the Latino community. Efraín became one of the most active of the initial members. He became our first president and began to bring many others with him. One day, Gilberto called me to say he was off to Mexico and that he'd be happy to serve as a MARCH liaison to facilitate bringing works and exhibits to and from Mexico. The idea was an exchange program that would bring Mexican art to the city and help send *mexicano* and other Latino artwork and artists to Mexico. The first works Gilberto helped us get were examples of El Taller de Gráfica Popular, including outstanding woodcuts by Leopoldo Méndez. We exhibited the work first at Lorraine Valley

Fig. 50. José Gamaliel González, Center panel of scale design for 135'×20' East Chicago mural, Maravilla Hardware Store, 1973–74. The mural no longer exists, but José has the scale designs in storage.

Community College, and then at Northeastern Illinois University in Chicago. That exhibit brought us some attention and brought some members to MARCH, especially when we took it to Northeastern Illinois.

Organizing the exhibit brought new people to our Centro de la Causa meetings. We all were supposed to bring people in to make our group function as an organization. Efraín had lots of University of Illinois at Chicago (UIC) connections; and from there he recruited two anthropology students, Santiago Boiton from Belize and his wife, Susan Stechnicj. In addition, he brought in a major artist, Ray Patlán (fig. 52). I'd known Ray in San Miguel, but now he was back from Vietnam and doing mural work and acrylics out of the Casa Atzlán neighborhood house in Pilsen. Ray brought in his teacher, Victor Sorell, a Chicago State University art historian with a keen interest in Latin American, Mexican, Chicano, and Latino art. At Chicago State, Sorell had a program called the University without Walls, where you did murals or other art projects in the city or anywhere outside the university. Ray had problems at the School of the Art Institute, and so he decided to get his bachelor's at Chicago State in Victor's program. When Ray connected with MARCH, he invited Victor to join in.

From the first, I was the leader of MARCH, even though my official role was secretary— Victor made a joke of it, saying I was "secretary general." And I guess I became a key recruiter after Efraín's initial work, because I brought in Mario Castillo. He and Ray Patlán had done the main outdoor Mexican murals in Chicago up to that time—Mario at Lakewood High School, Ray at Casa Aztlán. Ray moved on to San Francisco after a few years. But Mario is a major Chicago Mexican artist to this day. He is the one who got the academic education that I was trying to get, and I guess he was the first

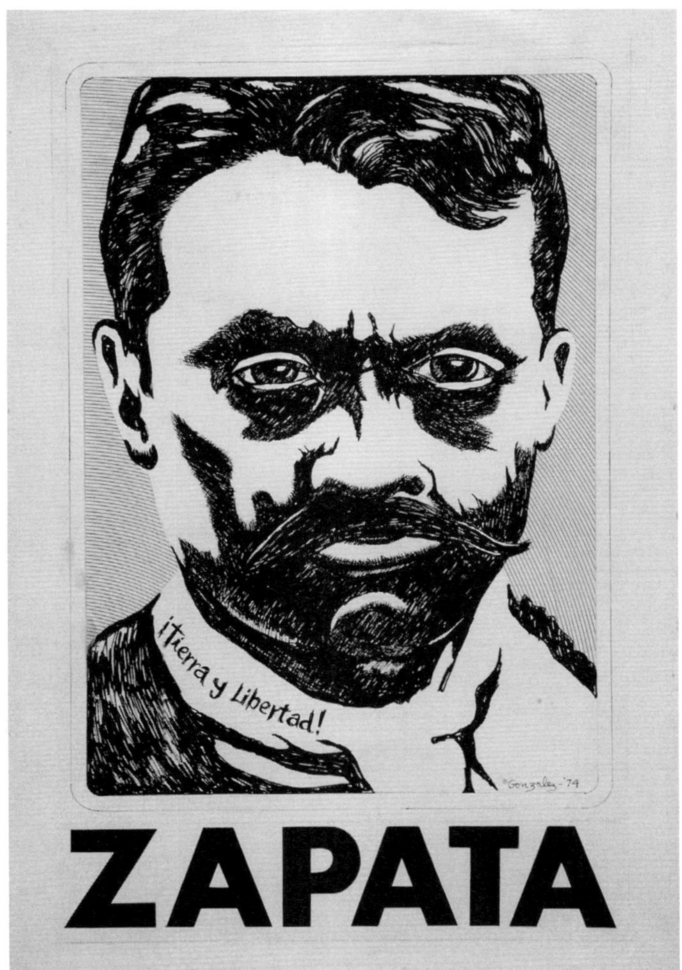

one to get it right, painting the first outdoor Latino community mural in 1968.[1] Muralism was a very important part of what I wanted to do and also public exhibitions involving the community. And Mario helped us find our way.

Mario was maybe my biggest recruit for MARCH. But when the Méndez exhibit moved to Northeastern Illinois University, lots of Chicago Latino artists saw it and began trying to join us. So our first woman artist, Marguerite Ortega, a student at UIC, joined and brought in her cousin, Salvador Domínguez, a grade-school art teacher. Frank Sánchez, a commercial artist, came in on his own after seeing the Northeastern Illinois University exhibit, and he brought in Rey Vásquez, an *indigenista* painter (fig 53). And then another artist joined. Carlos

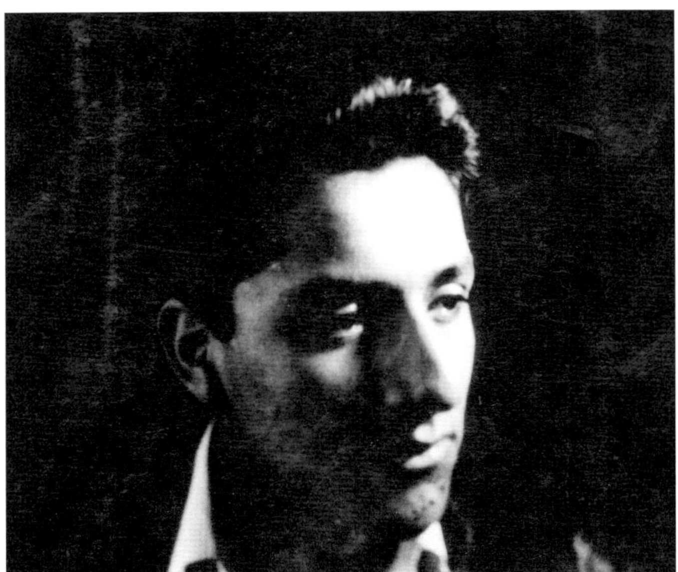
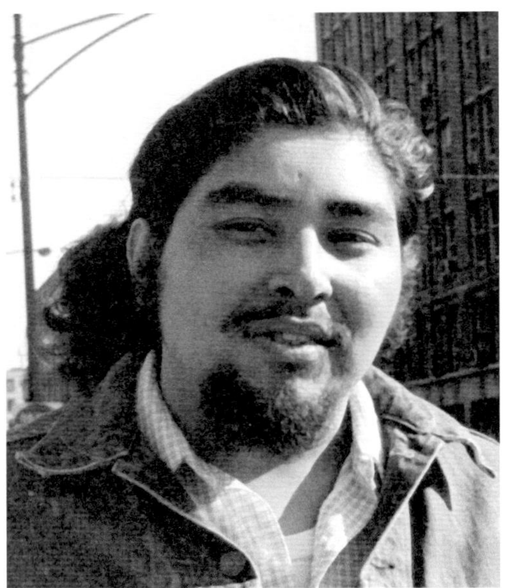
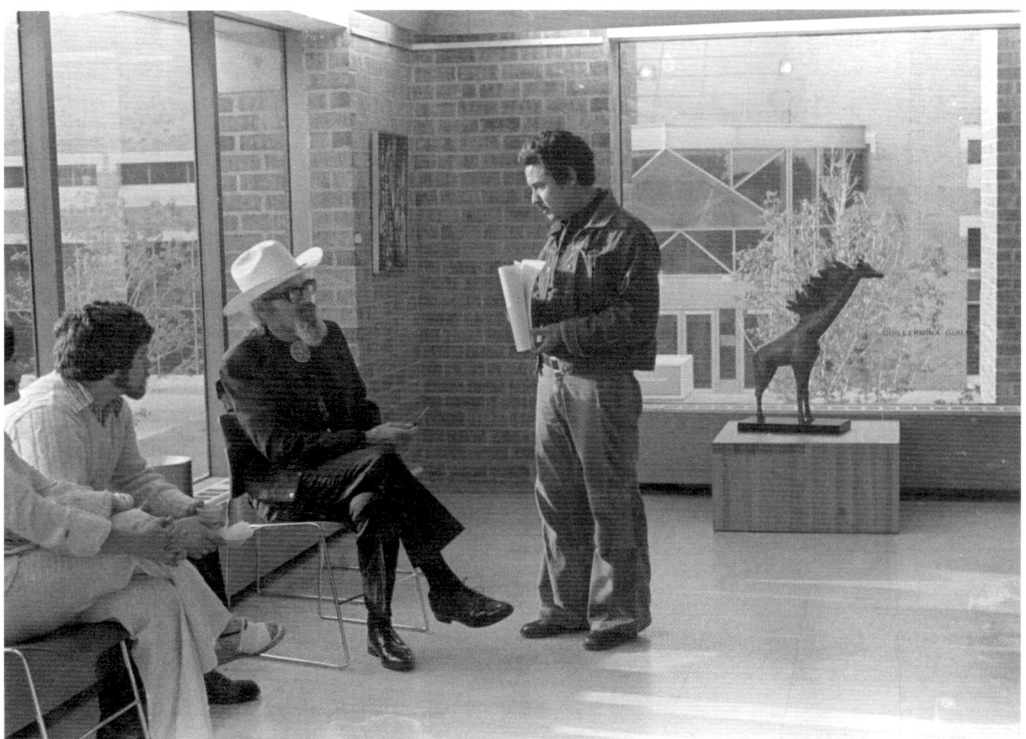

Fig. 52. Ray Patlán, 1975.

Fig. 53. Rey Vásquez, 1975.

Fig. 54. Victor Sorell, Carlos Cortez, and José. Exhibit opening at Chicago State University, 1975.

Cortez (fig. 54) also saw the Méndez exhibit at Northeastern, and he got interested in what MARCH was all about and whether he could join. He came up to me and said, very humbly, "I am Mexican, but I'm not a Chicano or even a Mexican artist." His art was to become more Mexican as a member of MARCH, especially through the influence of José Guadalupe Posada. But at first he came with a background in art from the International Workers of the World, or the "Wobblies," as they were called—basically an anarchist group fighting for workers' rights and socialism but from an anti-Communist point of view. He was Mexican

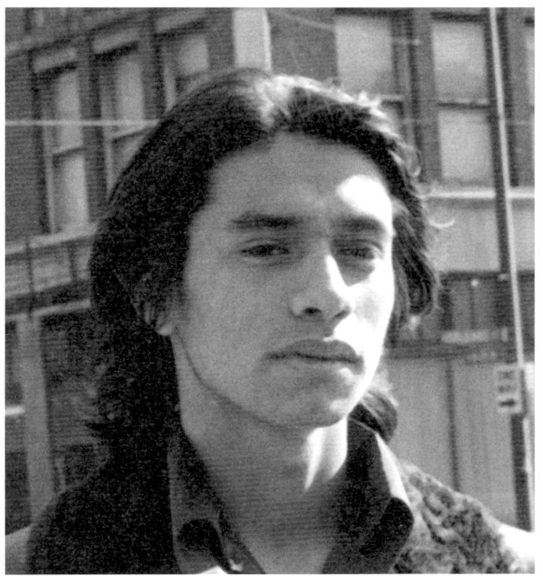 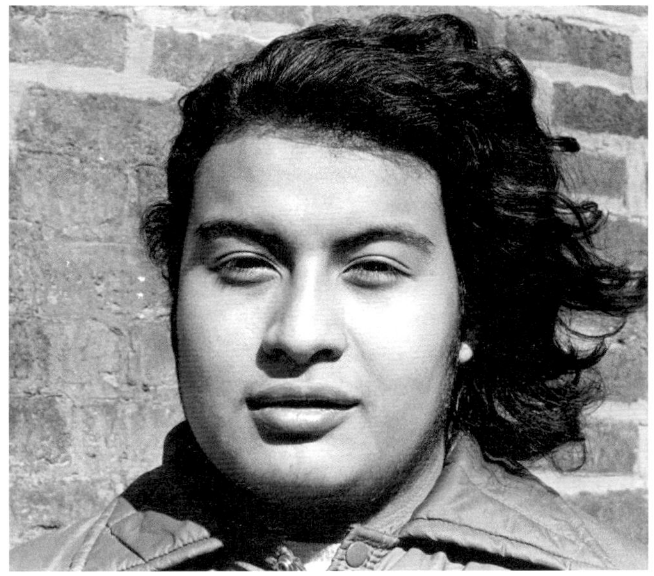

on his father's side and German on his mother's. He was brought up in a German community in Milwaukee, and even though he wrote early poems that dealt with Mexican and even Puerto Rican themes, those were things that he did as a political person working with the Wobblies; he could have been Chinese writing those things.

Still others came in, like Larry Hurlburt, an art historian from Wisconsin who joined, I think, through Victor. Then I brought in José Narrio and Francisco Blasco from Gary. I met Francisco catching the train to Chicago because he had a portfolio that he was carrying, and I approached him, and he said he was a student at the School of the Art Institute; so I told him about MARCH, and he joined up. Then in 1975, Aurelio Díaz (fig. 55), a Chicago Mexican painter, joined, and then Sal Vega (fig. 56), a young painter who would work at Casa Atzlán in the 1980s and do fine work, somehow mainly in the shadow of an artist who never joined us but was a kind of fellow traveler: Marcos Raya.

Aurelio came from an Indian village in Mexico. He got to California and then went to Texas. He came to Chicago, and I discovered him, I think in 1975. He had done some painting at a local restaurant, and I asked who did the work, and they told me, and I said, "Can I leave my phone number and tell him to call me?" And he did—he called me and showed me his work, with all his bright colors and Indian symbols; and he joined MARCH. We worked on many projects together, and in fact he made me an award of appreciation for my work with MARCH.

In 1975 and '76, MARCH was really on its way. Many of us were involved in arts projects of our own, with only some indirect ties to MARCH. So in 1975, Ricardo Alonso, who was coordinating community mural projects, asked me to produce a mural of eight panels depicting different pre-Colombian indigenous tribes on a wall between Sagamon and Hubbard Streets (see figs. 57 and 58 for two of the eight panels) and other ones depicting animals on the sides of trucks (fig. 59)—we called those portable paintings "moving murals." I hired Oscar Moya, a young Chicago Mexican artist friend of mine, to help me do the Hubbard Street murals. But they ran out of funds, and in the end, I didn't get paid a thing for any of the wall mural, which is a half a block long. The whole project was called *La raza de oro,* but for me, it was *La raza de nada*—at least financially. People now say it's my best mural work.

Anyway, Ricardo and I next teamed up to do the first Mexican American exhibit at the

Fig. 55. Aurelio Díaz, MARCH member, with portfolio, 1975.

Fig. 56. Salvador Vega, 1975

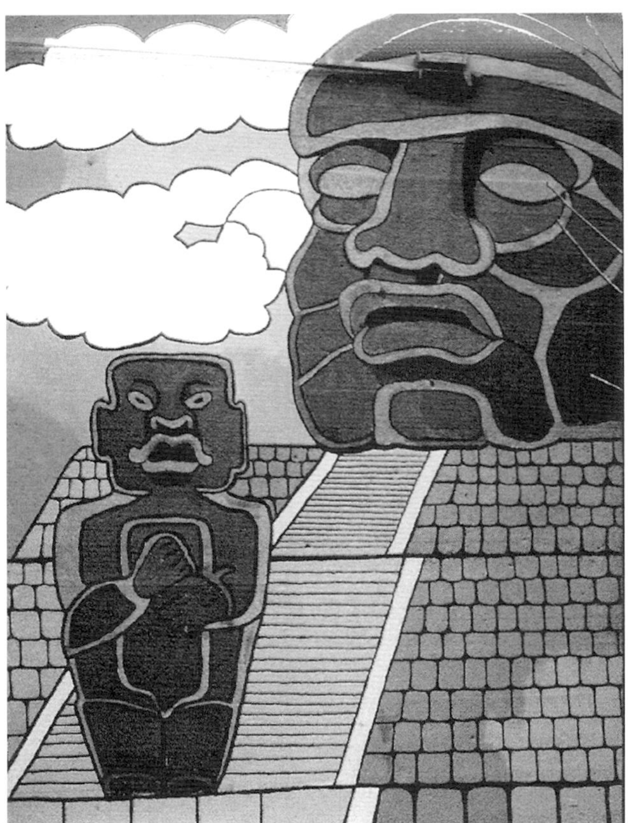

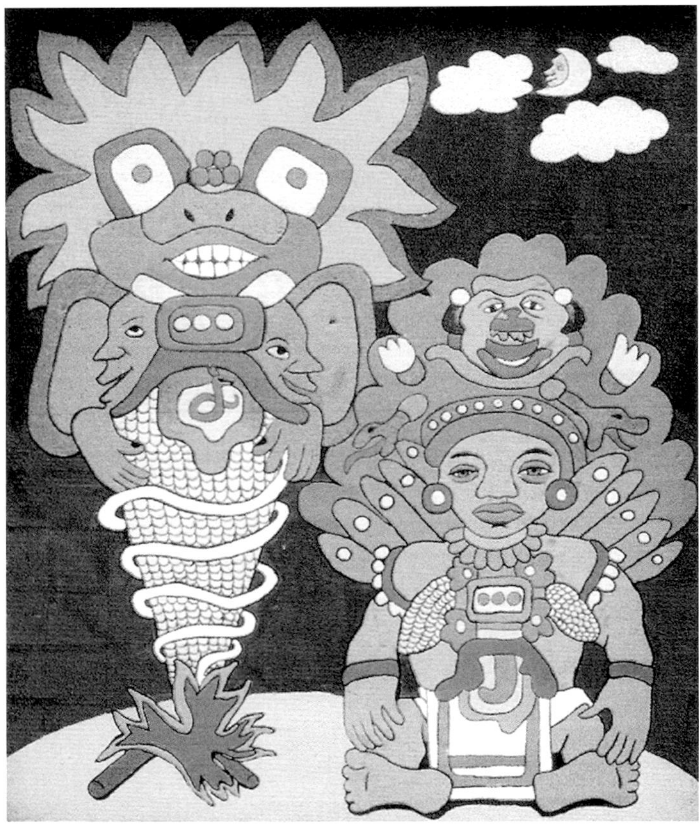

Museum of Science and Industry (fig. 60)—we were to do successive exhibits for them for about three or four years. So '75 was very busy for me because I was also working as a freelancer in Chicago. But also in that same year, Gilberto Martínez helped MARCH line up two exhibits from Mexico that we ended up doing at the Montgomery Ward gallery at UIC. First, we exhibited twenty-five paintings by the Mexican masters Orozco, Diego, Morado, Dr. Atl, Tamayo, and others—it was the first time a show of their work came to Chicago. For this show, we brought two artists from Mexico, Gilberto Ramírez and Jaime Mejía Servín, along with the show's curator and writer of the twenty-five-page introduction to the exhibit catalog, Adrián Villagómez. The show involved lots of packing and security measures (fig. 61). El Palacio de Bellas Artes de México stipulated that in order to have the paintings of the country's greatest artists, we had to have a special alarm system

installed in the gallery. Arranging that wasn't easy, first because none of us knew how to price the insurance for the artworks we had, though we knew the value was in the millions—I mean, just about every major modern Mexican painter was represented except Siqueiros, because he had just died, and they withdrew his painting to use for a special Siqueiros *homenaje* at the Bellas Artes in Mexico City. But in spite of all the problems and disappointments, the show was a huge success, as we brought all kinds of people to it and even got some attention from the Chicago arts community.

The show put MARCH on the map in a big way. It established us a major player in the Chicago Latino arts scene. Efraín invented a great subtitle for the show: *Mexposición*—a word he took from the Chicago Expo shows that hardly had any Mexican art, then we added the number 1, because we'd already lined up Mexposición 2—a show of Agustín Casasola's photographs

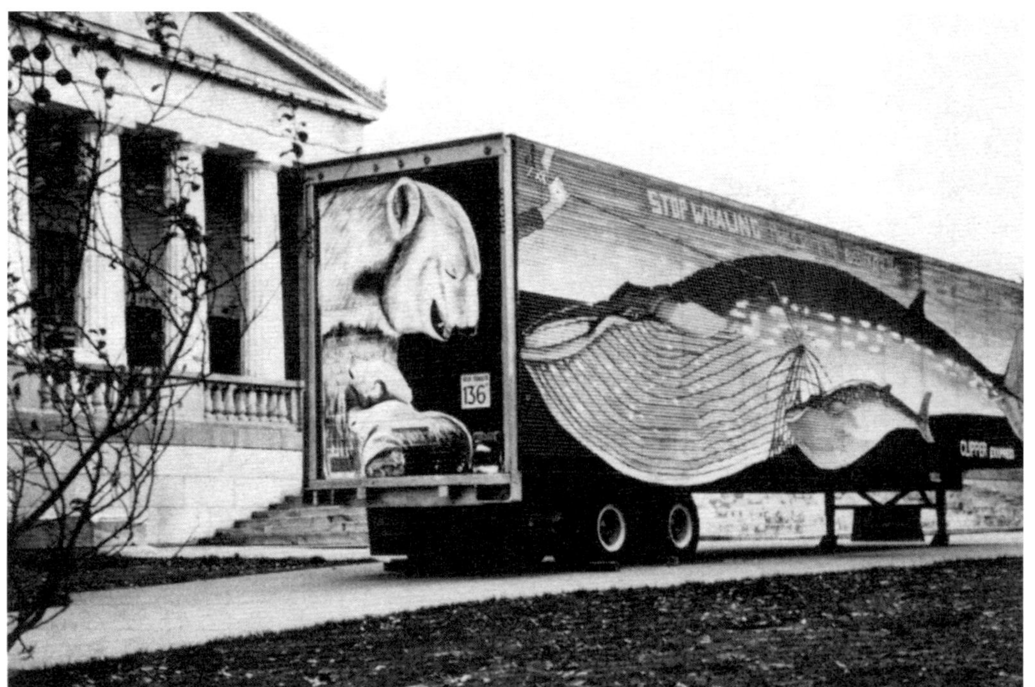

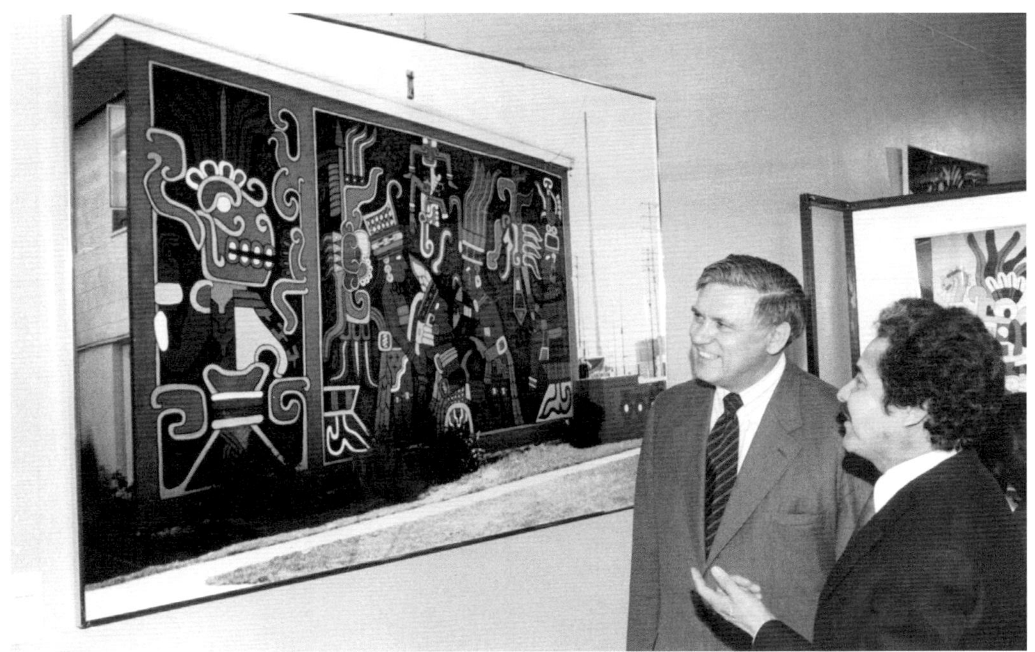

Fig. 59. José Gamaliel González, "Save Our Animals," truck mural (portable part of Raza de Oro Hubbard Street mural), 1975. Photo: Efraín Martínez.

Fig. 60. José as curator of the Mexican American exhibit of Chicago's Museum of Science and Industry, 1975, showing parts of his Raza de Oro mural design to Victor Danilow of the museum. Photo: Gini Sorrentini.

of the Mexican Revolution that we put together in 1976 (fig. 63). Gilberto went on his own to Mexico, and he met the great grandson of Casasola, and he brought personal photographs from him. He shipped them to his brother Efraín, who went with us to a place called U-Frame-It. You pay for the frame, but you do the framing yourself to save money. So we did an assembly job. And then we had to run complex security measures for this second show, too.

Maybe these two shows were the biggest exhibits of Mexican art in Chicago up to that time. The Montgomery gallery space was tiny, but we used every inch of it with panels so it was

The MARCH Years (1971–79)   **65**

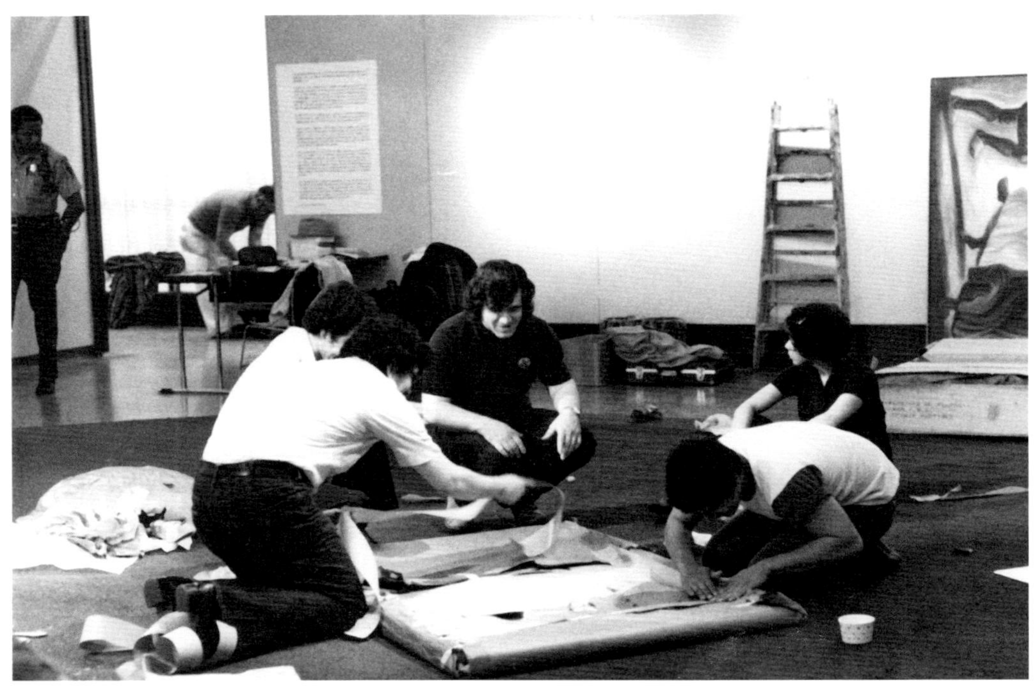

Fig. 61. Unwrapping the paintings from Bellas Artes of Mexico City, with Efrén Martínez. Victor Sorell, Francisco Blasco, and Sandy X, 1975. Photo: José Gamaliel González.

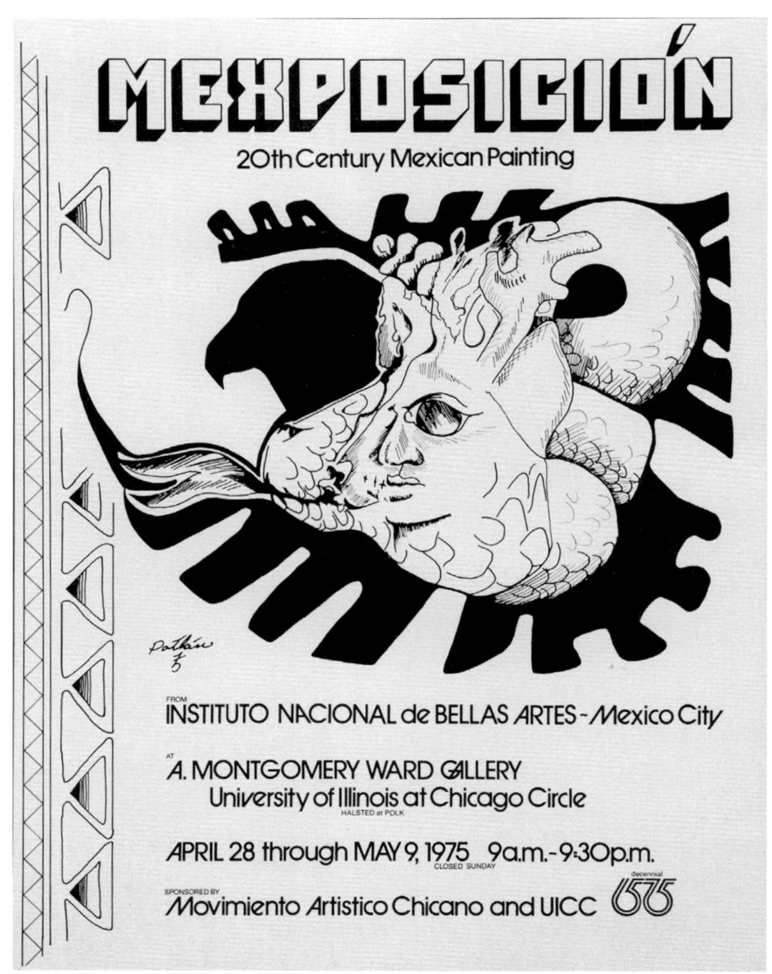

Fig. 62. Poster for Mexposición 1: Twentieth-Century Mexican Painting, May 9, 1975. Ray Patlán, poster art. Printed by the University of Illinois at Chicago Circle Art Department.

kind of a maze. And the shows got a big turn-out, with us bussing in kids from the schools—especially Mexican kids who learned as they walked around. UIC's Latin American studies program got deeply involved with the second show, with the chair, Otto Pikaza, giving us his blessing, and then professors Renato Barahona and Mary Kay Vaughan helping out. Their goal was to make the Casasola event significant in relation to Mexican history and I guess to show that their program was a center of Chicago Mexican studies. I was providing them with the vehicle to relate to community, I guess. Pikaza, Barahona, and other UIC professors helped us get together some of the elders from the community to talk about the Mexican Revolution. It was the part of the Casasola program we called "Los Ancianos," or "The Old Ones," and it was very moving—older people who might soon be gone, recounting before an audience and on tape their memories and impressions. As for Mary Kay, she was a historian of Mexico, so she wrote up all the notes on the revolution for the first issue of *Abrazo,* a publication I created to go with the exhibit (fig. 64). Mary Kay and I got really involved, as MARCH just marched on.

Those days were among the best I ever had. I was still freelancing and doing design work for *Revista Chicano-Riqueña.* I put together a collage of Chicago Latino mural images for an issue on the city's muralists (fig. 65), with a key article by Victor Sorell; and Nick Kanellos even got me a mural-painting class, which I taught at Indiana University Northeast. But my main energies were for MARCH, and I even got Nick involved with us by getting him to be the translator for the 1976 issue of *Abrazo.* The issue has a picture of a scene with Nick performing in the *Teatro del desengaño del pueblo.* It also has an image of Captain Chicano with the graphic artist David Torrez; and there's a drawing by Aurelio Díaz of Zapata. There's a staff list for the

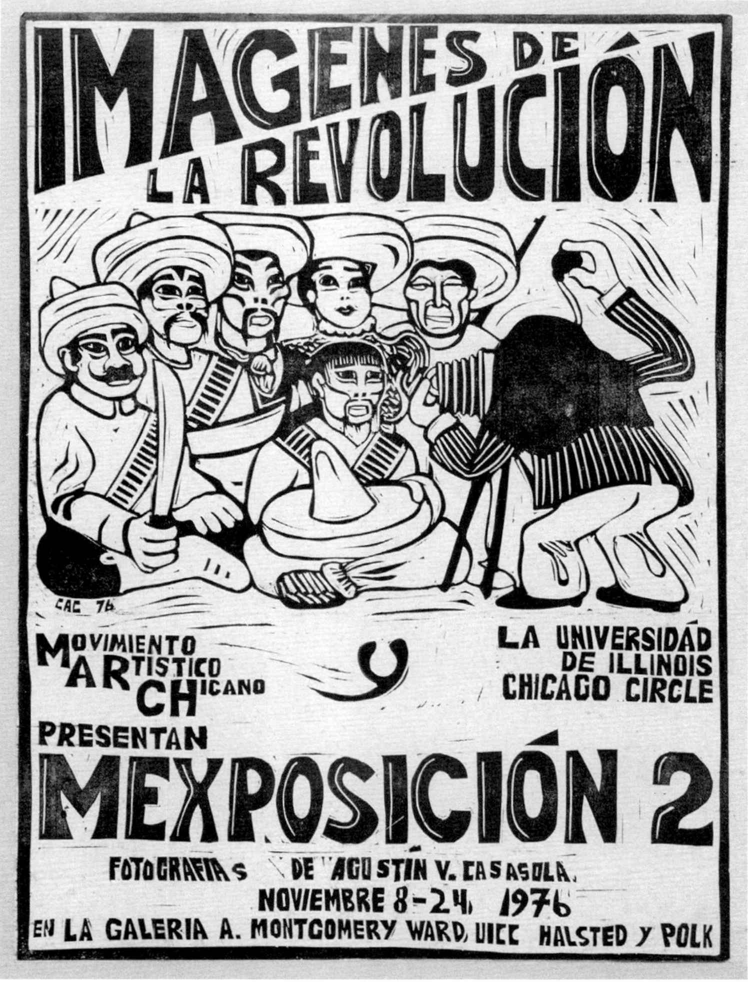

issue, including Nick as the Spanish translator. The issue's editors are Victor Sorell and Santiago Boiton; the associate editor is Susan Stechnicj; and I'm listed as art and design director. There's an editorial by Boiton and Stechnicj pointing out that in spite of the wealth of the country, Mexican, Latino, and Latin American artists were not doing well. There's a note on Companía Trucha, one of the local theater groups, in an article called *"Nuestra Gente,"* and there are images of Marguerite Ortega. It has a description of a Mexican Independence Day event in Michigan that was organized by David Torres from Michigan.

There's a discussion of an art-show boycott and the demand for "equal representation for Chicano Art"; and it lists a lot of different

Fig. 63. Poster for Mexposición 2: Imágenes de la Revolución, Nov. 8–24, 1976. Designed by Carlos Cortez for MARCH in conjunciton with the University of Illinois at Chicago and the estate of Augustin V. Casasola, Montgomery Ward Gallery.

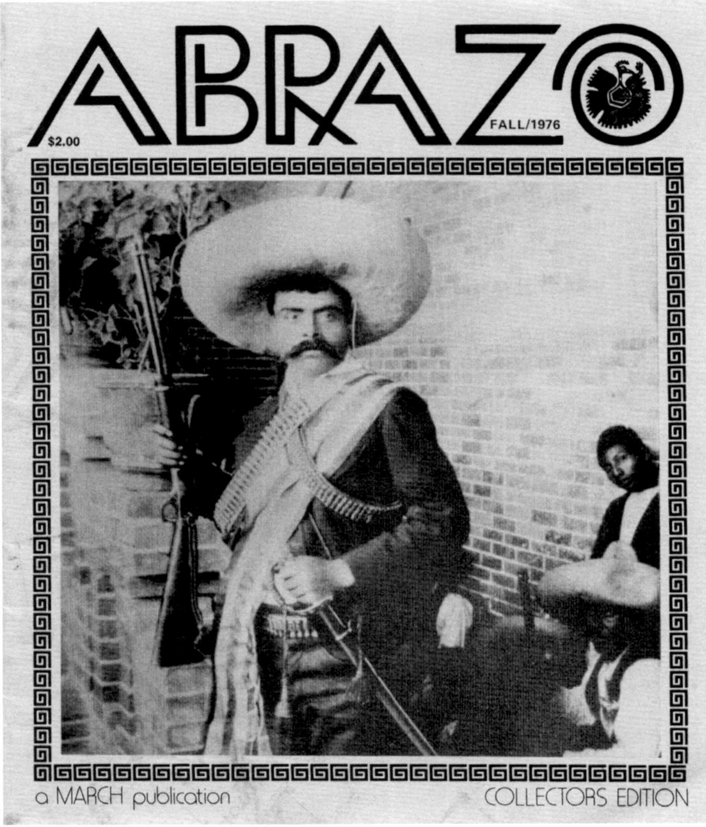

Fig. 64. *Abrazo* 1.1 (Fall 1976). Cover photo of Zapata.

also a notice about the new issue of *Revista Chicano-Riqueña* and the *Revista*'s forthcoming *Nosotros* anthology, which would appear in 1977 and stand as the first nationally produced issue about Chicago Latino poetry (more Puerto Rican than Mexican or Chicano) and arts, with several pictures by the Rican painter Gamaliel Ramírez, including a cover image of Gamaliel in a garbage pail, with the Chicago skyline behind him. (I designed the cover.)

In 1977 we did a show at Truman College, a community college on Chicago's North Side with a significant Native American student population. We called the show Anišinabe Waki-Aztlán (fig. 66), which was a Chicano–Native American art exhibit with performance, poetry, music, and visual arts. Carlos Cortez helped come up with the concept, but I think it was Lonnie Poco, an American Indian poet, visual artist, and leader of the local Indian guild, who first suggested the name, which is Native American for "Aztlán survivor." Lonnie worked with Carlos, Aurelio Díaz, and several others from MARCH to realize this project. I designed the poster, and Sal Vega did the poster art, featuring a framed *Toltec* warrior. We did a really strong and colorful show. The president of Truman College loved it very much, and at the end he was very proud that he could pronounce the show's name.

Then, too, 1977 was the year we produced the MARCH calendar, which tells you more about MARCH than anything I can narrate here. You just have to look at it, and it tells almost all you need to know about MARCH.[2] First the *calendario* features the cover I designed (fig. 67) and provides pictures of our thirteen artist members and four others who were not artists: Victor Sorell; Susan Stechnicj; her husband, Santiago Boiton; and Larry Hurlburt, our Wisconsin-based historian of Mexican art. There's a photo by Francisco Blasco, the Gary photographer I

Latino-centered or Latino-involved arts and cultural organizations in Chicago: the ACI, ALBA, Casa Aztlán, the Chicago Mural Group, the Public Art Workshop, the artists' coalition of *mujeres latinas.* There is poetry by Carlos Cortez, Anna Castillo, and Carlos Cumpián. There's work by Mario Castillo, featuring his beautiful image of birds; and there's Mary Kay's article, translated by Joséfina Cortez de Kramer—a long piece on Casasola's "Photography from the Mexican Revolution," with examples of his work. I did the photographs for the issue, showing the crowd of Mexposición 2 visitors looking at the pictures (some of them "old-timers" who cried when the saw those pictures of the revolution).

The issue also includes *El machetazo* by Carlos Cortez and an illustration by David Schwartz, influenced by Posada. It has information about different local events, and there's met on a train. And there's Efraín Martinez, an amateur photographer but a key MARCH member and our first president. The biographies give some really good details about the people, and the whole thing is something I've always been proud of. There are biographies and photos of Ray Patlán, José Nario, Frank Sánchez, Salvador Domínguez, Salvador Vega, Marguerite Ortega, Aurelio Díaz, Carlos Cortez, and Francisco Blasco. There's a wild picture of Mario Castillo, who did some very extreme things in school, like shaving off all his hair—and I mean even his pubic hair, his head, and everything—when he was going to California for his M.A. And here's me, José González: "Whether he is organizing Latino art exhibitions serving as art director of *Revista Chicano-Riqueña* or teaching a mural class at Indiana University Northwest or working as a freelance graphic artist, José González always utilizes his art originating projects that aim to show the importance of art and its role in life." And then there's some images of our artwork. Next to the photo, you can see my charcoal, "The Cycle of Man: Birth, Death, and Regeneration," one of the best pieces I produced during my School of the Art Institute days (see fig. 35 in chapter 2). There's photography by Efraín Martínez, Rey Vásquez, and Francisco Blasco, and there's a picture by Mario Castillo. Carlos Cortez has a very simple sketch of Mariana, his wife, with a dove. There's also a poem by Salima Rivera, "Indio."

In the calendar, there's also the common statement I wrote up for MARCH. You can read it all, but the main thing is that we were an arts group coming from, relating to, and working for our community, which we saw as oppressed, marginalized, and alienated from art. Our goal was to give expression to our concerns and needs and our history. It was to preserve history and project history from the standpoint of our people, including the peoples of Mexico and, more broadly, Latin America. These are some of the things I mention in MARCH's common statement, and it also had a Chicano ideology as part of it. I mean the ideology was Chicano and pre-Colombian indigenous as best as we could express it. In taking on these Indian identifications, we were trying to deal with the question of Aztlán. We were taking in West Coast and border Chicano experience and myths and extending them to Mexican Chicago. Not everyone in the group shared the same perspective, but it put some pressure on our group, if only at an unconscious level. Some of us also had a perspective on Chicano and Mexican concerns. We knew that in Daley's Chicago, the best chance for Mexicans was to unite with other Latinos

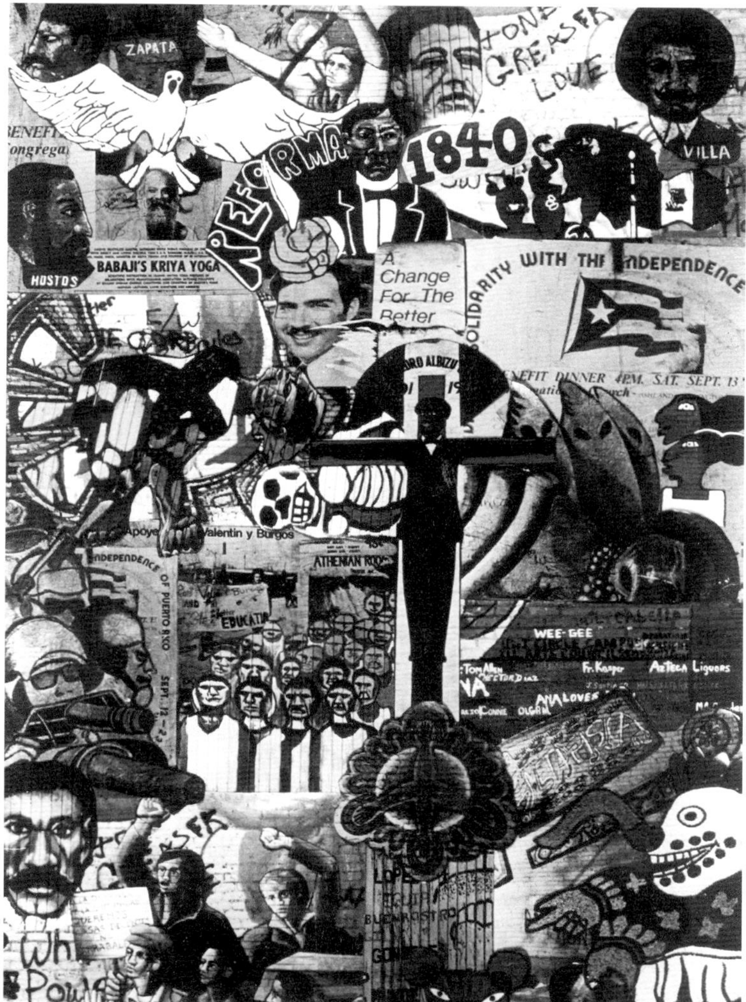

Fig. 65. José Gamaliel González, Collage of Chicago Latino Murals, designed and used as cover for bicentennial mural issue of *Revista Chicano-Riqueña* 4.4 (Autumn 1976).

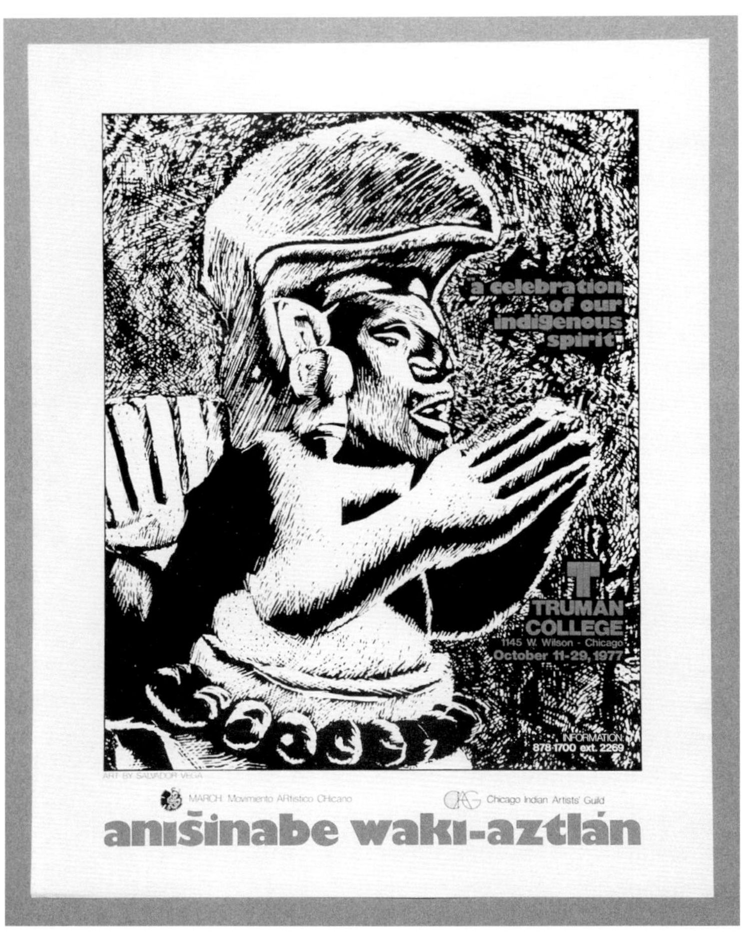

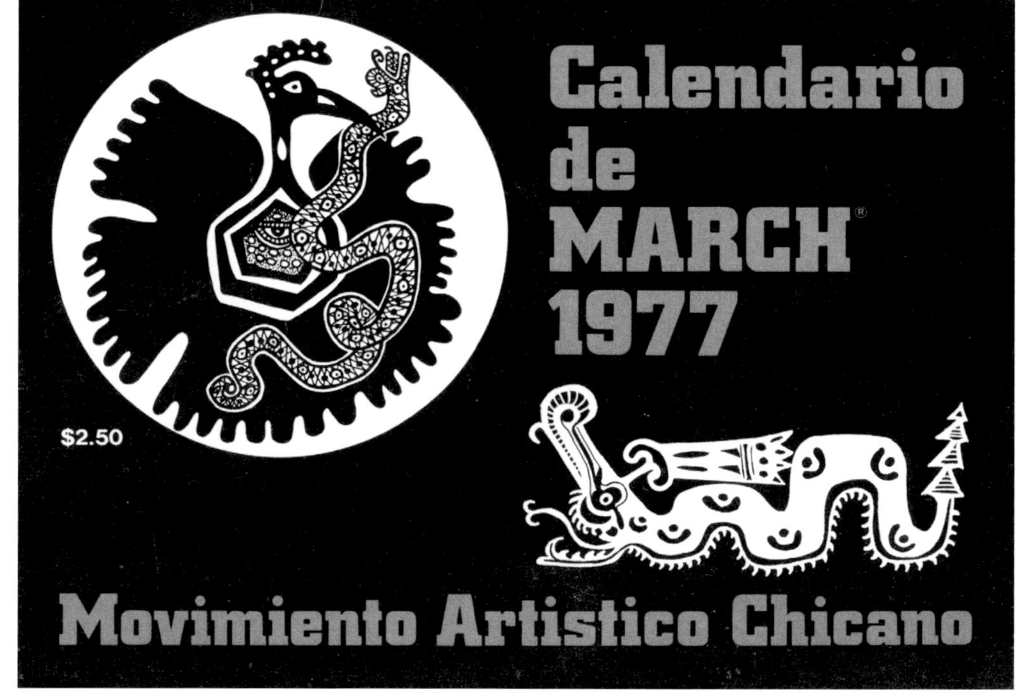

Fig. 66. Anišinabe Waki-Aztlán, Poster. Design: José Gamaliel González; drawing: Aztec Warrior, Sal Vega, 1977.

Fig. 67. Cover of MARCH Calendario 1977, designed by José Gamaliel González with reproduction of pen and ink images.

and also African Americans. Many of us participated in broader causes. But MARCH stuck to art, even though some members wanted more politics, and nonmembers might've thought we were all politics.

Another thing about us was our debate over using models. Ray Patlán didn't use models in his work—he pulled them out from his head. Cortez did a lot of that, too. The importance of not using models was that it meant we had to use our own inspiration, so it was more like poetic expressionism than any effort to render a copy of something seen or arranged. For myself, I worked with models for some of my pieces. But for something like "The Cycle of Man," I tried to be freer, to go from something out of or even beyond my head—from memory and emotion. But I always tried to combine some pictorial accuracy with vision. I always went beyond models, and maybe that was part of MARCH's code, too: to project Chicano experience but also imagine other options, other worlds.

THE BENITO JUÁREZ HIGH SCHOOL MURALS

One of the many exciting and controversial things that MARCH did in its few years as an art group was to meet with city officials and architects to work on the new Benito Juárez High School that was being built. The city called for input from the community and formed a committee to work with the contractors and architects.

At the beginning, they hired the famous Mexican architect Pedro Ramírez Vásquez to design the building. However, Fidel López, a Chicago Mexican architect, complained that it should be designed by a Chicago Mexican architect. You can be sure there weren't too many in those days, so we can pretty much guess who he wanted. Meetings were held with both architects, but in different rooms. They never met in the same room. The city couldn't work it out with either of them, and in time they were both dismissed. They then turned to a new firm that had three architects, and the firm chose Adrián Lozano, another Chicago Mexican architect, to design the school.[3] From the beginning, MARCH wanted the building to be designed with walls that could house both inside and outside murals. When the final blueprints were done, we were given a set to work with to design murals for given walls. I was one of the members, along with Aurelio Díaz and Efraín Martínez, that had approached the city. I went to Urbana, where Mario Castillo was living, and helped him a little in putting together a presentation board where we could post some of the mural designs. Mario had photographed the work, and I pasted it on the presentation board. For me, the most impressive designs of stone were done by Mario of the four elements—fire, water, air, and earth. But I never pushed the idea that those chosen to do the murals had to be MARCH members. To me, it was just important that the murals were done to enhance the building.

Finally, after some years, Casa Aztlán was chosen to organize a community committee and held a competition. The final design chosen for the outside wall of the gymnasium was by two people who were not muralists, Jaime Longoria, a painter from Los Angeles, and Malu Alberro, a Mexico City–born, Chicago-based photographer who'd studied at the School of the Art Institute. Their designs were for the Benito Juárez High School gym mural outside wall (fig. 68).

Since neither of them had ever done murals, they got Marcos Raya, Sal Vega, and Oscar Moya to do the painting. Aurelio Díaz was one of the youngest MARCH members and was very ambitious about painting murals throughout Chicago; you can see all of his murals throughout Pilsen. Many of them were done with young people, and some are on the viaduct on Eigh-

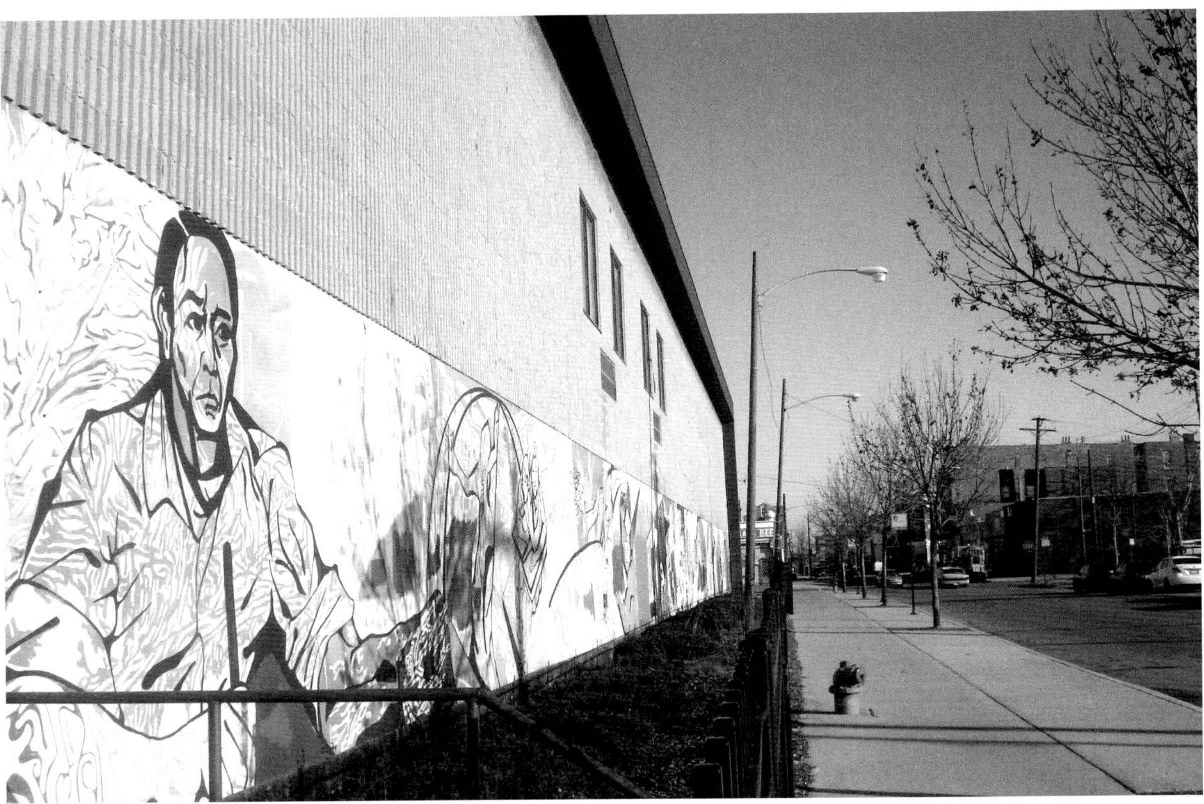

Fig. 68. Benito Juárez High School gym mural, outside wall. Designed by Jaime Longoria and Malu Alberro; executed by Marcos Raya, Salvador Vega, and Oscar Moya, 1977. Restored by Raya, Vega, and Juarez students in 1994. Photo: Marc Zimmerman, March 2007.

teenth Street. Aurelio, Marcos, Sal, and one other artist did an earlier mural in Dvorak Park, which has now been painted over by the summer program held each year by the city. Maybe all this explains why Aurelio was so upset with the outsiders' mural and its execution by some of his friends. But whatever the reason, before Marcos, Sal, and Oscar finished their work, Aurelio showed up one day with a group of young people and threw paint on the mural. Marcos claims that he took a photo of Aurelio in the act. All that created a scandal that tarnished Aurelio's reputation and maybe hurt MARCH as well. But it's also true that Marcos, Sal, and Oscar repaired the damage and completed their work; Marcos and Sal restored it in the 1990s.

A MAGICAL TIME: MEXPOSICIÓN 3 AND *ABRAZO* 2 (1978–79)

During and after our work on the calendar, things were happening fast and furious. In 1978, we did another exhibit, Mexposición 3, dedicated to *la mujer* and featuring work by and about Mexican women from Mexico and from Mexican Chicago, at the city's Cultural Center (fig. 69). Two older Chicago women in the exhibit were María Almontes and María Enríquez de Allen, mother of Mario Castillo. There were also two women artists from California, Linda Vallejo and Barbara Carranza.

Next we did *Abrazo* 2 in 1979 (fig. 70). And the issue turned out just fine. The Spanish translator continued to be Nick Kanellos, even as he was getting ready to move to Houston. The editorial was by Victor Sorell, who takes on the art world for not dealing with ethnic and Chicano arts. Then there's Aurelio Díaz, with an image of Sor Juana Inés de la Cruz. And the issue even has a picture of the mural that I did in Indiana for UNO.

In this issue, we had a poetry editor, Carlos Cumpián, a young Chicano writer, so there's lots of poems: one by Rina García Rocha, a

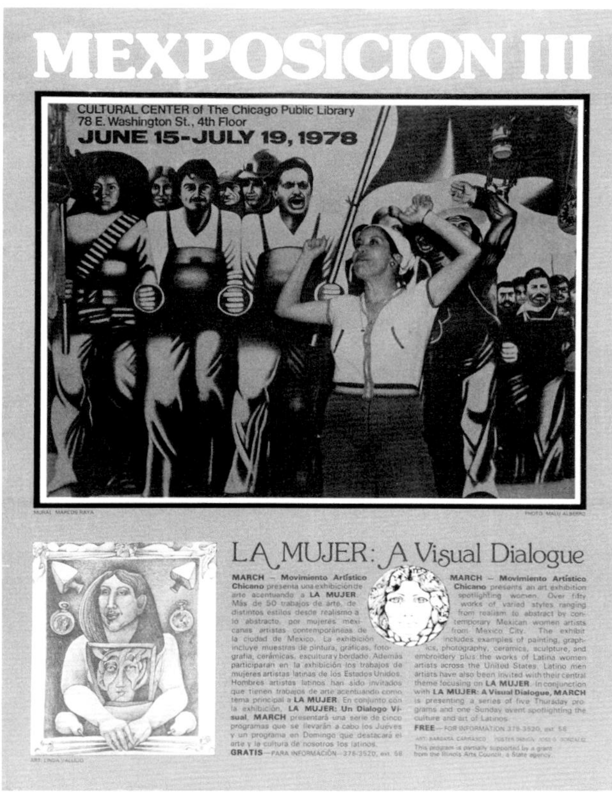

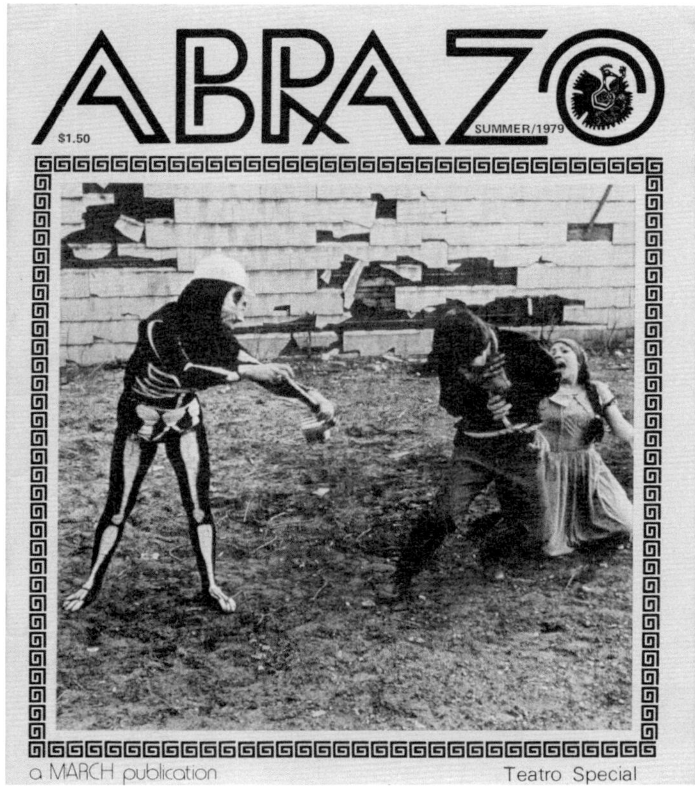

good piece dealing with her uncle Joe, a working-class Chicago *mexicano;* one by Rubén Sánchez, who published some work before leaving Chicago for California; one by Joyce Sato, a poet Cumpián found or maybe invented; one by Carlos Cortez, "This is the Land"—a long poem probably not written for this edition, but reprinted from his big body of Wobbly writings. There is also a poem by the Puerto Rican poet Alfredo Matías; and there's still another poem by Carmelo Romero, who, along with Matías, was a member of Taller, a Chicago poetry group mainly composed of Puerto Ricans (but also including the Chicana poet Yolanda Galván) and led by David Hernández, which developed on the North Side roughly at the same time as MARCH and came to include visual artists like Gamaliel Ramirez. The poems by Matías and Romero in *Abrazo* 2 would also appear in *Revista Chicano-Riqueña*'s *Nosotros* anthology, the collection of Taller poetry and images edited anonymously by Hernández in 1977.

In his poem, Matías asks, "Where are the Latin poets?" And the poem by Romero is about the Puerto Rican trombonist with Duke Ellington, Juan Tizol. So while we identified as Chicanos, we always reached out to others. I guess it's interesting and significant that early in the history of MARCH, we get into so much Puerto Rican poetry, and it just shows that you can't keep things segregated in Chicago for very long—-at least not in Latino Chicago. That was to become a significant part of MIRA in the 1980s: to promote all Latinos. It wasn't just Chicanos and *mexicanos.* I felt we should reach out to other Latinos, perhaps bring them at least as guest artists and writers. But then, too, from the beginning MARCH never was all Chicano, because we had Santiago Boiton, Susan Stechnicj, Larry Hurlburt, and Victor Sorell, none of them Chicanos.

Meanwhile, with all this MARCH work in the 1970s, I continued my design work for *Revista Chicano-Riqueña* and its offspring, Arte

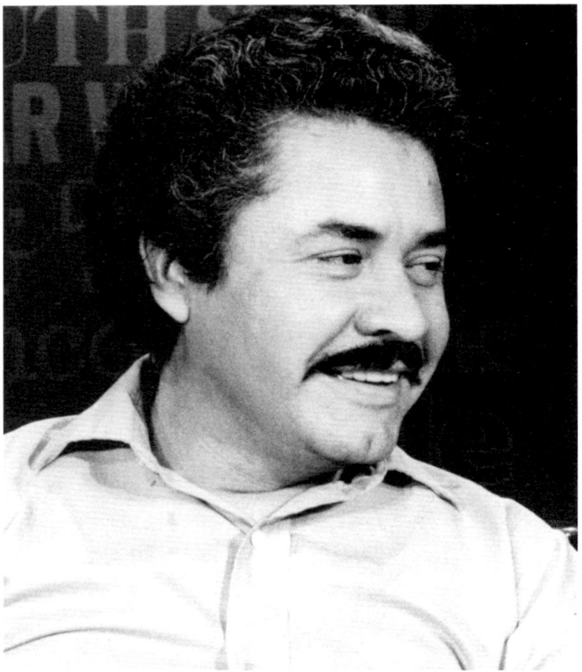

Público Press. I got appointed to a national Latino arts commission, and MARCH even got CETA funding. And during all of this, Mary Kay and I dated and finally got married, and then we had our baby, Alicia, in 1977. It seemed like a magical time. But then even as MARCH and life seemed to be going so well, things were beginning to fall apart—at least for me.

MARY KAY, THE WEDDING, ALICIA, AND THE END OF A MARRIAGE (1976–78)

I know I've mentioned Mary Kay, but I don't really get into enough detail about what Mary Kay meant to me, about marrying Mary Kay, and how that may have affected my work and my vision, and then how our daughter Alicia herself affected me from the very last years of my association with MARCH and down to this very day. So I think this is something I should talk about some more, even though I don't want to say too much.

First, I think I should mention my sense that I'm talking about a very special moment in the mid to late 1970s. For the first time perhaps, there was a Chicano consciousness in Chicago's Mexican community, and I was very much part of that. I was on the cutting edge of the artists who were trying to create a sense of identity in a time when *mexicanos* felt oppressed; and this consciousness was coming into Chicago, the largest U.S. city with a population that was more Mexican than Chicano and that had in general rejected the Chicano label. Only now, this more militant Chicano consciousness was coming to the fore in our lives—at a time when there was a national concern for Chicano and Latino community economic and cultural development. All this was going to lead to a new set of community leaders that would seek allegiances with other Latinos and Afro-Americans. It would lead to changes in Mexican Chicago and its artistic expressions.

I guess this is the story of how my local arts and community agenda got tossed around by both personal and national developments. As I've said, I'd met Mary Kay as we worked on Mexposición 2, the Casasola show of November 1976. She came to have a big role in the exhibit because she wrote about Casasola in the 1976 *Abrazo*. But she also took her turn just like the rest of us, watching over the exhibit, serving as a security guard, protecting the photos, welcoming people, and registering them for the visitor list. I appreciated very much what she did because she worked very hard, so I asked her if she'd let me take her out to dinner to thank her for everything. And we agreed to go after 6:00 P.M. if she could find someone to take her shift. And sure enough, she worked it out, and we met at Little Joe's, a little restaurant on Taylor Street, just walking distance from the UIC Montgomery Ward Gallery.

I got there about a half hour after she did, and she had already started on some drinks. So she was feeling very good when I got there. We had a couple of rounds and then dinner, and she said she wanted to invite me over to her apartment for dinner at a later date. And I said, "Well, that would be fine," and I realized I wanted to see her again. So about a month later, she cooked me a dinner at her place. And that was our second date. After that, we dated pretty often. We were seeing each other a lot—and before I knew it, we were going together.

It was a winter, cold-weather romance. And I remember we went to an art exhibit, and I was wearing a warm turtleneck sweater that one of the Mexposición 1 artists, Jaime Mejía Servín, had given me as a token of thanks for that show. And, sure enough, a photographer who was taking shots of the people as they arrived approached us, asking if he could take a photograph. "I could make a portrait of the both of you," he said. And I couldn't resist, so Mary Kay and I posed together in our sweaters, both of us smoking cigarettes and kind of expressing our relationship at a time when it was blooming (fig. 72).

So we dated, and we were going pretty steady once or twice a week. I still didn't have an apartment in Chicago; I still was driving back and forth to Indiana. But then finally, in January 1977, I got a basement apartment in a building owned by Santiago Boiton and Susan Stechnicj. And from then on, I was to live in Chicago, even though I would drive back to Indiana on most weekends to stay with my mother.

While I was in Indiana I was always thinking of Mary Kay. She had my mother's home phone number, so she would call me to make plans about seeing each other during the week. We were going steady all of wintertime '76–'77, and then I told her that I wanted to marry her. This was all in the beginning of 1977—it wasn't quite spring yet.

During all this period, I took on all kinds of freelance jobs trying to make ends meet during our courtship and upcoming marriage. Fi-

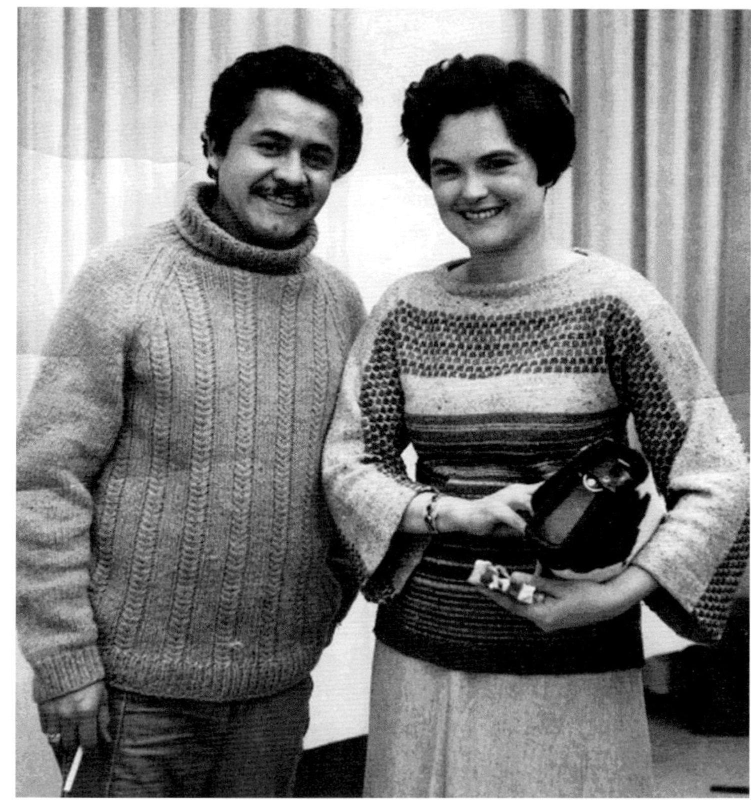

Fig. 72. José and Mary Kay Vaughan: a smoking couple, 1977.

nally, my experience as a volunteer worker for César Chávez in Indiana helped get me a steady full-time job with the community organizers Kathy Devine and Steve Salzburg working on the North Side at Hull-House as a counselor for people who couldn't afford housing. It was a good program and good work, but of course it interfered with my nonpaying job as the full-time head of MARCH. I took the Hull-House job for the sake of my marriage, though I personally preferred to be poor and fully committed to MARCH. But I was very much in love with Mary Kay. And she was in love with me— I'm sure of it. And so I tried to accept my new working situation.

The wedding took place on June 30, 1977. It was an outdoor affair at the home of her friend, Fanny Rushing, on the South Side. Mary Kay's sister Nancy came to town for quite a while so she could help plan and organize the wedding. Then, too, her father came to support her— which was an honor, really, with him cleaning up a dog-dirtied backyard for the ceremony. I'm the one who got the priest from Pilsen's Providence of God church. I also designed a pre-Colombian-style wedding invitation. It was printed by a small Mexican printing shop in Pilsen, and the invitations featured a tree with two indigenous people—a woman and a man—on each side.

Of course, lots of my family members were present at the ceremony, and a lot of MARCH members came. Frank Blasco and Santiago Boiton were the photographers. Carlos Cortez, Victor Sorell, Efraín Martínez, and other MARCH members came too. And I think the MARCH people saw the wedding as a kind of organizational event: the marriage between the Mexican artist and promoter and the professor of Mexican history. And that seemed to be a good thing at the time. But the relationship and the marriage didn't last very long—something like two years, 1976–78—that was about it.

Without doubt, this period was a major time in my life. Mary Kay meant a lot to me. I was very much in love with her and then with Alicia when she was born on Christmas Day, 1977. The Christmas date is why I wanted to call her Luz, "God's guiding light." But Mary Kay was afraid people would call her Lucy, so she added Alicia to her name. Luz Alicia: that's her baptismal and civic name. As it turned out, we always called her Alicia. She was like heaven-sent for me, the brightest star of my life then and now. And I was madly in love with both of them at once because Alicia was a part of Mary Kay and Mary Kay was part of Alicia.

By this time, we had an apartment together on the North Side, and the monthly rent was pretty steep. Mary Kay was making pretty good wages as a professor. And while I didn't make as much as she did, I made enough between my Hull-House job and freelancing to pay maybe half of our expenses. But it wasn't that easy, because I was still running MARCH, and the Hull-House job was getting to be too much. On top of that, I was freelancing on keyline-assembly graphic designs. I got paid very well for that work, and that's why I could afford not to work full-time at a regular job before. But now, with added expenses, I was trying to do everything at once, and I was running myself ragged. Of course, I was torn between doing the other jobs, doing work for the organization that I so much believed in, and also making a living as a new husband, I guess.

At the same time that I worked for Hull-House, I was super-active with MARCH; and the MARCH work became even more demanding when we became recipients of a grant from the Comprehensive Employment Training Act (CETA). Efraín Martínez somehow got MARCH lined up with the CETA grant, which provided funding for four full-time workers who could help us in any way we dreamed up.

With this new framework, Efraín and most of us thought that MARCH could really reach a new level. But the CETA experiment had some unforeseen negative consequences. With our CETA contract, MARCH had a real address for the first time, a rent-free office space of our own that Albert Vázquez gave us and that took up the whole fourth floor of the Little Village Community Mental Health Center, which Albert directed. It was unusual for an artist organization to get CETA workers. But it was the first time that they had a new program reaching out to arts organizations—and that was the ticket for us getting a contract. So we were fortunate to be offered four full-time federal workers and the office space, and we were also fortunate in that the city provided us with a very good full-time bookkeeper, who helped us with our taxes and kept the books for the workers and our projects. The only problem was that the whole CETA-driven operation required a full-time director to guide these people, develop the projects, and coordinate everything. That person was me as MARCH executive director, but the only problem was that I wasn't getting paid. They paid the workers, but not me. Part of my nonpaying job was to look for matching funds that would provide me with a salary, but that was easier said than done. People and corporations might want to fund projects, but they rarely wanted to provide salary for a director. I thought I'd still get something even as I tried to raise more. But it wasn't working out, and I found myself at a terrible crossroads.

Here I was married to a very intelligent, fiery professor who was very much fascinated with Mexican history and was taken also with the development of Mexicans in the community of Chicago. Mexican Chicago was late to the Chicano political movement, and late to the Chicano art movement. But now, as leader of MARCH, I was spearheading Chicago Chicano development in and through the arts. Mary Kay understood my ambitions for MARCH—she had become part of that. But then we came up against some limits, because I started choosing MARCH over what would bring me a direct income, I began to take a gamble, as my inner voice began to call out: *I want to make MARCH happen—this is my time. It happens now, or it doesn't happen.*

One thing leads to another, something gives, and before you know it, what is giving is the marriage itself—which blossomed in relation to MARCH but was now beginning to feel the pressure of my choices. There she was, saying things that were totally logical to say: We have a new baby, she says. You've got to take care of this baby. First of all, the baby needs attention. I'm a professor; I need to do my research. We need you to spend more time dealing with family; I can't have you running off to a meeting every five minutes. There has to be some order

in this situation, so that the baby gets dealt with. I loved the baby, but I was also fully caught up in my projects and aspirations.

Then, just to make things even more complicated, along came another opportunity I just couldn't resist—another option that would make it all the more difficult to keep my head above water. I got a call from Jacinto Quirarte, a professor at the University of Texas at San Antonio. He had been going around the country recruiting a group of twenty-five key Latino arts people to represent given areas in a new Hispanic Arts Task Force that he had been appointed to direct by the National Endowment for the Arts in Washington, D.C. And he asked me if I would be one of the twenty-five. Sure enough, he and his assistant came to Chicago to meet with me, and then they confirmed me as their choice to represent Chicago and the Midwest. Well, I talked it over with Mary Kay, and we both agreed that this would put me and MARCH on the national stage, and that it was just too important to turn down. But the unfortunate thing for me was that taking on the Task Force would be like taking on still another full-time job. Because we would have national meetings every two months in different locations—Texas, California, New York, Colorado, Washington, Miami, and even Puerto Rico—but in between these meetings, we had to cover our areas to assess needs and concerns. I had nine states—the largest area—to cover. And the problem was, they weren't going to pay a salary for this work, either—just travel expenses plus two hundred dollars per out-of-area trip. To make things even worse, the reimbursements would come every two months, based on my credit-card payments. Luckily, I had two credit cards to keep things rolling, but I'd probably incur credit-card debt while awaiting payment. Still, it was an opportunity to be center stage in the national and regional development of

Latino arts. How could I say no? And so I said yes, somehow knowing that this might be the straw that broke the camel's back.

It was impossible for me to handle MARCH's CETA program, serve on the Task Force, and still hold on to the Hull-House job. Faced with all this, I decided finally that I couldn't turn away from the opportunity to build MARCH, so I decided to leave Hull-House.

It's is not exactly clear to me, the exact day of the cutoff point, but I do remember that when I told Mary Kay of my decision, I sensed immediately that we had reached a limit. It wasn't so much that she was angry and disturbed—she was, without a doubt. She was upset because I wasn't going to have a full-time salary, and she was mad because I was going to depend on freelance work for my part. But she also knew that the CETA and Task Force assignments would chew up all my time and energy. She asked why I was quitting, why I was leaving the only steady and sure income-producing position when I should be more focused on supporting my family. And why hadn't I consulted her more clearly and consistently before taking such a big step? I guess the answer to everything was that I could not trade my dreams for a salary, and I hadn't discussed my decision with her because I knew what I was doing would make no economic or family sense. She was so upset. She and I realized, I guess, that we had drawn a line that would end us. I hate to recall this—it was a heartbreaking moment for me. She said, "Get out of my house. I don't want you anymore." That was in May 1978.

THE NATIONAL HISPANIC TASK FORCE AND MARCH (1978–79)

Of course, the marriage didn't end that smoothly. I tried to get back together. But I was under a lot of pressure. The pressure was so great that I began to drink pretty heavily, and maybe my mental health suffered too—that's what Mary Kay, and even some other people, said or thought: that maybe I was losing it. But at the time I think I was all right, even with the tension, because I had a lot of energy and lots of commitment to my work.

California had four members to cover their state. New York had the same. Margo Albert, an old-time movie star who had made her fame in *Shangri-La*[4] with Ronald Coleman and was married to the actor Eddie Albert, was the cofounder of Plaza de La Raza. She and a male cofounder were chosen for the Task Force. The other members from California were Judy Baca, a well-known Chicana muralist and director of SPARC, an arts group based in Santa Monica; and José Montoya from Sacramento, the cofounder of the Royal Chicano Air Force art group. From Manhattan's Spanish Harlem, Marta Vega, who founded a Hispanic arts organization, was the most dynamic member from her area; then there was a founding member of a theater group who only made one meeting in three years. There were two other male members—both of them photographers, one representing a large gallery, the other representing a very active organization. Carmen Lomas Garza was originally from Texas. So she represented that state, even though she lived in San Francisco. The other Texan was José "Joe" Rodríguez of Houston. There was also Luis Jiménez, who was originally from Texas but by then did his huge sculptures out of his studio in New Mexico. There were twenty-five members in total. I was the only one who covered more than one state—nine Midwest states overall.

I got really close with some other Task Force members, like Rodríguez, Jiménez, and Montoya. I also got to see the great fund-raising work Margo Albert was doing for Chicano Arts in the Los Angeles area. There were national meetings throughout the country. And once, when we decided to have a small, local meeting in Denver, we faced a demonstration against us, especially attacking Jacinto Quirarte for not including a Colorado artist in his book of national Mexican American artists. They also were not represented on the Task Force and wanted a member from their group to sit on the Hispanic Task Force. We agreed and chose Carlos Estebáns, who was a sculptor and the most vocal of the group.

Our national meetings were held every two months, and it was our task to reach out and gather names from our areas that had needs and concerns in the arts during the time between national meetings. I managed to travel and locate artists in five of the nine states. Those with the highest number of artists and arts organizations were Michigan, Minnesota, Indiana, and of course Illinois.

Each area was responsible for written reports to be included in the report to the National Endowment for the Arts (NEA). Only nine Task Force members were kept on to serve another year to bring together the total report. We were able to get the NEA to hire Joe Rodríguez for a three-year intern position as our "watchdog." I was also responsible for recommending Victor Sorell to be hired by the National Endowment for the Humanities (NEH). Victor stayed for about two years at the NEH on leave from Chicago State.

Through the Task Force, I was getting to know artists and arts promoters all over our region and all over the United States, and I thought that would lead to great things for MARCH and Chicago. So I did research with my CETA worker Salima Rivera on the Illinois Arts Council to find out how many Latino artists and Latino organizations had been funded. We found a very poor record with our community. With my presence there, I was able to get Latinos to sit on panels to review the proposals,

and I then helped get Eliud Hernandez hired for a full-time position with the council. He is still there.

In fact, that was only one of many good things we did with our MARCH CETA program. But some people said we could do more; some people felt MARCH was suffering and not gaining anything from my Task Force work. A series of events took place, which, in the midst of the pain of my marriage breakup, led to another terrible break—this time with the very organization I had founded and helped to develop, and which was such a source of pride for me.

THE BREAK WITH MARCH (1979)

It all started with CETA but ended with MARCH itself. The workers I chose for the CETA jobs were Carlos Cumpián, a young Chicano poet originally from Texas; Marta Ayala, his sister-in-law, who was a great outreach person and became our secretary; and Salima Rivera, a Puerto Rican poet who'd been brought up by a Mexican family and who related to all things Latino (at the time, she was a leading figure in ALBA, the mainly Puerto Rican arts group I've already mentioned). Finally, there was a woman named Carol Keating, who was the youngest of the group and helped us out with some of our projects.

These four workers helped with some of our key projects—developing our *calendario,* the Anišnabe Waki-Aztlán exhibit at Truman College, the Mujer exhibit at the Chicago Cultural Center, and *Abrazo* 2. But here came the negative consequences. All the support we received and every success we had was killing me. We were so good with our bookkeeping, cost control, and accountability that CETA officials considered us a model organization. And that was the worst thing that could happen to us, because then they wanted to give me another four CETA workers. And I thought, I'm getting killed here. How can I handle all this and everything else? I just couldn't see how. Now, with my marriage behind me, but with expenses before me, I was having to take on more and more freelance work just to keep afloat. By December 1978, I'd reached my limit. That's when I told Efraín, "Efraín, I just can't supervise eight people. In fact, I can't supervise four people anymore, and I'm going to transfer the workers to another CETA site." Efraín had fought so hard for us to get the positions, he complained to me, "José, what are you doing? It's Christmastime, and you're going to leave them out in the cold. It's a bad time to be out of a job," he said. And I told him, "Efraín, they're going to have jobs because they'll be transferred; and they're going to want to stay in the new jobs because they'll be on full-time salaries. But I don't have a regular job, and I can't support eight people without wiping myself out." The transfer was to Moming, an avant-garde Chicago dance group on the North Side. Salima decided not to go and dropped out of the program, but the other CETA workers made the jump. Later they were transferred to a Latino theater group that the Victory Garden Theater was trying to form; and one of them, Marta Ayala, actually joined the group and stayed with it when it broke from the Victory Garden Theater to form what would become the Chicago Latino Theater, or Teatro Latino Chicago. But I think some of the people, especially Efraín and Carlos Cumpián, were unhappy with the CETA cutback, feeling that I'd let my own agenda curtail a program that they felt would lead to a bigger and better MARCH. Above all, I think they felt my national Task Force agenda, as well as fears of problems with government contracts, had gotten in the way and that I was in the process of liquidating MARCH. But that was not my intent at all—I was trying to keep MARCH small enough to maintain its focus

and development, including its linkages with the larger network of Latino arts organizations that I was getting to know and help develop through my work on the Task Force.

Efraín was transferred to Texas at this time, and that was the end of his work with MARCH— I hardly ever heard from him again. But I began to have serious problems with Carlos Cumpián, which eventually led to my leaving MARCH. At first things seemed fine. Even after his transfer from the MARCH CETA job, he decided to join MARCH and serve as the poetry editor of the new *Abrazo* issue we were working on in 1979. He did a good job on that issue, but he was giving me a lot of trouble. He criticized everything I did, and maybe I criticized everything he did. The fact is, we just couldn't click together, and we finally had a falling out.

He was very young—much younger than me. And he was belligerent. I mean, he was a hothead with everybody, not only with me. It was difficult to keep him in check, and since he was in a position under me, that made him rebel against me. I think he felt I was too much the lord and master. "Caesar is too ambitious; Caesar is going too far. He is now building this national thing, and we want this local thing to work. It is time to get rid of Caesar." Maybe he thought it was time to assassinate Caesar. Even when the CETA program was on, he complained I was too much focused on money and bookkeeping and not on Chicano resistance. Then, when I joined the Task Force, he said I was showboating and not focusing on local concerns. When I warned him that we were being watched for being too radical, he said we were too conservative. When I warned that our Brown Beret connections and other activities might get us in trouble, he said I was paranoid, and we should be more political. When I pushed for more political kinds of activity, he said it was the wrong politics. To me, it was a question of control over the organization. He said that what I was doing to the organization was wrong, that I controlled and limited the organization too much. He said I wasn't open-minded and that I kept him and MARCH on a leash when he wanted a bigger role for himself and MARCH. He wanted to be the director. To put it frankly, he wanted to be me or a better version of me, maybe—at least that's how I saw it.

Part of Cumpián's job as a CETA worker had been to pick up the mail at our downtown post-office box. Even when the CETA job ended, he kept the keys, and he also had our master mailing list. In a way, that gave him some control of MARCH. I didn't understand what was happening, but suddenly I realized that he was communicating with MARCH members behind my back and even calling a MARCH meeting on his own, with the purpose being to oust me as the head of MARCH or, as I saw it and see it, to take the organization away from me.

I was depressed from the marriage breakup. And now I had this growing problem with Cumpián and MARCH. And he was right in saying the Task Force was crucial to me because I didn't want to be a poor example in the Task Force. We were supposed to solve problems in Latino arts communities, not make them worse. To create a mess over MARCH's internal problems would make me look like a bad representative. So yes, it was true: it was more important for me to be a figure in the Task Force doing this valuable national work on Latino art than to struggle for the control of our own local organization. I didn't fight Cumpián at all because, I felt, here I am, chosen to represent Latinos across the country, and if I had a fight with my own organization and caused a split, that would be the worst thing I could do locally and nationally.

I didn't even go to the meeting Cumpián called. But I understand he brought people with him, to side with him—and I never called on people to side with me. People who attended said Cumpián made it seem like it was his own organization, and I guess the majority agreed with Cumpián that MARCH should move on without José González. And I didn't fight Cumpián. I didn't fight at all, because I didn't think I could or should. I just sat back as he took MARCH over. As MARCH director, I guess I could have rallied my supporters. I could have said, "If you don't like the way things are going, you can resist. But you can't take over our organization." I had to make a major choice: I would either fight this breakup of my own organization, or I'd be kicked out. What founder of an organization would simply step aside and allow himself to be pushed out? People usually put up a huge fight to prevent that from happening. Maybe I could have gotten MARCH back by going through a lawyer. But I decided not to fight. And I made that decision mainly because of the Task Force. I guess I just felt that I was being hypocritical if I was having a fight with my own organization, with my own community of artists, for the sake of controlling an organization at least some of them identified with. I felt I could not both represent Chicago Latino artists and fight against those artists to hold onto the organization. So I just accepted the fact that Cumpián and his supporters had "released me" from MARCH, even as they stranded me from my own base in the community.

It was a terrible blow for me when Carlos Cortez went with Cumpián—I felt the virtual breakdown of my world. The break with MARCH involved some of my major friendships. These weren't just people I worked with—these were friends, and some of them were close friends, like Cortez (fig. 73). I might not have seen him seven days a week, but I had a kinship with him—the man was virtually my generation. I was at least one of the artists who made

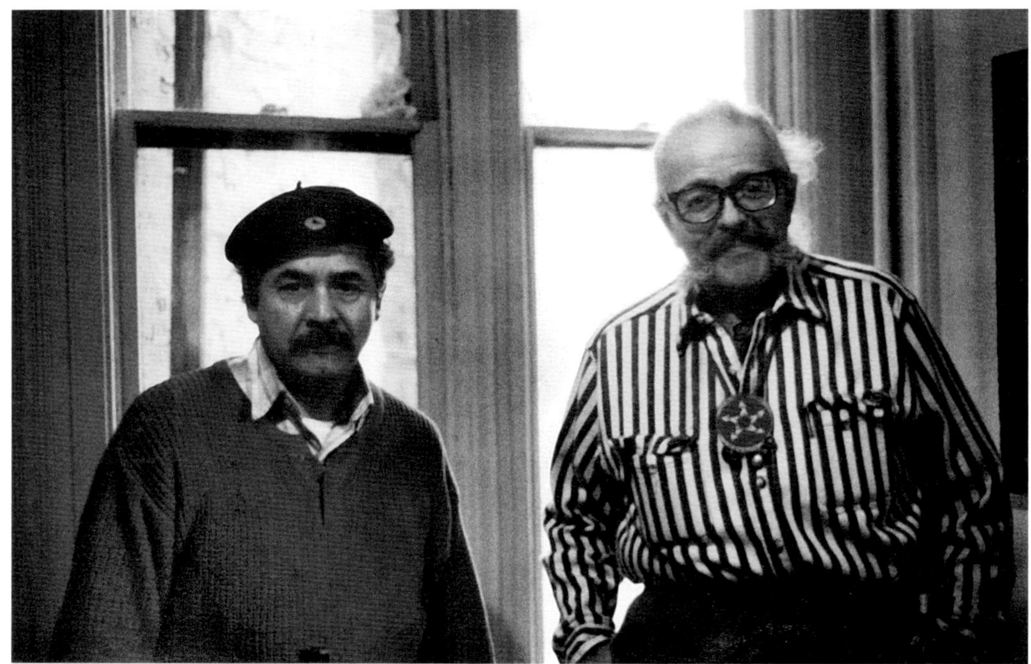

him aware that he was a Mexican artist, and not just any artist. He had his own political agenda. He was formed in wild and romantic Wobbly beliefs, and I couldn't share his politics per se, except to agree that Mexicans were underrepresented and oppressed, and something should be done about it. That was my point of contact with his politics, I think. I didn't care about his ideology, but we were friends, we were co–board members, and this young guy comes along and says, You've got to choose to be with José González or be with me. And it wasn't so much that Cumpián took Carlos away from me. Cumpián went to Carlos for support, and he got it. Cortez was a very calm person. And he was Cumpián's refuge, more or less. He was the one that Cumpián could talk to.

Why would Carlos Cortez support Cumpián, who was so young and always hyped up? Because Carlos was a graphic artist, of course, but he was also a poet. And so they had more in common on this score. Also they shared one core belief that I found difficult to accept, which was the idea that a Chicano arts organization should try to survive and thrive without try-

ing to get institutional grant money that would compromise the group's values and projects. That MARCH shouldn't go chasing after grants was one of the first principles in Cumpián's agenda. So he said to me, "Well, we don't really want grants." And I said, "Sometimes we need them for special projects." And he said, "Okay, for a special project thing we might do it, but we want to be as independent from grant life as possible, because we don't want to be tied down by Reaganite grant requirements and commitments." Well, we did get some grants from the city, but we hadn't gotten national grants for the arts—and my hope was that my Task Force connections would help us get some. I was opposed to Cumpián's view, which I saw as an attack on my role in the Task Force and what I thought would be important to MARCH in the future—its ability to get funding for collaborative projects with other arts organizations.

This was an important difference that surfaced at the end. However, above all this, Cortez was like a father to Cumpián. And I was not a father to Cumpián. Here he was looking for a mentor or a father figure, and he chose Cortez, not me. And

Cortez was more political than I was in the broad sense because he believed in worldwide anarchist revolution—that's another thing. My politics were more local and Chicano-driven—they were all about Mexican empowerment and art. I was too religious and mystical for Cumpián. I must have struck him as weird. Part of my work with the Farm Workers was out of my feelings for the Virgen de Guadalupe and the whole question of social justice. The fact that I went to Notre Dame had to do with my background. I fought at Notre Dame, but I was still part of Notre Dame—with a view of Catholicism that was related to liberation theology and Paolo Freire's pedagogy of the oppressed that was so popular among Chicago Latino activists in those days.

Looking back, I see now in fact that most of the artists and other people did not go with MARCH. Victor Sorell stayed a bit on the sideline during the breakup, leaving it to the core artists. But Victor didn't go to the breakup meeting. He just said, "Okay, let's say that they're now MARCH. Now what do we do?" In the long run, he went with me.

Really, from that point on, MARCH was mainly an organization of writers promoting Latino poetry. The only artist who stayed with MARCH in any significant way was also a poet. And he was one of my closest friends. Losing Carlos Cortez was almost like a second divorce on top of my divorce to Mary Kay. But of course, for me, the divorce from MARCH was a calamity on top of the other divorces I was already facing. I was deeply depressed. I guess my mental health problems started there—though some friends say that the problems had started and helped create the other breakdowns.

What can I say was my major achievement as the head of MARCH? Well, I'd say the exhibits and publications we did helped establish Mexican arts as significant in the city. And that is why I think that what I did was to open all these doors. I put Mexican and Chicano art on the Chicago map and put Chicago on the Chicano and Mexican maps as a center of Mexican art, along with Los Angeles and a few other cities. I was able to do that with MARCH, along with my Task Force connections.

But after all my successes, the need to leave MARCH so depressed me that I actually felt I was losing my way. The only thing that would save me, at least in the early 1980s, was developing MIRA, a new organization with many new artists but also with many of the same ones I'd worked with in MARCH who decided—some sooner, some later—that they couldn't continue with the older organization in its new form. But that's a story for the next chapter.

4

Raíces, MIRA, and the MFAC (1979–92)

RAÍCES ANTIGUAS, VISIONES NUEVAS

It seemed that most of what I'd been building was now in ruins, but that was really not the case. Most of the old MARCH group dropped out from that organization and waited to see where I or they might go. In the meantime, I was continuing my Task Force work, and my Task Force connections were keeping doors open as I began to dream up a new organization and project.

Even toward the end of 1979, in a moment of deep pain in my life, I got involved in bringing an important exhibit, Raíces Antiguas, Visiones Nuevas, to Chicago. The exhibit was put together by Marc Zuver of Washington, D.C. I had met Marc in New York City when we both attended a national mural conference. A well-known arts promoter and a real mover, he called me up to ask me to serve as his Chicago representative to bring the exhibit there.

Raíces had been put together in about three years, and it was set to travel to eight museums throughout the United States. Zuver and

Becky Crumbish, cofounders of Fondo del Sol in Washington, traveled throughout the country selecting artists. The greater number chosen were from the Southwest, and they included many good Chicano artists. But there were also a number of medicine men from Arizona and New Mexico, as well as video and installation artists from New York City. One Puerto Rican artist from New York was Rafael Ferrer, a brother of José Ferrer, the well-known actor and movie star. A couple of installations were from the Caribbean that also had videos to go with them. One large piece was a convertible car covered with mosaics. A lot of the art was shipped to Fondo del Sol. But they bought a used truck, and that's how they were able to bring the large collection to exhibit in different sites.

Zuver had already lined up Chicago's Museum of Contemporary Art (MCA), but he wanted me to provide the follow-up and see things through. Victor Sorell and I got called upon to serve on the planning committee because of our expertise and reputation. The MCA knew we knew a lot of local and national movers they wanted to involve. But then I got word that the MCA had won a grant from a corporation to hire a Latino community specialist to coordinate the exhibit. In fact, that's why they got the exhibit and the grant that went with it. But then they'd hired an Anglo woman who'd taken a two-month language course in Spain, and they figured that that was enough to qualify her to do the community-outreach work required for the show. As soon as I got wind of this, I called Marc and told him I thought it was a big mistake because this person didn't know anything about the community and the culture, and her Spanish was almost nil. Marc called John Neff, the director of the MCA, and recommended me for the position. He said Neff should talk to me if I wasn't working on something else because I was the

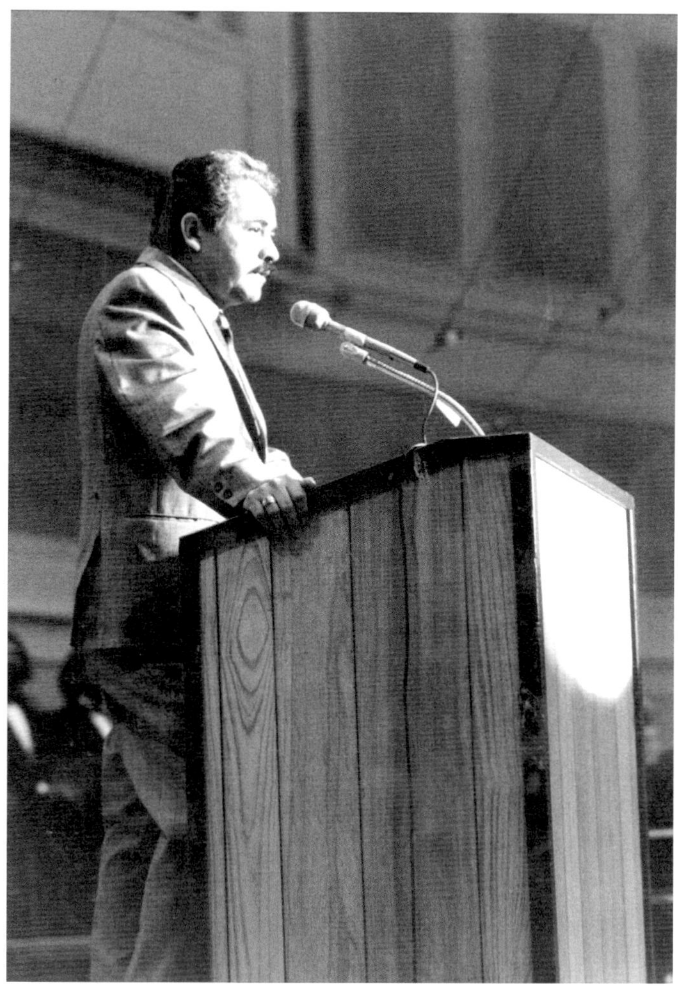

Fig. 74. José addressing the audience at an awards ceremony hosted by Mayor Harold Washington, 1985.

one who could do justice to the exhibit and make the outreach program a success. So they contacted me and offered me the job.

Raíces featured over sixty Latino participants, including painters, sculptors, and installation artists. Without question, it was one of the biggest Latino shows to come to Chicago. I hired Al Bonilla, a great P.R. and sales person, and Pat Michael, a great typist, office manager, and records keeper. At first they promised us a full-time space; then it was going to be a big cubicle with my own desk. We ended up with a table and chairs for all three of us. But that was fine. I didn't complain about that. So we had Al, Pat, and me doing the outreach; and then I established communications networks to do workshops in the community, to orient people about the show and get them to come on their own or in buses we could provide.

We went all-out in P.R. and community outreach, setting up three large locations for our neighborhood presentations. We reached over a thousand people, with artists also doing classes in the community, and we lined up Saturday mural tours in the Mexican and Puerto Rican communities.

In each city, Raíces included local artists to enhance the exhibit. So we added ten Chicago artists, including María Enríquez de Allen; Alejandro Romero; Jaime Rivera, a Puerto Rican photographer; John Asenscio, a Cuban graphic artist and sculptor; Dan Ramírez, a very popular avant-garde gallery artist; and MARCH's Sal Vega. The catalog supplement was designed by Frank Sánchez, and I did the keyline and assembly.

Alejandro's painting was the main work featured in the large brochure that was designed by a Chicago Peruvian graphic artist. The brochure was a large piece of work that included copies of some of the art pieces and a map of the museum. Also, to enhance the exhibit, Nick Kanellos helped me to produce a video that included Ray Patlán's mural at Chicago State University, a theater group with Al Bonilla and Marta Ayala, and María Allen demonstrating flower making. The video also featured David Hernández and Sandra Cisneros reading their poetry.

The opening-night reception attendance broke a ten-year museum record. We sold more liquor than anybody else in the past for a grand opening, and the men's committee was very happy about that because they were in charge of the liquor on opening nights. We had a mariachi group that played an hour extra when the people threw money in a hat to continue the fiesta. The whole thing was a big success

But then in the middle of all this, MCA officials got word that Pope John Paul II was coming to Chicago, so they right away called the New York Museum of Modern Art (MoMA) to get them to send a Polish photography show that the MoMA was finishing up and preparing to send back to Poland. The New York people arranged it so that the show would be on at the MCA during the Pope's Chicago visit. But this meant that they were going to have to take at least part of Raíces down and really shortchange our show.

I got wind of what was happening. I even heard that John Neff's assistant told Pat Michel that they were going to do the Polish show by hook or by crook, and that Pat should convince me to dismantle Raíces. But Pat told the assistant that she'd better talk to me about it herself, because she believed that I'd be less than thrilled with the idea. So the assistant called me in, and she said, "It's not positive yet, but we're thinking of doing the Polish show, and if we do, we're going to have to consolidate your show by taking out a lot of the work and putting up dividers to separate it from the Polish show." Raíces was crowded already; it was a big show, and I just couldn't go for squeezing it any further, Pope or no Pope. I was totally against the plan. Even though I supported the MCA, I couldn't support this business because it would look bad in my community and in U.S. Latino art worlds. I told the MCA officials that I wasn't going to put myself in the position of appearing to sell out the Latino show. John Neff was off somewhere finishing a book he was writing on Matisse. So I didn't know where he stood until he came back to work and told me the same thing his assistant had said, almost word for word: "José, it's not sure yet." And I said "No, John, come on. Let's be honest with each other—it's for sure that you're going to do the Polish show." And he answered, "Well, yes, it is, but we're not taking yours down. We'll simply put up dividers." I said, "You know that that won't work, John, that

that's going to be the death of our show. On top of everything, it'll be clear that our show and artists were disrespected, and people will see us as dupes or sellouts." So he said, "Well, José, the fact is, we make the decisions here." And I said, "Yes, and you already made your decision, but we have a contract." And he said he'd looked at the contract, and "it doesn't say that we can't move your show." "Okay," I said. "Maybe you can force me to move it, but I'll tell you right now that you're going to have problems with the Latino arts community." And he said, "We don't care about that." And I said, "Well, we do. Because for you it's not that bad, since you work in the Loop, but I live in my community. I'll have to explain to my local and national communities why the show was taken down and why they put up the Pope's show and why I'm still alive to explain it all."

Finally, he began to see how ugly this could get, and he relented a bit, saying, "Well, I'll see what I can do for you. Let's have a meeting with the local artists in about four days, on Monday at five o' clock. At the least, I'll explain why MCA has come to this decision, and I'll indicate that this is an MCA decision and not yours." I said, "Okay," but by the time I got home, I was really upset. And just then, Judy Kirshner, who later went to UIC but was then the MCA's assistant curator, called me. "José," she said, "I was at the meeting where we discussed the Polish show, and I want you to know that I voted against you too, because we make the decisions here, and I felt it was just not up to you which shows we did and how we did them." And I said, "It's okay, Judy, I understand your position." But I said to myself, "Oh, I'm not through yet, lady." Right off I got on my phone and called the artists in the show, plus key local Latino artists. I sent letters and telegrams, and I asked people to send letters to the president of the MCA board, Lewis Manilow. I even wrote a letter to the Pope with copies to the Polish consulate and Chicago's Cardinal Cody, saying we were going to have to picket the Polish show. I said to the Pope, "It's not against you; we respect you very much as our leader. But on principle, we'll have to oppose any effort to take down our show as a means of putting up the Polish one."

That same weekend I went to a Latino arts conference in Texas (Austin, I think). I had already written most of the representatives, and they all expressed their support. Danny and Joe Rodriguez let it be known that they had already written letters to the NEA newsletter criticizing the MCA; others had called the MCA leaving voicemails saying that they supported a strike against the Polish show.

So then Monday's meeting came with John Neff, and some of the local artists came in, including Aurelio Díaz and Cortez, too—and also some Puerto Rican artists showed up. So John Neff says, "Welcome to everybody here, and we want you to know that we want to take the show down to put a show up that we thought was very important and will bring a lot of prestige to the MCA. But we want you all to know that we have decided that Raíces is going to stay intact, and won't be affected at all." So I guess my weekend efforts had worked.

Our show was saved, but it produced a mess that strained my relations with the MCA and caused local waves anyway. Instead of dismantling our show, they took the second-floor Chicago gallery Two Women show down. They'd probably talked to the two artists and got them to agree to do their show later on. But when they took Two Women down and put up the Polish photography show, there were other local artists who began protesting against the MCA and the board; and Borg Warner, the MCA corporate sponsor of the Chicago Gallery, wrote a letter to Neff saying he had no right to take that show down to put up an "international" show—that Borg Warner had put up money for a gallery that only featured Chicago artists. Then the *New Art Examiner,* the primary publication for the Chicago arts scene, got wind of that letter and made a big thing of it.

The next thing I knew, I had to help save the *New Art Examiner* from retaliation. I sat on a key Illinois Arts Council panel at the time. And for years, almost all the panel members had bad-talked the paper, saying it was Communist-run, inflammatory, and everything else you can think of. Now they were about to defund them because they were upset with the views expressed against the MCA in their publication. That's when I said, "I know we're ready to vote, but I want to say one thing before we do it. If we don't give them any funding, first, they may not survive, and second, is there any other newspaper in Chicago that could take their place and do the job they are doing?" And sure enough, that made a difference, and they got their funding.

So my representing the community was very important. I don't know if the *New Art Examiner* has been very kind to Mexican arts over the years. And, of course, these victories always have their price. I got the reputation of being a real activist, troublemaker, and hothead just when MARCH broke with me for not being militant enough. I'm sure my reputation didn't help me in the eighties, when I was trying to get MIRA off the ground. On the other hand, it's very hard to do anything if you don't have the reputation for being a fighter. I became . . . maybe not a troublemaker, but maybe a provocateur. I was paying a large price for all the attention I was receiving—it was affecting my art, my productivity, my energy level, my mental health. I think it was all part of what eventually led to some breakdowns. In the meantime, even as I was maybe getting sick, I needed to have a regular community base to be fully effective. And this would be the idea behind MIRA.

OTHER NON-MIRA ACTIVITIES IN THE EARLY 1980S

I want to make it clear that during the early years of MIRA and really throughout its entire existence, I was also involved in lots of other things. Soon after the Raíces controversy, I took a job as Latino coordinator in the city's Council of Fine Arts, where I helped Latino artists write proposals for their projects and in fact coordinated their projects into an overall developmental program. But I ran into trouble with Jane Byrne's appointed council director, Mary Cunningham, who told me I was pushing too hard for Latino programs, when the idea was to go slow and mainly "integrate" Latino arts into the council's existing initiatives rather than starting so many "separatist" ones on our own. That is when I had my lawsuit. When Mary found I wouldn't play along, she fired me, and then to avoid being labeled anti-Latino and getting flack from the community, she hired Juana Guzmán, a *mexicana* artist who was also on one of the council's funding panels and whom Cunningham claimed would be more of a team player. There was a lot of protest over this. I filed a lawsuit, which I eventually won, but in the meantime I told myself, "I should focus on developing MIRA, and I can't get any help for MIRA if I push all the wrong buttons." The fact is, Juana ended up staying in that job for many years, and though I believe she tried to be fair, her being there in the long run had a negative effect on my efforts—though a positive one on the efforts of others.

Without a steady income again, I ended up picking up other gigs. I became the artistic coordinator for the Museum of Science and Industry's annual Hispanic art exhibit. First there'd been a Pan-American show featuring Latin American and Latino artists. Then some of us had pushed for a Mexican show, and that meant the Puerto Ricans wanted a show of their own. But the museum board was against having "a proliferation" of shows. So they called a meeting to tell all the Latinos involved that the museum was not going to have three shows but just one with all groups represented. And the Latino representatives agreed, but the museum wanted to call the show "Hispanic," because that was the name officially given to us by the government. I was against that, pushing for the word "Latino." But the president of the museum's board called us "Hispanics," and I agreed that it wasn't worth upsetting him and risking the project. So then we took a vote, and almost everybody voted for "Hispanic."

The person who recommended me for the Science and Industry job was my friend, Ricardo Alonso, a Mexican artist who ended up working with me on the shows, too. I didn't hang them physically, but I had to conceive each one, send out forms and contracts to participating artists, write up all the publicity, and so on. That was my job. But by the mid-1980s, after I had been chair for three or four years, I told the board that I could no longer do the show. The fact is, they ended up paying me nothing to run it, and in the end, I said, "If you want this show to work, you have to pay for someone to do it for some months a year, because it's hard—it's a full-time job, and you need to pay enough so that the person in charge can get paid for the time it takes to put it all together." And so they ended hiring a *mexicano* to do the job, but they didn't pay too much, and I guess he wasn't the best. Later on, they added a black show too. And eventually, when I wasn't involved with the show anymore, and he was serving as the director of the newly initiated Mexican Fine Arts Center, Carlos Tortolero joined the Science and Industry committee and helped change the name to "Latino" after all. I don't think the show exists anymore, but I don't think Carlos was to blame.

Another thing I did in those early MIRA years was to keep up with my design work for *Revista Chicano-Riqueña*. My Task Force participation had led me to emphasize a Latino as opposed to a narrowly Chicano framework, and Latino was what Nick Kanellos's *Revista* was all about. But now Nick accepted an offer to teach at the University of Houston, taking the journal with him. *Revista*'s leaving Chicago was another breakup for me on top of all my others. Nick left in 1980, taking Blasco with him. But he came in for a couple of his projects that were funded by the NEH, I guess, before his move—first a big program at the Chicago Public Library in 1981 on multicultural publications, I think, and then his theater exhibit at UIC in 1984, including a panel he moderated with Tomás Ybarra-Frausto, Rodolfo Cortina, and F. Arturo Rosales. But really his time in this city was over, and that hurt. Nick was important to me because he welcomed me into his developing project. He gave me a sense of self-worth even as things were going bad. He valued my work in his journal and in the first days of Arte Público Press, and those were important things I was proud to be a part of. I kept doing design work for the *Revista* and Arte Público even after Nick moved to Houston, and he paid my way to the city a couple of times—first for a few days to help Blasco design a photography exhibit for him, and then again to participate in the national exhibit kickoff for the Houston Museum of Fine Art's exhibit, Hispanic Art in the United States: Thirty Painters and Sculptors.

Of course, the world changed a lot in the eighties, and a lot of things broke up but also formed in Chicago, too. The main thing that happened was what I guess we could call "the Chicago Latino Political Awakening"—the development of Mexican and Puerto Rican political candidates in relation to the rise of Harold Washington. As far as Latino arts were concerned, many things developed, too. On the North Side, Diana Berticini, a recent arrival in the city, tried to start up a Latino arts project, winning support from Marcos Raya and other artists for her efforts as she tried to attract upper-end clients to Latino art, her gallery holding its own for a while but eventually failing. Then, too, with greater lasting success, Aldo Castillo, a Nicaraguan artist and entrepreneur with lots of capital, I guess, behind him, gradually set up his first gallery on Lincoln Avenue on the North Side and then established himself in the main Chicago gallery area near Huron and Superior Streets. A gallery even came to Eighteenth Street in Pilsen in the 1980s, Israel Hernández's Prospectus Gallery, which showed artwork by many of the local artists and had a special relation with Mario Castillo and his parents, Harold and María Allen. Other projects would also develop in the late 1980s into the 1990s, as I struggled to continue MIRA. But clearly the most important group would be the one that was meeting in 1983–84 and attempting to work out how to develop what they called the Mexican Fine Arts Center in Pilsen. That group's efforts would affect almost everything MIRA and all other Latino artists and groups tried to do in the next several years.

MIRA: ITS BOARD AND MEMBERS, ITS NAMES, GOALS, AND ACTIVITIES

The Hispanic Task Force was my inspiration in founding MIRA in 1981. MIRA came about because my Task Force experience had led me from Chicano and Mexican to Latino, but it had also led me to consider the economic as well as the artistic situation of Latino artists. It also led me to believe that Latino artists could be different from other artists by working more cooperatively, thinking and acting collectively,

but never surrendering their individuality. In this context they had to think regionally and nationally at the same time. Latino arts were weaker in Chicago and the Midwest because there was no infrastructure, no base for their work that could link them locally and also nationally. As my work for the Council of Fine Arts showed, local Latino artists needed help writing grant proposals, managing their careers, and finding places to show their work. In fact, they needed their own place—a gallery, some kind of center for Latino arts. These are some of the reasons why I founded MIRA almost immediately after I left MARCH, and they explain why MIRA members were everything—Central Americans, South Americans, Chicanos, Puerto Ricans. Even if the Puerto Ricans tended to struggle for their own organization, I often worked with Gamaliel Ramírez or Oscar Martínez. I also had a strong tie to the Cuban painter Paul Sierra, who was one of the early members of MIRA. Aurelio Díaz left the city for a while, but when he came back, he worked with MIRA, not MARCH, and we supported and participated in his own project, the Peace and Dignity initiative, involving a long-distance run in the name of indigenous peoples in 1991–92 (see chapter 5).

I tried to build a community board for MIRA that would help us develop the project and help also in the search for funds. Some of the people involved were teachers like Angela Miller, Humberto Rivera, Julio Naboa, a Chilean named Sergio Bézar, and Rosemary Bombela, the governor's Hispanic representative to the Illinois Arts Council. My friend Geno Muñoz also served on the board, and so did Amie Horton, a UIC community-outreach person who worked with us on antigentrification issues in the early 1980s and stayed on with MIRA even after she left the university. There were others who attended board meetings and seemed ready to join, and I certainly tried to recruit others, but it was hard. And I guess I can say that this was one of the biggest failures of MIRA—the people who joined our board were very good people, but they really didn't know how to help build a strong, committed, and active board, and they didn't know how to get us significant corporate resources. And I guess I didn't, either.

Still, MIRA received some funding and developed a whole series of projects of which I'm very proud to this day—even if in the long run, others took them up or even appropriated them, sometimes acting as if they had invented them themselves.

First, about our name: MIRA stands for Mi Raza Arts Consortium. In retrospect, I believe the abbreviation was fine, though less militant sounding than MARCH. But the inclusion of "Raza" gave some people the idea that we were connected with a major Latino newspaper in the city, *La Raza;* and even though the newspaper was owned by an Uruguayan, people also identified the title as an effort to establish something very Chicano, since the Chicano movement had picked up on the term, maybe as a U.S. adaptation of José Vasconcélos's idea of "la raza cósmica." But I was finally unhappy with the race or even specifically the Chicano emphasis the title invited, when our real intention from the first day was to establish something that didn't obliterate or sideline Chicano or even Mexican dimensions but that was pan-Latino in every respect. Maybe the name hurt us more than helped, leading non-Chicanos and non-*mexicanos* to feel that they were on the margins of a project in which they should have felt central.

In spite of these problems, MIRA did lots of great things. We developed a pretty special newsletter called *Mirarte* (fig. 75). We also developed a series of workshops helping artists to identify and apply for grant opportunities; and we produced a Midwest Latino artists and arts organization directory. We took the first steps in serving as a kind of not-for-profit agency or clearinghouse for Latino arts activities, recommending different artists for appropriate projects, never playing favorites or collecting even token fees. We did countless shows, some continuing the tradition of MARCH, but several others dedicated to local artists—and, among these shows, we developed what is now a Chicago tradition: art exhibits by Mexicans but also others centered on El Día de los Muertos, the Day of the Dead, in October and November of each year. Maybe I and the board should've done more to raise money for what we did, and maybe we should've had some modest fee structure for our many recommendation and referral services; but I guess I did what I did best, putting most of my energy into the publications and events I mention here.

First of all, the Illinois Arts Council funded us to develop *Mirarte* as a publication that would network national and local Latino arts projects. Each issue was carefully done, with lots of translation work commissioned among local writers like the poet Beatriz Badikian and many others—with Harold Allen proofreading the text in English. There were also Antonio Zavala's interviews with local artists and announcements about funding opportunities, new shows, and the rest. Maybe above all I took pride in deepening the layout skills I'd developed for the *Revista Chicano-Riqueña* and MARCH *Abrazo* issues. There was maybe something old-style about it—maybe a throwback to some of the Posada workshop publications—with paste-up boards and the use of traditional columns instead of the computerized mockups and manipulations that were still somewhat new in those days. It was all very artisanal, with hours and hours spent on detail work in my new apartment on Eighteenth Street just east of Halsted, making each number as perfect as could be. So really *Mirarte* not

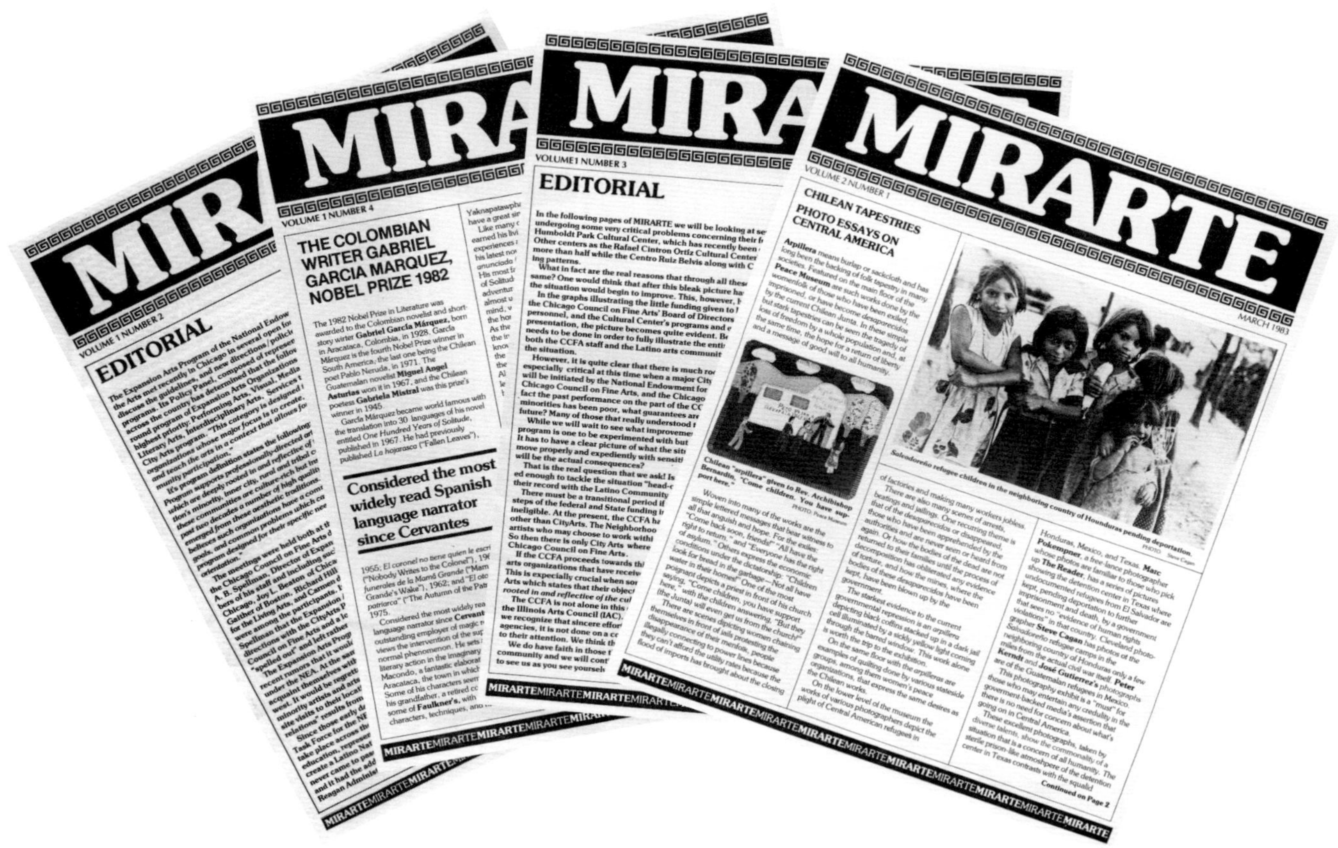

Fig. 75. Issues of *Mirarte*.

only reported on the arts but was an example in itself of contemporary Latino art—it won a lot of support and praise for MIRA, and so did our directory (fig.76), which provided background and contact information on almost every major Latino organization and artist in the Midwest and served as a valuable tool for several years before it was completely out of date. Some pretty well-known Chicano writers joined several artists in praising our efforts (fig. 77).

At the same time, where MARCH now opposed getting grants (though I understand they got some in the 1980s), MIRA tried to help artists get the grants they needed, organizing them for workshops in grant writing and career management. MIRA could also get some grants for our programs, but we had to compete and were sometimes successful and sometimes not. And it's true, the grants I got were very demanding and sometimes had more negative than positive effects, involving us in work and bureaucracy that led us away from our goals, but I had to do what our grants committed us to do or lose out in future proposals. And then too maybe we weren't applying for enough grants, since we didn't want to compete with the artists we were helping to write grant proposals. And at the same time, I was now getting competition from a new group that didn't know much about art or culture but knew a lot about getting grants and other funding support.

We held some start-up fund-raisers (fig. 78), and then a more formal reception at Margarita's Restaurant (fig. 79), and finally a full-scale fund-raising event at the Playboy Foundation mansion in Chicago's Rush Street Gold Coast area featuring the Negrete sisters and other performers (fig. 80), and later at the recently opened

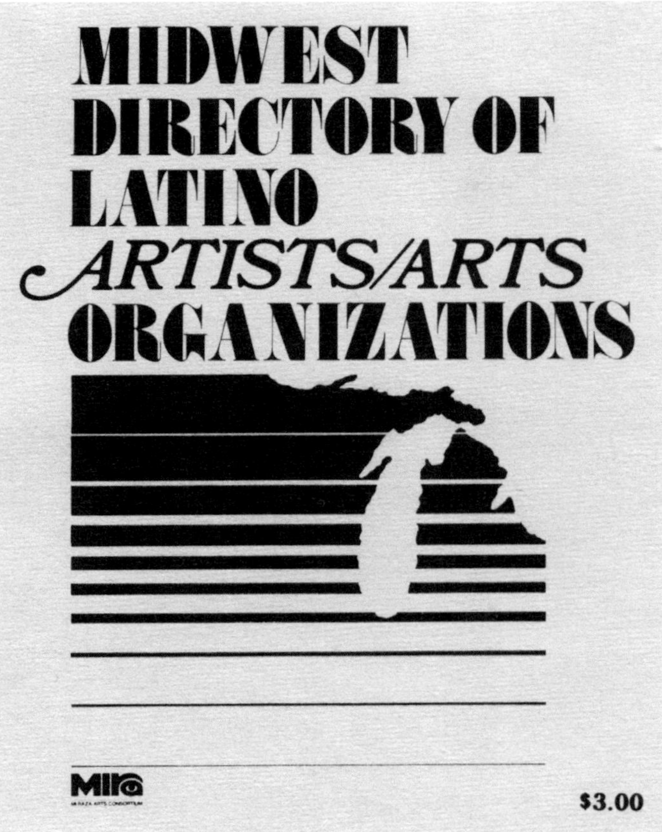

Decima Musa. There was one I remember that was cosponsored with the Latino professional organization HACE at the Latino Institute, and others I can hardly remember at all. Our shows included those we initiated and sponsored and also those we just supported. In 1982, there was our promotional work that Carmelo Díaz asked me to coordinate for the Chicago premiere of Robert Young's *Ballad of Gregorio Cortez,* with Edward James Olmos—a film we showed at an old Mexican movie theater in the heart of Pilsen and another theater in Little Village (fig. 81). At the same time, throughout the early eighties, we worked with the coordinator of UIC's Rafael Cintrón Ortiz Latino Student Cultural Center (Marc Zimmerman), and also Victor Sorell at Chicago State University in cosponsoring several events. First there was a showing of *Zoot Suit* at UIC, to go along with the *Gregorio Cortez* opening. Then there were the complicated arrangements for a visit to Chicago by the Nicaraguan/Sandinista poet/priest Ernesto Cardenal, including a reading at the Rubel Auditorium of the Art Institute, as the highlight of a series of events arranged by a committee that included Marc, me, Carol Becker of the Institute's School, Nena Torres, director of the Mayor's Advisory Committee on Latino Affairs (MACLA), and Michael Piazza, representing Artists against the War in Central America. We

Fig. 76. Midwest Directory of Latino Artists/Arts Organizations, cover designed by Paul Sierra.

Fig. 77. Cartas (letters), homage to *Mirarte* from two poets, Sandra Cisneros and Trinidad Sánchez (published in an early issue of the newsletter).

also worked on a Chicago visit of the Chicano activist Corky González and more than one Chicago appearance of the Chicano Teatro de Esperanza from Santa Barbara, California. We also had a couple of art exhibits of local painters when the city's Pan-American festival was held in Olive Park near Navy Pier. MIRA had a number of smaller exhibits that were not as large as the Raíces Antíguas show but helped make the organization's name known. At the annual Pan-American show, the organizers gave a small space to nonprofit organizations. I believe that we did it for two years. Diana Bertoccini and the MFAC were among those that showcased their organizations.

I did a group show with Nicole Smith, a woman from Haiti who still owns the Nicole Gallery in the River North Gallery Area. The gallery mainly features Haitian artists, but on this one occasion Nicole let me organize an exhibit of Latinos, which turned out fairly well.

We did a small group show at the Pilsen Little Village Mental Health Center, which was housed in what had been a huge mirror factory. The show featured about ten artists, including Arturo Miramontes from Hammond, whom I discovered at an exhibition at Indiana University Northwest in Gary. Arturo had training from a very fine artist who taught him to paint in oils. He learned very fast, and his teacher told him that he didn't need him anymore but to continue painting. Arturo worked a lot from memory, and many of his works were of famous people in Mexican history like Zapata, Cuauhtémoc, Juárez, Hidalgo, and many others. I was one that encouraged him to work, and I had him exhibit some of his pieces at the annual banquet of Chicago's Mexican Civic Society for September 15 at one of the large hotels in Chicago. He made a lot of good contacts and some very good sales that included one of his better Zapata paintings.

Another important exhibit that featured Arturo was at the new Margarita Restaurant on Polk Street near Michigan Avenue. I also featured Alex Galindo, a photographer, in the balcony space that they had. They had a mural by Alejandro Romero and another by his brother, Oscar. This time we weren't successful in selling any work, but we did get a lot of exposure. I designed a poster pamphlet that featured both artists.

Of all these events, perhaps I should say some more about our work with Edward James Olmos on the opening of *The Ballad of Gregorio Cortez*. He had decided he wanted to promote himself in the Mexican communities of a number of cities, and he chose Chicago to be one of them. Eddie contacted us and Facets Multimedia art cinema about his project. Aurelio, Jesús Gonzales, and I, plus a few others, worked to make flyers and other promotional materials.

The committee we formed worked to organize a dinner for Eddie and his community outreach coordinator in Little Village with a family that Aurelio Díaz knew. I worked along with Milos Stehlik, the director of Facets, for the promotion of *The Ballad of Gregorio Cortez* at their theater. Eddie's sidekick worked full-time from the theater to promote the movie in the Pilsen theater. All three sites were very successful, and I believe *Gregorio Cortez* broke the record at Facets for the longest run for a film there. I designed a flyer for the movie and also included a brief article about it in the edition of *Mirarte* that came out in time for the event (fig. 82). Eddie's assistant helped bring a large audience to Facets and the Mexican theaters. Geno Muñoz and I took Eddie and him around town and out to dinner near Rush Street.

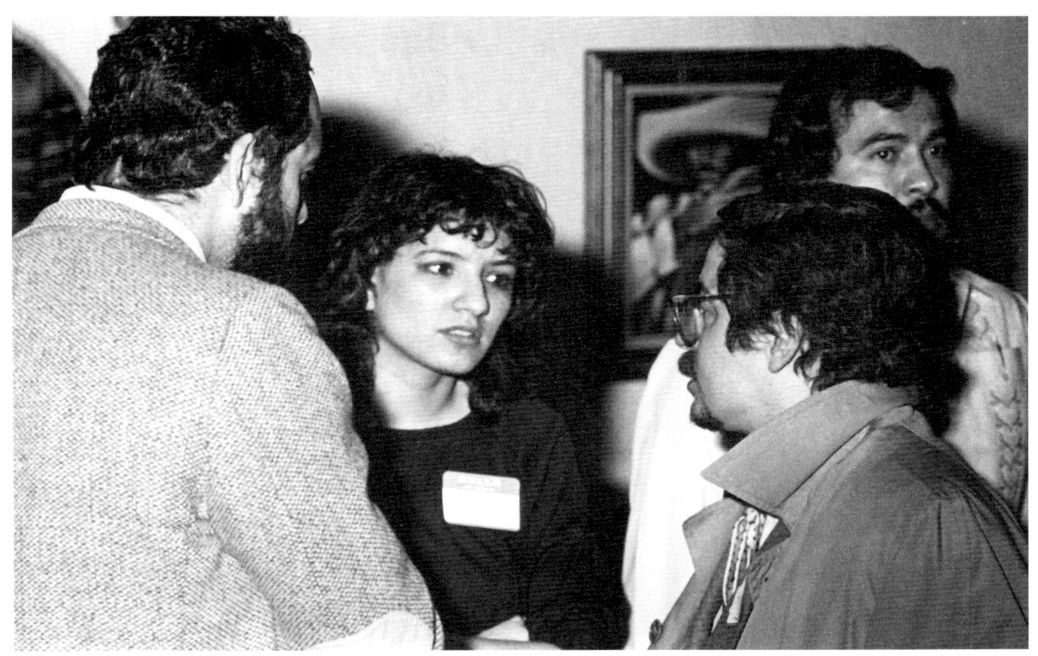

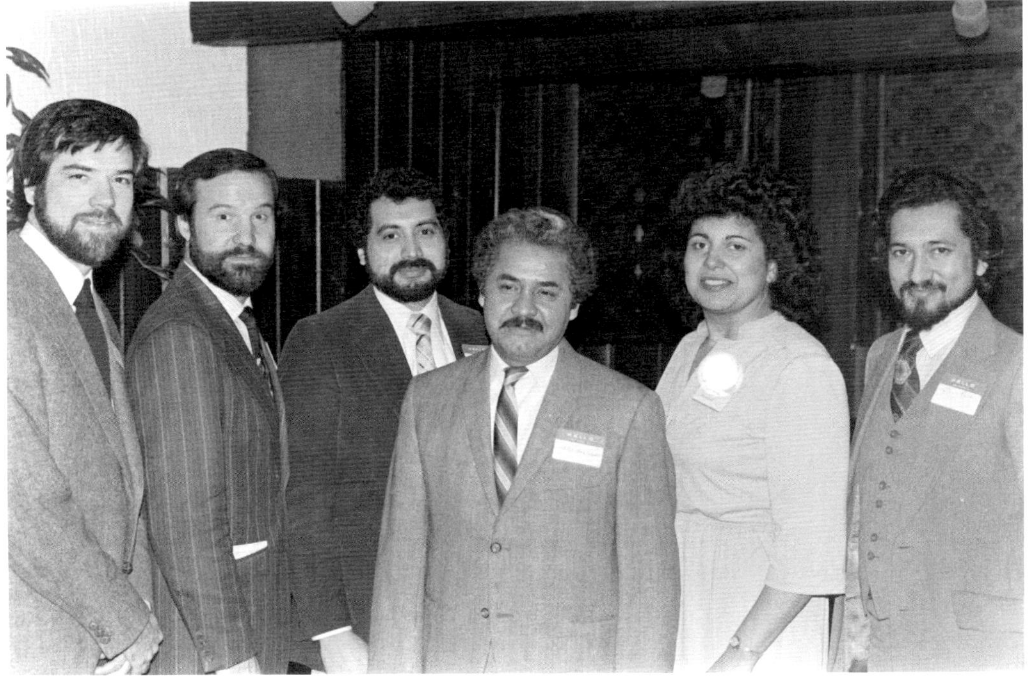

Fig. 78. Sandra Cisneros, Chicana writer, and Billy Zayas, Puerto Rican cultural promoter, at a MIRA fundraiser/exhibit, early 1980s. Photo: José Gamaliel González.

Fig. 79. From left to right: Paul Sierra, Sergio Bezard, Humberto Rivera, José Gamaliel González, Rosemary Bombela, and Julio Naboa, at the reception held by *La Raza* newspaper for MIRA at La Margarita restaurant on Rush Street in Chicago's Gold Coast, 1982.

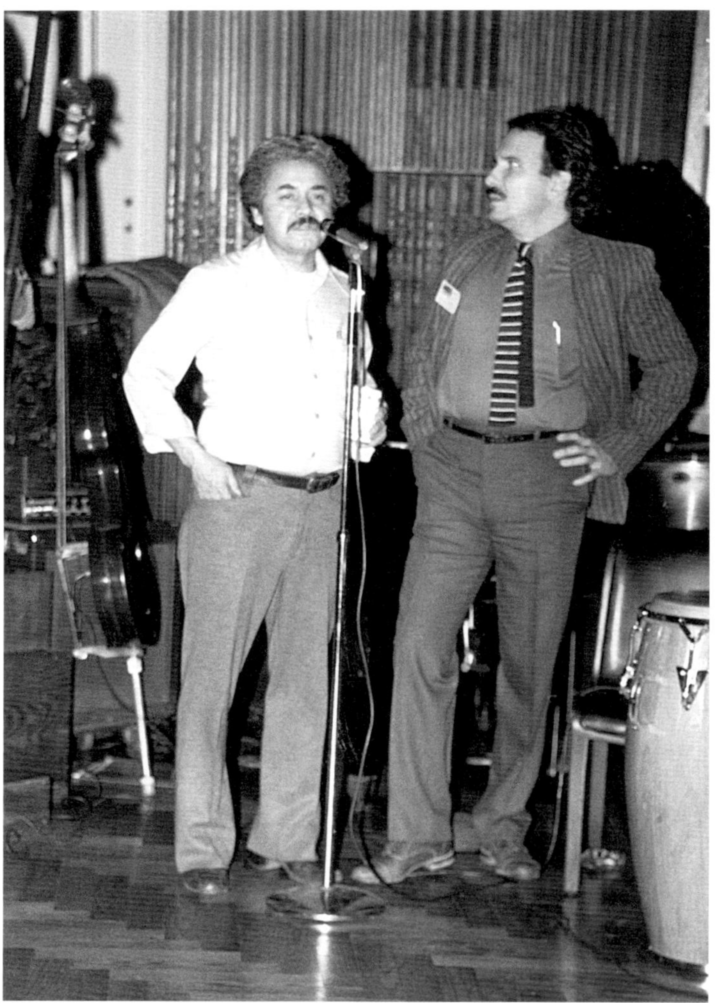

Fig. 80. José and Chicago
Cuban celebrity emcee
Juan Montenegro at
a MIRA fundraiser at
the Playboy mansion,
November 1983.

Fig. 81. José Gamaliel
González, *The Ballad of
Gregorio Cortez,* with
Edward James Olmos
(article in *Mirarte* 1.2
[1979]).

The Ballad of Gregorio Cortez

*"Gregorio Cortez, an unknown Mexican
ranch hand and W.T. (Brack) Morris, an
unknown sheriff, pistols in hand, blazed away
at each other on a farm a few miles west of
Kennedy, Texas. June 12, 1901, dates the
legend of a tragic misunderstanding. The
sheriff was killed and Cortez entered into
legend."* **Tomas Rivera**

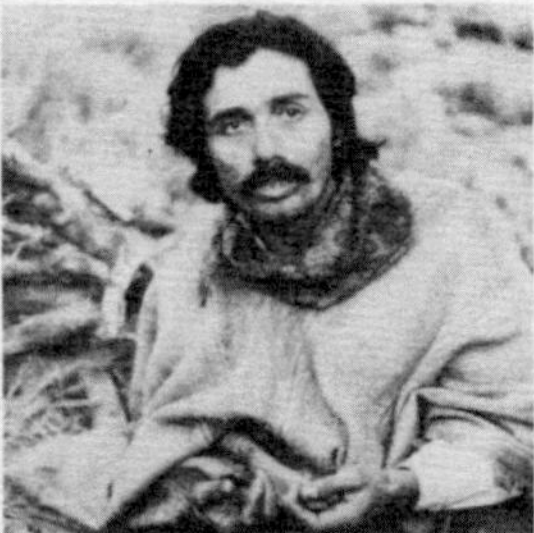

PHOTO:
Embassy Pictures

**Gregorio Cortez (James Olmos) is an
unwilling fugitive from Texas Rangers.**

The Ballad of Gregorio
Cortez, directed by **Robert
Young** and starring **Edward
James Olmos,** is a movie
depicting the story of this
tragic event, that is based on court transcripts
and newspaper accounts from that time.
The story has been vividly detailed by
Americo Paredes in his book **With
His Pistol in His Hand** (1958). The
scheduled for release in late fall of 1983, has
been well received because of its remarkable
book, although a scholarly study, weaves
several elements of the story from studies of
ballads written on the heroics of Cortez.

Edward James Olmos, better known for his
role of **El Pachuco** in the film **Zoot Suit,**
has been touring the country with his co-star,
Tom Bower, and his agent, **Daniel Haro** to
promote "The Ballad of Gregorio Cortez"
prior to its public release. Appearances have
been made throughout the country including
the Chicago/Milwaukee area back in May of
this year.

The film, a bilingual picture, which is
schedules for release in late fall of 1983, has
been well received because of its remarkable
quality. It also succeeds historically, with the
casting, the wardrobe, the background
scenary, and the railroad cars that have been
replicated for this movie. The finishing touch
of the film is the acting of Edward Olmos,
which is superb. Mr. Olmos, hardly speaking,
portrays Cortez excellently by his facial and
body language during the manhunt, eluding
Texas Rangers, local lawmen, and posses
dispatched on horseback and railroad train.
Cortez is finally captured after eleven days,
and, although innocent, he is sentenced to life
in prison but pardoned 12 years later.

The legend and *corridos* of Gregorio
Cortez continue to this day, and the movie
itself may well become a legend in filmaking.
J.G.G.

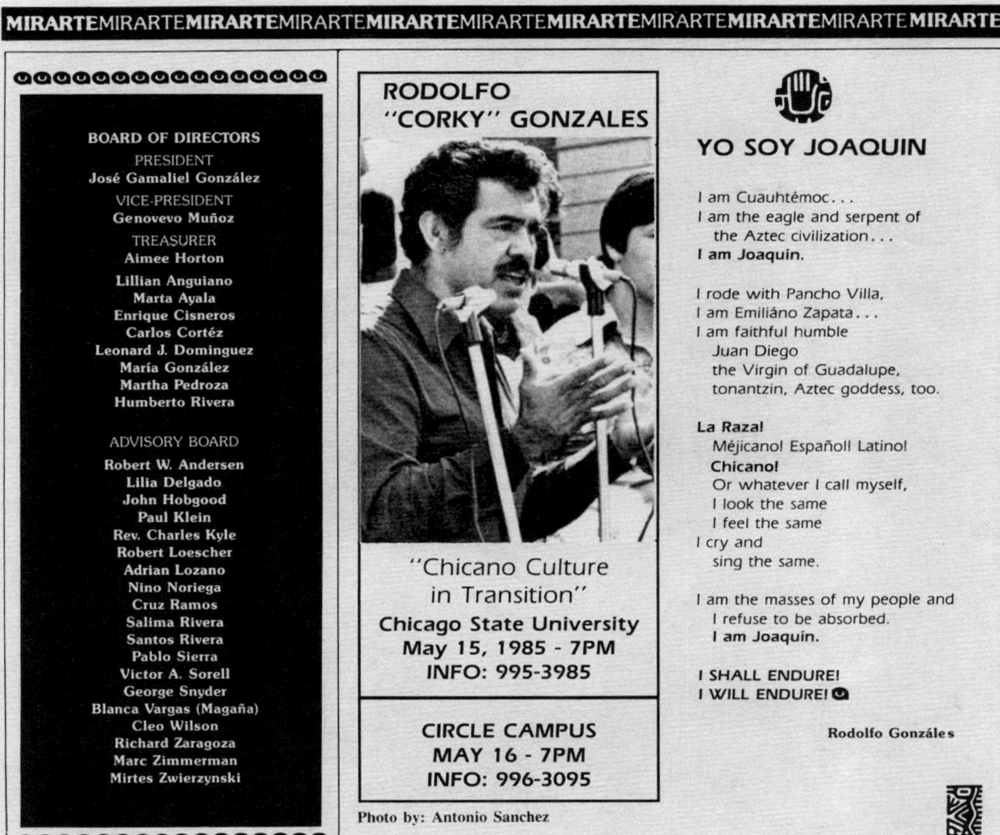

THE DAY OF THE DEAD

In spite of all the events we did, big and small, with or without stars from Mexico or Hollywood, I think that the most important events we developed were the art exhibits we did each year around the theme of the Day of the Dead. Each time we did one, the event got bigger, sometimes featuring older or newer pieces by me, sometimes featuring guest artists. All in all, Mira did a total of about twelve Día de los Muertos exhibits, starting in 1983, three years earlier than when the MFAC did their first Muertos exhibit. The only thing is that they began their show in September, and they made it really big, so that all the other Days of the Dead that are held around November 2 seem to be shorter and smaller and maybe offshoots of theirs.

Later on, it even seemed to people that the MFAC had invented the Day of the Dead in Chicago—and it's true that MFAC members seemed jealous of any individual or organization developing a separate show. MIRA's pioneer role was forgotten and overlooked. But at least I can try to set things aright here. We did not bring the Day of the Dead to Chicago—the first Chicago event I know of was Jean Parisi's Pro-Arts show of 1979, which took place in Dvorak Park and Casa Aztlán, with kids painted up as *calaveras,* live music, *pan de muertos,* and Mexican chocolate milk. The other show I remember was one developed by Clay Morrison at the Hubbard Street Gallery in 1981. I recommended Alejandro Romero to do the invitation image.

I'm pretty sure the two women who ran the popular Mexican handicraft store on Clark Street also had some Day of the Dead activi-

Fig. 82. The subsequent MIRA board structure (including Marc Zimmerman), an announcement of Corky González's presentations, and an extract from his poem, "Yo Soy Joaquín," a major work of the national Chicano movement, appearing in *Mirarte* 2.2 (1982).

ties. Later, many places, Mexican or not, had such events, some of them very good ones. And it's also true that no one could match the big shows at the MFACM. But it was MIRA that had made it a major event, bringing together art and handicraft; it was MIRA that first gave the event its cultural depth and dash.

The first Day of the Dead that I developed, and one of the most successful of all, was when I brought in the Mexican artist Felipe Ehrenberg to set up a big show for the occasion. Clay Morrison secured me a space in a large new addition to Ann Nathan's Objects Gallery in the heart of Chicago's River North gallery district. I went to Mexico City personally to talk to Felipe about doing this event to commemorate the dead in Central America. He was very excited about the idea and immediately produced a drawing, which I used in the postcard I designed for the show's invitation.

Felipe did a large installation of skulls, coffins, and helicopters. Marta Ayala, her artist brother Marcos, and others worked with him in putting the exhibit together. Marta, Susana Aguilar, and another Mexican woman dressed in black with skull masks designed by Marcos danced at the opening. I organized six lectures for Felipe and designed a flyer with his artwork. I had a little problem with Ann Nathan, who is Jewish like Felipe, and when I showed her the flyer, she said, "You should be more organized like Felipe." Felipe came to my defense and said that all of this organization was done by me. That shut her up.

We had a huge crowd at the opening, and Felipe was interviewed by media people. He was very impressive and talented with a great number of exhibits to his credit. But above all he was a great self-promoter. He had a great flair for the dramatic. He had skulls tattooed on his fingers and a big, deep voice that I think the women found sexy. He had lots of bright ideas that re-ally got people excited at each exhibit. MIRA brought him to the city, lining up a lecture for him at the School of the Art Institute and doing other educationals around the city for two hundred dollars a shot, except for a freebee at Casa Aztlán. He made so many friends and contacts in the city that when he got ready to return to Mexico, he brought a big crowd of people for a one-man show at his apartment and sold a number of works. I even bought one from him. Afterwards, the School of the Art Institute invited him to teach classes and do other exhibits so that for a few years he became a Chicago regular, though more and more distanced from MIRA. Still, with his help, we made the Day of the Dead a major Chicago event (fig.83).

In fact, from that point on we did Day of the Dead shows almost every year. In 1984, we brought Arsacio Vanegas Arroyo, the grandson of the printer for Posada's classic work and the owner of all of Posada's original plates, in a Day of the Dead show that featured some of the best Posadas and brought a lot of attention to MIRA. In 1985 we did Villa y Zapata Viven, a group show in Little Village with a poster designed by Carlos Cortez. Another group show followed in 1986, which was in Pilsen.

Then in 1987, MIRA sponsored two Day of the Dead shows. First we had one that honored Ritchie Valens, the young Chicano rock-and-roll singer who died in a plane crash with Buddy Holly (fig.84). We did the installation at Thalia Hall, the building where we had free space to do events for a year and where we dreamed of opening a museum. It was a huge installation with many salvage parts from cars arranged to imitate the form of a plane, along with a big motor that sounded like an airplane. Second, we did Frida y Diego—Una Pareja, with Carlos Cortez doing their images and me designing the postcard (fig. 85) and contributing a drawing for the show (fig. 86). We had two exhibits

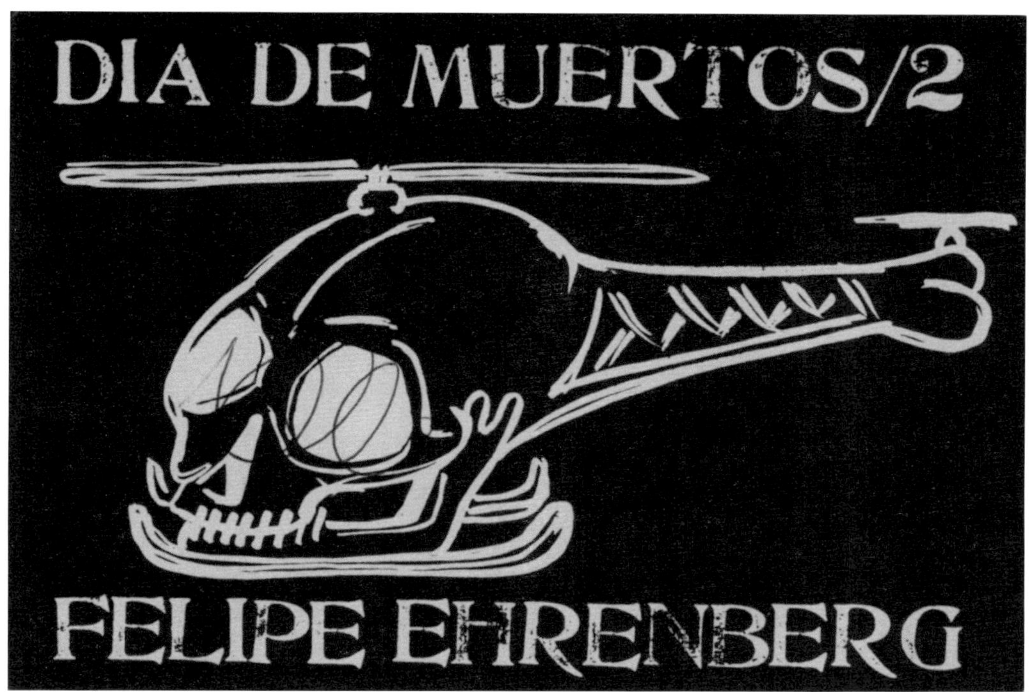

for this event, which we held at Prairie Avenue Gallery near Pilsen and at Artemisia Gallery. I invited the San Francisco artists Amalia Mesa Baines and Rene Yañez to do installations as the centerpieces for the two different exhibits, which also featured local artists in works evoking Frida and Diego. We had a panel discussion with Victor Sorell as the emcee.

In 1988, some years before the MFAC started their Sor Juana festivals, I honored Sor Juana Inés de La Cruz for El Día de los Muertos at the Prairie Avenue Gallery, featuring a large installation with flowers and antique furniture and showcasing works by some twenty-five artists. The postcard that I designed for the invitation was the one-thousand-peso bill that honored Sor Juana (fig. 87).

We also did an exhibit at Thalia Hall of prints of El Taller Popular de Grabado of Mexico City and an exhibit to honor La Virgen de Guadalupe. The painting for the poster was done by Aurelio Díaz, and a young girl I brought from Mexico City did an installation. Still another Muertos event I recall was an installation to honor Pedro Infante, including a tape recorder playing his songs at the Pilsen Little Village Mental Health Center. Finally, there were my four-gallery Van Gogh shows of 1990—perhaps our greatest success—where I used some of the antique furniture I'd acquired for the Sor Juana exhibit. But I'll leave that story for later.

With all this and more, we set the stage for the Day of the Dead to spread around the city and for the MFAC's making the Day of the Dead one of its core events. In fact, by the early 1990s there were so many Day of the Dead exhibits in Chicago that MIRA published a list designed so that people would know about all the shows. We tried to include information about the MFAC's show, which we considered very important, but they declined to give us information for our list. I guess they felt we were trying to steal their thunder and "put them in their place" on a list featuring what they considered minor shows that probably didn't merit mention at all. We just didn't see things that way.

There were other MIRA events I could list, and there were ones we developed even in the

Fig. 83. José Gamaliel González, postcard for Felipe Ehrenberg's MIRA-sponsored Día de los Muertos show at Objects Gallery, November 1983.

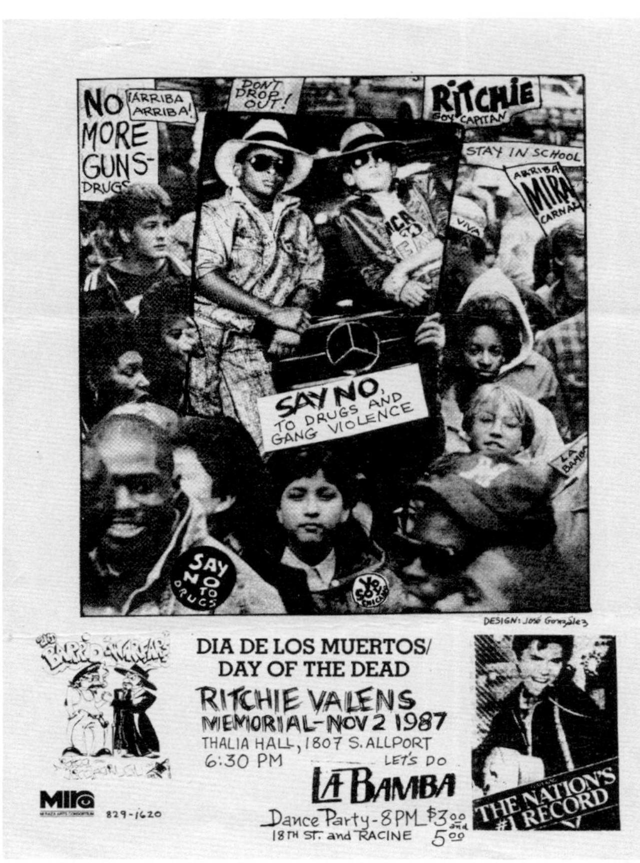

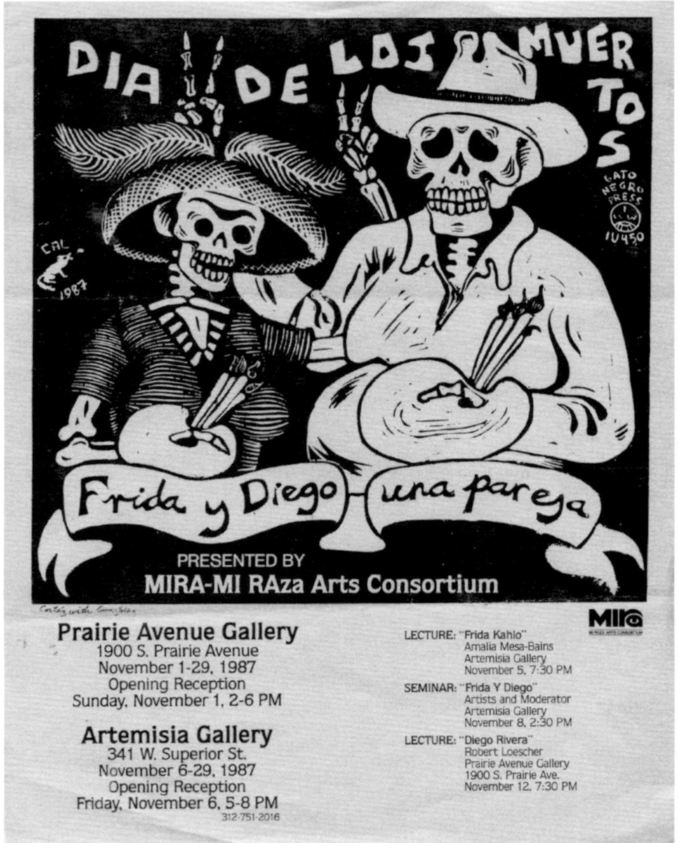

Fig. 84. José Gameliel González, collage, Ritchie Valens Dia de los Muertos flyer, November 11, 1987.

Fig. 85. Flyer for MIRA's Frida y Diego—Una Pareja Day of the Dead show, with drawing by Carlos Cortez and design by José Gamaliel González, November 1987.

Fig. 86. Frida, Diego, and nurse, 1980. 12"×10". Charcoal. Shown in MIRA show, 1987.

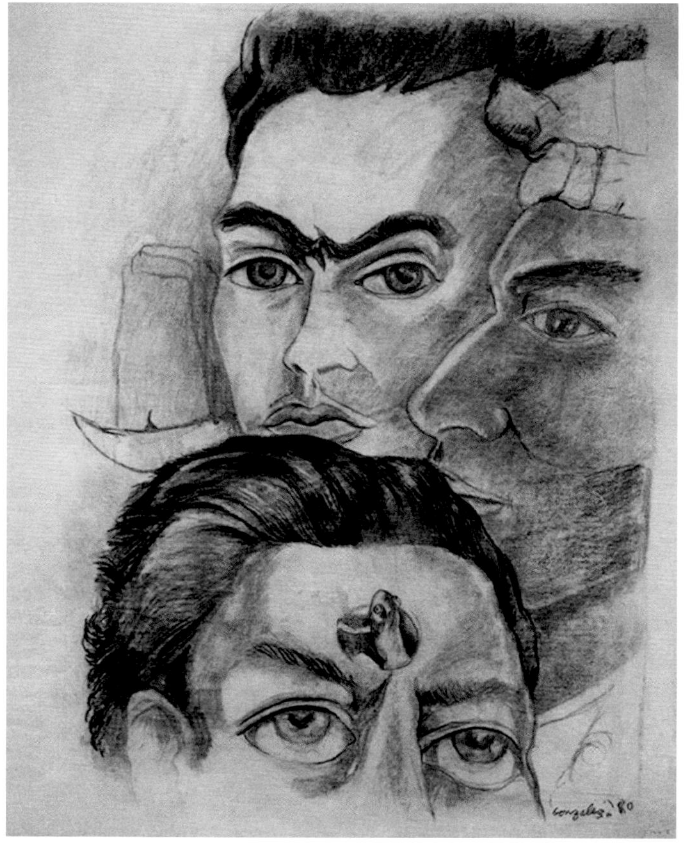

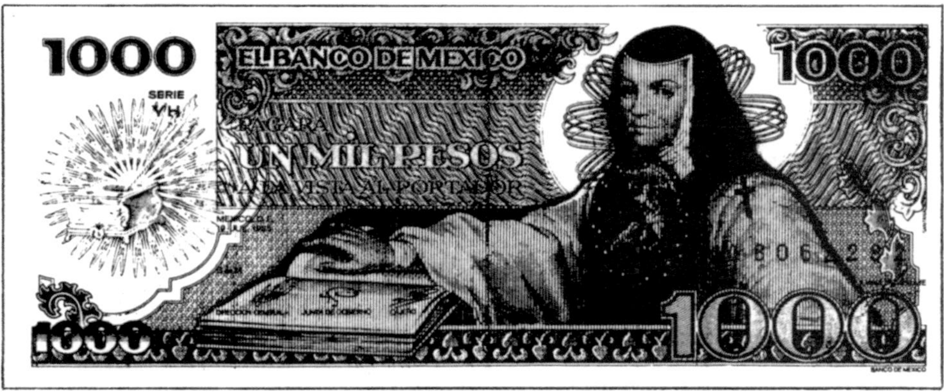

early 1990s. But there were also a series of core events starting in 1983–84 in which the tensions between MIRA and the MFAC became so severe that they became part of an almost a constant war, which I'm afraid to say we eventually lost.

THE SAN ANTONIO ¡MIRA! SHOW

In 1984, a San Antonio agency called me and indicated that a local artist, César Martínez, who knew me through my Task Force work, had recommended me as the Chicago contact to help him and a group of other San Antonio artists in finding a local venue and doing arrangements for a new show they had developed and wanted to take to Los Angeles, New York, and Chicago. By some coincidence, they called the show ¡Mira!,[1] and it had the added touch that I would be asked to add other, non-Texas Latino artists for the Chicago presentation. The name caused some confusion in itself, because it wasn't something we'd dreamed up—but it was the name the San Antonio agency had chosen. It was never even a MIRA show, even though I was involved and identified with it, so that many people thought it was our event. But it was clear from the beginning that I couldn't change the name of their show, nor could I put the MIRA label on it, nor could I say no to doing it (fig. 88).

In fact, I worked to the limit—making a list of artist show candidates throughout the country and then contacting them to send slides of their work to San Antonio. The agency designed the show poster, using one of César Martínez's well-known Pachuco paintings, with me making the invitations, drawing on MIRA's mailing lists and calling everyone on my phone lists to come (fig. 89).

¡Mira! was a big success, opening at the huge space of the Hyde Park Cultural Center. The show had a great funding base provided by Hiram Walker's Canadian Club, but they didn't pay me anything as a consultant. Because of the confusion from the name and my participation, though, I think the show added to MIRA's prestige and pointed toward a promising future. The show was such a success in Chicago and elsewhere that the San Antonio agency lined up a second show with the same name. But this

Fig. 87. José Gamaliel González, Sor Juana Decima Musa Flyer, fall 1988.

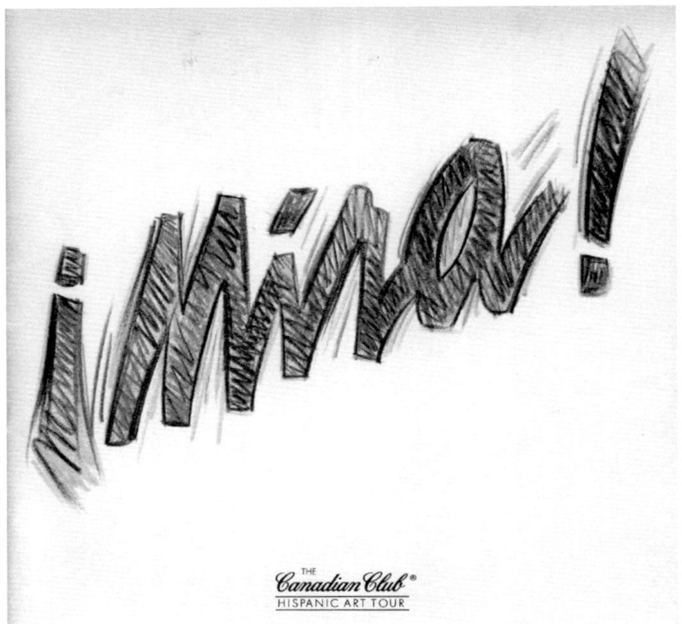

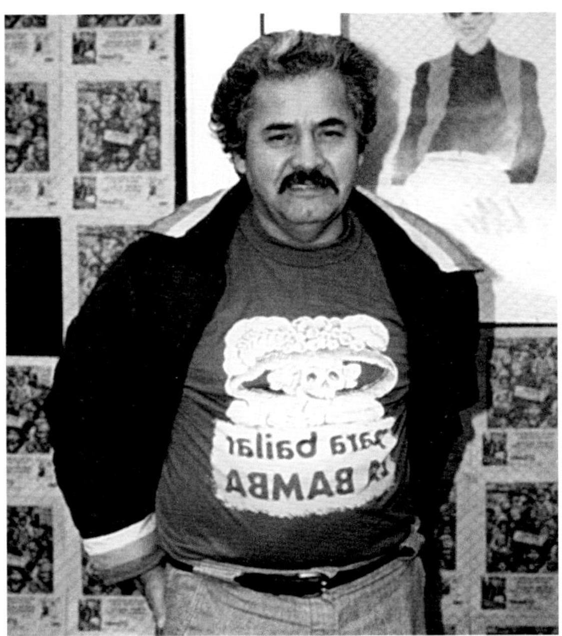

time, they got the prestigious downtown Chicago Terra Museum to house the show. And the people at Terra contacted the MFAC to help put the Chicago version together.

So this is where the real tensions began about who was going to represent Chicano and Latino art in Chicago. It was clear that the San Antonio agency overlooked me for their second show, and it felt like a slap in the face. I wrote a letter to Hiram Walker with a copy to the agency saying that I thought it was only fair that I be involved in the second show because I had made the first show and its success possible for them. I threatened to sue them for using the MIRA name for a Chicago show in which the head of MIRA was being unfairly excluded.

At that point, the Terra Museum called a meeting, which I guess I should have attended but was too proud to, in part because I figured it might be more of a lynching than a hearing. And sure enough, the MFAC people said I was not going to be part of the show and that I had nothing to do with it. Then, to avoid confusion and a suit, Hiram Walker decided that they wouldn't do another show with the name of ¡Mira! Maybe I should have held my

pride in check and gone to the meeting, but I just couldn't lower myself to go. I guess you might say I won that battle because Hiram Walker withdrew the MIRA identification, but in another way it was a defeat because MIRA would begin to lose out to the MFAC in other art shows and events.

THE CASASOLA EXHIBIT AND THE EARTHQUAKE

Then came 1985, which may have been the turning point for MIRA and me personally. Things were going along well enough, above all because of a new and richer Casasola show, The World of Agustín Víctor Casasola, which Marc Zuver had developed at the Fondo del Sol Gallery in Washington, D.C., and now wished to move to Chicago's Field Museum. Zuver designated me to serve as a coordinator, and I was hired for two months to reach out to the community. I worked my head off to make it a big show for Zuver, the museum, and MIRA (fig. 90). And in fact, the second Casasola show completed MIRA's link to the work I'd done with MARCH. But the opening night of the exhibit was also on the day of the earthquake in Mexico City, and at the opening I announced that I was going to raise money in one way or another to help the earthquake victims.

Soon after, I established a citywide committee that met at the Latino Institute, whose director, Mario Aranda, agreed to serve as the fiscal agent for the money we were going to raise. By this time, the MFAC was already on its way. The center's board members didn't have their building yet, but they already knew they didn't want anything to do with me or any activity that might seem to lend me some legitimacy, because somehow they saw me as a rival who might still question their role, their arts know-how, and everything that went with it. So here I was, this rival launching a big activity they should've thought of, this rival serving as chair of this fund-raising committee. I invited several Latinos to be on this committee to raise money. But who was one of the first people I asked to serve on the earthquake committee? One of the MFAC's founders and prime movers, my supposed enemy, Helen Valdez. I invited other Latinos to be on this committee to raise money. The initial work we did involved our getting donations from different groups of people for printing, mailing, and all the promotional work required for a major fund-raising event. We thought about several different venues for the fund-raiser, and we finally decided on a citywide concert at the Chicago Symphony Orchestra Hall. Two people were very important in helping to coordinate the ticket sales: a community outreach coordinator of the symphony and Kathy Devine, whom I knew from my days working at Hull-House and who was now doing a lot of freelance political fund-raising for several candidates, including Harold Washington.

For my part, I was able to obtain free typesetting for the poster-flyer from Handellan-Pederson, the studio where I began working

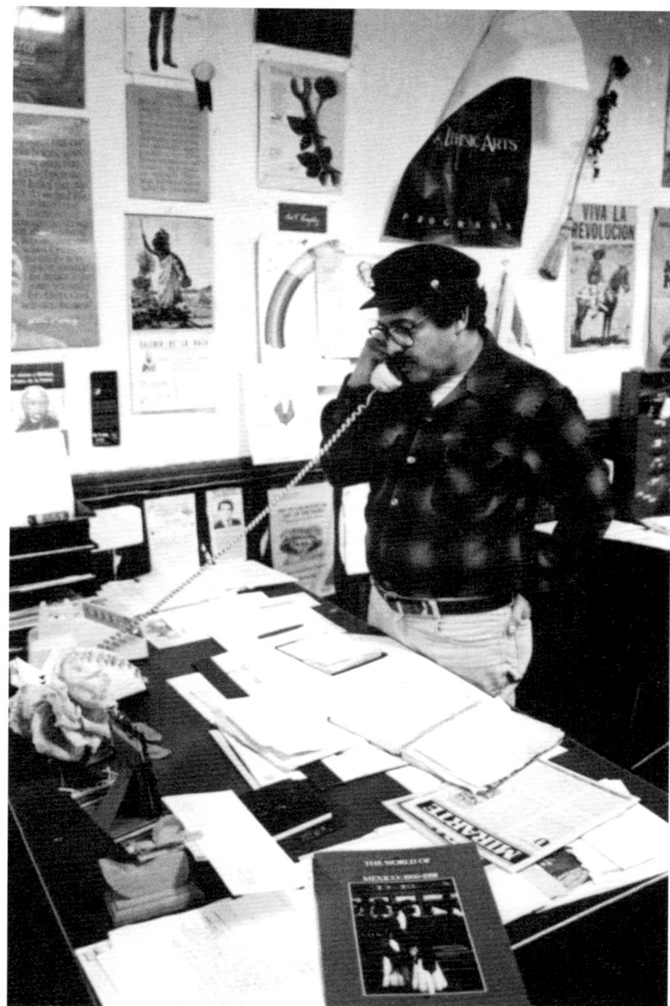

as an apprentice in the commercial art field in 1956. The poster contained all the information of the concert's participants and the price of the tickets. It was designed by the same Peruvian graphic artist that I had used to do the large brochure for the Raíces Antiguas exhibit held at the Museum of Contemporary Art in 1979. It featured the Stone Toltec Warriors that are at a pyramid site near Mexico City. It was printed green and red (fig. 91).

I chose the title of the concert, "Mexico Lindo y Querido," which is a very popular Mexican song. I was able to get a visiting Mexican opera singer, in town at this time to perform at the Lyric Opera theater, to sing the song at the concert. Other concert performers included Libby

Fig. 90. José at the Asociación Pro-derechos Obreros (APO) office on Eighteenth Street, working on the second Casasola show, 1985. The office would become a workshop area of Taller Mestizarte in the late 1990s.

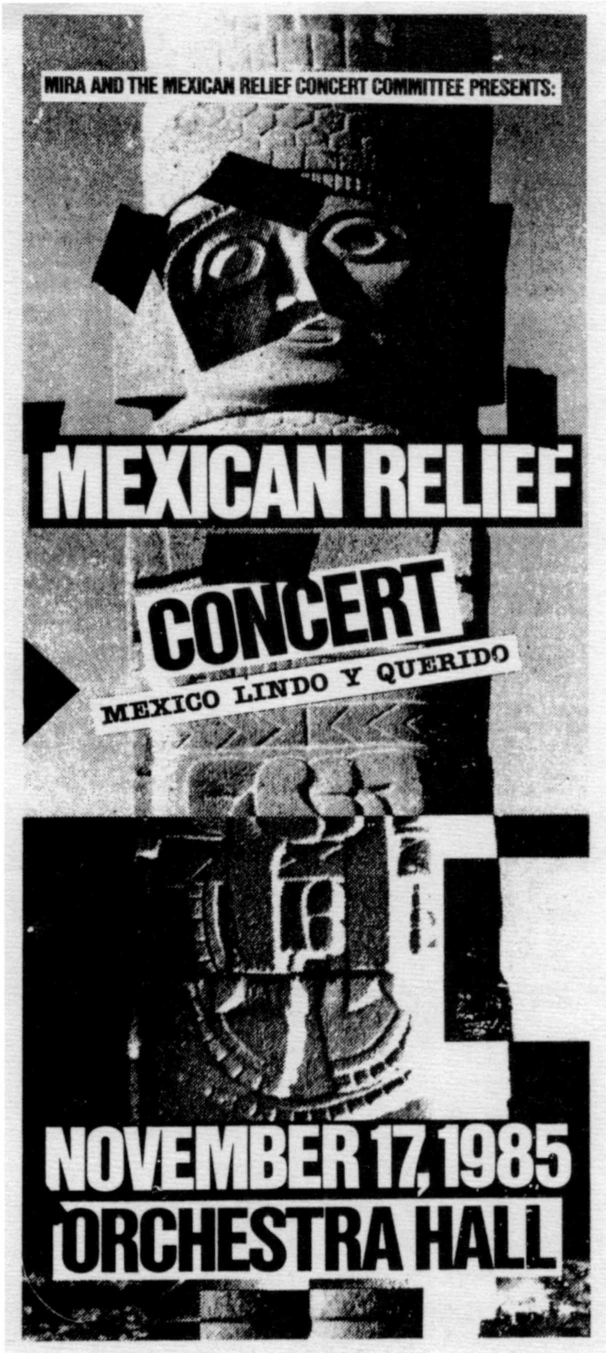

Fig. 91. José Gamaliel González, Mexican Earthquake Relief concert program, México Lindo y Querido (front cover).

better judges than me. We didn't sell out, but we had a good crowd. And after expenses, we raised just a little under ten thousand dollars, which really wasn't bad, considering the fact that just as we got under way, Mayor Harold Washington's people set up a broader committee and brought in Latinos through MACLA, which inevitably drew in most of the resources, eventually raising over a million dollars. But our committee decided that while we should back the city committee, we should also keep on with our own parallel and complementary effort, so we wouldn't simply get lost in the shuffle and so that people in Mexico would know that Chicago Mexicans and Latinos were not only contributing to the larger effort but trying to help at least some key Mexican sectors directly.

Harold Washington went to Mexico with a delegation that included Helen Valdez and me, as well as other hand-picked community organizers. But he didn't take the money we'd raised on our own. Helen somehow took her name off our support list, and it was Marta Ayala, now working as a key community representative on MACLA, who went with me as we took what we raised in the form of three checks, which we divided evenly among three groups: a women-seamstress organization fighting for their rights, Arsacio Vanegas's print-making workshop (the one that published Posada's work), and a cooperative that developed in Tepito, one of the poorer sections of Mexico City, where Felipe Ehrenberg was the general organizer and a man named José González was the hands-on coordinator.

All this looked good for me and MIRA. But I think it's also true that as I got my committee going, the mayor got moving on his bigger committee, with Helen Valdez on an equal footing or more with José González. And that can only mean that 1985 marks the relative decline of MIRA and the further development, entrenchment, and rise of the MFAC. But to

Fleming's Ensemble Español from Northeastern Illinois University, a group of Mexican folk dancers with a Mariachi band, a children's choir, gospel-music singers, ballet dancers, and of course George Solti's great symphony orchestra.

I felt that the price of tickets was too high, but Kathy and the woman from the symphony were tell that story fully, I have to set it in relation to the continuing development of local politics in the Harold Washington years and after.

LOCAL POLITICS, ARTISTS FOR HAROLD WASHINGTON, AND MIRA'S GROWING PROBLEMS

As strange as it seems, MIRA's decline and the rise of the Mexican Fine Arts Center really began during the Harold Washington administration, which I loved and supported. When I founded MARCH, I had felt that we were tied in spirit to the United Farm Workers movement. César Chávez was a big figure for me, and I did lots of work with the UFW in Indiana. But MIRA wasn't directly tied to the UFW or the national Chicano movement. First of all, it was a Latino as opposed to a Chicano organization. Second of all, as things got political in Chicago and the independent Latino movement began in the eighties, I felt close to that movement in the city, and that eventually brought me closer to the Latino/black coalition that formed in support of Harold Washington's campaign for mayor. But I was very careful to keep MIRA neutral, even as I worked for Harold Washington.

It's funny the way things turn out, but in the city, I became more political than Cortez or Cumpián—especially since Cumpián's spiritual father didn't believe in the possibility of any good coming from local politics. Cortez was interested in the international anarchist movement; while he seemed to like Harold, he wasn't deeply interested in the victory of any other local politician. But I was. So who was more political? They were more political in terms of political ideology, but I was more involved in *politics*—and especially the question of Latino empowerment.

I always had a good political relation with progressive causes in the Mexican community,

and I think MIRA was recognized as the artistic branch of community activism. I was always invited; I was always welcome. As time went on, I got involved with Juan Solíz and then Juan Velásquez in Pilsen, and then with Rudy Lozano in Little Village, until he was assassinated for reasons that were never made clear but were probably tied to his fight against corruption in the community. After Rudy's murder, I went with Chuy García, who picked up the baton. When Chuy ran, I went to some of the meetings too, and I was even a poll watcher for him and other Latino candidates. I also did a mixed-media portrait of Lozano that's become sort of an icon in the Chicago Mexican community, signifying committed militancy (fig. 92).

At the same time, I didn't wish to compromise MIRA's agenda for any political campaign or issue. There were members and friends of MIRA supporting various political positions, agendas, and candidates. So I decided that MIRA shouldn't get involved in those political things. I felt that it should remain very much in the world of the arts, and I decided that I was going to keep MIRA out of this.

But José González was another story; and as Harold ran for his first and then his second term, I helped form a separate organization which wasn't MIRA but which was the Artists for Harold Washington (AHW), a group trying to widen Harold's support base among the cultural sectors that had been so dependent on machine politics for support. The AHW had three cochairs—one white, one black, and one Latino, with me serving as the Latino cochair. In the second election campaign, I played a pretty big role, especially at a fund-raiser at the Moming Dance center, another one at the old Cross Currents Caberet off of Belmont, and then a major fund-raiser at Second City with the African American comedian and commentator Aaron Freeman and the Puerto Rican cultural promoter Billy Zayas, but

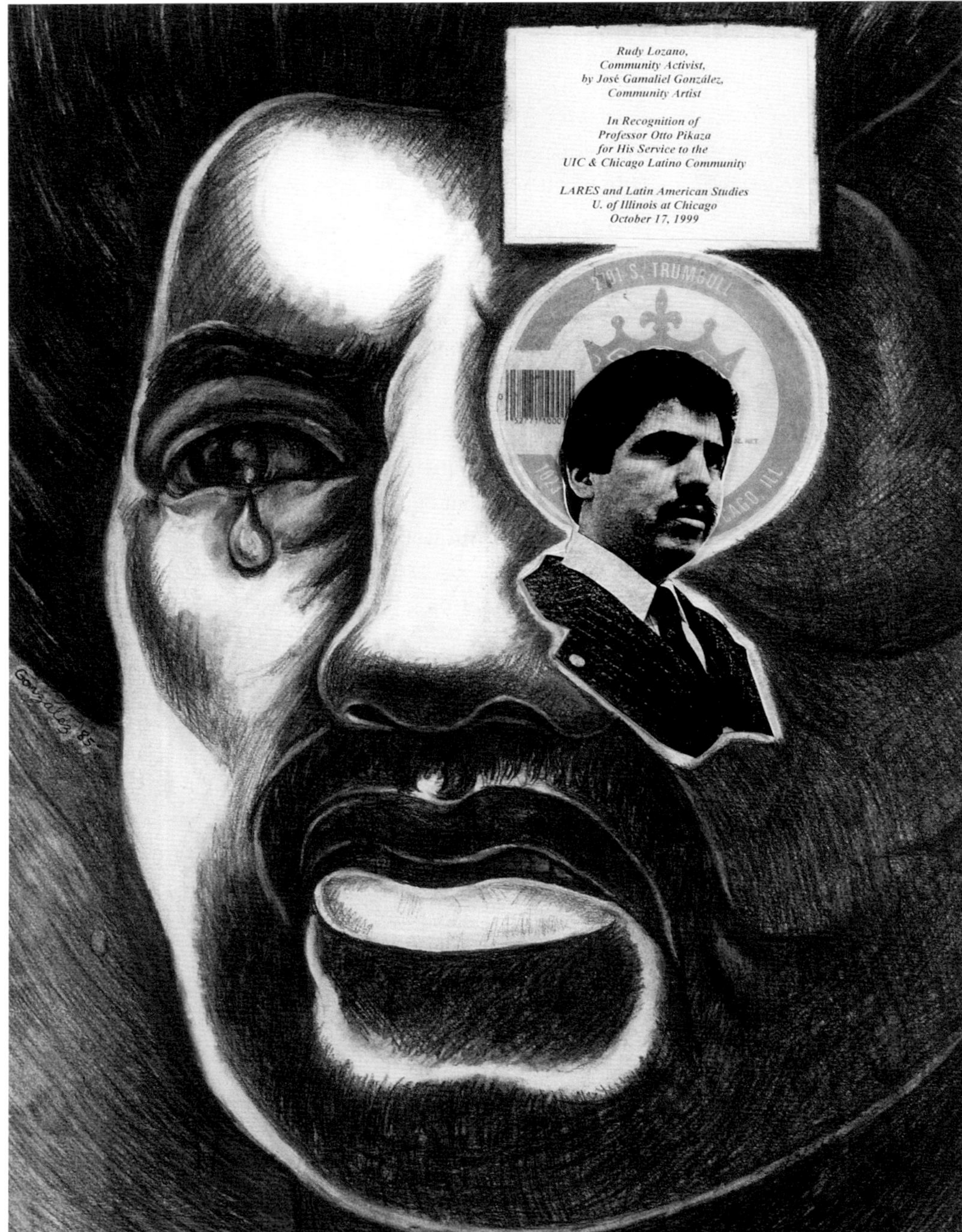

Fig. 92. José Gamaliel González, "Rudy Lozano, Community Activist," collage, 1985. José's collage features his painting and super-imposed photo of Lozano, a community leader murdered on the eve of Harold Washington's first mayoral victory in 1983. The dedication was drafted by Mary Kay Vaughan to honor Otto Pikaza, the longtime chair of the Latin American Studies Program (now Latin American and Latino Studies Program) of the University of Illinois at Chicago. The composite work is always on display at the office of the UIC's Latino American Recruitment and Educational Services at the Student Support Building at Harrison and Racine Streets.

also people like Studs Terkel and lots of other Chicago countercultural stars. And I think we helped Harold get reelected.

But as the Harold Washington Coalition began forming and reforming, MIRA was trying to develop, trying to find the means for a gallery space of some kind; and Harold Washington, toward the end of his first term and the beginning of the second, was getting more pressure to fulfill his promises to the Latinos—to do things for them. The Latinos were supporting him, but they were saying that he was not doing enough for the community. He had formed MACLA with my friend Marta Ayala as a key assistant to

Nena Torres, the director. And by this time, of course, Juana Guzmán, who'd taken over my job at the Chicago Council of Fine Arts, remained there when it became the Department of Cultural Affairs. Harold later appointed me to sit on the board. And that was important, because even though I tried to keep MIRA free from local politics, it was known for super-activism, and I think some people suggested that we were too militant and dangerous. And that was already seen as part of the political element in the community—and I'm having trouble; I'm not well. And all that created the opening by which a new group of people start meeting to form a group called the Mexican Fine Arts Center.

So here's an idea I've often thought about: I kept MIRA out of it, but if I had involved MIRA politically, maybe the MFAC wouldn't have been able to become so dominant. If, instead of it being José González the individual who worked with the artists, I had committed MIRA so that MIRA would have been defined as the Latino arts organization working with Harold Washington, maybe MIRA would have survived. Maybe I would have been able to block the MFAC just a bit so it couldn't lord over everyone else—so it would have had to share funding and credit. I always felt that the other organization was able to get support because Harold wanted to reach out beyond his base to a broader constituency. So of course, he helped out some of those in or close to his organization, but then, in an effort to extend his base, he helped out the people who had no visual connection with him, people who probably didn't support him but who could be wooed in his direction.

My guess is that the MFAC people were mainly for Daley. Some of them didn't vote because they lived in the suburbs, like Carlos Tortolero, who I think lived in Berwyn then as he does now. So he couldn't vote for Harold, but I don't think he supported Harold anyway. And I think what Harold did in his last years was reach out to those people who didn't support him in an effort to grow. That was probably good politics, but it meant that some of the people who worked the hardest for him were kind of left behind. I never worked for Harold in the hopes of getting personal favors or even support for MIRA, but I guess I couldn't help but feel kind of hurt as I saw his people give support to an organization that seemed to go out of its way to disrespect me. I was doing all the work people do to get money—to say, "Now that I helped get Harold elected, give me my patronage." And instead, the funds for the arts in the Mexican community—the money for everything artistic and Mexican—were flowing to the MFAC. And, of course, the support base and trend Harold's people established only extended itself as the new Daley era began.

I was recognized and honored by Washington and his administration (fig. 93). But at the same time, my situation began to decline. It's true, I was considered maybe not a troublemaker but a kind of provocateur, I think. I was also paying a large price for all the attention I had received and the waves I'd created over Raíces, the Chicago Council on Fine Arts, the Chicago Earthquake Coalition, and the Hiram Walker ¡Mira! show. And every time I got into a conflict with the MFAC it got worse, affecting my art, my productivity, my energy level, my mental health.

By 1985 I was already pretty sick, having blackouts, and some say I was maybe seeing things—having bad moments; and it got worse over time, affecting everything I did. I was sitting on so many boards at the same time, so that was depleting my energy. And I was also having bouts of illness so strong that some said I was maybe having breakdowns. So in spite of all the things I did in and outside of MIRA, we could

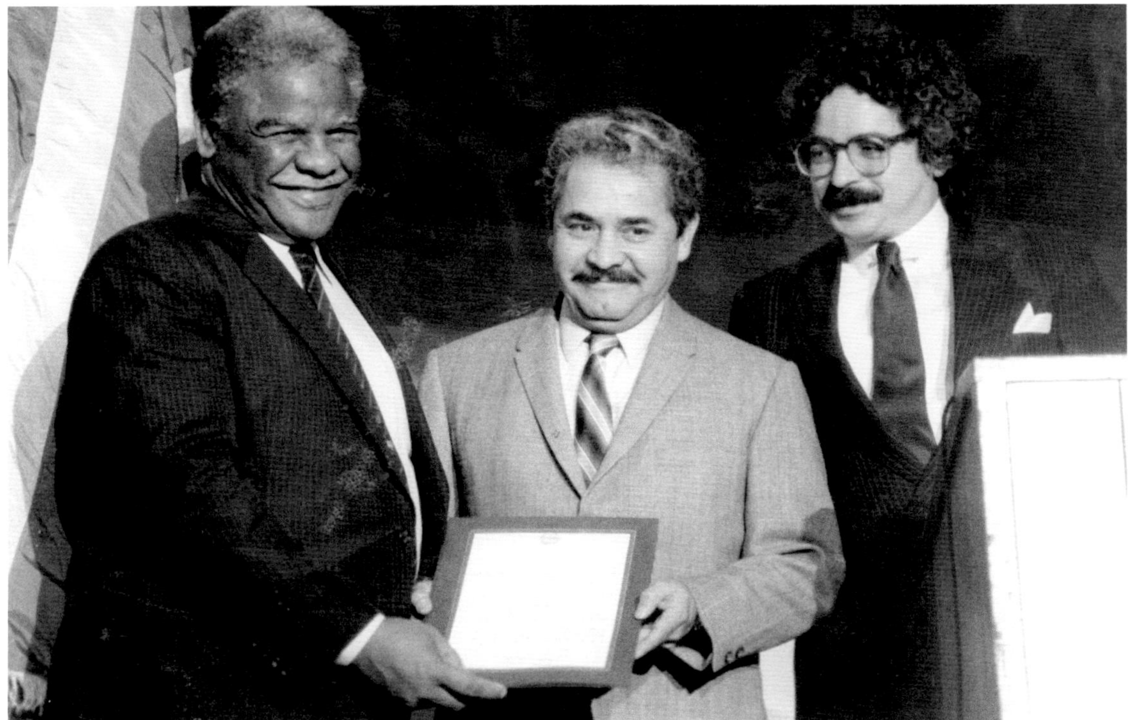

not compete with the rising star in the Mexican community that began to put down MIRA and other Mexican and Chicano projects in favor of their own.

THE RISE OF THE MFAC

The rise of the Mexican Fine Arts Center is the story I have to tell now, and it's not easy for me, because it's tied to the story of MIRA as well as the local political struggles of the period I've just mentioned.

When Harold Washington came into office and established the Department of Cultural Affairs with Madeline Rabbe as chair, Juana Guzmán retained the position she had held in the now defunct Council of Fine Arts. Although she might claim that she wasn't part of the struggle between me and the MFAC, she soon joined their Sor Juana Board developing programming on Mexican women, so I had no doubt about who she was going to favor.

Then there was another person who gradually supported the MFAC more than MIRA, and this is the cultural attaché of the Mexican consulate, Argentina Terán de Erdman, a very sophisticated and charming woman who was the ex-wife of Lorenzo Meyer, the famous Mexican journalist, and who seemed to know and escort every important Mexican cultural representative coming to Chicago.

At first, Argentina didn't favor the MFAC as opposed to me—she supported both of us and tried to help any and all organizations developing positive cultural projects in the Mexican community. But the fact is that the MFAC contacted her constantly asking for her help in everything. They knew how to talk to her, and they knew others who could also speak to her on their behalf. Then, too, as the MFAC got stronger and we got weaker, they were more organized and reliable; they knew how to move politically in the city; they were mainly school teachers with lots of ties in the Chicago donor community. Gradually, I think it just made her job that much easier to back MFAC projects and to channel financial and cultural resources from Mexico toward them, with her serving as a consultant and not having to develop things herself. Argentina knew that they were excluding other people in the community who had been working on arts questions for years. She also knew that the MFAC people knew little about art compared to us. They were part of this new wave—a Latino generation with degrees and special training who started belittling Latino grassroots leaders, saying they were no good, when in fact these people had been doing important work for years. But Argentina knew that they were very organized, persistent, and committed, and they were in fact delivering. If you gave them the resources, they were getting events together, they were getting the crowd together, they were learning how to do their business. Of course, one of the smartest things they ever did was to hire a trained artist and arts promoter, René Arceo, as their arts specialist and eventual curator. René made things work artistically and gave them some credibility where they were kind of lost without him.

And all this came at a time when the Mexican consulate was under orders to do more in and for the Chicago Mexican community; and it seems to me that it became easy for Argentina and the consul to see the MFAC more and more as the conduit for the goodies they could give towards the arts.

This is when the group began to get funding from the Chicago Department of Cultural Affairs, because Juana Guzmán was working there. So the group had Juana, they had Argentina, and over time they had access to almost all local dollars designated for the Mexican community, if not the entire Latino community. Elihud Hernández of the Illinois Arts Council helped them, and they began to build stronger connections with Chicago foundations and corporate sectors, as well as with the NEA, Rockefeller Foundation, and other national funding sources. Some of the funds they received were necessary matches for the resources coming from Mexico, but other grants made it possible for them to initiate projects in Mexico. Much of this story took place in the 1990s, but it had already begun in the mid to late 1980s, as Harold was reelected and then died suddenly.

The group was a good fit for the Daley clan, and the MFAC really took off in the early Daley years. So where they only had a post-office box when they started, under Daley, with Lois Wiseburg as the executive director in the arts, the group made contact with a park-district worker who got them the boathouse in Harrison Park, in the heart of Pilsen, for a dollar a year. And that gave the MFAC what MIRA never was able to get: a space to develop. They had a center now where they could operate and grow. Over time they ceased to be just a "center" and became the Mexican Fine Arts Center Museum (MFACM). There would be even a further name change down the road.

I supported the center and praised the staff's achievements even when I criticized the lack of grassroots participation; I became a member—even when they gave me and a lot of the local Mexican artists a rough time, and then gradually integrated one or another for a time at least, leaving me out at every turn. And, of course, there are many initial supporters who never came back to them and who said they would never step into the museum again. A key supporter was Bill Goldman, an expert on Mexican handicraft, who built up a wonderful handicraft shop for them, only to lose his job when they'd learned almost all he had to teach them—even though he came to several Día de los Muertos exhibits, he never entered the store again. Another offended party was Helen Valdez, the cofounder, who resigned and quickly began to fade in the museum's memory. And then there was Rene Arceo, who also left, but I don't know under what circumstances.

I do know that he did a fine essay on Carlos Cortez's artwork, based in part on a great interview he did with Cortez's wife Mariana, but Victor Sorell couldn't include it in the book he edited for the MFACM on Cortez (2002)—even though he cited it time and again.

Of course, over time there were even more people who swore by the MFACM and felt that they were doing something good by supporting them. And the MFACM did much. I'm probably a pretty good judge when I say that I think they did remarkable and praiseworthy things, including many things I'd dreamed of doing. But I can't help seeing a story we all know: how a group comes in and takes over a given place. They step on a bunch of people's toes, and a lot of people get hurt in the process, but they make the place really nice, so that even some of the injured parties have to admit that the place is pretty good—even though sometimes you can still feel the wounds.

WHAT'S IN A NAME? THE STRUGGLE FOR ZAPATA PARK

From 1987 to 1989, one of the important series of MIRA events had to do with our leading a movement to change the name of Harrison Park to Zapata Park. During those years, we collected signatures to support this movement, and we collected many more signatures at the annual Fiesta del Sol in the summer. In 1989, sensing we might win the battle, I designed t-shirts of Zapata and also a button.

The idea of changing Harrison to Zapata began many years earlier, when Elgin Watches brought out a new ad in the *Chicago Tribune* stating that its new watch was one that Zapata "would kill for." A huge group gathered at Harrison Park to protest, and they marched all the way to the *Tribune* towers on North Michigan. Some of the demonstrators went to jail when

it got out of hand. So the residents of Pilsen began calling the park Zapata, but it had never become official. Some years later, other activists began their own campaign to rename the park. Unfortunately, the movement died down, and so the park was never renamed.

Zapata has always been a hero to me when I discovered Mexico again in 1966 during my time in San Miguel de Allende. Then, of course, when we brought the Agustín Víctor Casasola exhibit that showed the Mexican Revolution with Zapata and Villa, Zapata became an idol of mine. I identified so much with his struggle for land and liberty. So I guess it's not surprising that in the midst of my struggle with the MFACM, I took up the Harrison Park Zapata movement. MIRA began the campaign with articles in the *West Side Times* and with the backing from Antonio Zavala, who was a reporter for the newspaper. Later, a t-shirt design of Zapata, calling him a "bandito," was being sold at a large store in Little Village. I organized a picket line and talked to the manager of the store to take the t-shirt off the shelves. Antonio covered the event and was there to report in the *West Side Times* with a photograph of the picket line and of the manager. Another community paper that wrote in Spanish did a large article for the front page. The store was a Zayre's, and we finally succeeded in making them remove the t-shirt from their chain.

In the summer of 1989 at the annual Fiesta del Sol, which was always held in late July with about a million people attending, we were still collecting signatures and selling t-shirts and buttons. Then we were informed by some of the people there that we had won and could stop the campaign. But I still continued to collect signatures.

Finally, about a week later, I was informed that we had won a partial victory—a kind of consolation prize. It turned out that the city had a policy making it almost impossible to change a park's name. But the new recreation center they were planning to build was going to be named the Zapata Cultural and Recreational Center. They called me up to invite me to the opening of the center and to unveil a sculpture bust of Zapata done by an artist from the state of Morelos, which was the home state of Zapata (see figs. 94 and 95). We had the unveiling of the bust on a Sunday with a number of people that attended the ceremony with the Mexican consulate and Ambrosio Medrano, the Twenty-fifth Ward alderman present with me for the event. But in the meantime, another building had opened in Harrison or Zapata Park that was going to have a much bigger effect on my mind and soul and on the future of Mexican art in Chicago.

THE CARA SHOW AND THE DECLINE OF MIRA

The year 1987 was also when the MFAC opened its doors as a building after developing their organization from the mid-1980s on. In this same year, MIRA sponsored three field trips, including one to the Detroit Art Institute to see Diego Rivera's murals paying tribute to the Ford Company technology and workers, plus two other trips to Mexico, one involving ten couples visiting Mexico City, the pyramids, and Oaxaca, and the other involving another ten couples in a trip to Chiapas and Yucatan, including San Cristóbal, Mérida, and the ruins in Yucatan. We also had big auctions at the Décima Musa and the Prospectus Gallery, selling off lots of paintings and drawings that were donated to us. We had good crowds for the auctions, but we didn't make as much as we'd hoped. And the fact that we had to have the auctions is an indication that we were losing our funding base. Of course, these shifting fortunes came about gradually and involved many of the things I've already described, but maybe they can be seen as coming to a head in the period from 1985 to 1988, during the last Harold Washington years, in the struggle over still another arts event, the CARA show. If there was ever a war between José Gonzalez and MIRA on one side and Carlos Tortolero and the MFACM on the other, the battlefield for that war became the CARA show.

CARA stood for Chicano Art, Resistance, and Affirmation. It was one of the most ambitious exhibitions of Chicano art to have been presented up to that time. I think that the general idea for the exhibit came from Shifra Goldman, an art historian from Los Angeles. Shifra had a long history of writing about Chicano art, but she was in bad trouble with the California Chicano artists because of her know-it-all attitude. She was smart to take the idea to UCLA's Wright Art Gallery, but the name of CARA didn't come from her; it came from a well-organized national committee that included some of the key people who had been part of the national Hispanic Task Force on the Arts, including Jacinto Quirarte, Tomás Ybarra-Frausto, and Amalia Mesa Baines, with some very famous people as honorary members, like Edward James Olmos and César Chávez. Ybarro-Frausto was an early member but resigned when he was offered a big position at the Rockefeller Foundation in New York. Most of the artists were from California, like Judy Baca, Carmen Lomas Garza, José Montoya with his *pachuco* drawings, John Valdez, and many others. Texas was well represented with many painters and the sculptor Luis Jiménez, along with folk artists from New Mexico. Victor Sorell and I had established national credibility and recognition, so we were the ones called upon to represent the Midwest on the planning committee and, if possible, to bring the show to Chicago's Field Museum.

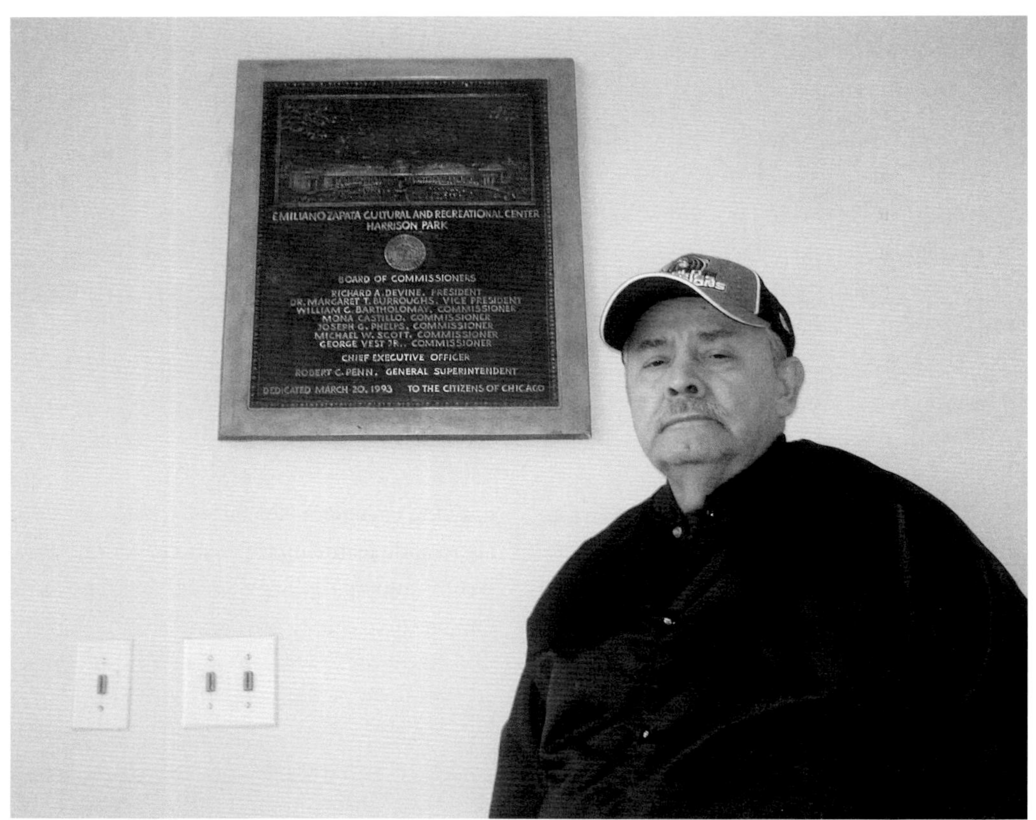

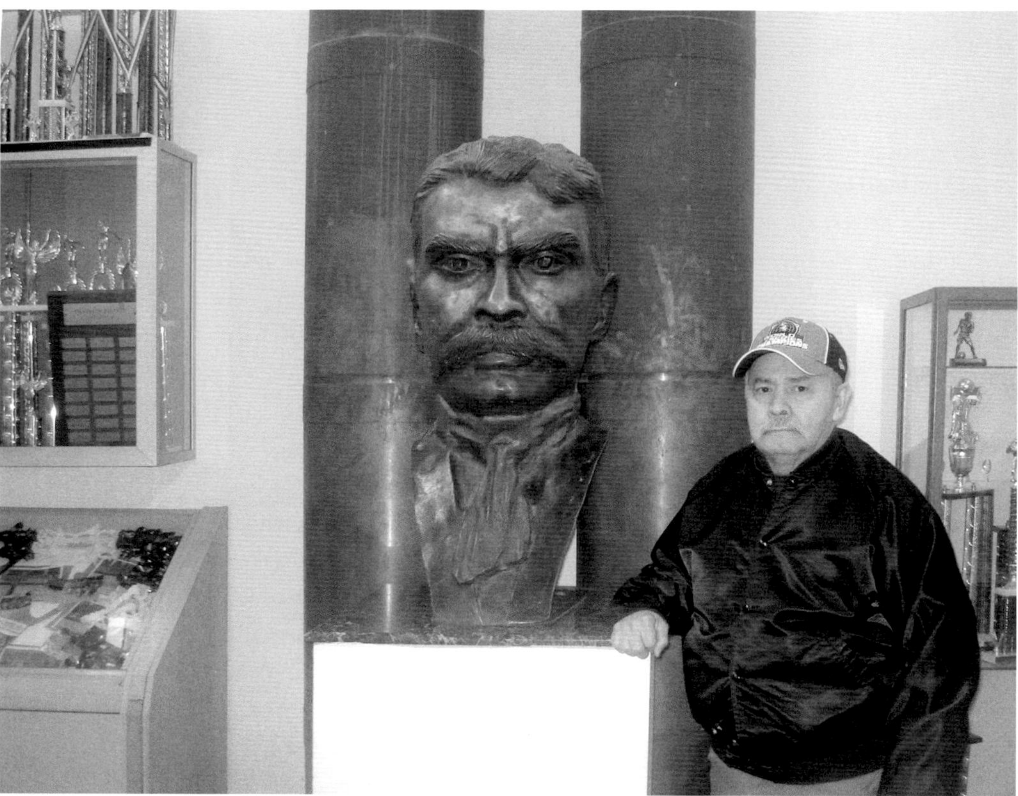

Fig. 94. José with plaque dedicating the center under Zapata's name. Photo: Marc Zimmerman, March 2007.

Fig. 95. José between the trophy case and Zapata bust in the Zapata Cultural Center. Photo: Marc Zimmerman, March 2007

I know a lot of people might have assumed that just because the CARA organizers turned to us, they had designated MIRA as the prime organizers. But the fact is that we were asked as individuals and not as members of MIRA—which isn't to say that *Mirarte* didn't cover the CARA story (see fig. 96). But the Chicago CARA show was not supposed to be a MIRA activity or the activity of any Chicago organization; it was supposed to be a joint enterprise involving many members of the city's Mexican arts community.

On the other hand, the MFACM wanted to be included directly on the national planning committee and be a part of the organizing. As always, they claimed their expertise, and Tortolero wrote a letter to the committee chair recommending Helen Valdez. But the MFACM had never before recognized the Chicano name and had never put on a Chicano exhibit at their locale, and this might have played into the decision of CARA planners to turn to Victor and me and to exclude the MFACM people from the national committee. Sure enough, as soon as we were named and they weren't added, that became the turning point for the MFACM in claiming Mexican American as well as Mexican turf. Not Chicano turf—they still didn't like the word "Chicano." Carlos didn't know much about Mexican or Chicano art, and he didn't know the artists either. But he did know how to get things done. I was told by a Latino community artist that he said negative things about CARA to the museum, letting on that it wasn't a worthy exhibit. I don't know if he talked to Sandy Boyd, who was then president of the Field Museum, or to Michael Spock, Dr. Benjamin Spock's son, who was the museum's vice president in charge of special events. But I do know that CARA plans couldn't seem to get off the ground in Chicago.

It took a couple of years to put the national CARA show together because we wanted to include the best Chicano artists and have it tour the country, Mexico, and the 1992 World's Fair in Sevilla. In the meantime, we tried time and again to involve the community and raise the first ten thousand of the fifty thousand dollars needed to guarantee the Chicago showing. We also went about getting our local contribution to the artwork ready. I brought my 1974 ink drawing of Zapata (see fig. 51 in chapter 3) and also a slide featuring the first panel of the Raza de Oro murals I'd done on Hubbard Street. The exhibit had three installations by different Chicano arts groups, Sacramento's Royal Chicano Air Force, Los Cuatro, and Asco.[2] They added a mural section to the exhibit that was shown by a projector built behind the wall. CARA also involved the making of silk-screen posters designed to promote the exhibition, and Mario Castillo produced one of the silk screens.

Then there was the catalog—a large one with color and black-and-white photos. All the work was reproduced in the catalog, and my mural was featured on a full page. Victor was chosen as cochair for the catalog along with Tomás, until he stepped down, and Alicia González, who worked at the Smithsonian Institute. Essays for the catalog were by Jacinto Quirarte, Amelia Mesa Baines, Victor, Tomás, and others.

The head of the Wright Art Gallery came along with two other people who worked with her to meet with Carlos Cortez, Marcos Raya, and Alex Galindo, who were chosen along with me to be in the exhibit. Since the MFACM was so close to Marcos's house, I recommended that we visit the museum because we still didn't have a Chicago venue. Victor was also with us, and he went with us to the museum. Tortolero was kind of cold to Victor, and Victor resented that for a long time. We saw the facility and

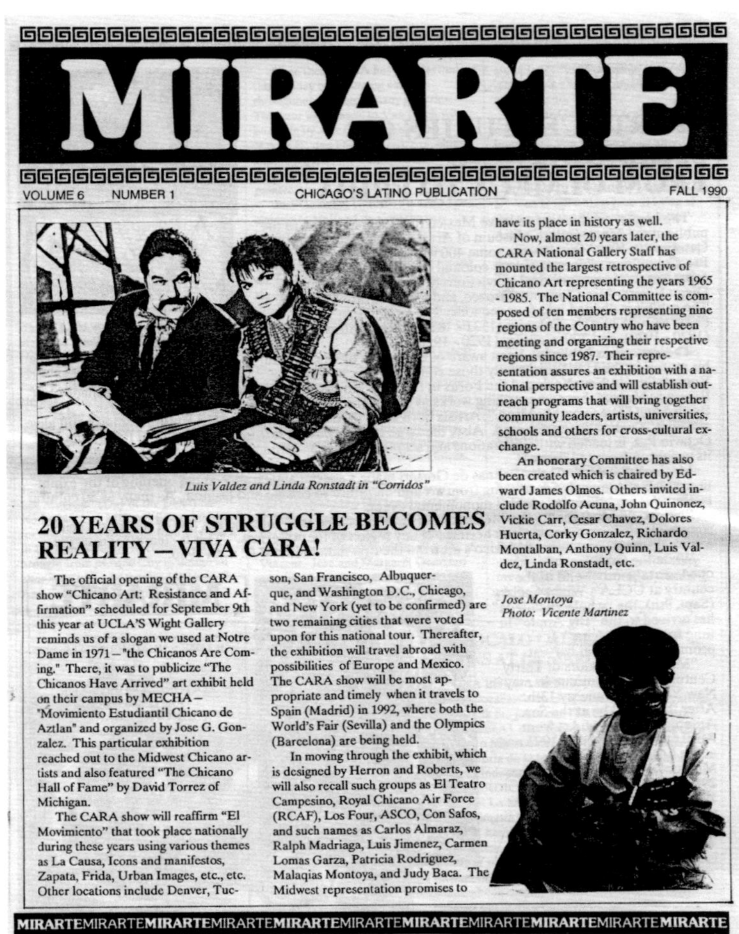

stayed only a short time. This was before they expanded the museum, and it was clear that the space available just wasn't big enough for the CARA show. So the museum wasn't included for the tour.

That's when Carlos Tortolero really got upset and did just what he had said he would do. I don't know all the details about how he did it, but he stopped the show, pushed Victor and me off the map. And the Field Museum, faced with such Mexican-community conflict, just decided that it was wise to bail out and cancel the show.

The CARA exhibit traveled to about eight museums throughout the country, but we weren't able to get a venue in Mexico City in the end, and Sevilla turned it down to do something else. As you may guess, it never came to the Field Museum, which had shown such an early interest. And some people even blamed MIRA, saying that we had failed to include or cooperate with the MFACM.

This CARA mess spelled the beginning of the end for MIRA. We had started with a lot of problems, and we weren't able to advance as far as we wanted to go in developing a program or establishing a space. In the meantime, another organization grew up and established a space at least partially on the basis of being very Mexican as opposed to Chicano. Then once they established their space and began to get more and more support from funding sources, it became clear that entering on Chicano turf would enable them to get even more. And the way they did this was to discredit me, MIRA, and our national and local connections, block the Field Museum's CARA show, and then mount their own rival show taking on dimensions, without using the word, of Chicano culture and art. And I'm not trying to knock them: they were changing things, they were doing things; they knew how to go after money, and they got it. All kinds of organizations funded the MFACM because eventually it became the only game in town.

Once the MFACM blocked the CARA show, they began to mount an alternative show called The Other Mexico, a smaller, rival event that could be handled in the MFACM space, and so they invited about one third of the original CARA artists and then invited Jacinto and Amalia themselves to do the catalog. The show was good enough, but nothing like the great CARA show. As it turned out, Jacinto didn't like what they were doing, so he dropped out of the catalog project, even though he left an essay that appeared in the published version.

Victor was very upset with the interference of the MFACM in the CARA show, but I think that in the long run he learned, "If you can't beat 'em, join 'em"—at least by the late 1990s, when he began editing the volume on Carlos Cortez for them (Sorell 2002). But as for me, the CARA show's failure was the turning point in which my health problems and my energies gave way and I was not able to overcome this attack made upon my efforts. I was deeply affected; and even though I tried once more to bring CARA in 1990 and would succeed with other significant exhibits in the years that followed, the CARA show was my last major effort and probably marked the beginning of the end of MIRA and in some ways José González as the center of Mexican and Chicano art in Chicago.

By the early 1990s, I was about ready to give up the MIRA ship, though not quite without some last efforts. I was depressed by my defeats and also about the members of MIRA because they were not putting in their time. Geno Muñoz as board president wasn't doing much of anything except coming to see me now and then to see what was up. So I had to be constantly after them to come together, and I was forced to do things on my own, and not in the name of MIRA. I still did an occasional show, but MIRA was suffering from my own personal problems.

In the meantime, the MFACM began doing some of the things that MARCH and MIRA had always done—which was to bring in at least some of the other local artists, but often with tension and resentments about the way they went about doing their things.

THE LAST DAYS OF MIRA

MIRA ended when I left my apartment at 1842 South Carpenter Street in 1995. But it had already faded when I moved to Carpenter from East Eighteenth Street in the late 1980s and stopped producing *Mirarte*. Over the years, I had taken on teaching duties at the Latino Youth Alternative High School program, and I had served as director of APO (la Asociación Pro-Derechos Obrero), working out of the APO office in the Smyrna Temple on Eighteenth Street and Bishop and even doing MIRA work out of there. But my health and funds were making it harder for me to continue with MIRA or anything.

I was still trying to set up another center. Even after the MFAC established its museum, I felt there was still room for another space. If the MFACM had already developed the Mexican dimension, which was part of MARCH and continued in MIRA, still I felt there was room for a second center that would feature the development of Chicago Chicano and Latino arts. I already had two potential sites in mind—the APO's Smyrna Temple site itself, and Thalia Hall on Eighteenth Street and Alport. APO's Smyrna Temple site was built by the Croatians in the 1890s to be a cultural center (fig. 97). Years later, when the coalition moved out to the suburbs, the building was used as a church until APO bought it for only thirty thousand dollars. Thalia Hall was built by the Bohemians for the World's Fair held in Chicago in 1891. The hall had several storefronts, apartments, and a movie theater. It was bought by Franciso Rodríguez's father, who later sold it to his son and daughter. In time Cisco became the sole owner and rented the storefronts to Mexican businessmen and the apartments to some undocumented residents. A large space on the first floor went to the Cuban boys who sold magazines and newspapers. Both buildings had their theater, but the one at Thalia Hall was in better condition, and it had the capacity to house an opera company. So Thalia Hall became the dream space for our museum (fig. 98).

I got to know Cisco through Serafín Trejo, who had gone to school with him. Cisco gave us free space if we were able to make the building feasible for remodeling and use as a great

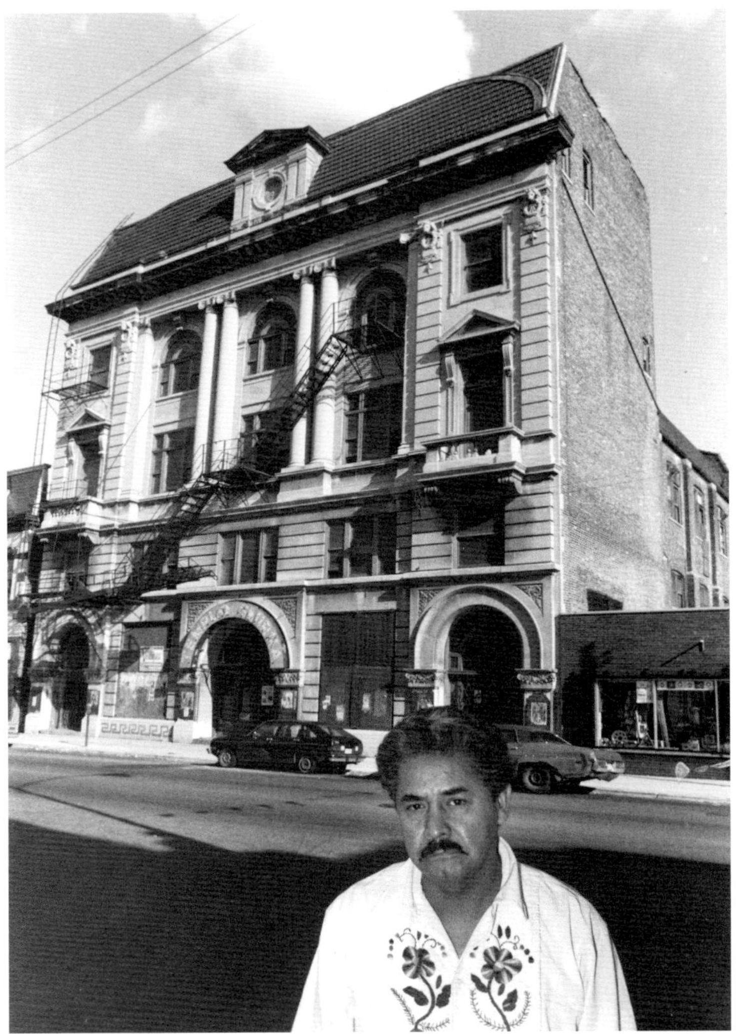

tectural group that did complete blue prints of the building. I also raised money to use a Mexican firm to do a feasibility study for the need to create a new cultural center for Pilsen. But we never received the larger grant that would have paid for remodeling and that would have made the whole effort possible.

The building was in bad shape and would take way over a million dollars to redo, even if we could get some startup money. It came to feel like too much. We struggled and struggled to make our dream a reality. But with the MFACM already in full swing and downgrading anything that they thought touched on their turf or funding possibilities (and it seemed just about everything did), we couldn't convince enough funders of the need for another center, even if my idea was a kind of not-for-profit space for contemporary local and national Latino and Chicano as opposed to Latin American or Mexican arts. It was also true that, starting with The Other Mexico, the MFACM outflanked any other group's efforts as they began expanding into at least dealing with local and national Chicano arts, which they'd avoided before. So finally, after a little more than a year, we had to face reality, move out, and let Cisco put the building for sale.

In 1990, Victor and I even made a further effort to bring the CARA show to Chicago. We had been working up a coalition of community organizations like Casa Aztlán and Mujeres Latinas to cosponsor the event, and now we'd arranged a meeting for these people to get together with representatives of potential funders and indeed with the Field Museum itself as represented by Michael Spock.

But I missed the meeting, because I had won a grant to go to Amsterdam and visit the spectacular one-hundredth anniversary Van Gogh retrospective held that year, all expenses paid, and with a special letter from Vincent Van

cultural center. I said I would try and then designed a brochure on the Thalia Hall project with beautiful photographs by Roberto Arredondo of me, the building, our past efforts, and future plans, including a fine photo of my work at the School of the Art Institute on the *Cycle of Man* drawing and sculpture project.

We held several exhibits there, starting with woodcuts from the Taller Popular de Grabado in Mexico City. Others were the Virgen de Guadalupe and the Richie Valens Día de los Muertos exhibits, which I've already discussed. One important thing that MIRA did was that we obtained a grant from the National Landmarks Preservation Council in D.C. to save the building from demolition. I hired a Mexican archi-

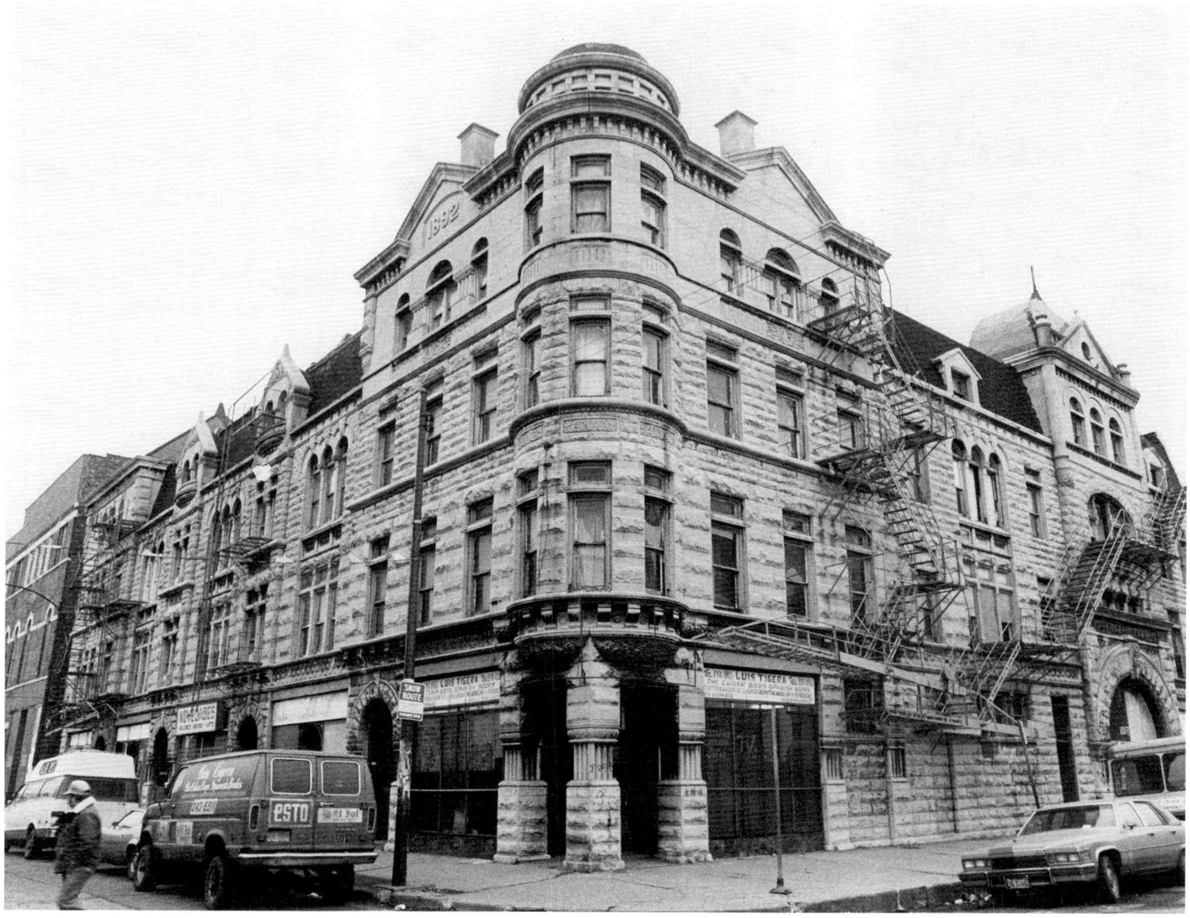

Gogh Jr., the painter's nephew, that permitted me to go to the two major shows for free.

I guess I should have been at that meeting, but I just couldn't resist going to the Amsterdam exhibit. My mistake was not telling Victor and other key players from MIRA and the Field Museum that I would be gone for at least a week, so maybe things wouldn't have fallen apart during the time I was out.

But for some reason, Michael Spock got very upset with one thing or another and even cussed at the group. Ana María Balmas from AT&T and Cynthia Rodríguez from Casa Atzlán were very insulted because he used a very bad word. So the meeting broke down, and that was it— that was the end of CARA in Chicago.

Who knows what might have happened if I had been at the meeting, or if I'd talked to Victor or the museum president Sandy Boyd or other museum officials who never even knew I'd been invited to the Van Gogh exhibits. I know this was a big error on my part. But the deck was already pretty much stacked against me in terms of the future of Mexican arts in the community. And maybe it was best that I went to Amsterdam, since the Van Gogh retrospective distracted me from the CARA show I had wanted so desperately but probably couldn't bring off. Besides, it was the fulfillment of my near lifetime love of the artist, and it led to a series of four Van Gogh Día de los Muertos shows at four different galleries—an event organized by MIRA presenting interpretations of his paintings by a wide variety of Chicago artists.

One show was by three Mexican painters (Héctor Duarte, José Guerrero, and a third

Fig. 98. Thalia Hall, the site of José's last dream for a major Chicano arts museum, 1990. Photo: Roberto Arredondo.

painter whose name escapes me) at Name Gallery; another was Jim Mesple's one-man ceramic sculpture show at Objects Gallery; still another was a show with thirty additional local artists, more women than men, at ARC Gallery. And there was also my own one-man show, Vincent and I, at Artemisia Gallery featuring my Van Gogh images (figs. 99–102) and my photos of Amsterdam. The Chicago Arts Coalition (of which I was cofounder but no longer an active member) voted our four-show Van Gogh project as the best exhibit of 1990.

Then came Cuba USA, a show Marc Zuver organized in Washington. Zuver asked me to coordinate community outreach for the Chicago presentation at the Museum of Contemporary Arts in 1991. This show featured some of the best Cuban American artists like Paul Sierra and Nereyda García from Chicago along with Ana Mendieta, a well-known New York–based installation artist who imposed self-images on sand surfaces. It looked like we were to have a big opening, but it poured that evening, and the opening ended early because it couldn't compete with the Baghdad fireworks for what was also the spectacular opening night of the first Gulf War.

It turned out that we'd lost our own war to maintain a place for MIRA's work on Mexican arts. By the late 1980s, and especially after our failure to bring the CARA show to Chicago, it was already clear to others that things Mexican and even "Mexican American" if not Chicano were most represented by the MFACM. MIRA had become a minor player, and in fact we were without funds. I was very sick off and on through the early 1990s, and I was central to MIRA. We just kind of faded away as the MFACM expanded and took up all the turf. They certainly had the connections and know-how to build the infrastructure they had to build. They were

maybe ruthless sometimes in their methods. But the fact is, the MFACM did excellent work, did many of the things we'd dreamed of doing, created and developed projects we'd wanted to develop. It was hard to accept it all because they did it over our own bodies, claiming as firsts things we'd thought of or actually done before, incorporating or integrating one art project or artist and another but never fully serving the local Mexican community as some of us felt they should.

Another thing that occurs to me as I think about the decline of MIRA was that while I was taken with the big Thalia Hall project, I could not realize or visualize that the space that I was living in until I moved in 1995 could have been a modest version of the gallery of which I had dreamed. Maybe it was because the place was so cluttered with my artwork and my MARCH and MIRA archives that I just couldn't see the possibility as I lived there. Maybe it was because I was so sick now, as MIRA faded away. And yet José David, a Chicago Honduran artist, would see that possibility some short time later and would make it into a reality for the Calles y Sueños art group (see fig. 2 in introduction). Of course, he didn't have the things I had in my place. He didn't have my history or past. He didn't have the furniture and all the books and archives that I had. He had a lot of empty space so he could make a gallery. I guess it may be interesting to think what might have happened if I'd had a place to store my things and used my home space as a gallery, but there's no sense in crying over spilt tequila.

I guess every *mexicano* dreams of a space all his or her own, but not all of us can see it or realize it. I guess I was one who couldn't. But those were rough times for me, and that may explain it all. Again, we're talking about a matter of establishing an arts infrastructure,

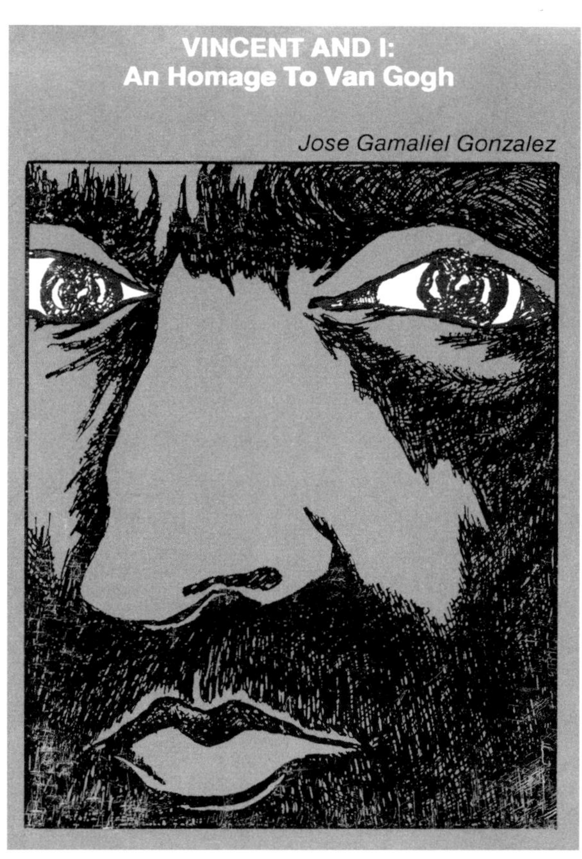

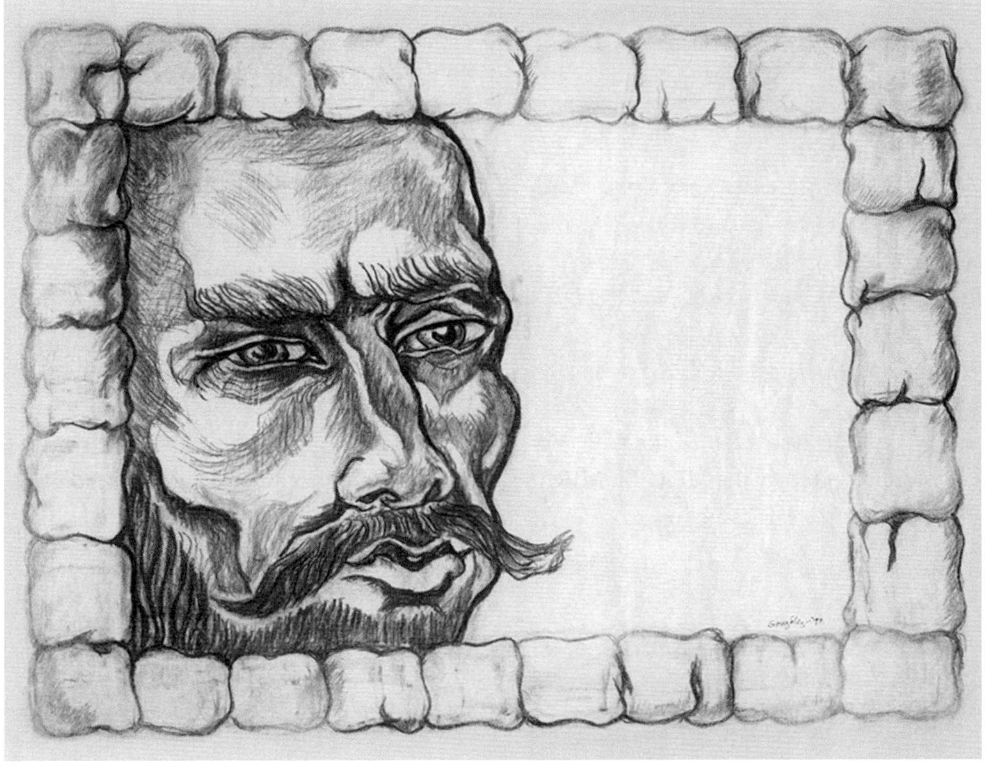

Fig. 99. José Gamaliel González, Vincent and I postcard (featuring his 1990 ink drawing).

Fig. 100. José Gamaliel González, Van Gogh framed in teeth, charcoal drawing for Vincent and I show, 1990.

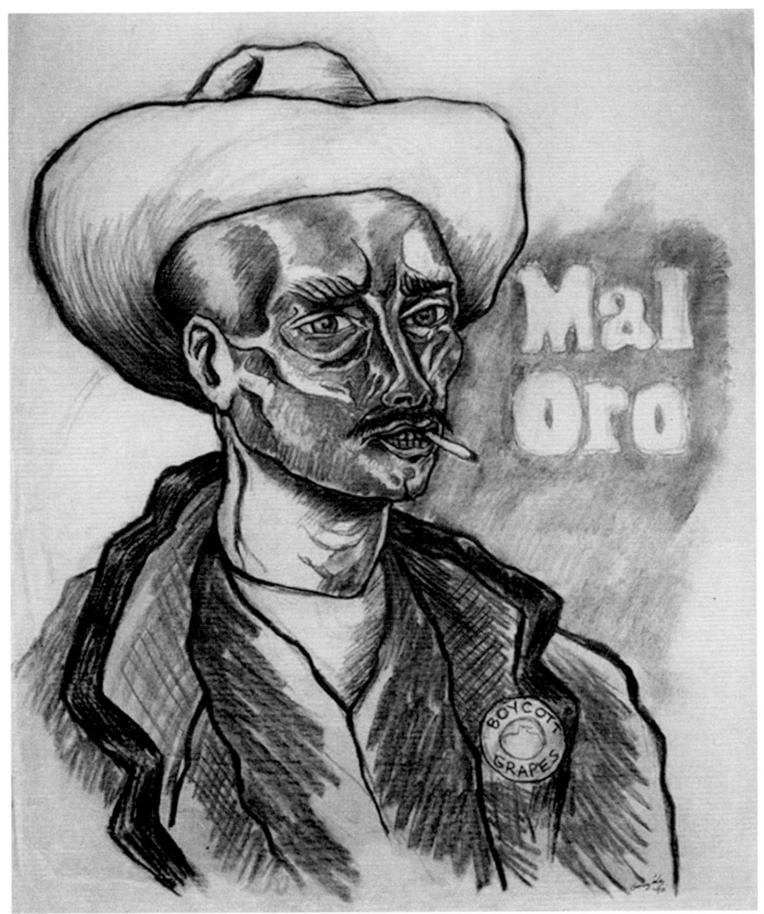

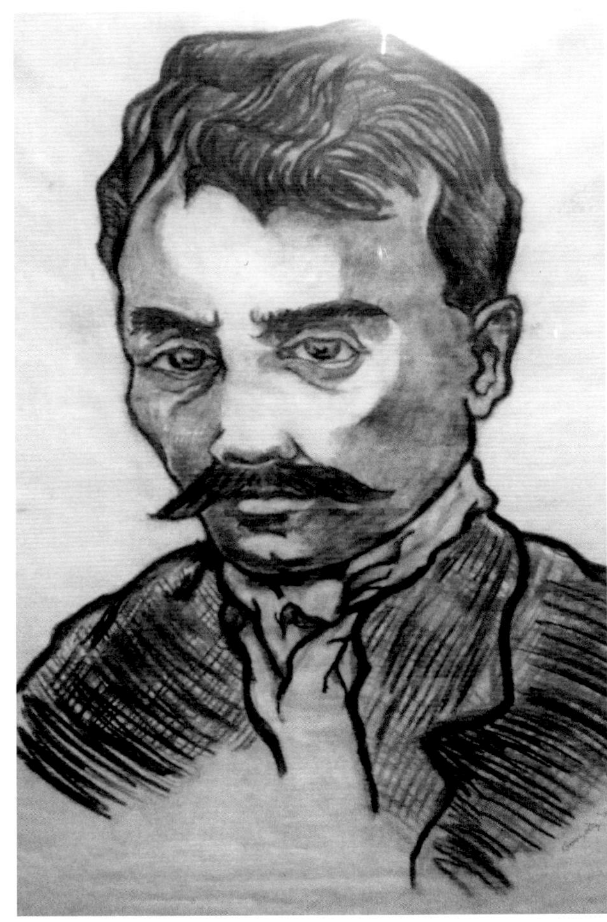

which has to be called a failed passion in my life. It is sort of like Moses taking his people out into the desert and into the Promised Land, but he doesn't go into the Promised Land himself. Maybe that is a key way to understanding the story of my life. Somehow the story of Aztlán became mixed up with Zapata's call for land and my own search for a creative space and my very soul. But it was not to be.

Fig.101. José Gamaliel González, Van Gogh as Chicano, for Vincent and I show, 1990.

Fig.102. José Gamaliel González, Zapata as Van Gogh, charcoal drawing, 1990. Photo: Alicía González (framed drawing in her Logan Square apartment).

5

Art, Work, and Health (1990–2007)

During the period of MIRA and for years afterward, my struggle was going to be like being thrown in hell. I was dealing with a series of attacks or breakdowns. I was in and out of hospitals, body- and mental-health facilities, and halfway homes. There were times when I had intense visions, when I walked the streets also unconscious without a coat on in thirty or even minus-thirty degrees. Sometimes I'd get all hyped up and then put on downers that led to depression, trembling hands, and even some states of sleep that bordered on unconsciousness. Then, even as I learned to keep my hallucinations under control, even as I learned to accommodate, I had to deal with what they later diagnosed as Parkinson's disease. All the while, I was dealing with diabetes and even a period of dialysis for kidney problems that came to sap and depress me and keep me from my work. Gradually my career as an artist and

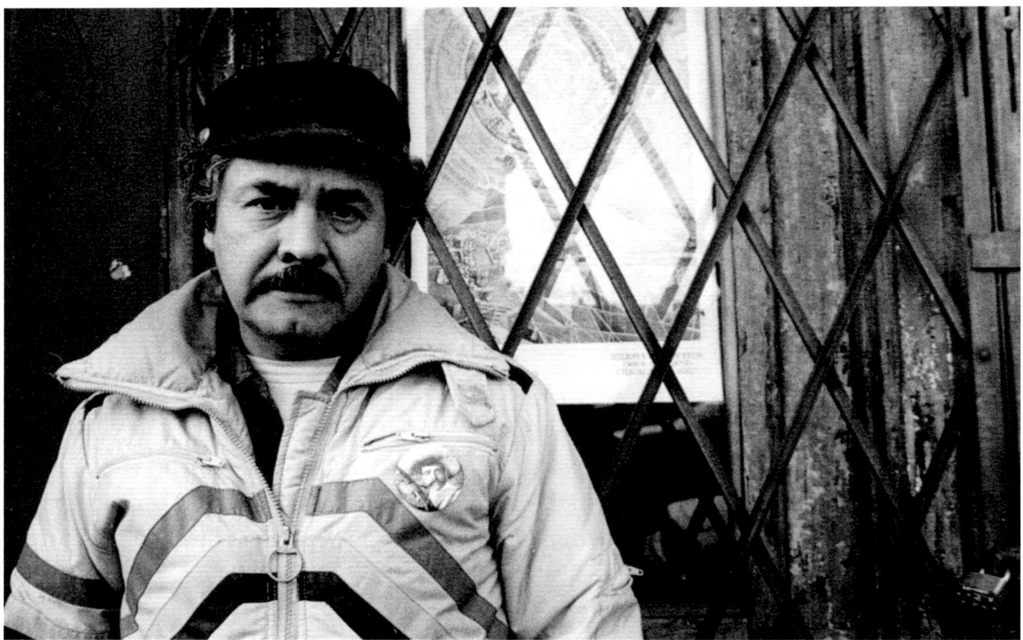

a promoter of events in the city really slowed down, and at the same time I was trying to deal with the MFACM, both supporting it but also criticizing it for the way it swallowed up the artists and the resources for Mexican and Chicano art in the city.

And there's no question that the MFACM did great things, building an infrastructure of activities and support that would keep it going for years to come. With René Arceo as curator, they developed an annual Day of the Dead show into the key one throughout the city involving visits by students throughout Chicago's neighborhoods and suburban areas. They developed a series of women's events under the name of Sor Juana Inés de la Cruz. They developed an annual Christmas sale. Like MARCH before it, they brought one major show after another from Mexico, becoming the main place where Mexican cultural figures would appear in Chicago, including Octavio Paz, Carlos Fuentes, Helena Poniatowska, Ofelia Medina, Amparo Ochoa, and countless others. They had any number of great exhibits—on ex-votos; on colonial art; on Mexican handicraft; on women artists like Frida Kahlo, Remedios Varo, and María Izquierdo. In

between all of this and much more, they weaved in some showings by U.S.-based and even local Mexican and Chicano artists. But the way it worked was that the MFACM encouraged or discouraged the local artists, praised or ridiculed them, sought to incorporate or neglect them as they saw fit, sometimes exhibiting and sometimes failing or even refusing to exhibit their work. One case I remember was their effort to convince the Taller de Grabados to become part of the museum. The Taller members voted against it—they didn't want to become like the student radio station the MFACM had taken over and controlled. That created some conflict for René Arceo, I think, because he was an artist with the Taller but an employee of the museum, and he didn't want to give up his job or the Taller.

At first, the local artists tried sticking with MIRA to see if we could get some new energies, but we just couldn't do it. Then they tried to get support from the MFACM, but they found only sporadic help when it was in the organization's interest to call on them for one show or another. Seeing that they had no place to go, some of the top veteran artists, like Mario Castillo, Alejandro Romero, and Marcos Raya, tried to go it alone, seeking alternative mainstream or offbeat forms of support. Several of the other artists, young and new, suffered from marginalization and began to develop or enter different organizations outside of the MFACM— what you might call guerrilla artist groups in some ways, following the model of MIRA, like the Taller del Grabado or its successor Mestizarte, Calles y Sueños, Polvo, and others as the 1990s came and went. Then there was a new group of Mexican and other young Latino writers who came forward in the 1990s as the literary journal *Fe de Erratas,* the newspapers *Zorros y Erizos* and *Tropel,* and now most recently as the cultural magazine *Revista Contratiempo,* which often features some of the local artists.

As time went by, new artists came from Mexico, and younger artists in the community came forward. Hector Duarte, a Siqueiros-trained muralist and excellent painter, came from Michoacán. Gerardo de la Barrera, a poetic landscape painter, and Filemón Santiago, a disciple of Rodolfo Morales's magical realism, came in from Oaxaca. Nicolás de Jesús, a master of *amaté* drawings, came in from Guerrero and joined Duarte, Carlos Cortez, René Arceo, and others in doing great work in the Taller de Grabado. Among the artists, veterans like the actress Susana Aguilar and the photographer Diana Solís and younger people like Miguel Cortés, Esperanza, Gama, Jesús Macarena, and many others began to exhibit paintings of quality. Later, Roberto Fereyra, along with Monserrat Alsina, a talented Venezuelan artist, opened up a gallery on Eighteenth Street west of Damen and close to the MFACM. Meanwhile, the artists supported themselves as they could, Raya making it into a major Chicago gallery, Duarte and others taking on new mural projects, and others coming and going from one part of the city to another, as they sought the broadest

possible exposure. Unable to find major venues, they turned to the Prospectus Gallery, the Rudy Lozano Library, Calles y Sueños at my old 1900 Carpenter apartment, and Polvo's gallery space, as well as at the Jumping Bean and other Pilsen coffee shops. Then, on the North Side, they could exhibit at Esther Soler's handicraft store and art gallery, Collage; a Mexican art furniture store; Casa Loca; Mi Casita Restaurant; and a small but active Mexican gallery, La Llorona, near Lincoln Park across from the Webster Cineplex. The artists could get some space in Pilsen's annual Fiesta del Sol or in John Podmajersky's annual East Pilsen art show. They could exhibit at Around the Coyote on the North Side or at the Pan-American Summer Festival, which moved from Olive Park near Navy Pier to South Grant Park. And of course there were other occasional gigs and places, including Aldo Castillo's gallery, where my Cuban friend Paul Sierra could show his work, or the Mexican Consulate's Mexican Institute space at 704 North Wells, in the gallery district. Collectors like Sandra Cisneros's brother Alfredo and Erasmo Salgado sometimes did shows, if only to highlight what they'd bought from different artists. But it was never easy for most of the artists, and many left the city after some years here, disillusioned and often poor.

As for my artwork, the one good thing that occurred for me in 1990 was the Vincent Van Gogh Day of the Dead exhibits, including my own show at Artimesia Gallery. I had been sick, but now I was back, at least for a time. I also played a minor role with Gamaliel Ramírez, Aurelio Díaz, Roberto Velásquez, and others on the mural project inside Benito Juárez High School. And there were other things I did.

But there's no question that my health really made it difficult for me to work as an artist. Rather, I showed my solidarity with different active groups. I was especially close to the initial Taller de Grabado and stayed close when the group changed its name to Mestizarte and moved from Halsted and Nineteenth to the old Smyrna Hall building, formerly the site of APO, on Eighteenth and Bishop. Once, a friend of mine, a nephew of Siqueiros, went to Mexico to see his aunt and brought back a large number of engravings from the Taller de Gráfica Popular in Mexico City, which he gave to me for MIRA. But MIRA was just about over, so I donated them all to Mestizarte. That's how I supported them. And I continued to work with them as best I could, even as I wrestled with my mental health and the pills I had to take, which kept me even, but made my hands shake and tremble so I could hardly sketch or draw.

In the meantime, I sought different jobs just to keep myself active and involved and to have enough to barely live on, even while I was in and out of hospitals and resident units. For a long time, I continued giving English and citizenship classes at Pilsen's Latino Youth Alternative School, where I also helped adult students get jobs. And I also gave art and art-appreciation classes for three years at the central campus, Humboldt Park, and Little Village branches of St. Augustine College. Then, in 1991, Louise Año Nuevo Kerr, a Mexican-Filipino woman who had written an important dissertation on Chicago Mexican history, had a key position at Loyola, and was now a UIC administrator, invited me to lunch and offered me the job as interim director of the Rafael Cintrón Ortiz Latino Student Cultural Center.

There's no doubt in my mind that I had been between somewhat and very sick for several years, and I think that had Louise worried, and that was why she wanted to check me out at lunch. She knew it was a tough job, because the last coordinator was a student, and the students might have had the idea of the center's always having one of their own as coordinator. But

Louise and I both knew that while the center was important to the students, it could also play a significant community role as it had done in the early 1980s, when MIRA worked with the center on given projects. She wanted to try to make something positive out of it. And so did I, with both of us hoping against hope that my health would hold out.

In my new position on campus, I developed many activities and even made that final try to bring the CARA show to Chicago. MIRA was still not quite completely dead, but it was dying. I was working full-time for the center, but I still had to complete my other teaching commitments. When I finally resigned from my Latino Youth job, my students took me out for dinner, and they bought me a radio—it was a beautiful gift. But the students at UIC were very difficult to work with—especially at first, because of the way I'd been appointed. I gradually won over many of them—especially when I did what turned out to be my next to last Día de los Muertos show in November of 1991, featuring a procession of Hernán Cortez's men coming through the city of Tenochtitlán to establish his power over the Mexican people (fig. 104). The last one would be La Risa y la Esperanza (The Laugh and the Hope) in 1993, in honor of the lives of Mario Moreno (Cantínflas) and César Chávez, both of whom had died the previous April (fig. 105).

AMERICAN ME, THE BENITO JUÁREZ MURALS, AND THE PEACE AND DIGNITY RUN

In the quincentenial year of 1992, Eddie Olmos released a film he had directed about the Chicano mafia, *American Me,* and he asked me once again to help him promote it. Eddie arranged for the preview to be shown for free at two Chicago locations. One showing was at the Ford City The-

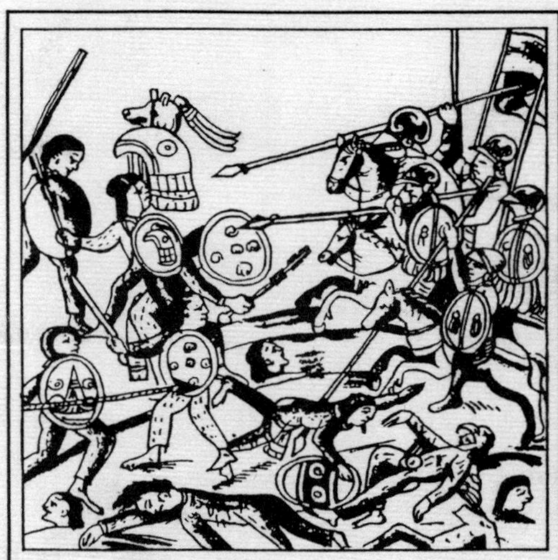

Rafael Cintron Ortiz
Cultural Center at UIC
and
Mi Raza Arts Consortium (MIRA)
invites you to the
Opening Reception
for the exhibition

**"470 YEARS AFTER
THE DEATH OF THE
MEXICA (AZTEC) EMPIRE"**

THURSDAY, NOVEMBER 7, 1991
5:00 to 8:00 pm

Exhibition Continues thru November 17, 1991

Rafael Cintron Ortiz Cultural Ctr.
University of IL at Chicago
Lecuture Center B-2
750 S. Halsted St.

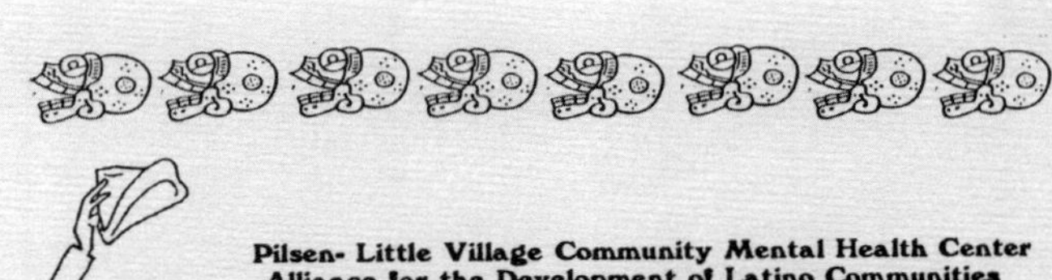

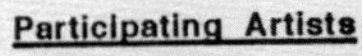
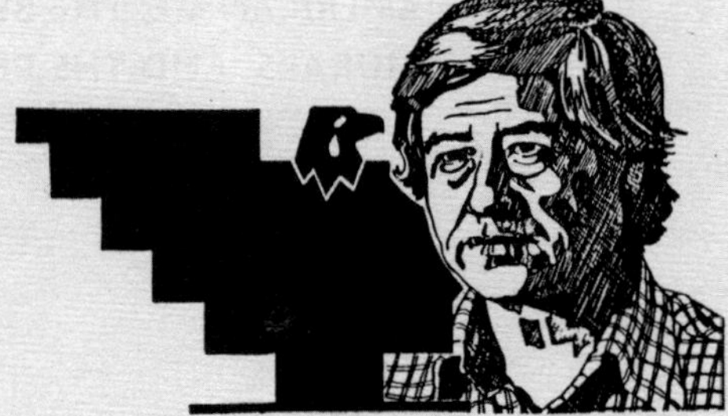
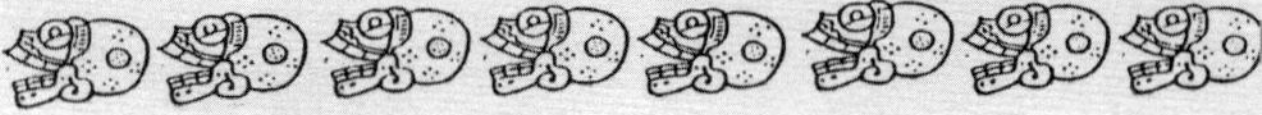

Fig. 104. José Gamaliel González, postcard, MIRA/Rafael Cintrón Ortiz Cultural Center, 1991.

Fig. 105. José Gamaliel González, flyer for La Risa y la Esperanza (The laugh and the hope), 1993.

ater, where we arranged to bring in large groups of young people who in fact turned out to be too young for such a violent and sexually explicit film. (The film includes a male/male rape scene in which Eddie kills the rapist with a knife.) The other screening was arranged for students from Columbia College at the Fine Arts Theater, a popular movie house on Michigan Avenue. And it seemed even too strong for many of the college students. In both cases, Eddie was there to answer questions from the audience, as he had done with *Gregorio Cortez.* There was a strong comment from a friend of his, Victor Villaseñor, the writer of the script for *Gregorio Cortez,* saying that he'd gotten so sick from watching the picture that he had to go the washroom to vomit. Eddie agreed that it was strong but said that the second time around it would be easier, like a roller-coaster ride. For me, the film was very depressing and fed my worst thoughts about what was happening to Mexicans in the United States. But I also thought it was a brave and necessary film with a story that had to be told, just as I feel that today I must tell mine.

On a visit to Chicago some years earlier, Eddie had given me a three-thousand-dollar award at a Little Village dinner for my work on *The Ballad,* but I asked him to rewrite the check in the name not of MIRA but of the Eighteenth Street Development Corporation (ESDC) because even before the early 1990s, MIRA was all but a thing of the past, and the ESDC was an organization with which I was becoming identified. Meanwhile, other things begun in the 1980s were coming to fruition in the new decade.

In spite of the mural-defacing scandal that haunted his name, Aurelio Díaz never gave up on the Benito Juárez High School mural or the Peace and Dignity Run. He was fortunate later to get the outside wall on the west side of the gym. He organized community people and students to do a very striking mural of Juárez; and he also included Juana Negrete in the project (they were married at the time). But he still wasn't finished. He met with the school principal to paint murals in the patio. This was now in the mid-1980s. But when he didn't succeed, he went to the Pilsen Neighbors Community Council and met with Mary González, who was one of the strong cofounders of the organization. He finally got her support, and they agreed to raise the money to pay the artists and to pay for the paint and other materials, like the scaffold that was needed.

Aurelio called a meeting, and we met at Casa Aztlán and worked on ideas using the concepts Siqueiros had developed in "How to Paint a Mural." Finally, we had Gamaliel Ramírez, a Chicago Rican artist; Antonio Dos Santos, a Brazilian artist; along with Aurelio, Roberto Valadez, and I, three *mexicanos,* working out the design for the first wall. Pilsen Neighbors decided that we would do one wall each year, at the time of Pilsen's Fiesta del Sol, held during the month of August. The theme that we used was the same one that Mario Castillo had designated years before: the four elements—fire, water, air, and earth. Ray Patlán was in town during the first mural, and so he also did some work. I only helped paint the first mural and worked with the design of the second one. The MFACM complained to Pilsen Neighbors that no women were involved. And this time they were right. So the last three murals did have a woman in the mural team. They are very impressive, and when I did mural tours of Pilsen I always included those walls.

Aurelio's other pet project, the Peace and Dignity Run, had to do with the completion of a fifty-two-year cycle on October 12, 1992, and the start of a new cycle on October 13, as recorded on the Sacred Stone Calendar of the Mexican people. The idea of the event was a run that would start from various points North, picking up people

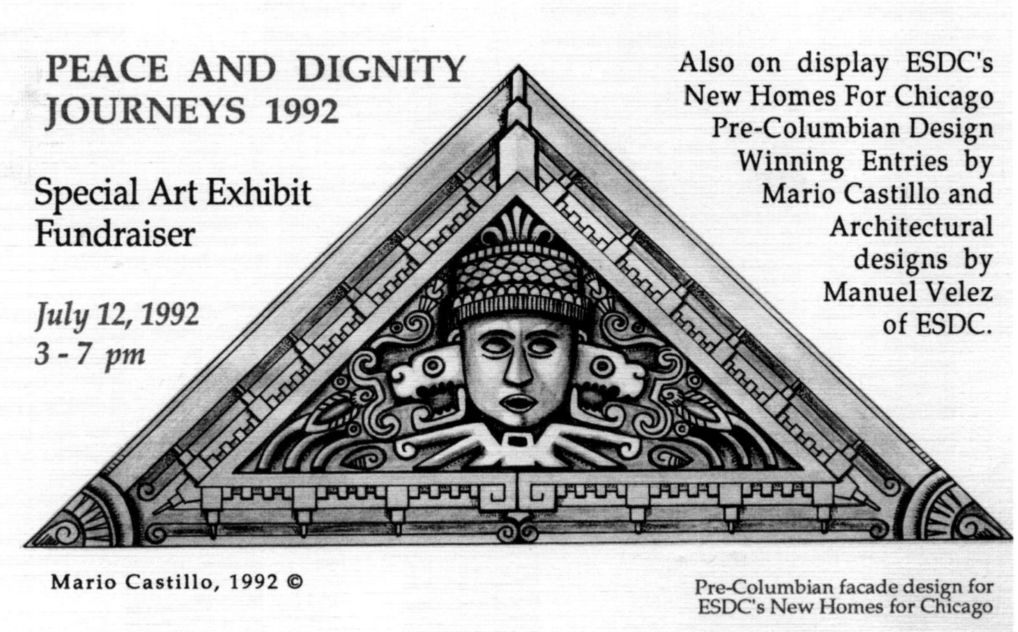

from the South, and end in Teotihuacán near Mexico City, while simultaneously there would be a run from Central and maybe South America to Teotihuacán, where symbolically the indigenous peoples of the Americas would declare their rights to peace and dignity (fig. 106).

Aurelio served on the central committee for the event and asked me and others to join a local committee that he founded with his friend, Alfonso. The run took a lot of intense organizing. So we met every week from late 1989 to October 1992, when the run took place. We also attended some regional meetings so that we could report on our progress and coordinate our efforts with other local committees.

Organized by two *güeros,* the run from the North went from Canada, Boston, and the Northwest, with runners from Texas and the Southwest joining in. We never were able to get runners from South America, but we did succeed in getting some from Central America, mainly through the efforts of Jesús González, who was responsible for Central American participation.

During these years, we'd sometimes have sweat baths held at the *güeros*' farm. I only went to a couple of them. I must confess that I couldn't take the heat as the others could. Also I didn't go to the peyote ceremonies that took place during these years.

For our local meetings, we met at Aurelio's house on the outskirts of Pilsen, and a round table was designed so that there was no head person, although really Aurelio was the one who headed the meeting. We had a computer that was donated to us to commemorate five hundred years since the arrival of Columbus. Jesús and others designed t-shirts and buttons to sell and to commemorate the run. Those meetings at Aurelio's were mainly held in Spanish because he and Alfonso spoke that language better. I had to interpret after the meetings to my old friend Ramón Cruz, who had a hard time understanding Spanish. Ramón was always late to the meetings, even though his house was only four blocks away. But he did his part by going to the Indian powwows, where we sold the buttons and t-shirts.

Ramón and I were among those who didn't run the long distance. We flew to Mexico City, and we were driven to a village outside Teoti-

Fig. 106. Postcard, Peace and Dignity Journeys, with image by Mario Castillo.

huacán. I was among those who ran with a small jeep that would stop and pick us up when we got tired. We arrived at another village outside the pyramid grounds, and by this time we had hundreds of people who gathered to walk the final miles to the pyramids. We formed a procession that took over an hour to get to the final ceremonial site.

There was another Indian group that met us there for the day and night ceremonies that took place. Tents were set up outside the grounds of the pyramid site, and they also built the sweat-bath tents. Ramón and I chose to go to a hotel instead of staying there on the grounds. One ceremony lasted a long time into the night, but we were able to get a ride from Alfonso, who had a small truck someone lent him.

We didn't stay a long time there—only a few days, during which I was able to contact some friends and see the large parades held in Mexico City for el Día de La Raza, October 12. Ramón was very disorganized, and I needed to translate for him on many occasions. When it was finally time to get our flight back to Chicago, he was lagging behind, and by a miracle we caught a taxi that got us to the airport on time.

Aurelio, Alfonso, and others remained a longer time to conduct more ceremonies and to meet the press. Aurelio is a Tarascan Indian, and both he and Alfonso, who's light-skinned, were using peyote in the ceremonies. So when they got caught, it was Alfonso who went to jail, while Aurelio and others tried to get him out. But the fact is, they failed, and Alfonso remained in jail for quite a while.

Aurelio was married to Juana Negrete, but he had two illegitimate children from two other Mexican women. When he came back from Mexico, he brought his girlfriend from Denver, divorced Juana, and married the girl-friend. Of course, Aurelio always had trouble in Chicago after he was accused of defacing the Benito Juárez mural. Soon after his divorce, he left Chicago for good. Later, his second wife died at an early age, and Aurelio, who had become an Aztec high priest, continued with his ceremonies. I heard later that after Alfonso got out of prison, he had married a *güera* and did ceremonies in Europe. Both of them are no longer in Chicago, but I heard that Aurelio came back once for a visit. But he never visited me.

ANTI-GENTRIFICATION EFFORTS, APO IN THE EARLY 1990S, AND THE FATE OF THALIA HALL

In the late 1980s, I had gotten involved in a conference on gentrification that I did with Professor Teresa Cordoba and other people at UIC. Now as the coordinator of UIC's Latino student center, I got even further involved with the question of gentrification in Pilsen—a matter partially related to my earlier efforts to save Thalia Hall from the developers and make it work for MIRA.

I formed a small ad-hoc committee to re-name Pilsen as Pilsen-Aztlán. We only did some work for about half a year. I designed a poster flyer called "Gentrification: The Human Earthquake." I got some support from the urban studies researcher Pat Wright of UIC and Antonio Zavala of the *West Side Times*. But the project folded up, and it wasn't until I joined the board of the ESDC and moved into their building at 1900 South Carpenter (see fig. 2 in introduction) that I could focus on gentrification issues. In about a half a year, I was voted president of the board, working with the executive director, who soon moved to Milwaukee and was replaced by Arturo Vásquez. I remained as president for three and a half years, and during this time we built thirteen brick homes in Pilsen. The first one was next to my building, and the other twelve were west of my building and took up a two-block area, with prices affordable to middle-income Mexicans.

We had problems with these homes because Arturo used non-union bricklayers who were trained at our organization. Former ESDC trainees organized picket lines against us. We supported Arturo, and things worked out so that the buildings were completed and rented out.

Arturo was a great director, and we did some good things with him. But the labor conflict hurt, and there was also the fact that he was against the Catholic church. We had joined a coalition that was headed by the Catholic churches in Pilsen called the Resurrection Project. One of the prime movers was Father Chuck Dam, and Arturo gave him a hard time. We eventually dropped out of the coalition because of Arturo, and they had to continue the work of building low-income housing without our organization.

Arturo finally retired, left Eighteenth Street, and bought a house in New Mexico. Very shortly after moving there, he died from a stroke.[1] As for me, I didn't die, but nothing I did seemed to go too far. It was a difficult time because of my deepening health problems, and I finally had an attack that led to the end of my job at UIC and really put me out of commission for quite a while.

What happened was that as MIRA faded and my last jobs ended, I was becoming disabled, and certainly less able to keep up with all the antigentrification and community-development projects I had been involved in. Not that I could have really succeeded in my efforts, because the Pilsen area was slated for big-scale development that would be almost impossible to stop.

John Podmajerski, the local land developer, owned most of East Pilsen, catering to the artists and becoming a millionaire with the many buildings he owned. Podmajerski made great inroads into gentrifying all of East Pilsen. He set up blocks of artist homes and studios, plus a large building space that he used as a gallery. Marcos Raya rented two spaces from John— one for his residence and one for his studio. He also began participating in the gallery for its fall open-house walk. In the meantime, Podmajerski and others were also working on Pilsen itself, and then UIC bought up and gentrified most of the land between the campus and the barrio, so that things were getting tighter and tighter.

APO's Smyrna Temple, my first choice for a museum, survived, as Taller Mestizarte took over the space. But as far as Thalia Hall was concerned, Alderman Danny Solís gave Cisco Rodríguez a hard time because he wanted to take the building from him. Cisco located some potential buyers, and finally he found one that came through. He sold the building for only over one million dollars to get Danny off his back, giving the new owners lots of time to pay off the whole amount. The new owners worked on the building, but their rental prices were too high. The storefronts that Cisco rented for one thousand dollars went up to four thousand dollars, and the apartments went even higher. I don't know if the theater has been worked on, but I believe it hasn't. It's my understanding that the building owners wanted to work with Prospectus Gallery in doing cultural events and exhibits, but someone recently told me they were in the process of making most of the apartments into condos. So much for my fight against the gentrification of Pilsen and my dreams of a Chicano Center.

ILLNESS, HOUSING MOVES, AND A RETROSPECTIVE (1996–98)

I didn't die, though many of my dreams did, and I've already seen many friends and foes make their goodbyes. The fact is that between me being hospitalized, going in and coming out of different facilities, I was on medicines that were so strong I couldn't do any artwork. How many times was I getting things together, getting ready to do new exhibits and projects, when my health fell apart, and I ended up in one facility or another? It seems I got to know half the treatment places in Chicago—hospitals, mental-health clinics, halfway houses. I've been in many facilities, good and bad. In the midst of all this, I lost my mother, who had been a great pillar of my life.

For years, I had moved from place to place in Pilsen, returning to some, going to new ones after each major bout with my demons. First, Zorine Arnold, a former mural-art student of mine at Indiana University Northwest in Gary, found me a warehouse apartment owned by Podmajerski on 567 Eighteenth Street, several blocks east of Halsted and Providence of God church, homebase for the priest who married me to Mary Kay. Since the apartment wasn't as well-finished as his other lofts, I only paid $250 a month. I stayed there for a good time, producing most of the issues of *Mirarte* there, but I finally moved out when Podmajerski told me he was going to work on the building and would have to raise the rent. I moved to one of the two buildings that Aurelio and Juana Negrete owned on Nineteenth Place west of Ashland, before finally moving to Nineteenth and Carpenter to the building rebuilt by the ESDC. When that building was sold, I moved across the street to 1842 South Carpenter.

The last place that I lived in Pilsen was on Eighteenth Place near Morgan. This was in the early 1990s, and I no longer had a car to get around with. It was getting harder for me to live by myself, even with health workers coming to my house. I bought a dog named Chula, and she helped me for a while, but soon my illnesses made it hard for me to take care of her, so I gave her to my cleaning lady. After that, when I came home from different illness centers, I felt the weight of loneliness.

At times with all my moves, I felt alone, sensing my life flowing away. But in all my bouts, I've had support from a girlfriend who I began seeing in the heydays of MIRA and who still calls me, visits me, and goes with me for a meal whenever we can get it together. Efrén Beltrán, who was a MIRA member and designed t-shirts and light running jackets to sell at the Fiesta del Sol, has been one of my strongest supporters.

Then I've also had great support from my sister Helen, my brother Arturo, and Helen's husband, Cayetano, who's taken the trouble to organize and protect many of my paintings and drawings and who's helped Marc Zimmerman with some of the final images needed for this book. I've had great help from my daughter, Alicia, even when she was a young girl, and now that she's a mature young woman. And I also had help from Mary Kay, who turned out to be a great ex-wife, showing her concern and even involving her doctor husband, Harold Fineburg, in helping me qualify for better medical care and being there for me until his death in the late 1990s. Mary Kay also bought some of my artwork, and she gave me some money for some time to help me with part of the rent. Harold was also a generous soul. Once, he picked me up from the hospital when I was released and took me to Walgreen's to get a prescription filled. The price was $250, and I didn't have that much money with me. Harold said the price was highway robbery, but he immediately took out his credit card and charged the medicine to his account. Later, when he died, Mary Kay brought a friend from Mexico who cooked a large meal and made a wonderful *ofrenda,* or altar, which included Harold's old camera. Many people came out for this event, including some of his relatives—all of them Jewish, but they appreciated the *ofrenda* made to remember and honor Harold.

It was also Harold who got a friend to recommend me to Dr. Denson, a psychiatrist who prescribed me medications. But the fact is, I really didn't need a psychiatrist. All Denson did was ask me three questions: How did you sleep? How's your energy? And how are you going to pay for the help you need? He helped me identify some resources I was entitled to. But he said, "You don't have Parkinson's," and I said, "Yes, I do." The one who said I had Parkinson's was a neurologist who visited me when I lived at 1842 South Carpenter Street after 1995 and diagnosed me. He could hardly make out my writing because it was no tiny. And I could hardly read my notes either, and he said, "You've got Parkinson's. So what you have to do is open your mouth, write and write, and you will be able to control your hands, and also take your medication."

One thing I want to make clear is that I'm not bipolar, even though that's what my daughter Alicia keeps thinking is my problem. And she even said so in print, when Hugh Hefner—I mean, Jeff Huebner (that's a Freudian slip, isn't it?)—was working up an article on me for the *Chicago Reader.* Jeff interviewed Alicia, and that's what she told him—which is what Denson thought, and he prescribed me Depakote. I took it, and I got sick. I started to break out in a rash, and I called him at the hospital; but instead of helping me, he went on a skiing vacation, leaving another doctor in charge—a woman whom I threatened to sue unless she took me off that medication, which she finally did. I never took that medication again, and I didn't need it because I never was nor am I now bipolar.

Whatever I had, by the late 1990s I was pretty much disabled but not eligible for many benefits, often ending up short of cash and needing lots of help. Here I was, unable to produce much, now without my UIC or other jobs, watching the MFACM doing fine things, many of which I'd wanted to do, and watching them not do other community things that I thought were essential. But I was unable to do much of anything. And another bad part of this was that the MFACM tried to eliminate me from its own history of Mexican art in the city before they existed. But a funny thing happened when they did a major retrospective on Carlos Cortez, where the MARCH connection meant that even I somehow appeared. That at least was better than the fate of Helen Valdez, one of the founders, who seemed to have been erased like Trotsky when she left the MFACM some years back. But I must say I've had better relations with the MFACM in recent years, and some of their recent publications have had some praise for me as a community-arts pioneer activist. Somehow, though, it seems that they began honoring me when they thought I was too old and sick to do anything else.

But the fact is, I did some work even in the worst of times, promoting the artwork of Nicolás de Jesús (until he had a fight with the Taller and went back to Guerrero) and drawing some images in my sketch book in the nineties—most of them are like the Diego Rivera–style drawings I'd practiced in San Miguel so many years ago. I also did some linoleum cuts with Cortez's help, including one of Siqueiros that appeared in a Mestizarte retrospective on Siqueiros's work. Maybe most important for me were the sketches I made of patients during one of my last times at Northwestern Hospital's loop facility (see figs. 107 and 108), even with a new wave of Parkinson shakes that turned my drawing off again.

In fact, I think it was then, gradually, after the Siqueiros and Cortez retrospectives, that people started remembering me, with Hector Duarte leading the way and Victor Sorell and others getting involved in a show of my work at Mestizarte in the summer of 1998. Alicia was there with me. Then Mary Kay came with her friend, Fanny Rushing, Marta Ayala—and even

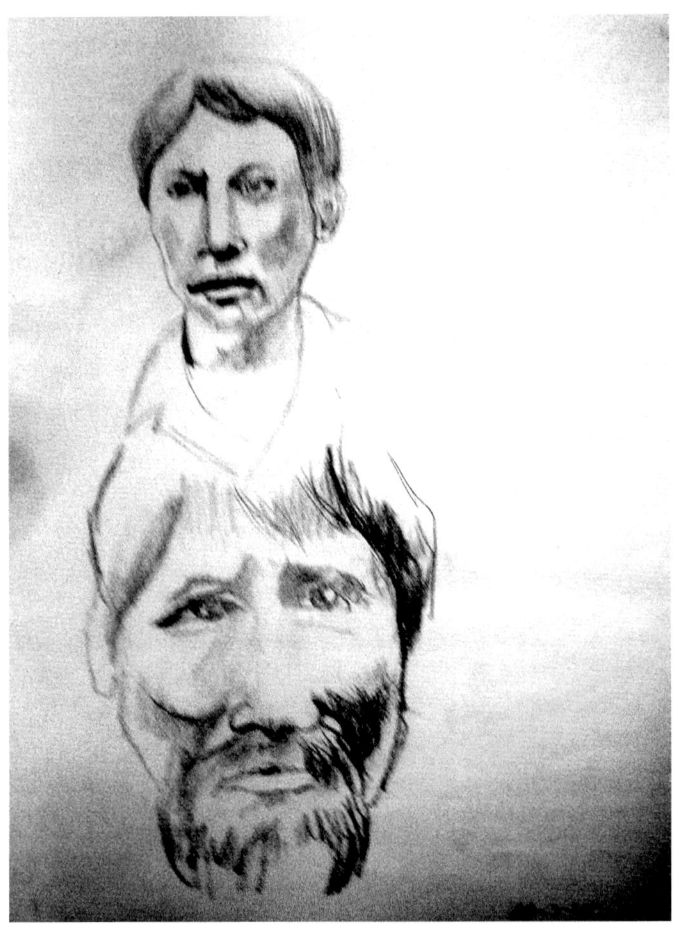

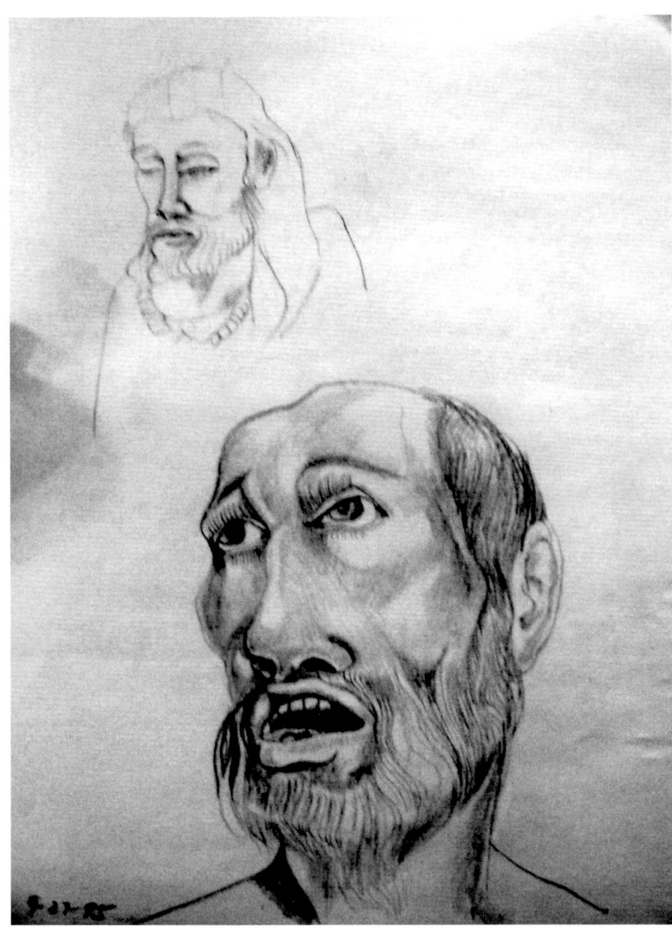

Fig. 107. José Gamaliel González, Old Man Dreaming of His Youth, 1995. 8"×10". Pencil.

Fig. 108. José Gamaliel González, Old Beggar Dreaming of Christ, 1995. 8"×10". Pencil.

Esther Soler and Marc Zimmerman showed up. It was a very moving event for me, seeing some of my best sketches mounted and people there to celebrate my work, and a nice program, with my "Cycle of Man" charcoal on the cover and an essay by Victor Sorrell inside. I remember Victor reading his essay, which was maybe too complimentary, but I felt good hearing it and seeing others impressed by it too. And then Héctor, a really talented artist, declared me an honorary member of Mestizarte for life (see figs. 109–11).

EVENTS INTO THE NEW CENTURY

I had another big medical crisis, and when I finally came back from the hospital, I moved over a few blocks to Eighteenth Place and Mor-gan, just down the street from where Alejandro Romero and his family lived. I started going to shows again, but I also got stronger and started participating in and even putting on some. I remember showing my three-dimensional sculpture piece in a Day of the Dead show at Collage. I remember a big exhibit I did with my friend Efrén Beltrán and other artists on South Michigan Avenue, and then an important one at Café Revolución on Eighteenth Street and Carpenter, with Chuy Negrete singing *corridos* at the opening and Dr. Rita Hernández joining in, with Victor Sorell serving like an emcee and *padrino*. Of course, there were other shows, too—like one in Seattle, where they showed my portrait of Zapata that had been in the CARA exhibit. But the Café Revolución show was special to me because I had such a big hand in securing the materials.

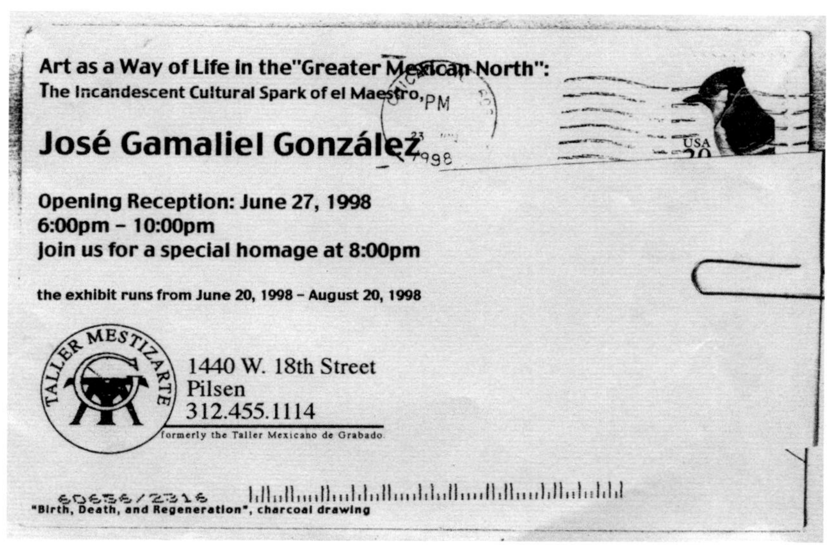

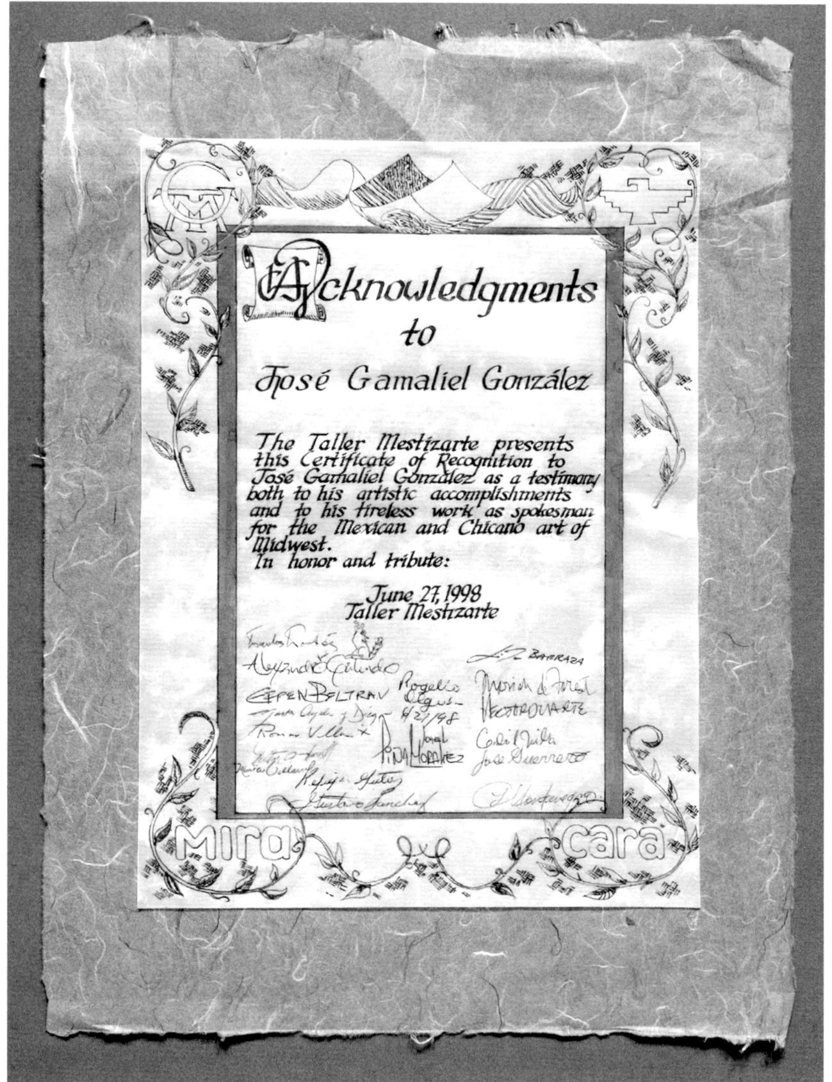

Fig. 109. Invitation to José Gamaliel González retrospective, June 1998.

Fig. 110. Acknowledgments, signed by Mestizarte artists and friends and presented to José at the retrospective in his honor at the Mestizarte office (formerly the APO office) on Eighteenth Street, June 1998.

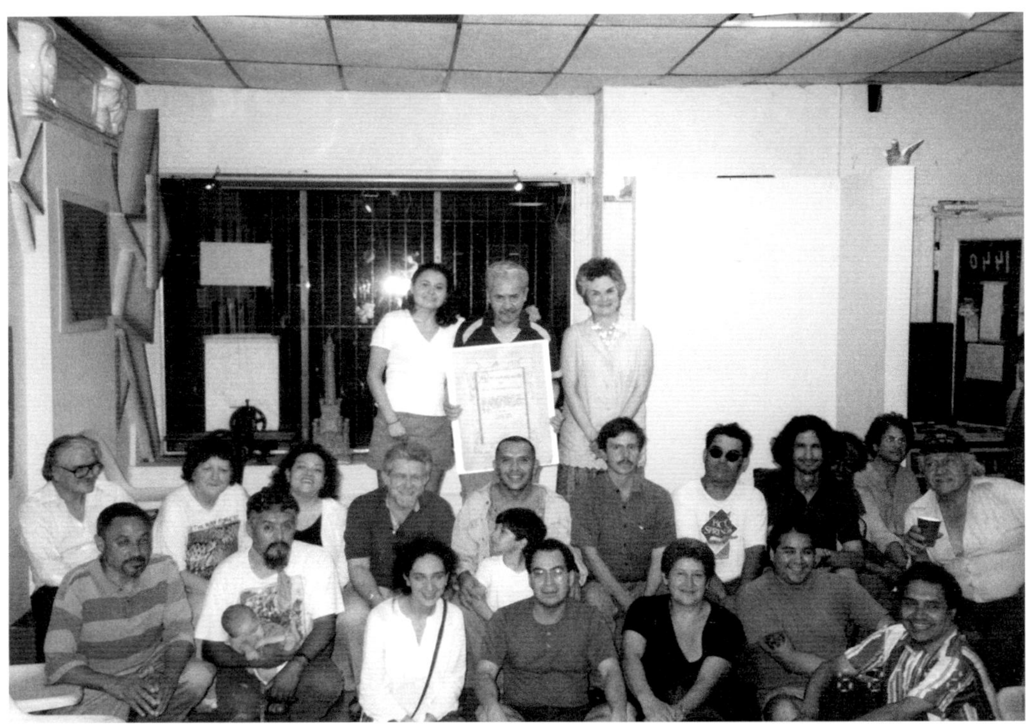

I included a painting of a crucified Zapata that Nicolás de Jesús sold to me when he arrived in Chicago with his wife and baby. I showed a large painting of Zapata by Arturo Miramontes and a photo-collage that Oscar Moya did of Subcomandante Marcos. I exhibited a large photo of Zapata that the Field Museum gave me because it was somewhat bent. The owner of the café wanted it for his collection, and I sold it to him for a very low price.

Locally again, one of the most important events I took part in during the new century was a two-man show with Cortez in 2004 that we held at La Llorona art gallery, where I've had a great ongoing relationship with the owner, Arturo Avedaño, who continued to support me in my lowest moments. Of course, I've helped him, too, when I added my mailing and phone list to his—we get very good turnouts for events in his space. I gave Arturo a copy of the MARCH calendar so he could get some idea of the kinds of things we'd done, and he agreed that we could do a series of events, starting with the two-man show. The calendar has two photos,

one of Cortez and one of me. So Arturo cut up the calendar, taking the photos and making the postcard, with the two of us together, for the two-man show. I had some twelve sketches that I did for the Raza de Oro murals on Hubbard Street, plus I had ten other pieces (mainly ink and pastels)—twenty-two altogether, making up about almost half of the show. Cortez had produced so much, and so he showed a few pieces more than me. But the exhibit attracted a lot of attention, and people were actually talking about Carlos and me as two founding fathers of Chicago Chicano art. I was so happy that my sister Helen could be with me at the last event I would do with Carlos (fig. 112).

My next show opened in 2004 at Kristopher's Café, opened by a Salvadoran named Carlos with his wife from Guadalajara, Mexico, on Halsted and Eighteenth Street, right in the heart of John Podmajerski's kingdom. Carlos immediately made friends with John and the local artists to put exhibitions at his place. He also got involved with the annual Artists' Walk held in October where participating artists opened up their studios as the artists do in Wicker Park's annual Around the Coyote art show.

Most of the art Carlos was showing at his café was by Anglo artists from East Pilsen, but he also had a number of works from outside the East Pilsen area that were by Mexican artists. Among those that have exhibited in one-man shows were Mario Castillo, Jeff Maldonado, a cousin of his wife, and me.

The fact is, I was one of the early patrons at Kristopher's when he'd just opened up, and I brought a portfolio of my work to show him. This was in the first years after 2000. He liked my work, and we arranged a date for my exhibit. Since I didn't have a car, Efrén helped me to bring the artwork in his van. He also helped me to mount the exhibition.

The exhibit contained drawings I did in San Miguel de Allende, three abstract water colors that I did at the Chicago Academy of Fine Arts in 1953, the design of the Hubbard Street Raza de Oro mural panels, the design of the mural I'd done in East Chicago, Indiana, for UNO in 1974, a poster that I did for MARCH, and an early oil painting I did in the 1950s of Elizabeth Taylor in a kind of nightmare scene with a mouse and many other images surrounding her—one of my best color pictures to survive (see back cover).

We had a large turnout for the opening that included my cousin Terry and her husband, my sister Helen and my brother-in-law Cayetano, and Alicia and her boyfriend at that time, Ángel. Gilbert Cárdenas from Notre Dame and many others came. My sister brought some cookies and a cake, which made Carlos upset because he had his own baked goods to sell.

My works were very low-priced; each black-and-white water color was only forty dollars. A *güero* gave me the money immediately for one, and when the exhibit closed a month later, he came right on the date to pick it up. Gilbert bought the other two watercolors, some draw-

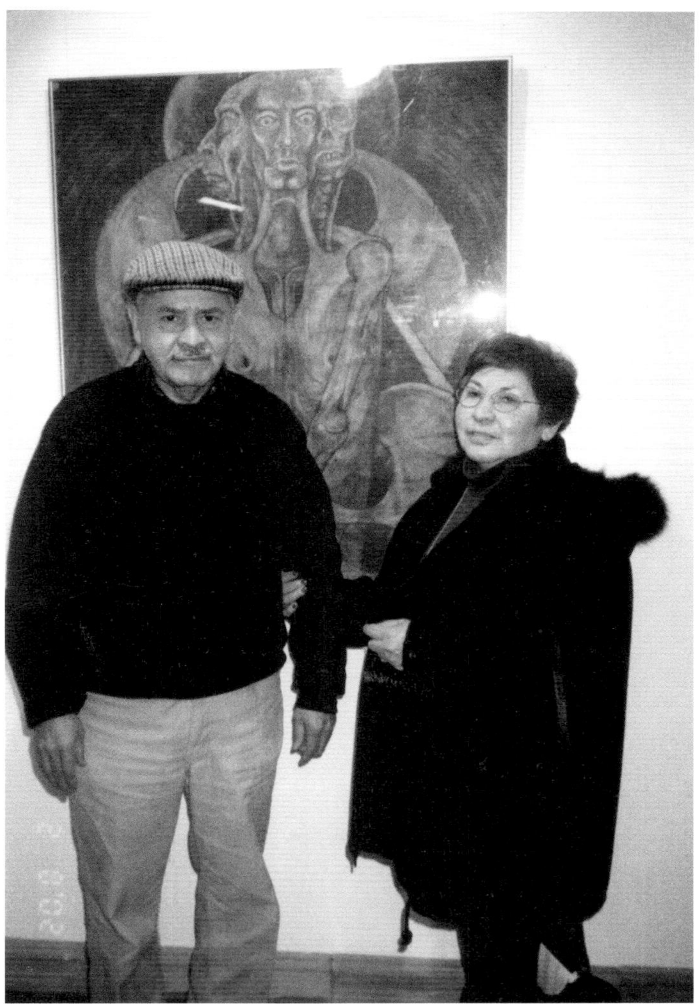

Fig. 112. José with his sister Helen at the Cortez/González exhibit opening, La Llorona gallery, November 16, 2004.

ings from San Miguel, and the Elizabeth Taylor oil painting. The article by Jeff Huebner in the *Chicago Reader* came out at that time, and that also helped to bring people to the exhibit.

I was very pleased at the result, and others promised to buy some work at a later time, but they never came through. Carlos and his wife were very pleased with the reception, and we became good friends. Carlos is a mover, and he caters for the MFACM as well as for Pomadjerski and his people. In fact, he catered the food for the recent Mayan Textile exhibit held in January 2007. One great dish he may still have at his café is the Mayan tamales. I haven't been to the cafe for a few years now, but I'm sure that Carlos is doing well.

Just around the time I did my one-man show at Kristopher's café, I also organized the Frida y Diego exhibit at La Llorona gallery. I called it Número Dos because it was the second exhibit featuring these two artists. This was not a Day of the Dead event. The exhibit had about twenty artists, with Esperanza Gama, Nora Chapa Mendoza, Jeff Maldonado, Luis de La Torre, me, and others. Jeff Huebner called his story on me "Battling Fridas" because of my disputes with Carlos Tortolero of the MFACM. Carlos and my daughter were interviewed by Jeff for the article.

We didn't have a postcard invitation as we had when I had a two-man show with Carlos Cortez. The crowd this time wasn't as large because we depended mostly on e-mail and word of mouth. Some of the works were well done. I especially remember the one by Luis de la Torre.

On Saturday, I organized a panel discussion that featured me giving a talk on Diego. Gail Werblood, who was then a student going for her Ph.D., focused her dissertation on Frida's handicapped life and her sketchbook. Gail is also a handicapped person who was accepted by Columbia College with a special grant for disabled people. The other person invited as a panelist to talk on Frida was Judy Kirshner, who is at UIC but was curator at the Museum of Contemporary Art when they brought an exhibit of Frida Kahlo's work. The emcee was Victor Sorell.

Judy never showed up, and Victor was very angry about this. Actually, the turnout was bad, and it was just as well that she didn't make it. Still, it was not right. I had a pencil drawing of Frida that was taken from the photo of Salma Hayek when she played Frida in the movie made of her life. The drawing of Frida wasn't very good, but the one of Diego, based on one of his self-portraits, captured the artist's ability to laugh at himself (fig. 113).

This was the last exhibit that I organized at La Llorona, but I went to other exhibits that Arturo Avendaño had at his gallery. Efrén Beltrán took me there all of these years, and he continues to support me. The last exhibits that we went to together were in January 2007 at the MFACM and at Prospectus Gallery. Since then, other people have taken me to events, and I've sometimes met Efrén at them.

During the first years of the decade, the MFACM had expanded its facility. They had started developing their collections of art from several of the local artists, including a complete set of Cortez's plates that Carlos donated. They seemed to be entrenched for the new century as the major Mexican arts organization in the city and a real force nationally. After all our problems, they now seemed to honor me by asking me to donate my "Cycle of Man" drawing to their collection. I guess I was flattered that they finally felt secure enough of their future to include me even a little bit, but I was also kind of broke and needed some money, so I told them I just couldn't afford to donate the piece. And at that point, Gil Cárdenas—a man so tied to my life and my alma mater, now a member of the MFACM board—bought it and donated it to the museum to honor his recently deceased aunt.

Some articles have even appeared about me in the past few years: a really complimentary one that some bright young Mexican kids did for the MFACM history project (they call me "a great man"); another on my role in civil rights struggles; and then, to top it all off, that big piece by Jeff Huebner for the *Chicago Reader,* where I talk about my life and struggles. Of course, that article reached thousands of people in the Chicago area—so I guess that's important (see Zimmerman forthcoming).

All these happenings made me feel like I was going through some sort of little renaissance. I was flattered and pleased. It was like I was back in the limelight, so to speak. Arturo Avedaño and I started planning another show, and I was getting all revved up, first to do the show and also to help Gary Chico's aldermanic campaign. Maybe the excitement was too much for me, because in the middle of it all, I had a heart attack, followed by a double bypass heart operation. My health had gone downhill, but I recovered very quickly and went right to work as a volunteer for Lenny Dominguez, who was running for Cook County commissioner. I needed a car for this work and tried buying one with Bill Luna of the Mexican Historical Museum in Little Village. But things didn't work out, and I was running around when I wasn't well. And before long, I ended up in the street. I was picked up by an ambulance and taken by emergency to Mount Mercy Hospital in 2005. I was there for about a month, when my sister Helen and Alicia decided that I needed to go into a home. So I ended up in the Casa Central Center home for the Hispanic elderly, a place run up to recently by a local Cuban couple, serving mainly Puerto Rican patients in Chicago's Humboldt Park area.

It was hell for me, of course, to lose my apartment and be "institutionalized," as they say—with all my artwork, books, and archives put into storage and with no idea what would happen to any of my things. It also killed me to leave the Pilsen neighborhood, but Alicia wanted me to be someplace that was close by to where she lived and easy for her to get to from home or work.

As time went by, I felt good enough to do drawings of some of the nurses and did a drawing of Zapata taken from the photo by Agustin Victor Casasola that appeared in a special issue of *La Raza* newspaper to advertise the Casasola exhibit at La Llorona (fig. 114). In November 2005, I did a pretty good colored-pencil drawing of La Virgen de Guadalupe and Juan Diego.

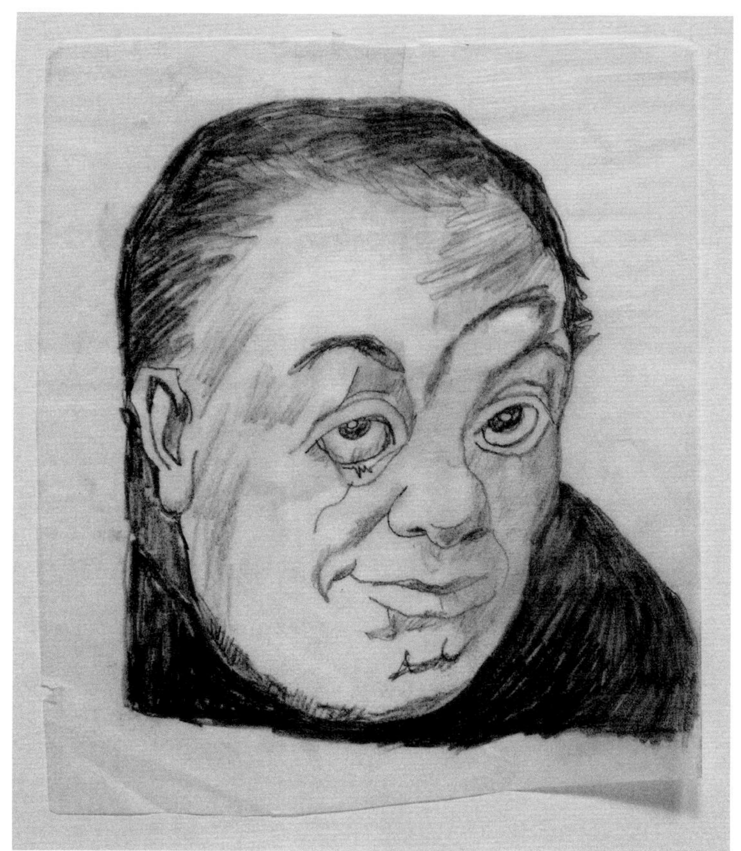

And I decided to do an event to honor her in December, the month when she appeared to Juan Diego. The event was a small one held at Sabor Latino, a restaurant right across from my church, St. Procopius. I had gone to the MFACM for El Día de los Muertos in September, where I met an old friend, Lillian Anguiano, who had returned to the city and was now working for Barton Beers, which handled Corona and Modelo in several countries. Lillian helped me get some Corona beer donated for the event that was held on December 2, 2005. José Piña, the director of my old APO office, which was now called Casa de la Cultura—Carlos Cortez—Mestizarte, came to the Casa Central nursing home, where I gave him the artwork and a rough layout for the poster and flyer. The reproduction of the Virgen didn't come out as fine as I'd hoped, but he did a good job on the poster and flyer (fig. 115). The priest that I'd in-

Fig. 113. José Gamaliel González, Diego, based on Rivera's self-portrait. Pencil drawing for Frida y Diego II, La Llorona gallery, March 28, 2003.

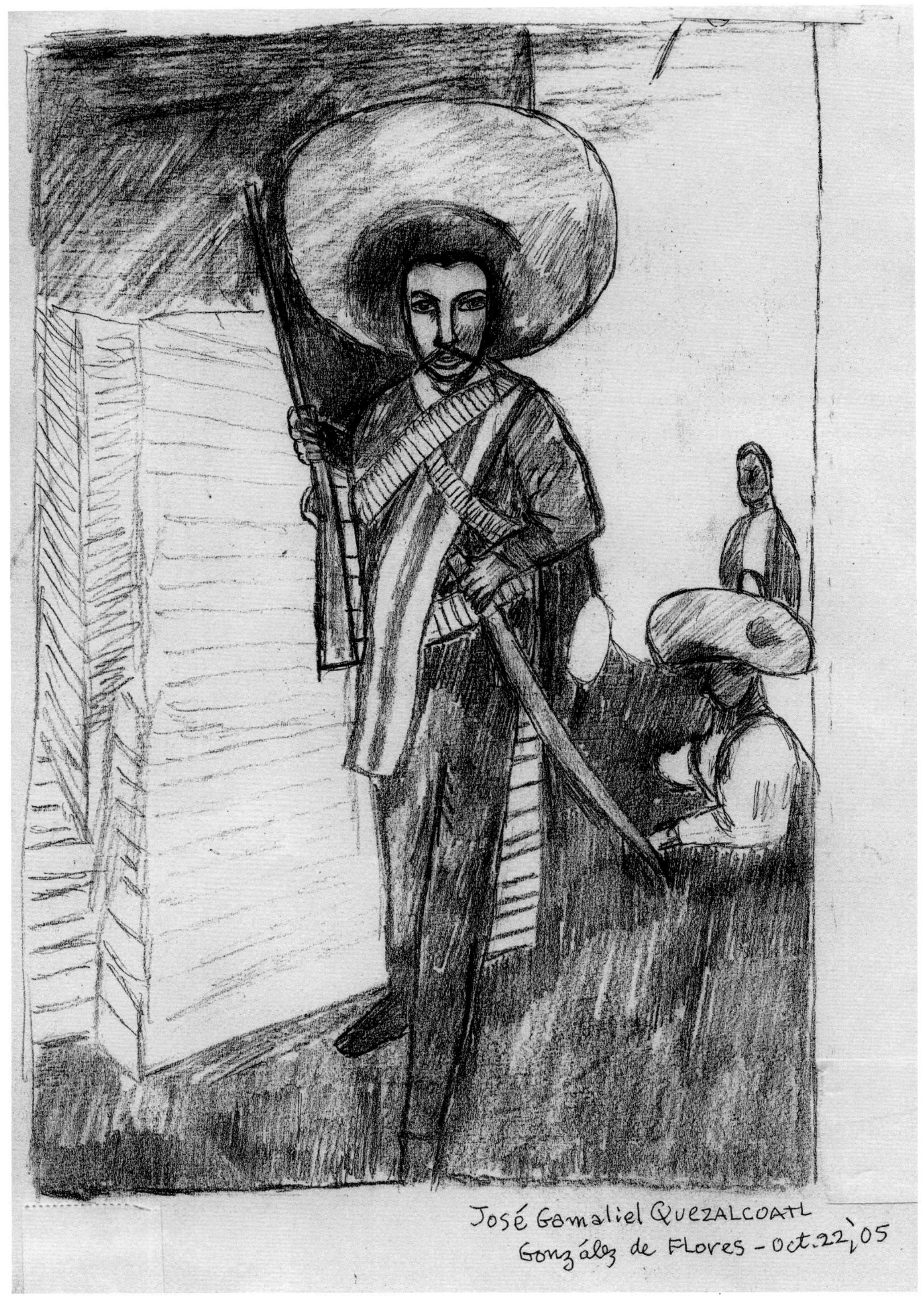

Fig. 114. José Gamaliel González, Drawing of Zapata with special signature, October 22, 2005.

vited from St. Procopius never showed up, but another priest, who was a closer friend, came. Only a few people showed up, but that meant there was plenty of beer for the faithful.

After that, I was moved to the second floor of the nursing home and found less inspiration to draw. I guess I started to feel the routine of waiting for Puerto Rican food and the dominoes games, waiting with fellow residents for the next church meeting, the next outing in Humboldt Park or around town, the next ballgame, movie, or *telenovela* installment, the next visit, the next time out with a relative or friend. I did do a decent portrait of Carmen Benítez, a certified nurse's assistant at Casa Central who had studied with Carlos Cumpián at Farragut High School, but I'm sad to say that my portrait didn't capture her beauty. That was among the last artworks I did at Casa Central.

In the meantime, I wait for the Cubs or the White Sox, the Bulls or the Bears on the TV. My dominoes playing is getting better all the time. I wait for Alicia or Efrén to take me out for a Mexican meal, a movie, or a gallery opening. Many of my old friends have forgotten me, it seems, or just don't have time to visit or call. Others visit whenever they can, no matter what it takes. Arturo Avedaño from La Llorona gallery has been good to me, encouraging me to think of new shows and picking me up to do work at the gallery once in a while. For a long time, Alicia said that she had me on the waiting list for the Resurrection Project Home for the Elderly in Pilsen because she was also interested in moving to Pilsen. I guess I would rather be there, in a place that stands against the forces of Anglo-dominant gentrification, close to the site of my deepest defeats, but also my greatest victories. But now I wonder if she'll ever move there and if I'll ever live again in Pilsen.

Here I sit in Casa Central remembering all that has happened over the years, the friends

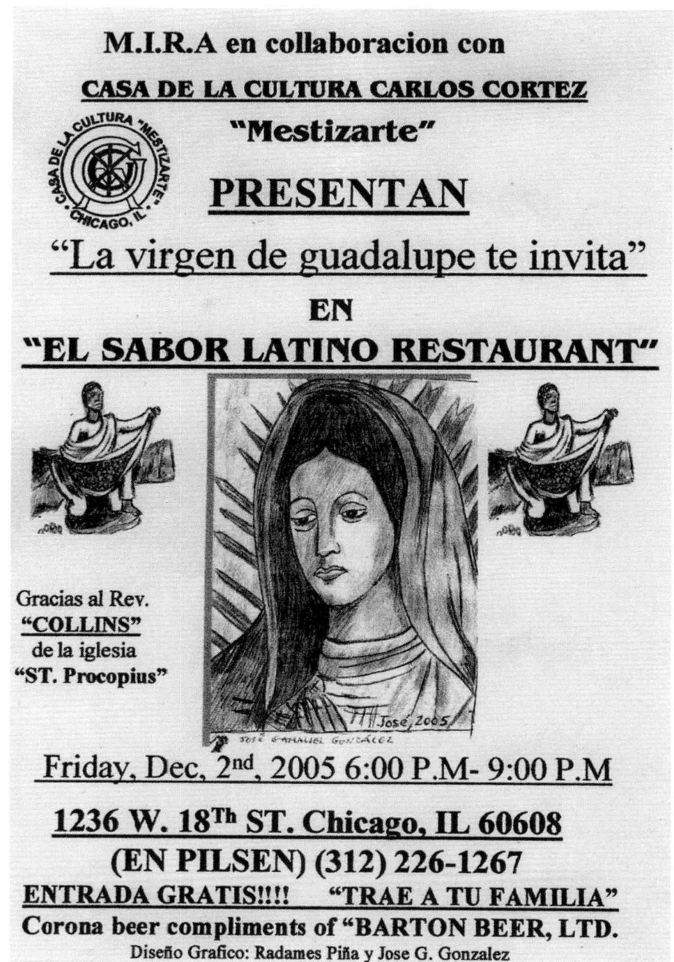

Fig. 115. MIRA reborn in "La Virgen de Guadalupe te Invita," with drawings and codesigned by José Gamaliel González, December 2005.

and loves I've had and lost, the fights I've won and the ones I didn't. I sit here knowing that I'm in my last years and wondering about what I can accomplish between now and the time when I will be gone. But I'm not ready to go yet. I'm getting stronger as I recover from my illnesses. I'm recuperating, and I'm very excited about this book—it's taken so long for us, working on it bit by bit, year after year. And now that we're coming down the home stretch, I can almost see the reactions of family and friends and even total strangers as we show the book and maybe have an exhibit of the pictures to go with it. They're still in storage, along with a lot of other works I wish we could've had for the book. Maybe we can show them in the exhibit, if we can locate them and pull them out.

I want to list some of the awards that I received, starting with the UNO Award for the mural in East Chicago, Indiana, in 1974. Then came the award given to me by the Museum of Science and Industry in 1975 for the Quinto Sol exhibit of Mexican Americans. Then, in the early 1980s, there was the award for civic leadership from the Mexican American Legal Defense Fund (MALDEF). In the late 1980s I received a Midwest Latino Leadership award from Cristina Saralegui, who hosts the famous *Cristina* TV program on Univisión. Geno Muñoz nominated me, and I was one of the two candidates selected. Geno and Alicia, my daughter, were both present at the Univisión award ceremony that attracted many media people. Along with the recognition came a check for over two thousand dollars, which I had Univisión make out to the ESDC when Arturo Vásquez was the executive director.

A lot of other awards and recognitions came my way, and at the same time I was a member of several boards, including Casa Aztlán, Hogar del Niño, and the ESDC, plus a couple of other organizations that I can't remember.

The most recent award was from the Chicago Public Art Group in October 2005. A fundraising event was held to honor the community pioneer muralists Marcos Raya, Mario Castillo, Ray Patlán, Carol Yasko, and the legendary Bill Walker—though only Marcos and Carol joined me to receive the award, a brick with an engraved brush. This was the second time this organization had honored me, the first being in 1977 when their name was the Chicago Mural Group. But still another honor came to me in September 2005: the special issue of *La Raza* newspaper to commemorate Mexican Independence with a special cultural section in color

that featured the works of Alejandro Romero, Oscar Romero, Marcos Raya, Mario Castillo, Carlos Cortez, Arturo Miramontes, Esperanza Gama, Nora Chapa Mendoza, Héctor Duarte, and myself. In fact, they gave me the biggest space—almost a full page of the Toltec panel of the Raza de Oro mural on Hubbard Street (see back cover). Nevertheless, thinking of all the recognitions I've received, still the one I cherish the most was the award given to me by Mayor Harold Washington for the work I did with the Earthquake Committee I formed to raise money for Mexico City in 1985 (see chapter 4).

Finally, I should mention my appointment to the board of the Chicago Council of Fine Arts and to the board of the Department of Cultural Affairs by Mayor Washington. I sat on panels for nine years for the Illinois Arts Council and helped fund many Latino arts organizations and individual artists. On a national level, I sat as a panelist for the National Endowment for the Arts. Finally, I was appointed to sit on two more important panels, the Department of Public Works and the Department of Economic Development. Each of these panels gave the MFACM fifty thousand dollars to develop their gift shop and to expand the museum. So you may say with some justice that, whether they liked it or not and in more ways than one, I was part of getting them toward where they got.

ACHIEVEMENTS OF CHICAGO'S
MEXICAN ARTISTS AND MY
OWN LEGACY

The Chicago Mexican painters of my time who will be most remembered are Alejandro Romero, Marcos Raya, and Mario Castillo—full-time artists who developed a huge body of good work. Cortez will have a special place as a printmaker. Héctor Duarte was our greatest muralist, and Nicolás de Jesús's *amaté* series on

Chicago should always have value in Chicago Mexican art history. Ray Patlán, Aurelio Díaz, Salvador Vega, Oscar Moya, Diana Solís, Esperanza Gama, and many others will have their place. And José González? What is my place? What did I do?

Looking again and again at the artwork that still remains with me, sitting on my tables or propped against a wall, as we have developed this book, it has become clear to me that my main achievements were not my paintings as much as some of my sketches and much of my work in black and white. I think people will always point to my portrayals of Zapata—that some say are haunted and haunting, his eyes staring out, asking us what happened to our Mexican revolution and our greatest hopes for the Mexican people. And then I think people will remember some of my portrayals of Mexican women and above all my pictures of the dead—my "Cycle of Man" drawing and even my four-headed "Cycle of Man" sculpture—which was badly repainted but was recently redone by Rey Vásquez, so it is close to being what it was.

As I developed my artistic skills, the greatest influences on my work were Michelangelo, Van Gogh, and Orozco. I was very fortunate to study Renaissance painting as a young boy. But I found Van Gogh in the late 1940s, and he remained with me in all I did. Michelangelo and Van Gogh were religious artists, dedicated to a vision of salvation. I was overwhelmed by all Michelangelo did and by Van Gogh's Paris paintings—the ones he painted in dark, amber colors—and the exciting colored paintings he's most famous for. In 1966 I found Orozco; his technique and his vision of the revolution and modern civilization had the greatest impact on me. All the major Mexican muralists and painters like Tamayo and Kahlo influenced me, but Orozco affected me the most, because of his expressionism. Like Van Gogh, his work expressed

turmoil, *lucha*. It showed the struggles of people and the violence of our history. His art is intense, visionary, and real at the same time. It's not like Diego's work, which is designed, tight, and pretty, even musical. My work is not like that—it's not musical, and neither is Orozco's.

I guess it's true that I never did enough with my artwork—that art organizing and my illnesses consumed much of my artistic time and talent. I don't think I produced as much as I could or should have because I was doing so many other things, and that cut down on my output. If it had not been for that, I think I would have produced a lot more work. I didn't produce many murals, either, though there are some so-called mural painters who haven't done as many as my eight or nine. There are paintings and collages of mine that are incomplete. And I'd have to say that I produced far more work in color (oils, pastels, watercolors) that are in storage and that would be too difficult to get at before this book goes to press. I know that having these works might change how my overall opus is seen, which is one reason why I hope we can show at least some of them when the book comes out.

There's no doubt that some of the most important contributions I made were to Chicago's Mexican community and above all the artistic expression and life of that community. In this sense, I think that I helped to put us on the map. I made our work and needs known in the art world—that we needed to get funding, that we needed space, that we needed our own cultural centers. I can say that I helped establish the need for those centers, even though I never established one myself. I believe I did help other organizations become known and to get funding. I guess I can say in a way, too, that even though we had our conflicts, I helped to demonstrate the value and need for the space and many of the programs of the MFACM. I made it clear that such a center was needed. I couldn't bring it about myself, but I think I was maybe the key person who had laid the groundwork to establish such a place in Chicago. I know some people may say that my conflicts with the MFACM were motivated by jealousy and sour grapes. But early on, I became a member of the museum, and I guess you can say that I was a critical supporter, one who praised the many good things they did but criticized them when I thought they could and should do better for the community. I dreamed big, and they did too, so that what started as the Mexican Fine Arts Center and became the Mexican Fine Arts Center Museum has now changed its name again, as of December 2006, to the National Museum of Mexican Art (fig. 116). There's no doubt that Carlos Tortolero has provided the leadership with his organization to establish this museum. May he continue in having further success.

As for me, I think I made it clear that artists must be involved in community and even in politics. I'm proud of my role in the Washington years and even my efforts to help failed candidates in the years that followed. I guess I had a dream that there was a person who could unite the community, and maybe the ones who came along weren't really able to do that. Changing things in Chicago isn't easy, but we have to keep on trying. That's why I was proud of my daughter Alicia when she was working for Chuy García, and when she was trying to help bring a cultural museum to Little Village, which really needed one. And even though she had to leave that work, I think she helped plant a seed as her father did and in his honor. She is still planting seeds, and I am proud of her.

I tried to show things from the perspective of a U.S. Mexican, someone living in the United States and working within a Mexican community. One thing is to make people aware of Mexican art, which has been part of my life as a whole, but another is, as an artist, to bring a vision of the Mexican world and connect it to the other Mexican and Latino communities in the United States. I think that was part of what I was trying to do with my work. I certainly did everything possible to call attention to the fact that we were producing a body of important artwork that was valuable to everyone, not just ourselves—that our community was part of a larger Latino community and the community that is Chicago itself, and that there would be women who in the next generation would come forward (as they did) and be among the better artists in our community, and that would help create great images and richer lives for us all.

I always felt that art was both religious and revolutionary and tried to instill that belief in my art and community work. I recognize that what I have done I have done through the grace of God, and with the intervention of the Virgen de Guadalupe, who has helped me in my darkest moments, when illness and death were knocking again and again at my door. She and God have been with me through all my bouts of illness and now in my final years. But I know they want me to keep on trying—to do something, to make clear what I have done for my daughter, my sister, and brother and the larger world.

I admit to having many faults and having committed many errors. Among the faults, I consider excessive pride to be my worst, since it doesn't let me defend myself as well as I defend a friend, which lets me absorb insults without showing that they hurt and without reacting in the necessary time.

My errors are mainly due to pride, like when I turned down an offer from Juana Guzmán to help me raise money for the CARA show; or when I failed to fight back at showdowns with Carlos Cumpián over MARCH or with Carlos Tortolero over CARA; or when I kept on fight-

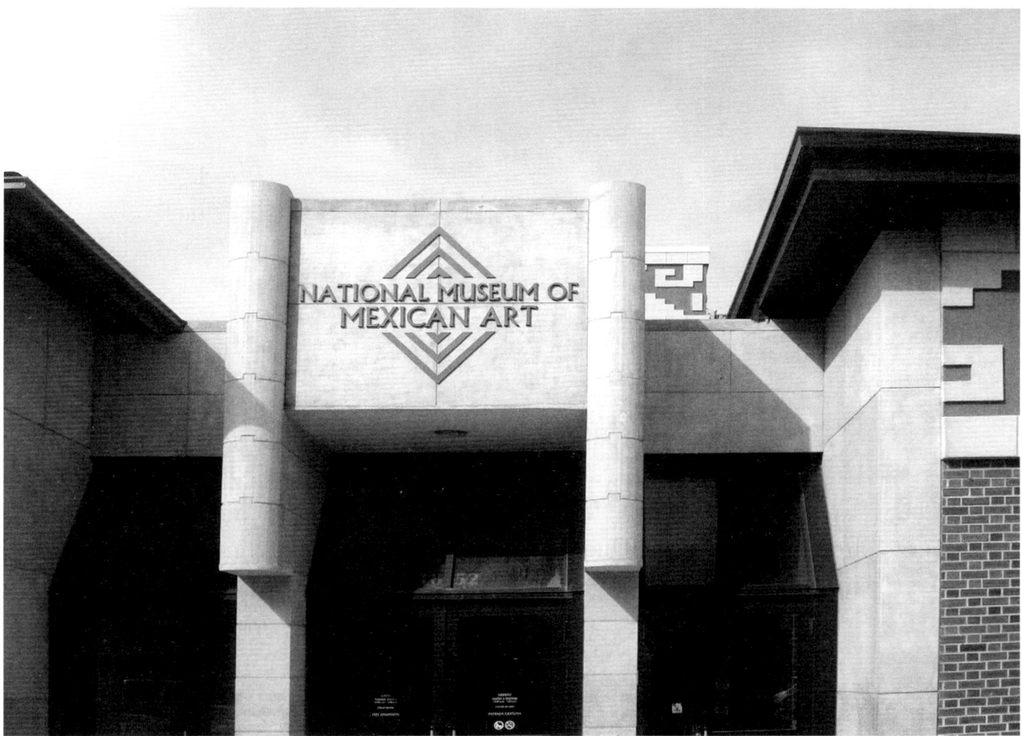

ing for a new museum even as the MFAC was working to establish their own.

May I be forgiven for my sins and remembered for my works.

FINAL WORDS: MARCH 24, 2007

This book has been a long journey, and I find I can't end it if I don't make a few more additional points. The first is about my religion and the love that I have for our Lord Jesus Christ, his saints, and our Blessed Virgin, who has appeared at many places, including Mexico City, when she appeared to a poor Indian, Juan Diego, almost five hundred years ago and who was finally canonized by Pope John Paul II.

As I mentioned earlier in the book, I was very close to the church in my youth. A priest gave me an old book with the lives of five hundred saints. There are many saints that I love—John, Peter, and Paul. There are also popular saints like Theresa of Avila, Rose of Lima, Catherine of Sienna, and St. Martin de Porres of Brazil. But the ones closest to me are Francis of Assisi; Anthony of Padua; the Curé of Ars, Jean Baptiste Marie Vianney; and Augustine. Saint Francis talked to the birds and tamed a lion that was about to attack him. Saint Anthony was my mother's patron saint, and she loved him because he was known for his many miracles of finding lost objects. The Curé of Ars, France, became famous for the many hours he put in throughout the day hearing confessions. Saint Augustine was a great sinner until he was converted by his mother, Saint Monica, who prayed for him for forty years, as did my mother, praying to Saint Anthony to tame my demons, to find my lost socks, and to save her lost artist son.

I have visited many sacred, ancient, and historical places in Mexico and Europe. I regret that I never made it to Lourdes, France, or to Yugoslavia, where the Virgin is still appearing every day. I did make it to Fatima, Portugal, where our Lady appeared to three children and made the miracle of the sun. In Mexico, I did go to Zapópan, to San Juan de los Lagos, and to

Fig. 116. National Museum of Mexican Art, formerly the Mexican Fine Arts Center Museum. Photo: Marc Zimmerman, March 2007.

the old basilica as well as the new one designed by Pedro Ramírez Vásquez.

I have come close to death on four different occasions but have been spared by my Lord and our blessed mother. I had a stroke when I lived on 1842 South Carpenter. Thanks to my landlord, I was taken by ambulance to St. Mother Cabrini Hospital. I remained in a coma for several days. My sister Helen and my girlfriend prayed the rosary over me. Helen called a priest, and I was given Last Rites. My girlfriend bought a beautiful large purple pearl rosary at the gift shop there and gave it to me.

In the past several years, so many close friends and relatives have passed away. Ron Wieburg, whom I worked with in the commercial art field and who was a great dancer of Latin music, especially the mambo, died some years ago after he finally got married and settled down. I was very close to David Torres of Midland, Michigan, who probably painted his first community mural in the 1950s—even before Mario Castillo painted the two murals on Halsted Street that are no longer there. David initiated many projects that included his small museum and his Captain Chicano comic strip. When David came to Chicago, he always stopped in to see me. On one of his trips here, I took him to a book fair in Printers Row; and since he knew that I loved Van Gogh's work, he bought me a large book on Van Gogh with many of his works in full color. David later left the Catholic church with his wife, Alicia, when they simultaneously received the gift of tongues at a charismatic session. David later became a minister and led his own church.

Other close artist friends who died include María Almonte and María Enríquez de Allen, the mother of Mario Castillo and the wife of Harold Allen, Mario's photography teacher at the School of the Art Institute who met María at Mario's graduation. There was also Aaron Ker-low, my doctor for several years who also did artwork, examples of which appear as the covers for a series of books Marc Zimmerman has been publishing while working on this book. Aaron died in 2006, as did Luis Jiménez, the Chicano sculptor from New Mexico, and Michael Piazza, another friend and collaborator with Marc and others, who did a lot of work in Chicago's Latino community. Both Jiménez and Piazza had *ofrendas* in the MFACM's 2006 Día de los Muertos show. Of course, I'm haunted by the memory of Carlos Cortez, my longtime friend, a very special artist and poet, who was a member of MARCH and MIRA and passed away in 2005, not long after his wife, Mariana. Carlos was the central figure of MFACM's Day of the Dead show that same year.

There have been over fifteen deaths among the residents at Casa Central in the time I've been here. I was especially close to Emiliano Hernández, with whom I played dominos. Emilio was very religious and gave me a bible that we read together. He played the guitar but only sang religious songs.

There have been many deaths in the family. Most painful, of course, was the death of my mother. But I should also mention two tragic deaths: my cousin Manuel committed suicide when his wife left him, and my Uncle Joe was killed in his home by an explosion caused by a gas leak in his stove.

Marc Zimmerman has put in endless hours of work on this book, which began with many hours of taped interviews. Then came my corrections and additions, small and huge, some given verbally but more and more by my hand. It was all a question/answer format that Marc changed into a narrative. Marc has been like a brother to me since we became acquainted. It was hard to develop this book because of my illnesses but also because Marc now lives in Houston. But he always visits me on his trips to

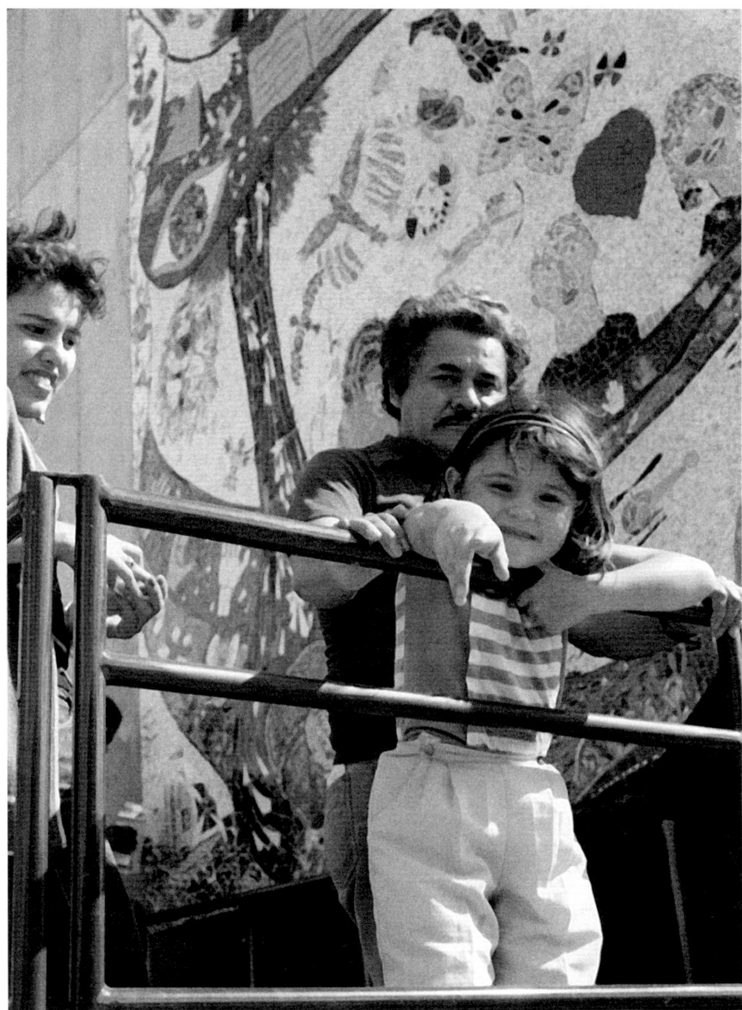

Chicago. We get together to work on the book, and he always takes me out to eat. His wife, Esther Soler, has also been very good to me. God bless him, Esther, and their whole family.

Coming to the end of my story here, I wish to express my gratitude again for the support I receive from my brother, Arturo, my sister Helen, and her husband, my brother-in-law Cayetano, who is storing my work and putting some copies and originals for sale. I also wish to thank Efrén Beltrán, Arturo Avedaño, and Nancy. And Marc has gotten help down the stretch from Victor Sorell, Nick Kanellos, Jeff Huebner, Mario Castillo, Juan Mora, Frances Aparicio, and Gil Cárdenas. God bless them all.

And, of course, above all, God bless my daughter, Alicia, who provides me with her love and attention: Alicia, Luz, light of my life, whose every passing year glows within me (see figures 117–22).

I feel almost rejuvenated again, reading over these words, waiting now to see how my book and the pictures come out in print, waiting now to open another show or two featuring the book and my work. Again I take comfort in imagining all the reactions of loved ones, acquaintances, and strangers as they read these pages and see my images. I can see me signing copies of the book—I can sense my growing pride, knowing that my story and art will be there for those to see and know even after I have said goodbye to this life and all I've loved (figs. 123 and 124).

Fig. 117. José with his daughter, Alicia (age four), backgrounded by José's lost mural, "Chicago's Dream," at the YMCA building, 3600 West Fullerton.[2]

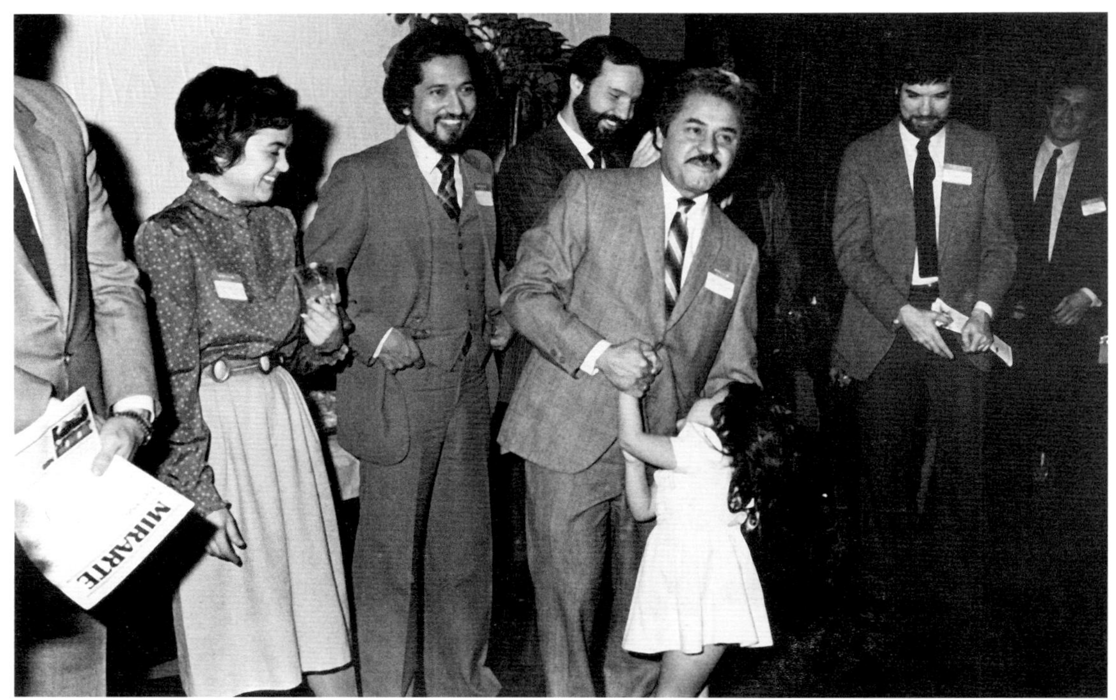

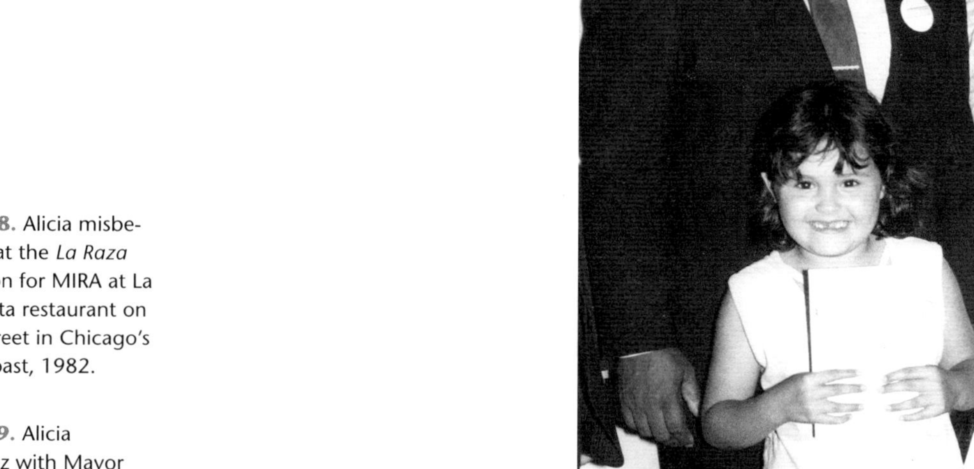

Fig. 118. Alicia misbehaving at the *La Raza* reception for MIRA at La Margarita restaurant on Rush Street in Chicago's Gold Coast, 1982.

Fig. 119. Alicia González with Mayor Harold Washington and Madeline Rabb, director of Chicago's Department of Cultural Affairs, 1986 (photo autographed by the mayor).

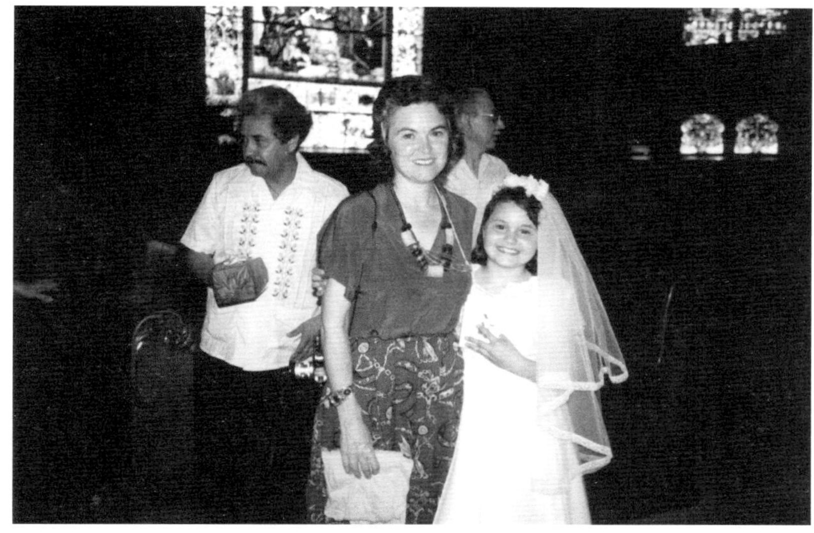

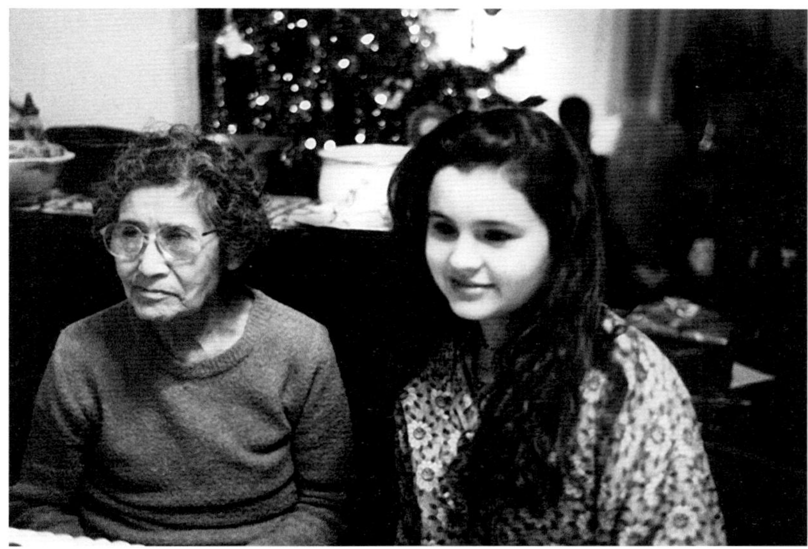

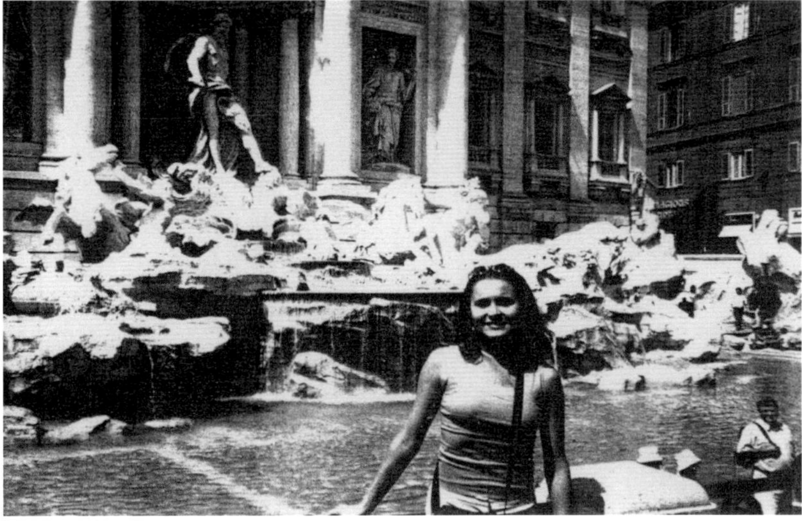

Fig. 120. Mary Kay Vaughan with Alicia and José in the background at Alicia's first communion, Notre Dame church, 1990.

Fig. 121. José's mother, Conception González, and his daughter, Alicia. Photo: José Gamaliel González.

Fig. 122. Alicia in front of the Trevi fountain in Rome, 2000.

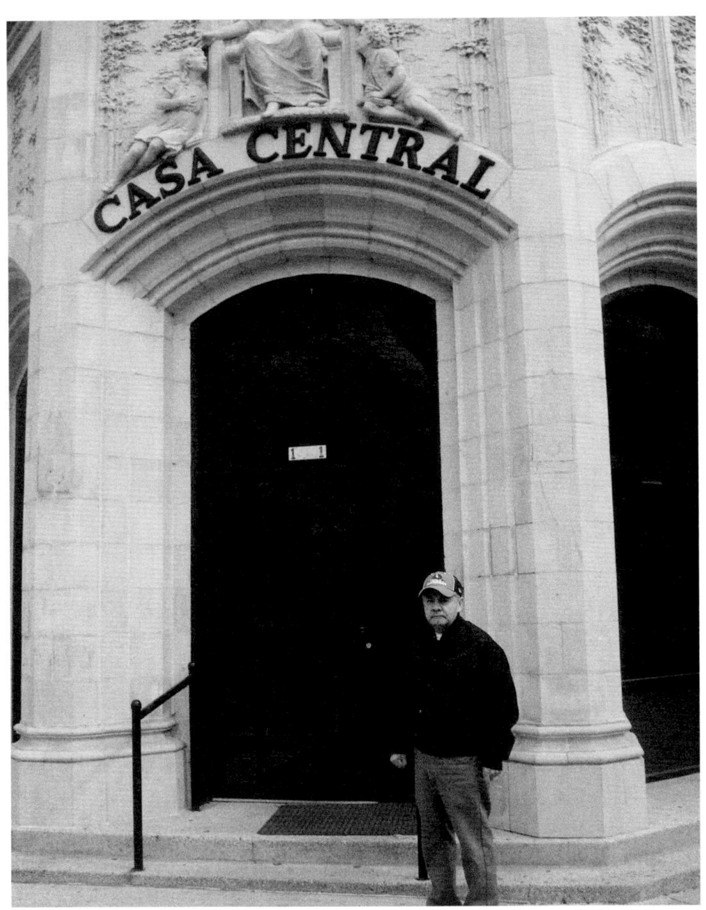

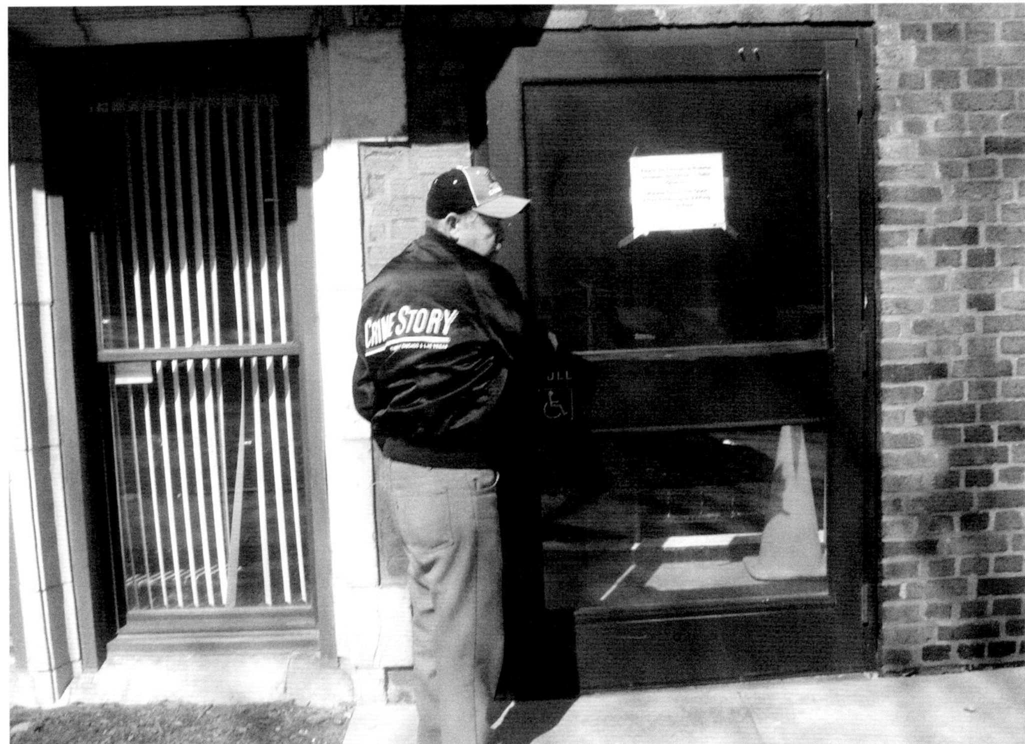

Fig. 123. José at the front door of Casa Central home for the elderly, Jose's residence on California Avenue facing Humboldt Park from Winter 2005 to Winter 2008. Photo: Marc Zimmerman.

Fig. 124. José opening the door to the Casa Central entrance. Photo: Marc Zimmerman, March 2007.

Notes

Preface

1. This other publication, referred to in this text as "Zimmerman forthcoming," is entitled *José Gamaliel González: Documenting the Life of a Chicago Mexican Artist/Activist* and is due for publication in 2011. It is a collection of documents, pictures, newspaper articles, and a wide range of other materials featuring key articles about José written by Jeff Huebner and published in the *Chicago Reader;* an essay by his longtime associate, Victor Sorell, which was written as part of a program for a retrospective of José's work in 1998; an essay by Nicolás Kanellos on José's role as art editor for *Revista Chicano-Riqueña;* and an interview of the late artist-writer Carlos Cortez—perhaps the last extended interview with this iconic figure who died in 2004, focused not on himself but on his longtime friend and former MARCH associate, José González.

2. For two examples of the growing literature on Latino autobiography, see Olivares 1988b and my section on Chicano autobiography in Zimmerman 1992: 92–93.

3. The two previous examples are those by Dr. Jorge Prieto (1989) and Gabriel Aguilera (2000).

4. The other two are Victor Sorell's edited volume on Carlos Cortez Koyokuikatl (2002) and Francisco Piña's on Marcos Raya (2004).

5. See, for example, Marquesa Macadar's interview with me (1999). I should also note that the only fictional treatment, however partial and veiled, that I know of about Latino Chicago's artistic world from the mid-1970s to the early 1980s is in Ana Castillo's novel, *Sapagonia* (1990).

Introduction

1. For a study of Saul Alinsky's influence in Mexican Chicago, and especially on Danny Solís and his United Neighborhood Organization (UNO), see Wilfredo Cruz 1987. This Chicago organization should not be confused with UNO of Northwest Indiana, with which José worked in the early 1970s. Chapter 3 of this volume recounts how José left the Concerned Latins of Lake Country (CLLC), which indeed bore the Alinsky influence, to form UNO of Northwest Indiana, which diverged from Alinsky tactics. The section in question outlines José's indirect relation to and view of Alinsky, as José discusses the role of the community organizer Ernie Cortez. Unfortunately, José's Indiana activism is not referenced in the key book that should have detailed it (Lane and Escobar 1987), even though Ernie Cortez's organizing style, affiliation, and efforts are mentioned briefly (254).

2. For an extremely positive portrait of the Mexican Fine Arts Center Museum and its evolution, see Dávalos 2001. Another positive account is found in Herrera 2008: 59–62.

3. See Arias Jirasek and Tortolero 2001: 155. For the interview, see Backley, Davis, Hernández, and Nava 2003: 22–27.

4. In English, "Prints Workshop"; it was later renamed and reformulated as Mestizarte and most recently as Taller Carlos Cortez Mestizarte.

5. For work on Mexicans in northwestern Indiana, in addition to Lane and Escobar 1987, see Samora and Lamanna 1967; Rosales 1976 and 1978; and Rosales and Simon 1975. For Mexicans in Chicago, see Kerr 1976; Arias Jirasek and Tortolero 2001; and De Genova 2005.

6. On the transition in Chicago ethnic politics from Washington to Daley, see Betancur and Gills 2004. On Chicago Latinos and economic restructuring and gentrification, see Betancur, Córdoba, and Torres 1993. On Mexican Chicago and globalization, see Mora 2007. It must be noted, however, that Mora's statement that José was a Brown Beret leader who, in 1970, joined with other activists to occupy Pilsen's Howell House and rebaptize it as Casa Aztlán (6) is apocryphal—apparently based on misleading comments made by Marcos Raya in an interview with Mora. José had strong, fundamental ties with Casa Aztlán, but he did not participate in the protests that led to its founding. In 1970, José was involved in Chicano activism at Notre Dame. His limited relation with the Brown Berets is spelled out at the beginning of chapter 3.

7. For a pioneering look at intensifying national identifications and general Latinization not as contradictory but as complementary processes in Chicago, see Padilla 1985.

8. For the best treatment of space in Cisneros's work, see Olivares 1988a; but also see Saldívar 1990.

9. I myself may have first suggested this Anglo trope to José. If so, it is an instance of how an interviewer's own background can distort the cultural bases of an interviewee. But it would be naïve to conclude that José could not embrace the trope and make it his. Robin was, after all, a guerrilla bandit fighting Anglo-Saxon abuse of power, and José's work refers to several canonical English texts—such as Aldous Huxley's *Brave New World* and Oscar Wilde's *The Picture of Dorian Gray*—thus providing a clear instance of the transcultural and transnational processes involved in Chicago and U.S. Latino identities.

10. I owe this question of "masking" to the commentary of one of the anonymous readers of this book for the University of Illinois Press.

Chapter 1. The Early Years

1. On Mexican repatriation in East Chicago, see Simon 1974.

2. See Rosales 1978. See also Rosales and Simon 1975. In *Chicano!* (Rosales 1999), the author briefly describes Conception's life and the family's involvement in repatriation and subsequent processes in a way that varies with José's account.

3. It is interesting to compare José's account of his relationship with his brother to the stories by Hugo Martínez-Serros about steel-mill Chicago Mexican youths in the late 1930s and early 1940s. See especially "David and Victor" (Martínez-Serros 1988, 129–73).

Chapter 2. From High School to Notre Dame

1. A Chicago Mexican in love with Cuban mambo, Parra played timbales Tito Puente–style. With the Chicago Rican Billy Zayas, he coproduced "Mambo Express" on public radio in the 1970s; he then led a band called Mambo Express in the 1980s and beyond while earning his living as a janitor at the University of Illinois at Chicago. Once, in his janitor uniform, he gave a lecture in my University of Illinois at Chicago Latino cultural studies class about Oscar Hijuelos's novel *The Mambo Kings Play Songs of Love*.

2. In my interview with Carlos Cortez (to appear in Zimmerman forthcoming), Cortez refers to Mela as Mel and speaks of their relation in the 1970s.

3. Cárdenas indeed has provided some photos documenting the exhibit José describes here; they are somewhat faded, but they will appear in Zimmerman forthcoming.

Chapter 3. The MARCH Years

1. David Badillo (2004) asserts that the first Mexican mural in Chicago was painted by Adrián Lozano (51–52)—a matter confirmed, and with a photo of his mural, in Arias Jirasek and Tortolero 2001. Badillo provides valuable information and images about Lozano's Jane Addams Hull-House participation. But Lozano's mural is indoors, while José is here giving credit to Castillo for developing Chicago's first outdoor Mexican mural.

2. For a reproduction of MARCH calendar materials, see Zimmerman forthcoming.

3. José adds this comment: "Adrián Lozano later designed the Mexican Fine Arts Center Museum and the building housing the Manuel Pérez Elementary School."

4. José is referring to the film adaptation of James Hilton's novel, *Lost Horizon*.

Chapter 4. Raíces, MIRA, and the MFAC

1. José insists that the show was called Mira, Mira, Mira, but the Internet and hard-copy materials I have been able to find indicate that the two successive shows he describes both had the official name ¡Mira!: The Canadian Club Hispanic Art Tour Program. In the taped interview, José remembers the corporate sponsor to be Seagram's, while the program materials indicate it was Hiram Walker.

2. Asco was an East Los Angeles artists group. The name means "disgust," expressing the group's rejection of commercial and mainstream art.

Chapter 5. Art, Work, and Health

1. This discussion of Arturo Vázquez raises an issue I failed to explore with José, which has to do with the relationship between his artistic efforts and those of the political organization with which Vázquez was long associated and had a particular importance in the development of the Mexican left in Chicago: the local branch of CASA (Centro de Acción Social Autónoma), whose members included Linda Coronado and several figures who came to the fore (or faded) in relation to the development of Mexican independent politics in the 1980s. CASA opposed the UFW's negative stance toward undocumented workers in the name of international worker unity; José agreed in general with CASA's slogan "Sin Fronteras," or "No Borders"; but he never wavered in his admiration for Chávez. CASA itself broke away from its founder, Bert Corona, in the 1970s to take on more radical positions. These matters, as well as the relation of CASA to APO, UNO, and the ESDC, will be explored in Zimmerman forthcoming.

2. In an email (May 18, 2007), Jeff Huebner, a freelance writer on Chicago's art scene, notes that the mural "Chicago's Dream" was designed and executed by José along with Pedro Silva, a New York community artist, as the result of an exchange with Silva sponsored by MIRA. Huebner comments that "the mosaic appears to have been lost or destroyed—it's not in the new YMCA building., either, near [the corner of] Armitage and Lawndale, because I went looking for it. Maybe I didn't talk to the right people; maybe it's still somewhere, in storage, whatever. Another mural mystery."

Works Cited

Aguilera, Gabriel. 2000. *Gabriel's Fire: A Memoir.* Chicago: University of Chicago Press.

Anzaldúa, Gloria. 1999. *Borderlands/La frontera: The New Mestiza.* San Francisco: Aunt Lute Books.

Arias Jirasek, Rita, and Carlos Tortolero. 2001. *Images of America: Mexican Chicago.* Charleston, S.C.: Arcadia Publishing.

Backley, Andrew, China Davis, Esmeralda Hernández, and Sergio Nava. 2003. "Building History." In *Telling Historias: 2002–2003.* Chicago: Mexican Fine Arts Center Museum.

Badillo, David. 2004. "Incorporating Reform and Religion: Mexican Immigrants, Hull-House, and the Church." In *Pots of Promise: Mexicans and Pottery at Hull-House, 1920–1940.* Ed. Cheryl Ganz and Margaret Strobel. Urbana: University of Illinois Press.

Betancur, John J., Teresa Córdova, and María de los Ángeles Torres. 1993. "Economic Restructuring and the Process of Incorporation of Latinos into the Chicago Economy." In *Latinos in a Changing U.S. Economy: Comparative Perspectives on Growing Inequality.* Newbury Park, Calif: Sage.

Betancur, John J., and Douglas Gills. 2004. "Community Development in Chicago: From Harold Washington to Richard M. Daley." *Annals of the American Academy of Political and Social Science* 594.1 (July): 92–108.

Bruce-Novoa, Juan. 1982. *Chicano Poetry: A Response to Chaos.* Austin: University of Texas Press.

———. 1990. *RetroSpace: Collected Essays on Chicano Literature.* Houston: Arte Público Press.

Castillo, Ana. 1990. *Sapagonia.* New York: Anchor Books.

———. 1995. *My Father Was a Toltec and Selected Poems.* New York: W. W. Norton.

Cisneros, Sandra. 1991. *The House on Mango Street.* New York: Vintage.

Cruz, Wilfredo. 1987. "The Nature of Alinsky-Style Community Organizing in the Mexican American Community of Chicago." Ph.D. dissertation, University of Chicago.

Dávalos, Karen Mary. 2001. *Mexican American Museums.* Albuquerque: University of New Mexico Press.

De Genova, Nicholas. 2005. *Working the Boundaries: Race, Space, and Illegality in Mexican Chicago.* Durham, N.C.: Duke University Press.

De Genova, Nicholas, and Ana Y. Ramos-Zayas. 2003. *Latino Crossings: Mexicans, Puerto Ricans, and the Politics of Race and Citizenship.* New York: Routledge.

Ganz, Cheryl, and Margaret Strobel, eds. 2004. *Pots of Promise: Mexicans and Pottery at Hull-House, 1920–40.* Urbana: University of Illinois Press.

Hernández, David, ed. 1977. *Nosotros: A Collection of Latino Poetry and Graphics from Chicago.* Special issue of *Revista Chicano-Riqueña* 5.1 (Winter).

Herrera, Olga. 2008. *Toward the Preservation of a Heritage: Latin American and Latino Art in the Midwestern States.* South Bend, Ind.: University of Notre Dame, Institute for Latino Studies.

Kerr, Louise Año Nuevo. 1976. "The Chicano Experience in Chicago: 1920–1970." Ph.D. dissertation, University of Illinois at Chicago.

Lane, James E., and Edward J. Escobar, eds. 1987. *Forging a Community: The Latino Experience in Northwest Indiana, 1915–1975.* Chicago: Cattails Press.

Lefebvre, Henri. 1991. *The Production of Space.* Oxford: Blackwell.

Macadar, Marquesa. 1999. "Chicago y el arte chicano: Entrevista con Marc Zimmerman." *Tropel* 3 (Oct.): 16–17.

Martínez-Serros, Hugo. 1988. *The Last Laugh and Other Stories.* Houston: Arte Público Press.

Mora-Torres, Juan. 2007. "Pilsen: A Mexican Global City in the Midwest." *Diálogo* 9 (Fall): 3–7.

Olivares, Julián. 1988a. "Sandra Cisneros' *The House on Mango Street* and the Poetics of Space." In *Chicana Creativity and Criticism: Charting New Frontiers in American Literature.* Ed. Maria Herrera Sobek and Helena Maria Viramontes. Houston: Arte Público Press.

———, ed. 1988b. *U.S. Hispanic Autobiography.* Special issue of *Americas Review* 16: 3–4.

Padilla, Felix M. 1985. *Latino Ethnic Consciousness: The Case of Mexican Americans and Puerto Ricans in Chicago.* South Bend, Ind.: University of Notre Dame Press.

Piña, Francisco, ed. 2004. *Marcos Raya: Fetishizing the Imaginary.* Chicago: Mexican Fine Arts Center Museum.

———. Forthcoming. *Chicago Mexican Artists.* Chicago: National Mexican Museum.

Prieto, Jorge. 1989. *Harvest of Hope.* South Bend, Ind.: University of Notre Dame Press.

Rosales, Francisco Arturo. 1976. "The Regional Origins of Mexicano Immigrants to Chicago during the 1920s." *Aztlán* 7.1 (Summer): 187–201.

———. 1978. "Mexican Immigration to the Urban Midwest during the 1920's." Ph.D. dissertation, Indiana University.

———. 1999. *Chicano!: The History of the Mexican American Civil Rights Movement.* Houston: Arte Público Press.

Rosales, Francisco Arturo, and Daniel T. Simon. 1975. "Chicano Steel Workers and Unionism in the Midwest, 1919–1945." *Aztlán* 6.1 (Summer): 267–75.

Saldívar, Ramón. 1990. *Chicano Narrative. The Dialectics of Difference.* Madison: University of Wisconsin Press.

Samora, Julián, and Richard Lamanna. 1967. *Mexican Americans in Midwest Metropolis: A Study of East Chicago.* Los Angeles: UCLA Study Project Advance Report.

Simon, Daniel T. 1974. "Mexican Repatriation in East Chicago, Indiana." *Journal of Ethnic Studies* 2.2 (Summer): 11–23.

Sorell, Victor, ed. 2002. *Carlos Cortez Koyokuikatl: Soapbox Artist and Poet, a Catalog.* Chicago: Mexican Fine Arts Museum.

Villa, Raúl Homero. 2000. *Barrio Logos: Space and Place in Urban Chicano Literature and Culture.* Austin: University of Texas Press.

Zimmerman, Marc. 1992. *U.S. Latino Literature: An Essay and Annotated Bibliography.* Chicago: MARCH/Abrazo Press.

———, ed. Forthcoming. *José Gamaliel González: Documenting the Life of a Chicago Mexican Artist/Activist.* Houston: LACASA Books.

Index

JOSÉ GAMALIEL GONZÁLEZ is an artist and arts organizer living in Chicago.

MARC ZIMMERMAN is the director of world cultures and literatures in the department of modern and classical languages at the University of Houston. His many books include *Orbis/ Urbis Latino: Los "Hispanos" en las ciudades de los Estados Unidas*.

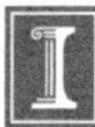

The University of Illinois Press
is a founding member of the
Association of American University Presses.

____

Designed by Kelly Gray
Composed in 10/14.5 Adobe Minion Pro
with ITC Stone Sans display
by Jim Proefrock
at the University of Illinois Press
Manufactured by Bang Printing

University of Illinois Press
1325 South Oak Street
Champaign, IL 61820-6903
www.press.uillinois.edu